The History
of The Book
in 100 Books

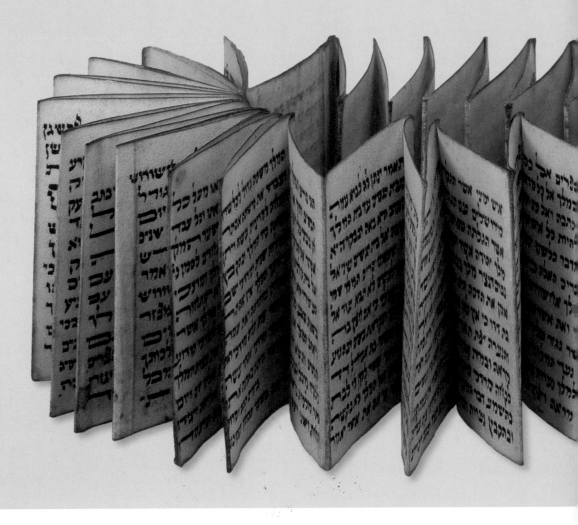

ABOVE **Esther scroll, or *Megillah***
The Hebrew text of this Book of
Esther—intended for reading aloud
at Purim celebrations—is finely
inscribed in pen and ink on parchment,
concertina-folded into an elaborate
repoussé silver case. Its silvermark
denotes import control to the
Netherlands. It is a fine example of
a book much-prized for its content,
its material and aesthetic value, and
latterly, for its provenance and history.

The History
of The Book
in 100 Books

Roderick Cave & Sara Ayad

FIREFLY BOOKS

A FIREFLY BOOK

Published by Firefly Books Ltd. 2014

First printing

Library and Archives Canada Cataloguing in Publication

Cave, Roderick, author
   The history of the book in 100 books / Roderick Cave.
Includes bibliographical references and index.
ISBN 978-1-77085-406-2 (bound)
1. Books—History. I. Title.
Z4.C39 2014   002.09   C2014-900612-8

Publisher Cataloging-in-Publication Data (U.S.)

Cave, Roderick.
   The history of the book in 100 books / Roderick Cave.
[288] pages : col. photos. ; cm.
Includes bibliographical references and index.
Summary: The e-book age has taken the paper book to a turning point. But in fact, casting off old technologies and taking on new ones has been part of the history of the book since Egyptian times. At this time in the history of books as we know them today, this volume tells the story of the book from the very beginning.
ISBN-13: 978-1-77085-406-2
1. Books – History. I. Title.
002.09 dc23 Z4.C384 2014

Published in the United States by
Firefly Books (U.S.) Inc., P.O. Box 1338, Ellicott Station, Buffalo, New York 14205

Published in Canada by
Firefly Books Ltd.,50 Staples Avenue, Unit 1 Richmond Hill, Ontario L4B 0A7

Color separation in Hong Kong by Bright Arts (HK) Ltd.

Printed in China by Shanghai Offset Printing Products Ltd.

Conceived, designed and produced by
Quarto Publishing plc, The Old Brewery,
6 Blundell Street, London N7 9BH

FOR QUARTO:
Project editor: Victoria Lyle
Designer: Hugh Schermuly
Design assistant: Martina Calvio
Picture researcher: Sara Ayad
Picture manager: Sarah Bell
Copy editor: Sarah Hoggett
Proofreader: Ruth Patrick
Indexer: Helen Snaith
Art director: Caroline Guest
Creative director: Moira Clinch
Publisher: Paul Carslake

CONTENTS

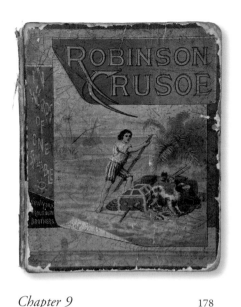

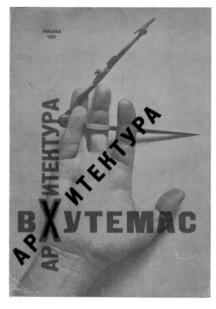

Foreword

People love lists. In the book world they have reached the status of a genre: the best books of the century; 100 books to read before you die; and so on. The present volume is one of these; it is a wonderful listing of wonderful items that provides the reader with comparisons and connections across different cultures and periods of time.

There are few people with the breadth and depth of knowledge to compile such a list. Roderick Cave has been publishing in this field for decades, and has books and articles by the dozens behind him. His knowledge of the book in all its manifestations, along with its place in history, is practically unparalleled. So it is no surprise that the present volume touches upon topics that few authors writing on the history of the book have looked at. Cave has been joined in this fascinating volume by Sara Ayad, a scholar in the literary and visual arts, and in publishing and book history. Ayad and Cave are a strong team, together weaving the tales of the books they have selected into a tapestry of beauty and intrigue.

There are, of course, the standard entries in a volume of this sort: texts written on cave walls and animal bones, clay tablets and palm leaves, bamboo-strip books, the *Iliad*, *Beowulf*, medieval illuminated manuscripts (naturally including the *Book of Kells*), the Gutenberg Bible, the *Nuremberg Chronicle* and so forth. But we also get an Andean khipu from Peru (predating the Incas), papyrus scrolls, the *Tripitaka Koreana* and the Ethiopian Bible—better known as the Garima Gospels—to name just four examples.

The list is punctuated with short essays putting all of the books into their historical contexts, from the earliest times to e-books. Clearly this is a special compilation, containing an extraordinary list of important—though often overlooked—books in a huge range of areas of scholarly and popular interests. The originality of concept and assortment of topics and individual items, along with the superb illustrations and their articles and captions, make this a fascinating study.

Unlike so many other books of lists of books, this one is bold and insightful enough to consider texts on dance, cryptography, graphic novels, miniature and nano books, palimpsests, pharmacology, divination and a host of other topics important in book history and in Western and Eastern culture, drawing upon the literature of more than a dozen countries.

The amount of history and lore, literature and science, popular culture and erudition displayed in these 100 books is a tribute to Cave's broad understanding of history, the world of printing and the world of the book. This is a fascinating, informative, valuable compilation, and it belongs on the shelves of any historian of the book, of history and of culture.

SIDNEY E. BERGER &
MICHELE V. CLOONAN

Introduction

In a time when talk about the death of the book is now trite, there are good reasons to look backward at what books have been in the past, as well as at the many speculations about the future of written communication. Some journalists and librarians, as well as computer enthusiasts, believe that the coming of the e-book marks a total and complete revolution. They anticipate an imminent future of publishing that will be entirely electronic. Despite the continuing failure of the paperless office to appear (so confidently predicted 20 years ago), they expect no paper, no printing; all information being accessed from images on a screen.

Perhaps the popularity of e-books is rising; perhaps the printed-paper book will disappear (just as the clay tablets of Babylon and the papyrus scrolls of ancient Egypt have long since dropped out of use). We are by no means persuaded that the future form of the book will be entirely electronic; what is certain is that, over the past 10,000 plus years of history, humankind has developed ways of preserving and transmitting information which are deeply embedded in our subconsciousness.

Our emotional connection to physical books will be clear from our selection. We have decided, reluctantly, not to include bookbinding or any consideration of newspapers and magazine publications in this book, important though they are. If we took a chronological approach, it would allow only one picture for every century, so we have had to be very selective in our choice of the books to illustrate. One or two books to represent drama? One for invention? How many for banned books? Choosing our 100 took a lot of thought and debate with people advising us.

We have not attempted to produce a collection of the 100 best books (however best may be defined). Nor the 100 earliest in this or that way. Nor the most famous, the most beautiful, the most influential or the most valuable; though these all have had an effect on our selection. Nor the most obvious, though it was hard to avoid selecting the earliest examples of printing in Asia and in Europe, and some other books.

Our principle in selecting books has been to range widely, with books from every continent except Antarctica. Books that illustrate the huge range of formats and styles, with books of string (khipu), or written on bone, bark or palm leaves as well as the better known clay tablets, papyrus scrolls and vellum or paper more familiar in Europe or North America. We have tried to select books that are characteristic of particular genres, but not necessarily the most obvious.

As the pictures in this volume show, we have passed over some books so well known that they needed no further publicity (no King James Bible, no Shakespeare). Instead, we are illustrating several other books equally important or influential in their milieu. Instead of the King James Bible, we include the Gustav Vasa Bible (so important for the spread of Lutheranism in Northern Europe, the formation of the modern Swedish language and the spread of Germanic typography) to stand for all national Bibles.

It has been said that if you want to understand a particular area or period, you should not look only at the great and the good: you will learn much more from looking at the less great and the not very good. This volume has a mix of these, which are intended to stimulate readers' interest enough to persuade them to go farther. There are so many treasures to be found!

In a period when more "real" printed books are being published, and it is becoming steadily easier to self-publish, is the day of the printed book over? Our answer has to be no! What is certain is that there will be more new developments, sometimes very different from (and better than) the e-books to be published. But even in the 21st century, as our illustrations show, some people are creating new forms of the written or printed book, using methods that may seem deliberately backward-looking and wayward, and ignoring digitization altogether. The traditional book will still be produced for a very long time yet.

RODERICK CAVE & SARA AYAD

CHAPTER

1

In the Beginning …

RIGHT **El Castillo cave**
These Paleolithic paintings
in Northern Spain date back
at least 40,800 years, making
them Europe's oldest known
cave art—10,000 years earlier
than previously thought.
Painted by the earliest humans
(or Neanderthals), some 50
paintings of handprints and
disk shapes blown or spat onto
the rock have been found in
11 caves. See pp. 14–15.

The origin of the book is as hard to pin down as the origin of language itself. This chapter spans many hundreds of centuries (from prehistory to about 1000 BCE) and reviews how, in several civilizations, different cultures developed ways to capture and preserve knowledge and information.

L et us start with a confession: we have almost no knowledge or understanding whatsoever of when, or how, or where "the book" was first created. The text of a book has to survive—and the chance of ancient writing surviving is slight. Where it has survived (as in Mesopotamia, Egypt and China) and we can actually read what it says, humankind has already moved from prehistory to history. But before that, the development of speech was one of the things to distinguish us from any other group of primates. Speech was vital, but the development of organized memory was also essential.

We learned to externalize our knowledge, as well as to memorize words, and this was primarily through graphic means. Such means were usually pictures, or symbols that would allow the originator to repeat and pass on the content of the message. Prehistoric peoples throughout the world turned to making marks and pictures where they lived, and these are often preserved only in cave paintings. Whether abstract patterns or descriptive drawings, they carried meaning for their maker and for their "readers."

Ways of Communicating

Some contemporary scholars interpret pictorial elements in paintings in caves as possessing a developed and widely understood meaning, as if they were a kind of visual language (see pp. 14–15). Although this theory is still far from widely accepted, these scholars see symbols in the cave paintings that were used and repeated over tens of thousands of years. Are these the first glimmers of proof that people were moving toward a system of writing? If this were true, it was perhaps 20,000 years or more ago: in archaeological terms, not long ago at all.

Beyond the meanings attributed to cave paintings, possibly the first attempts at recording information were quite simple. Humankind learned to number very early. Some of the oldest surviving records are the Lebombo bone from Swaziland and the Ishango bone from the Democratic Republic of Congo about 20,000 years ago (around 18,000 BCE), on which their owners made marks (see pp. 16–17). Were they mathematical marks, or perhaps astronomical calculations? Measuring time was as important to our ancestors as it is for us today. The use of **tally sticks**

survived into recent times, showing that such apparently basic tools have great practical advantage.

If thinking "a book" had to be a **scroll** or a collection of leaves (a **codex**), with pictures or words transferred to the surface that could then be read by another person, we assume a considerable advance in understanding and culture. First, there has to be the graphic representation of words: sounds that carry meaning, and that could be understood. Learning how to write made our ancestors more successful than other groups, and this was recognized early. In many cultures, gods were venerated for the gift of writing: Thoth and Seshat in Egypt; Nabu by the Babylonians; Cadmus in Greece; Quetzalcoatl in Mexico.

Forms of Record Keeping

All societies turned to whatever materials were readily available. We might think that impressing marks into slabs of clay is a laborious method of writing, but it had the advantage of durability—one of the reasons that we know as much of Babylonian history as we do. For peoples who used **papyrus**, its fragility meant that the texts had to be copied and recopied. The Incas developed the only major empire to lack a system of writing, but their knotted strings, **khipus**, assisted memorization and allowed some information to be stored and transmitted. This system survived for thousands of years, partly because the materials lasted well (see pp. 20–21).

Writing was not seen as an unmixed blessing. For many centuries, conservative-minded people condemned the use of writing as wrong, because it was thought to make people lose the power to retain their memories. And that act of memory took an enormous level of commitment. For example, in Britain the Roman emperor Julius Caesar reported in his *Commentarii de Bello Gallico* (written in the 50s BCE) that the course of study for an educated Druid might spread over 20 years. Because of the Druids' distrust of writing and their reliance on oral means alone, we have now lost all access to their lore and knowledge. And, fast-forwarding 2,000 years, we shall likewise lose access to the content of large quantities of written and printed records and electronic records—unless they are transferred to current and future media.

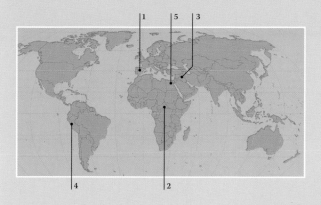

For writing surfaces, mankind used stone, clay tablets, bark, leaves, papyrus, bones, animal skins and **paper**, and many other media. We discovered how to transfer marks to these surfaces, using dyestuffs for ink, and sticks, reeds, quills and pieces of lead as "pens." We have devised efficient systems to write, replicate, store and retrieve many artifacts of our modern civilization. In books, through conventions of layout, by adding sophistication to the shapes of the letters of our alphabets and by the use of technology, we can now read an amazing array of literary creations. Through the development of punctuation, authors can precisely convey their message so that all can understand—or deliberately choose to flout the rules (see pp. 166–167).

ONE NEED, MANY SOLUTIONS

Almost unconsciously, we recognize the interplay between the medium and the message it carries. The history of the book is not a single development from a single source. Many societies developed their own writing systems. The availability of clay in Mesopotamia, papyrus in Egypt and **lontar** palms in India and Indonesia—plus the variety of writing surfaces that were available in China and Southeast Asia—enabled all these areas to develop their own systems of writing and bookmaking (see pp. 22–23).

These developments occurred in different places and at different times, partly because of the continuing inventiveness and ingenuity of humankind, as the later sections of this book show. Some peoples developed their own local methods, instead of adopting more advanced ways: the future of books and e-books worldwide will probably show as much variety as there was, *in the beginning.*

Cave Paintings

In the earliest days of mankind, people left painted traces of their time in caves. Whether abstract or realistic, the paintings had a meaning for the artists. What were they saying?

Throughout the world, people sheltering in caves left traces of their presence. Sometimes they left bones and shells from the animals and fish they hunted, or traces of the implements they used to kill their prey, or the fires they used for cooking, warmth or light. When they died, their own skeletons formed part of the remains through which modern archaeologists sift to try to find out about our ancient ancestors.

There are differences between the cave paintings made in warm areas portraying buffalo, lions and giraffes, and those from cold climates sometimes showing bears, mammoths and elk that then roamed the earth. There are also marked similarities in cave paintings from sites throughout the globe. Some come from the media used: pigments made from earth or charcoal left from fires. Many seem to reflect the localized experience, feelings and beliefs of the people who made them.

In many cave sites, there are pictures of hands— sometimes just of a single hand, more often many images of hands—usually made by a "spray-painting" technique in which the artists spat or blew dissolved ocher over a hand that was held to the wall as a stencil. In some caves, archaeologists have found fine, hollow bone pipes, stained by the pigment blown from them.

Such paintings were often made from the hands of young children, but also from adults whose hands were sometimes maimed by accidents. You can see them in the painting from El Castillo in Spain, thought to be from about 16,000 BCE (shown opposite). The more recent Cueva de las Manos in central Patagonia (Argentina) of about 9500 BCE, and an Indonesian example of about 3000 BCE at Leangleang cave near Moros in southern Sulawesi, are all very similar. They were saying, "We were here!"—but what other meanings or messages did they contain?

RIGHT **We are here!** One can almost feel the excitement in the making of this cluster of hands at the Cueva de las Manos in Santa Cruz Province, Argentina. The "prints" are in negative—silhouettes made by blowing mineral pigments (iron oxides) through a pipe across the hand held against the rock surface.

Connections

For other effective use of pigments, see

Batak Pustaha, **pp. 38–39**

Garima Gospels, **pp. 50–51**

T'oros Roslin Gospels, **pp. 66–67**

RIGHT **First impressions**
A rock face at El Castillo, with the outline of a buffalo and hand markings. Static, site-specific information for a localized audience, it's a world away from crowd-sourcing and other modern means of conveying information, yet instantly recognizable to every human being. Handprints remain, for many children, the first means of artistic expression.

Earliest Evidence of Mathematical Knowledge

Many survivals from prehistory are found in archaeological digs. One of the oldest "books" is this baboon bone, which a prehistoric man used for recording information.

BELOW **Tally sticks** These 13th-century hazel sticks are Exchequer receipts, notched to show the amount paid. The shaft was split lengthwise, each half having the same number of notches. One was given to the payer and the other to the payee. When accounts were audited, they were fitted together to see if they would "tally."

When archaeologists investigate caves, they are just as interested in what they find underfoot as they are in the markings and paintings on the walls or ceilings, or (as in areas like Pompeii, buried by volcanic eruptions) the evidence of what people ate, wore and worked on, and what they threw away.

Several cave searches throughout the world have revealed bones that had been deliberately marked: radiocarbon dating shows that some of them are very old indeed. One bone dating from 25,000 to 20,000 BCE was found in 1960 by a Belgian archaeologist at Ishango near Lake Edward in the Democratic Republic of Congo, buried under a volcanic eruption. Called the Ishango bone, this fibula from a baboon has a piece of quartz fitted into its end, making a tool. On the sides, it has marks scratched onto it.

At first the bone was thought to be a **tally stick**—commonly used until modern times in Europe—but research suggests that it was possibly a lunar calendar covering six months. Some researchers claim that the marking was done by women and related to their menstrual cycle; others believe that these arguments over-interpret the data, believing that these bones were simply mnemonic devices, used like the **khipus** of South America (see pp. 20–21). Skeptics assert that the markings on the bones were simply to make gripping the tool easier.

Several other older prehistoric lunar calendars are known, including the Lebombo bone from Swaziland, in many ways like the calendar sticks used in modern times by the Bushmen (San) of southern Africa. The Wolf bone found in 1937 at Dolní Věstonice (Czech Republic) was of the same kind. But the Ishango bone is often regarded as more important than these, and it is evidence of the first development of mathematical calculations.

Connections

For other (very different) astronomical calculations, see

Al-Sufi's Book of Fixed Stars, *pp. 86–87*

Tycho Brahe's Astronomiae, pp. 136–137

Banneker's Almanack, pp. 170–171

For other books using bones as the medium, see

Batak Pustaha, *pp. 38–39*

BELOW **Ishango bone, Congo** The three rows of 168 grouped notches etched on this baboon fibula seemingly correspond, although their meaning is unclear. We have no clue as to its author or knowledge of its real use, but dating to around 20,000 BCE, it is often considered the earliest evidence of mathematical knowledge.

Cuneiform Tablets

*Cuneiform writing on clay tablets had a very long life. Many of the earliest books including medical, legal, mathematical and others were in **cuneiform**—and the oldest epic of all is the tale of Gilgamesh and the Flood.*

Marking symbols in a sheet of damp clay seems unlikely to succeed as a vehicle for creating great literature. But in the fertile crescent on the rivers Tigris and Euphrates, clay was abundant—and it had some strong advantages over most writing systems. Readily available, easily manipulated and marked, the cuneiform tablets were almost indestructible when baked. (They lasted far longer than the **papyrus** used in Egypt and later in Rome.)

The use of clay disks for counting first appeared about 8000 BCE; by about 3100 BCE, an early form of cuneiform was being used at Uruk in the Sumerian empire. Cuneiform documents were written in a variety of regional languages such as Akkadian, Sumerian and Babylonian. They were so widespread that they were used for diplomatic contacts with the Pharaohs in Egypt (the Amarna letters of about 1340 BCE). The first legal codes, medical guides, mathematical texts, astronomical studies, dictionaries and even an early cookery manual (describing methods of boiling) are known. Many administrative, trade and fiscal records needed in the development of city states have survived. The latest known datable cuneiform tablet is an astronomical almanac from 75 CE.

Sumerian and Babylonian writing included many proverbs, and the tale of King Gilgamesh caused great excitement when a Victorian amateur first deciphered the tablet because of some similarities to the tale of Noah and the Flood. It is now regarded as one of the high points of literature. We do not know its author, but we have the name of the scribe who compiled and incized the clay tablet: Sîn-lēqi-unninni, a priest (*mashmashshu*) who lived in Mesopotamia between 1300 and 1000 BCE.

Our understanding of cuneiform texts is advancing fast. The digitizing of texts and the creation of dictionaries by the universities of Oxford, Chicago, UCLA and others has made the study of ancient Mesopotamia much easier—even if we are unlikely to discover another Gilgamesh.

LEFT **Epic of Gilgamesh: the "Flood Tablet"**
This Neo-Assyrian tablet formed part of the library of King Ashurbanipal (reigned 669–631 BCE), who collected thousands of cuneiform tablets in his palace at Nineveh. It describes Gilgamesh meeting Utnapishtim, a Noah-type figure who built a boat and loaded it with people and animals.

RIGHT **Assyrian scribes** Palace scribes, each holding a stylus, conduct a head count after battle, on this exquisite Neo-Assyrian alabaster slab, carved at Nineveh for the south-west palace of Sennacherib, 640–620 BCE. The bearded scribe writes on a hinged board, probably covered with wax.

Connections

For very different writing surfaces and methods, see

Sulawesi Lontar, pp. 252–253

Other equally famous European epics are

Homer's Iliad, pp. 48–49

Bruges Roman de la Rose, pp. 72–73

Aldine Virgil, pp. 108–109

An Andean Mystery

Most civilizations devised memory systems by putting marks on surfaces. Spanish invaders arriving in Peru found that the Incas had a different communication method, using knotted, colored cords.

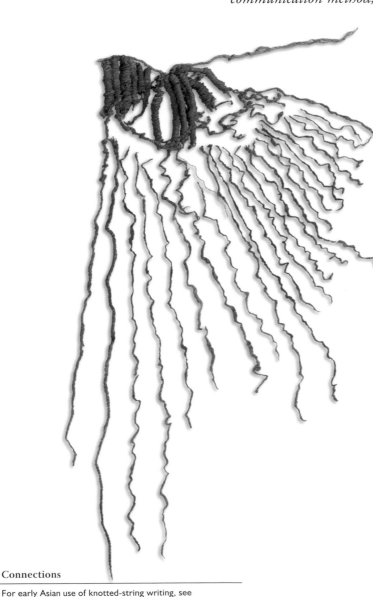

About 5,000 years ago, long before the Sumerian culture emerged in Mesopotamia or the pyramids were erected in Egypt, the first known center of civilization in the Americas was Caral-Supe with its own pyramids about 125 miles (200 kilometers) north of Lima, Peru. It was, in many ways, a rudimentary development—but while the people of Caral-Supe had apparently not started making pottery, they were developing a system of using knotted and dyed cords for making records or in communication. These were called **khipus**. The Caral site has been known since the 1940s, and recent excavations reveal when the pyramids were built and quite a lot about how Caral developed, but we still know little about the people or their language.

A very early khipu was one of the important archaeological finds at Caral-Supe. The method of using them survived for 4,000 years and into the early days of the Spanish conquest of the Inca empire in the 1530s. The khipus fascinated the Spanish. Having looted some of the goods carried by the Inca officials, the Spanish could not understand how, by re-knotting some of the strings differently, the Quechua officials recorded what had been removed—as clearly for them as if making an alteration in the spreadsheets we use today.

The understanding of the "language" of khipus is still incomplete, but recent research by American scholars suggests that possibly these knotted cords were used as a mnemonic device, and it is argued that their inventors had started using a binary system in computation.

In Inca times, there were several descriptions of khipus, as in the *Historia de los Incas* by the Galician explorer, Pedro Sarmiento de Gamboa, in 1572. There are several pictures made by Guamán Poma, a Quechua aristocrat who, in about 1615, wrote his *Nueva Corónica y Buen Gobierno* (*New Chronicle and Good Government*). Kept in the Royal Library in Copenhagen since the 18th century, this manuscript is so fragile that it could hardly be used by scholars. The Royal Library digitized its content in the 1990s, making it available for all to read.

Connections

For early Asian use of knotted-string writing, see

Guodian Chu Slips, pp. 28–29

For other very rare early Amerindian books, see

Bay Psalm Book, pp. 128–129

Codex Mendoza, pp. 130–131

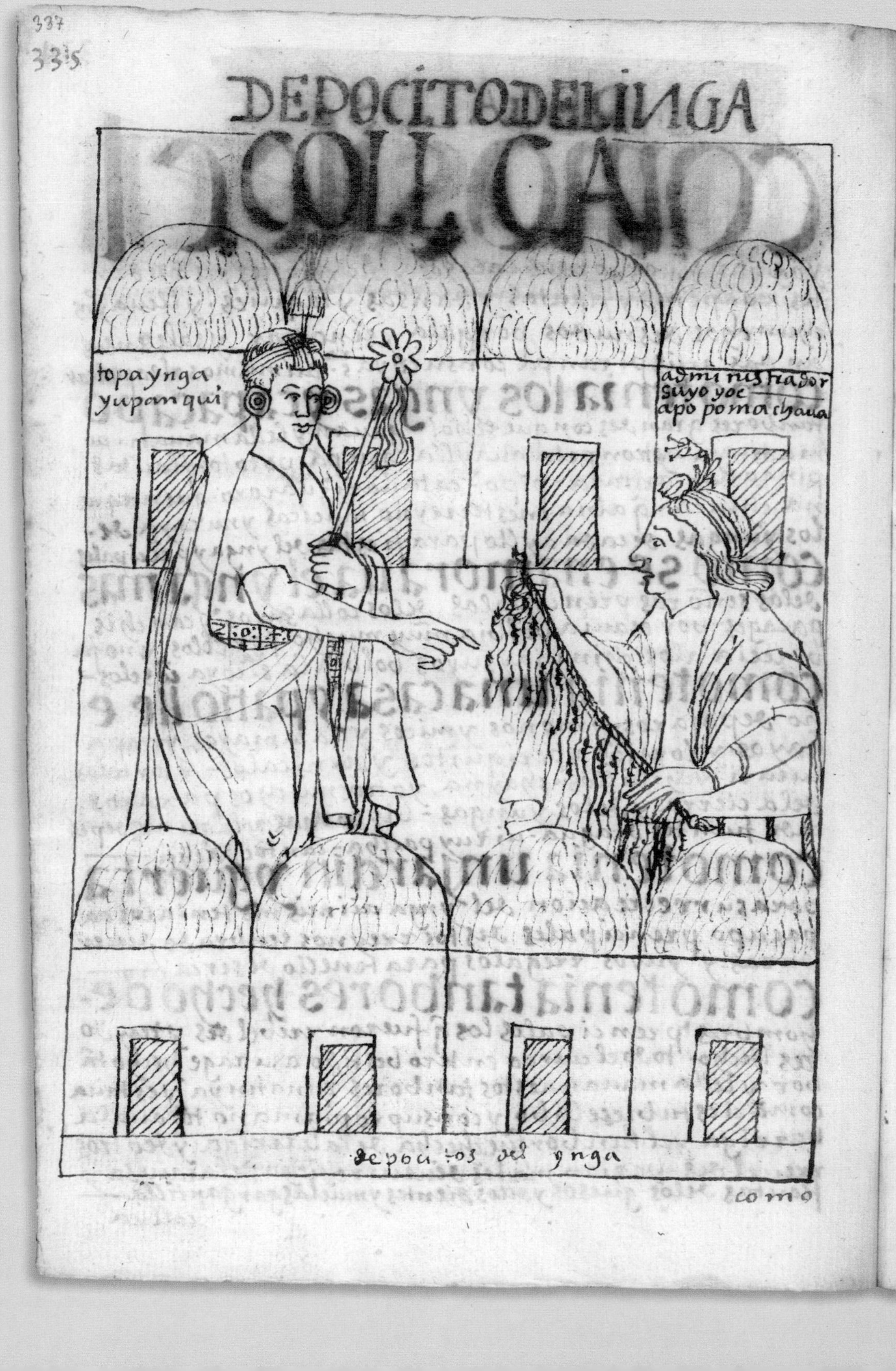
DEPOCITO DEL INGA
COLLCA
topa ynga
yupanqui
administrador
suyo yoc
apo pomachaua
depocitos del ynga
como

RIGHT **The Inca's storehouse** Quechua nobleman Guamán Poma's *New Chronicle and Good Government*, 1615, is the longest sustained indictment by a native of Spanish colonial rule, and contains 398 full-page drawings. Depicting a khipu being worked in a storehouse context, this suggests their use for accounting.

LEFT **Caral khipu** The Caral-Supe site is the oldest known center of civilization in the Americas. This khipu, the earliest known, dating to 4,600 years ago and predating the Inca form of "narrative thread," is made of knotted cotton wrapped around sticks.

Book of the Dead of Ani This papyrus, reading from left to right, depicts the Judgment of the Dead before Osiris. Ani and his wife are attended by Anubis, god of embalming. At the center, Ani's heart is weighed against a feather, symbolizing *maat*, the principle of order.

Egyptian Books on Papyrus

The ingenuity of the ancient Egyptians enabled them to invent **papyrus** *as a writing surface, and it became standard in the Egyptian and Greek worlds for centuries. The* Book of the Dead of Ani *is one of the most important Egyptian manuscripts.*

The clay tablets used in Mesopotamian **cuneiform** lasted well, but were cumbersome. In about 2900 BCE, the Egyptians found a way to make a relatively cheap and portable writing surface, which scribes and painters could use easily. The pithy stems of a sedge common in the Nile delta, papyrus (*Cyperus papyrus*), was used for making boats, furniture, boxes, bags, rope and for writing surfaces. As a writing surface, it became popular. It was exported extensively for use in other countries around the Mediterranean, though the damper climate away from Egypt reduced the life of Greek and Roman papyrus manuscripts. Papyrus could not be folded: it was used in **scrolls**, usually up to 12 inches (30 centimeters) high, and pages of text would be written (on one side only) on the roll. Rolls

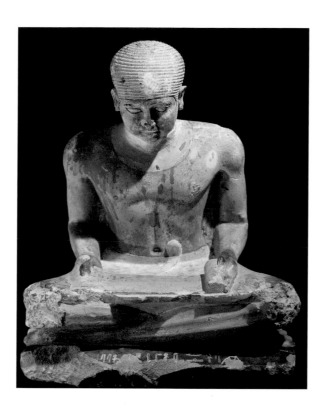

ABOVE **Egyptian scribe** Many statues exist of scribes working on papyrus, both in stylized form and astonishingly lifelike. This painted limestone figure of Ptahshepses, a prominent fifth-Dynasty scribe, comes from a tomb at Saqqara, and dates from around 2450 BCE.

would be of varying lengths: as long as 33 yards (30 meters) or even more.

The dry Egyptian climate was propitious for the survival of papyrus scrolls. The thousands of surviving documents show that the Egyptians were interested in law, medicine, mathematics and astronomy, and death. The finest were those written for funerary purposes—scrolls that went with the dead into their tombs. Their purpose was to guide the Egyptian soul "going forth by day" to the afterlife; and they contained prayers, incantations and spells that were intended to preserve the mummified body and to help it in the afterlife (with matters such as providing servants for physical work). Over 100 such scrolls survive. The cost of having a scribe prepare one was substantial—as much as a year's salary.

The Book of the Dead of Ani, written in cursive **hieroglyphic** script in about 1275 BCE, was bought

in Egypt for the British Museum in the 1880s, before modern ideas of conservation. For safe transport, it was cut into 37 pieces, which were then framed. Recent conservation and digitization enable viewers to see it in something closer to its original form.

Connections

For alternative vegetable surfaces, see

Nalanda Perfection of Wisdom Sutra, *pp. 34–35*

Batak Pustaha, *pp. 38–39*

Boke van Bonang, *pp. 92–93*

For another book of funerary rites, see

Dunhuang Diamond Sutra, *pp. 80–81*

CHAPTER

Eastern Approaches

The East Asian civilizations developed in a different way from those of Mediterranean countries. The Asian developments in writing, paper and printing were the foundation of the modern book world—but some of them appear quite strange to those from the West.

ABOVE **Batak divination book** This
extraordinary object known as the *Great Book
of Magic*, was made in north central Sumatra,
c. 1850. According to notes by Father Promés,
a Batak-speaking missionary, it contains spells
such as "instructions on acquiring Strength and
Support during important endeavors and armed
conflict." See pp. 38–39.

There is a discontinuity in the production of books in Mesopotamia and Egypt. **Cuneiform** and the Mesopotamian languages dropped out of use. Though the use of **papyrus** spread to the Greco-Roman world, the decline of the ancient Egyptian civilization meant that the plant became extinct in the Nile valley and, over time, the ability to read **hieroglyphics** also disappeared.

China had no papyrus, its ingenious peoples and those in other Asian countries created other surfaces and ways to write. Some archaeologists claim that marked tortoise shells dating to 6600 BCE show that the Chinese were already using writing. Most researchers regard that dating as anomalous, but agree that as early as 1400 BCE the Chinese marked shells for divination for the Shang emperors.

In Chinese myth, writing is stated to have been invented by the four-eyed **Cangjie**, in about 2650 BCE. By the seventh century BCE, writing on bamboo strips and on silk was extensively used (see pp. 28–29). The form of the bamboo strips dictated the later design of Chinese books, with characters written from top to bottom and from right to left. The religions observed in China (Buddhism, Confucianism and Daoism) were the driving force behind many of their books, as Hinduism and Islam were in other countries.

The Coming of Papermaking

As well as using silk, the Chinese also used a process of converting the inner bark of paper mulberry (*Broussonetia papyrifera*) into a writing surface, using stone or wood beaters. In China its production died out nearly 2,000 years ago, but it continued to be produced in the Nanyang (the countries to the south) for much longer. As *dluwang* in Java and under the Polynesian name *tapa*, bark-paper continues to be made in parts of the South Pacific. In China by 105 CE it was starting to be replaced by the use of **paper**, by tradition invented by Cai Lun, who is still revered by Chinese papermakers.

The papermaking process spread to Korea and Japan in the seventh century CE. Reputedly some Chinese papermakers captured by Abbasid troops at the Battle of Talas River in 751 CE took the techniques of papermaking to Samarkand. By the 12th century CE, knowledge of papermaking spread to Europe.

Japanese papermaking and printing, which took a slightly different form, was also heavily influenced by the Buddhist religion. As well as using paper mulberry for papermaking, the Japanese started to harvest other plant fibers like gampi and mitsumata, and adopted different ways of **sizing**, producing papers of superb quality. They learned the techniques of printing quite early, and a famous example of mass production dates from about 770 CE (see pp. 30–31), but manuscript production remained the standard process for Japanese books for several centuries.

Korean book production and papermaking was also heavily influenced by China, and the local devotion to Buddhism ensured a remarkable survival—of the blocks for printing what is known as the *Tripitaka Koreana*, originally cut in 1087 CE (see pp. 32–33).

Other Writing Surfaces

India was even more strongly influenced by Buddhism, as Gautama Buddha (c. 563–483 BCE) was from South Asia. Although oral transmission remained important, the teachings of the Buddha and most other forms of written communication were carried out through the use of **lontar** leaves. Like papyrus, they were readily available, but in the long term these palm-leaf manuscripts present enormous conservation problems.

The shapes of the leaves used caused many peoples to adopt a very different format from the one used for papyrus (see pp. 34–35). Knowledge of papermaking was introduced via Tibet and Kashmir about 800 CE, but the use of lontar for manuscripts continued in India, Sri Lanka and Indonesia for many centuries, and for this reason printing was not widely adopted in India for many years.

The Book Trade Develops

Chinese government was highly centralized, and its emperors (or their officials) planned on a grand scale. As with many Western rulers, there was often a wish to bring books under control, through both censorship and patronage. Attempts at all-comprehensive collections of religious, literary and scientific texts were made, the most famous being the *Yongle Dadian* (*The Great Canon of the Yongle Emperor*) of 1403–1408 CE, probably the biggest work ever produced (see pp. 36–37).

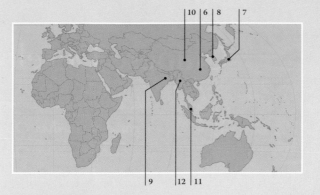

There were always exceptions to general rules for the making of books. Though minor linguistic or cultural groups often borrow the scripts, styles and methods of neighboring countries, some isolated societies developed their own individual styles—particularly noticeable in Indonesia, for instance, in the extraordinary reeled manuscripts of the Bugis people of southern Sulawesi (see pp. 252–253). The bone and bark books of the Batak peoples in Sumatra were also markedly different from anything produced by neighboring societies, until European colonization introduced other methods (see pp. 38–39).

In Southeast Asia, the local civilizations and language groups often adopted the same writing surfaces and formats as other countries, with Buddhism and Hinduism having a marked effect on what was written in Java and Bali, and with the same use of lontar leaves as the writing medium. The use of their local bark-paper, dluwang, or later imported European paper was normal for the Islamic groups. In Burma and areas under Burmese control, the **parabaik** was developed. This concertina-form book, probably based originally on the palm-leaf manuscripts, was widely used, and Buddhist parabaik manuscripts are still written today. Parabaik formats, and the use of Burmese scripts, were commonplace for manuscripts written in the Laotian and northern Thai languages (see pp. 40–41).

SIMILARITIES AND DIFFERENCES

To people used to modern Western books and their formats, the writing surfaces, scripts, subjects and formats used in early Eastern books often seem strange. The **ideographic** forms of Chinese writing undoubtedly caused some serious difficulties for printing as compared to the simpler European alphabets. Technical difficulties in casting types for Indian scripts also delayed the development of printing in the East. Western imperialism has tended to mean that Eastern modes of the book have been replaced, and its developments in book production (such as type-casting) were to change the ways in which books are made. But despite these drawbacks, the Eastern methods and styles have lasted much longer, and are as fit for purpose as most Western methods.

Chinese Developments in Bookmaking

The bamboo books written about 300 BCE, found recently in a grave at Guodian Chu in Hubei Province, are recognizable ancestors of modern Chinese books. But Chinese writing was developed much earlier.

In legend, the Yellow Emperor Huangdi united China about 2650 BCE. Dissatisfied by the "rope knot-tying" system (**khipus**), the Emperor instructed the four-eyed **Cangjie** to invent writing to convey meaning. This was the legend: by that period, there was an effective Chinese way of writing using a large number of **ideograms** to record and transmit information. Their advantage is that they can be read irrespective of the dialect used by the writer; their main drawback being the huge number of characters needed, and the problems for people learning to read them.

The origin of Chinese writing can be found on stone inscriptions, in bronze dishes cast in the 11th century BCE and also in the symbols scratched on bones and tortoise shells as early as the 12th century BCE, which some archaeologists believe to be much older. Bamboo was abundant and cheap, but it decays and is subject to insect attack, except in exceptional conditions, as when sealed in tombs.

The Guodian Chu bamboo slips (shown opposite) are much more recent, taken from a tomb of about 300 BCE. Thousands of other books on bamboo slips are known: the 804 slips from Guodian include excerpts from several classic works, including the fundamental text for Daoism, the Confucian *Book of Rites* and other texts important to the history of Chinese civilization and thought. Discovery of these survivals has improved our knowledge of early Chinese civilization, and current digitizing programs of the slips' content assist in this.

Like others excavated in recent finds, the Guodian Chu slips show how the design of Chinese books, written on silk or **paper**, was modeled closely on the form dictated by the use of bamboo slips, on which the ideograms were written down the slip and continued on the next assembled to the left. The division of the pages into columns in modern Chinese books is still done in the same way.

LEFT **Oracle bones** This petrified tortoise shell or *plastron*, c. 1400 BCE, bears oracle inscriptions, used in late Shang-dynasty China for pryomancy (divination by fire). Diviners inscribed questions onto the surface, applied intense heat and then interpreted the resulting cracks. Much early Chinese writing is found in oracle form.

RIGHT **Guodian Chu slips** Discovered in 1993 in Guodian tombs in Jingmen, Hubei Province, these ancient bamboo strips have small seal characters written the length of the slips; they describe both the practical and the inner life, according to Confucian philosophy. They would have been written before or close to the time of burial.

Connections

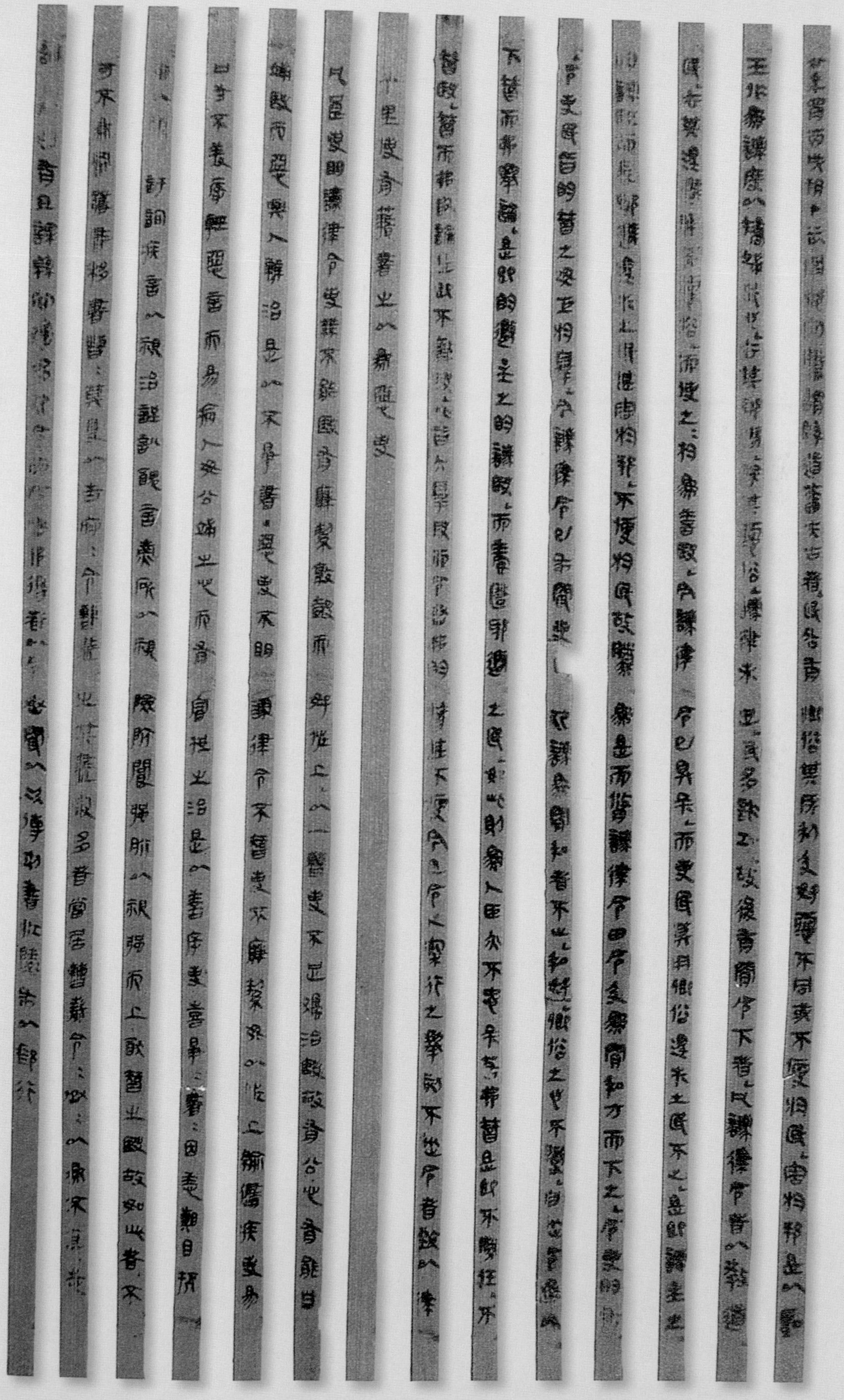

無垢淨光經
自心印陀羅尼
南謨薄伽伐
帝納婆納伐三藐
底喃一三藐
三佛阤俱胝
那庾多設多
索訶薩羅喃多
一羅汦列

Mass Production in Japan

The earliest example of mass production was the preparation of a million dharani, *or incantations, ordered about 770* CE *by the Japanese Empress Shōtoku. Was their production because of a guilty conscience?*

LEFT **Japanese *dharani*** The miniature pine wood pagoda, just 8 inches (20 centimeters) high, containing its block-printed Buddhist prayer scroll, is one of the Hyakuman (Japanese for "one million") pagodas commissioned by the Empress Shōtoku in the eighth century.

Female rulers throughout the world had problems in gaining and maintaining their power. The Japanese Empress Shōtoku, also known as Empress Kōken, had an eccentric and tumultuous life. As the 46th imperial ruler, she succeeded her father Shōmu when he abdicated, and she ruled Japan from 749 to 758 CE. She suffered from bouts of depression and abdicated in favor of her young cousin, who ruled as Emperor Junnin, under the control of a courtier, Fujiwara Nakamaro.

Through friends, or on the advice of Nakamoro, she put herself under the care of a young, charismatic Buddhist monk, Dōkyō—and made a rapid recovery. With her support, the monk was appointed Master of Healing, and accumulated unheard-of secular and religious power. There was civil war: Junnin was deposed, Nakamoro was killed, and in 764 CE Shōtoku resumed rule, and became the 48th ruler. The Empress seemed infatuated by the monk and there was a faction that supported Dōkyō to succeed her. Shōtoku allayed her doubts about her actions by turning to religion, and ordered that small wooden pagodas containing incantations printed on **paper** be made for distribution to temples. A million sets were made and finished about 770 CE. Many still survive in temples and museums around the world.

The enterprise was a marvel of organization: the woodturning for the pagodas; the papermaking; the printing of the incantations. The paper was made of hemp fiber. For printing, the Japanese are thought to have used eight cast bronze plates—1,000 years before the European use of **stereotyping**. Using hand inking and burnishing on the back of the paper, the printers took 125,000 prints from the plates. But the enterprise was the last undertaken by the Empress: she died; Dōkyō was exiled and died in obscurity in 772 CE. There was no further printing in Japan for many years, and the Japanese relied on imports of books from China.

Connections

For other early Asian printing, see

Tripitaka Koreana, *pp. 32–33*

Dunhuang Diamond Sutra, *pp. 80–81*

Monumental Korean Undertaking

Korea was the first country outside China to adopt printing and was a leader in developing printing from type. Its most famous book is the Buddhist Eighty Thousand Tripitaka *(the three main canons of Buddhist scriptures) of the 13th century* CE. *The printing blocks for it are preserved in the Haeinsa monastery in Korea.*

ABOVE **Haeinsa Temple, South Korea** Behind the wooden shutters and over dusty floors, rows and rows of shelving house the 81,258 *Tripitaka* blocks (of 1,496 titles) in the long halls of the temple in Gyeongsang Province, South Korea. One of the country's most prized cultural treasures, it is now a designated UNESCO World Heritage Site.

Korea was long closely tied to China, and frequently the channel through which knowledge and technical innovation passed to Japan and the wider world. Despite many invasions and occupations, Korea stubbornly maintained its own language and culture.

Papermaking was introduced to Korea at about the same time as in Japan, in the seventh century. Recent research has shown that the Japanese charms printed in 770 CE were not the first example of printing: a Korean *dharani* charm of about 700 CE was discovered in 1966.

Korean printing was closely associated with Buddhism. In 1087, seeking the Buddha's support in the course of a war against the Khitans (who occupied a large area in Manchuria and Mongolia), the Emperor undertook to print the entire Chinese Buddhist canon. This was done, but the blocks for printing it were destroyed by a Mongol invasion of 1232; now only a few fragments of the prints taken from them survive. The Korean Emperor Gojong then ordered a new edition to be prepared, and under the direction of two monasteries the whole work was done by a team of 30 woodcutters from 1236–51.

More than 80,000 woodcut blocks are still preserved in Haeinsa Temple, to which they were removed in 1398. The maintenance of the blocks and their buildings has successfully preserved the whole collection, forming a UNESCO World Heritage Site. Described as the most important and most complete corpus of Buddhist doctrinal texts anywhere in the world, these Korean texts are used as the base also for Japanese, Taiwanese and Chinese editions. Their texts have been digitized, and there is a special research project for this important work.

ABOVE ***Tripitaka Koreana*** Made in the
Goryeo Period (1237–48) for King Gojong,
the *Tripitaka* recreates texts destroyed by the
Mongols in 1232. A monumental undertaking,
each birchwood block, finely engraved in Hanja
script, measures 9½ x 27½ inches (24 x 70
centimeters), up to 1½ inches (4 centimeters)
thick and weighs around 6½ to 8¾ pounds
(3 to 4 kilograms).

Connections

For other printed Buddhist works, see

Shōtoku's Dharani, pp. 30–31

Dunhuang Diamond Sutra, pp. 80–81

For another early Asian book on paper, see

Yongle Dadian, pp. 36–37

For Asian alternatives using "proto-paper," see

Boke van Bonang, pp. 92–93

Indian Palm-Leaf Manuscript

Palm-leaf manuscripts written and decorated in India are often beautiful, and evidence of the religious fervor in making them is clear in this ancient Buddhist text. And we are lucky any survived.

In India and in wide areas of Southeast Asia, writing on prepared palm leaves (**lontar**) was the standard way of making books for many centuries. Although easily damaged by insects, such books have a good shelf life and last for hundreds of years. As with the earlier **papyrus** rolls, recopying (or nowadays digitization) is essential if the texts are to be preserved.

When leaves had been prepared for writing, the letters were written with a reed pen (as above) or by using a sharp stylus to score the leaves' surface, with

black pigment rubbed in to make the text visible. The holes made for the cords used to fasten the leaves together limit the design possibilities, either interfering with reading or forcing scribes to divide their "page" into three columns: in the case of this famous palm-leaf manuscript, written about 1120, the design and execution are superb.

In the development of Mahayana Buddhism, by about 100 CE the *Astasahasrika Prajnaparamita* (the *Perfection of Wisdom Sutra*) of 8,000 lines was one of the most significant texts. Many other manuscript copies were made in a wide range of scripts and styles across India, Tibet and beyond, but few of such quality.

It is believed that the book was a gift by a layman, Udaya Sinha, and probably executed at Nalanda (Bihar), an important center of Buddhist culture. In the East, Nalanda is famous for its library, which was comparable to the great library of Alexandria. Like Alexandria, it was deliberately destroyed—in this

case by a Muslim warlord, Bakhtiyar Khilji, in 1193. (A contemporary Persian historian reported that, "smoke from the burning manuscripts hung for days like a dark pall over the low hills.") The decline in Buddhism in India is ascribed to this catastrophe—and many hundreds of thousands of palm-leaf manuscripts recording early Indian work in medicine and science were destroyed. This is a rare survival.

ABOVE ***Astasahasrika Prajnaparamita***
This 12th-century sutra from Bihar depicts: at center, Bodhisattra Padmapani (white) seated on a multicolored lotus on his pink lotus throne; at left, Syamatara, the green Tara, with two goddesses and a blue lotus; at right, Mahakala, god of wealth, surrounded by flames and holding a mongoose.

Connections

李淳風小巷推崩洪搏換　搏骨換龍之法起天狐天角二星天狐雀巷
如勒馬發足如飛幡天角偃俛如犀午發足如競渡二星相照號曰正崩
洪成大地在五十里之外大都山勢成龍形勢直奔不慕祖宗走挽江水
窮極之下自然有樹石井泉陂堰社廟橋梁津渡寺觀神壇之類靈異變
怪接引連帶如飛鴻泊江如天虹貫水如鬥牛疾趨如龜蛇相顧如圭璧
之巧如倉廩之實至如吞漢無蹤氣脈沉寂其間有馬迹崩洪字崩洪
螺蚌崩洪交角崩洪莫石崩洪沉五敗石肌理相貫毛髮形狀相同
交互崩洪已上十大崩洪筋血崩洪川字崩洪之字崩洪
嚴惡醜怪人居逃移疾病神愚送性妖祥號為毒龍其處天角崩洪
深蓬妖精龍蠶旋是為崩洪之處也夫天狐天角二星正照龍神之地
主成大州郡或為王侯之都亦應仙之道如二星不正照則不滿五里
內有大地內密則居上上密則居下下供客則居其中更尋彼天關地
十大崩洪有以形象言者馬迹螺蚌者也字川之字是也真石者石露
軸為門為戶照對而定之自然龍神現矣　崩者山之明洪者水之共也
水面也沉石者石隱水中也交角者為吉山禍福師法別有十崩洪
血者以名取也然此十說與所為吉山禍福師法別有十崩洪一曰天角

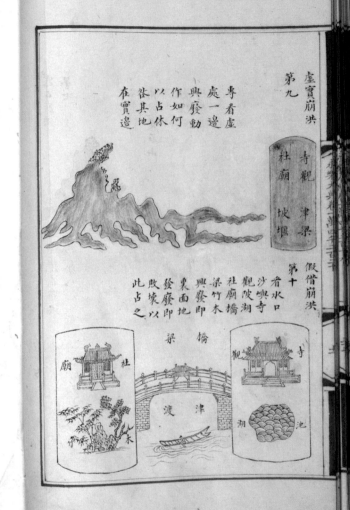

虛實崩洪
第九
寺觀津梁
專看虛
處一遍
與發動
作如何
以占休
咎其地
在實邊
社廟坡堰

假借崩洪
第十
看水口
沙學寺
觀陂湖
社廟橋
梁竹木
興發即
裏面地
發嶐即
敗壞以
此占之

廟　社
津　渡

ABOVE *Yongle Dadian* This general encyclopedia, an ambitious undertaking commissioned in 1403, encompassed history, the sciences, art and philosophy. This volume is from the third copy made in the Jianqing period (1562–67). These pages discuss flooding, illustrating the "actual situation" and "flood management." The red edges bear the title (*Yongle Dadian*), volume and page number.

The Biggest Books Ever Written

In 1403, the Chinese Ming emperor Yongle ordered the production of an encyclopedia, the Great Canon. *It was the biggest work attempted— until the Qing emperor, Qianlong, decided he could do better.*

Perhaps because of its long tradition of both literacy and centralized government, China has frequently produced massive collections of books of importance, more like complete collections of the information content of libraries than the summaries usual in Western encyclopedias. Soon after Emperor Yongle came to the throne, in 1403, he commissioned a large compilation on the whole range of knowledge, from religion, science, technology, astronomy, medicine and agriculture, through to drama, art, history and literature. Over 2,000 scholars were put to work analyzing and editing over 8,000 texts, completing their task in five years.

To write out the text, completed in 1408, the scribes used more than 370 million characters, filling over 11,000 volumes. Theoretically it would have been possible to have blocks cut to print the text (a much larger task than for the *Tripitaka Koreana*, see pp. 32–33), but instead only two manuscript copies were made. They were nearly destroyed by fire, so in 1557 the Jianqing emperor ordered a third copy to be made. Over the next 400 years, fire, war and looting reduced the holding of the three manuscripts to a mere 400 volumes, scattered in libraries and museums around the world.

The fame of the encyclopedia was remembered by the Qing emperor Qianlong, and in 1773 he instructed a team of scholars to prepare a new work, known as the *Siku Quanshu* or *Complete Library of the Four Treasuries*. Its production involved a lot of censorship: many works the editors believed were anti-Manchu were destroyed in this attempt to rewrite history. Learning from the past, the emperor Qianlong had seven manuscript copies made, and the scribes' work, completed in 1782, filled nearly 37,000 volumes, using 800 million characters. The devastation of wars has reduced them to four surviving sets, held in China and Taiwan.

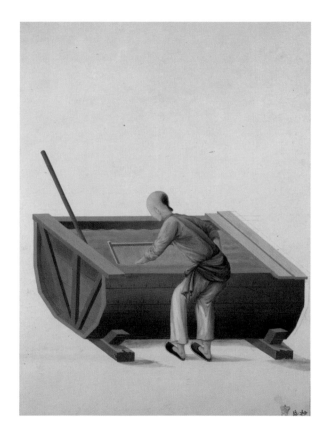

ABOVE **Chinese papermaking** This illustration of papermaking—showing the pulped fibers being raised on a mold, allowing water to drain through and a sheet forming on the mold's surface—comes from a 19th-century album of export paintings (intended for the foreign colonial market) depicting Chinese trades. The technique of the maker would have changed little since Yongle's day.

Connections

For other massive works of scholarship, see

Complutensian Polyglot Bible, **pp. 118–119**

Johnson's Dictionary, **pp. 154–155**

Diderot's Encyclopédie, **pp. 158–159**

For other Asian use of paper, see

Dunhuang Diamond Sutra, **pp. 80–81**

Bone, Bamboo and Bark

When these artifacts were first seen in Europe in the 18th century, the extraordinary books of the people of Sumatra astonished Western scholars.

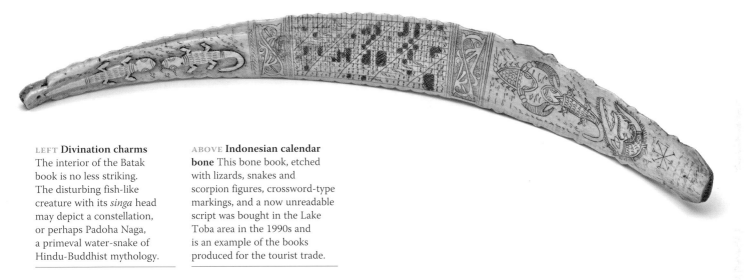

LEFT **Divination charms** The interior of the Batak book is no less striking. The disturbing fish-like creature with its *singa* head may depict a constellation, or perhaps Padoha Naga, a primeval water-snake of Hindu-Buddhist mythology.

ABOVE **Indonesian calendar bone** This bone book, etched with lizards, snakes and scorpion figures, crossword-type markings, and a now unreadable script was bought in the Lake Toba area in the 1990s and is an example of the books produced for the tourist trade.

Marco Polo and other earlier European travelers to Sumatra described the Bataks as a savage cannibalistic group, much feared by the Muslim people of Aceh to the north. There were cases of ritual cannibalism, much emphasized by Christian missionaries in the region in the nineteenth century.

Numbering some millions today, centered on Lake Toba, the Batak people had their own language and their own script, an **abugida** whose letters are of consonants modified by vowels (as also in the Ethiopian Ge'ez language). Before **paper** was introduced by Europeans, for casual use the batak script was scratched on bamboo pieces or sections, with black pigment rubbed in to make the letters more visible: the same method is now used also for writing on water buffalo bones, making "books" that are very different from those in other parts of the world.

It was reported that in the 1840s adolescent boys would send notes written on bamboo to girls, praising their glossy hair, their full breasts and their strength in stamping rice, but such bamboo love letters seem extinct. Instead, one finds *pustaha*, books used in medicine and religion for ritual divination. Sometimes incised on bones, these divinatory books are often written on the inner bark of the **alim** or agarwood tree

(*Aquilaria malaccensis*), now an endangered species. The pages are folded in concertina form, with writing and pictures on both sides, and written using pens made from buffalo horn, bamboo or sugar palm (*Arenga saccharifera*).

These *pustaha* were made only by a priest (*datu*) or his acolytes, and the ability to read them was limited to those who helped in their production. Such books are still prepared today—but only for the tourist industry. The Batak people have lost their old religion and their script has also dropped out of use, but these books remind us of alternative ways of conveying information and are valued in European research libraries.

Connections

For another use of bark in books, see

Boke van Bonang, pp. 92–93

For an earlier use of bones, see

Ishango Bone, pp. 16–17

For other calendars, see

Banneker's Almanack, pp. 170–171

Burmese Folding Format

*Palm leaves were used for manuscripts in Burma; when indigenous papermaking developed, a folding format—the **parabaik**—was adopted and used for books. These were so successful that they were still being produced at the end of the 20th century.*

In a wide area in northern Thailand, Laos and the Shan states of Myanmar (Burma), one sometimes sees unfamiliar oblong formats for texts and pictures, *kamawa-sa*, which are used in religious services in Buddhist monasteries. They are red lacquer panels, bearing texts painted in black tamarind-seed lacquer, with plentiful and often beautiful gold decoration.

Poorer relations of the *kamawa-sa* of religious texts (which were written on **paper** by young monks as part of their education) were *parabaiks*, accordion-style books on a stout cream paper made from the inner bark of the paper mulberry. Intended for religious instruction only, there were no illustrations. These usually ranged in size from about 5 ½ x 14 inches (14 x 36 centimeters) to 7 x 16 ½ inches (17 x 42 centimeters). With the edges of the folded sheets stained red, and covered in a reinforced red paper cover (with identifying text written on a central panel), they are light, portable book blocks, commonly still to be found in rural villages and therefore subject to insect attack.

One sometimes finds older *parabaiks* on a thick black paper, with text and pictures written with a steatite stylus (white on black). Used like slates for teaching, or as notebooks, the **sizing** of the black paper was tough enough to allow the text to be wiped off, so the *parabaik* could be used again.

In the past, the format was used for many purposes, and in the most sophisticated examples the brilliant colors and lively pictures of major events gave illustrated *parabaiks* an exuberance seldom found in other societies' manuscripts. The convenience of the format led the Burmese to produce how-to manuals for medicine, fashion and a variety of other topics, as in this 19th-century manual for tattooists. In traditional Burmese society, it was important for young men to be tattooed. The images of the tattoos (and their position on the body) would bring good luck. The artist's skill and delicacy in illustration is clear in this heavily used and worm-eaten manuscript.

Connections

For other how-to manuals, see

Al-Jazari's Mechanical Arts, **pp. 88–89**

Markham's Cavelarice, **pp. 140–141**

Helm's Art and Industry, **pp. 142–143**

Soyer's Modern Housewife, **pp. 202–203**

For other use of folding formats, see

Batak Pustaha, **pp. 38–39**

For very different uses of paper folding, see

Meggendorfer's Grand Circus, **pp. 198–199**

Prieto's Antibook, **pp. 250–251**

RIGHT **Burmese *parabaik*** Interspersed with the text in this 19th-century Burmese tattoo manual, roughly 15½ inches (40 centimeters) square, are mythical and real animals (a tiger, a dragon and an elephant) and a Burmese Nat-like figure. The circles below, enclosing animals and other symbols, probably represent planets.

ဒုံနဟဲံသာဗဲ့လှုကပွါနိဗ္ဗူဒဝံသာ သာလိကာသိနွာအောတုံးစီးရှင်နဲးကြား၌ခွံသာ တပါ့ကိုဘာတဏ္ဍာပိုသ့ ၍ပြီလှုတစက်တစ်ရွေးစိုင်ရှင်ကလှုပ်ဝါစ်တ်တွင်းသာဘ်ပန့် ရှိ၍တ်ထု့

အိုအောလွှုံ "ရွှေးပျံုစုးများ "သာလိကာဝမ်းထဲတွင်းယတလုံးရဲနောက်တော်ဟွမ့်မွှ်ဖြတ်"ပြင်တဘက်ကဗိးယ်းပိယ့်ရာရေးခေါ်တခနမ္မသာလိကာပဲးကာ့ ပုံ။ိုးထုံ

ကဝိတ်တိုနဲုဟာသာကားရဲကိုလ့ခုံ နဲ့ထုလုံးရဲ့ပြင်တဘက်ကသလ္လပ်ဆွီးရဲ့ ပြီးလ်ျာ"ရုပ်ရမ္မဒ်ဠ္ဘာ "သဗ္ဗေမတ္ထါကဏ္ဍာဏဗ်ပိယ်ကဏ္ဍာဆျွိဟိဝက်ဲယလ

မသာဒ်ဆိုနိုစိုရ်ျာရဲ့ ၊ ၌ဂရုံ ပံပြီ။ ၇ိုပ်ိယ့်ဒ်ဖှ် ၌ရဲ့ နဲ့ဘုရား၇ွံတွင်ဆုမ်ံသိ'ပေါ်န့ိုးဆ္ဇုပ်ား ပြင်၉ိုကာလကဏ္ဍ်ိုးစိုဟ်စိက်ကာ ကျုလျှင်မသနုံးမ'သ်ထိုင်ိုရ်ျာရဲ့ရ

မူတကာဏ္ဍာဏတ်ာလုံးသွင်းလေဥၥသ ယ်ဲဒ်ဖှ်းဒျိုရ်ရုံဆ္ဇုံတ်ို င်ပွ့ိုနာ ပြ၇ှ်ပြီ ၎ျူနရုပ်ရမ္မဒ်ႀ'ကြား ၅ဒ်ဟ်မေတွံ့ဥ္ဇသာဟ်တ်ံယထာကာရိ်ိကတ်ဖံဲနုု ပိးယာပုဏ္ဍာသ်ိဖ်ရိုး

ပွူံစွ ထ္ၱုုဘားလုံးသ့ဲလ်ျ့ဲ့ချိုး၍တ် ယန္တမဖစိုဂွံ'သ်နေဟဲ်းပိုယ်ဒါလ္တသရွေ၊ ချုးကူ၌ဲ့သ့သ္ဗ၀ဝတ်ိုး ၎ုဲ့နရုဒ္ဓုသ်မွံမွံရုပ်လ ပြီ'လ ့ုကာလဂ.်ဒ်ိုဲ့ ်ုရဲ့ နဲ့စိုး

ရဲ့အပါ့၊ဏ်ာ ့ပြီဲ့ ့ နိ၇ှ်ထား ပြီးလ်ျ့ဲ "လေလ၀ြမ္မဒ်ဆ်ိုး်ကား ်ပန့်ပေါ် ်ုံ်ုဆ်ုးပေါ် ်ုဏ်ေ်လ်ဲ်း်နွာ ့းုဲ့ ်ုကိုဲ့ မ္မဒ်ိုသ်ိလာ်ုပ်ား်ုုုံ်ဒ်ေ်ုမ်ုဏ်ျ်းကို်လ်

ရာသ္ဂိစ အ္ၱုုဲ်ကျ္ကြ္ကာလ ့ဲႀ်ိုုရ်ိုလ်းပါးသံသ်ဲ့ုွ့းဒ်ုနှာ်စိုိုး်ြ ုပြီၛီုလ်ျ့ဲ့ ်ုဥ္ၱ်ုးပ်ရမ္မဒ်မွ်ုဲကား ်ဒ်ုုလမ်ဲ်ု်ုႀ်ုဲ်ရ်ုႀ်ု်မ်ဲ်ုႀ်ုႀ်ုုႀ်ုႀ်ုဲ်ုႀ်ာ်ုႀ်ုုတ်ိုးေ်ာႀ်

တိရ်ိုဆ်မ်ိဲ်ုေ်ုဲ်ာႀ်ြ် ်ုဒ်ာေ်ာဖ်ုုုာလုံးအ်ုႀ်းုအ်ုသ်ု ်ကိုုႀ်ုသ်ုႀ်ုန်ု ်ုနွ်ုႀ်ာလိုင်းႀ်ုႀ်ုသ်ုုပ်ုုပ်နုုဲ်း ်ုေ်ုုႀ်ိုုႀ်ုာမ်ုႀ်ု်ုႀ်ုကိုဝ်တ်ုရ်ုဲ်ုေ်ာုရ်ုႀ်ုႀ်ုုု်ု်

ိုႀ်ုႀ်ုုႀ်ုႀ်ုုႀ်ုႀ်ုုႀ်ု်ကို ်ုပ်ုႀ်ုႀ်ုုႀ်ုႀ်ုုႀ်ုႀ်ုုႀ်ုႀ်ုုုဲ်ာ်ုႀ်ာလ်းုႀ်ုုုပ်ိုင်ုႀ်ုုႀ်ုုုႀ်ုုုႀ်ုုူႀ်ုုုႀ်ုႀ်ုုႀ်ုုုႀ်ု ်ုႀ်ုုုုု

်ုႀ်ုႀ်ုုုုုုုုုု်ေ်ုုႀ်ုုုုုုုုုုုုုုုုုုုုုုုုုုုုုုုုုု

်ု်ုႀ်ာ ်ုးုုု

CHAPTER

RIGHT **Homer's *Iliad*** The 10th-century Venetus A codex, in the Marciana Library, Venice, is the manuscript on which all modern editions of the *Iliad* are primarily based. Made probably in Constantinople c. 950 CE, it is writen in a fine minuscule script and the work has annotations in several hands. See pp. 48–49.

The Great Classics

In the 1,000 years from about 600 BCE, book production, authorship and information control all started to become standardized in the Greek and Roman cultures in a way we still understand. But worries about authority, censorship and access to information (and information loss) emerged.

δαῖμων· οὐδέ τι μ οἱ δ᾽ ἀλλήλοισι πος ἔϊπον·
οὐ μὲν δ᾽ ὁρμῆσοι περὶ καμβεος. λιω ὃ χ᾽ ἀπόλλων·
μουσάωρ τ᾽, αἵ ἄειδον ἀμειβόμεναι ὀπὶ καλῆ·
αὐτὰρ ἐπ᾽ κατέδυ λαμπρὸν φάος ἠελίοιο·
οἱ μὲν κακκείοντ᾽ ἔβαν οἶκον δὲ ἕκαστος·
ἧχι ἑκάστω δῶμα περικλυτὸς ἀμφιγυήεις
ἥφαστος ποίησεν ἰδυίησι πραπίδεσσι·
ζεὺς δὲ πρὸς ὃν λέχος ἤ᾽ ὀλύμπιος ἀστεροπητ
ἔνθα πάρος κοιμᾶθ᾽ ὅτε μιν γλυκὺς ὕπνος ἱκάνοι·
ἔνθα καθεῦδ᾽ ἀναβάς, παρὰ δὲ χρυσόθρονος ἥρη·

✻ ────────────── ✻

ΙΛΙΑΔΟΣ Β

Ἄλλοι μὲν ῥα θεοί τε καὶ ἀνέρες ἱπποκορυσταὶ
εὗδον παννύχιοι, Δία δ᾽ οὐκ ἔχε νήδυμος ὕπνος·
ἀλλ᾽ ὅ γε μερμήριζε κατὰ φρένα ὡς ἀχιλῆα
τιμήσῃ· ὀλέσῃ δὲ πολέας ἐπὶ νηυσὶν ἀχαιῶν·
ἥδε δέ οἱ κατὰ θυμὸν ἀρίστη φαίνετο βουλή·
πέμψαι ἐπ᾽ ἀτρεΐδῃ ἀγαμέμνονι οὖλον ὄνειρον·
καί μιν φωνήσας ἔπεα πτερόεντα προσηύδα·
βάσκ᾽ ἴθι οὖλε ὄνειρε θοὰς ἐπὶ νῆας ἀχαιῶν·
ἐλθὼν ἐς κλισίην ἀγαμέμνονος ἀτρεΐδαο·
πάντα μάλ᾽ ἀτρεκέως ἀγορευέμεν ὡς ἐπιτέλλω·

I t is easy to make a superficial distinction between prehistory, which had no written records, and history, in which records were written down. For prehistory we have information we have gathered from archaeological digs, and (for example) using forensic analysis of ancient corpses to learn what diseases they suffered from or what food they ate. We have masses of information gathered from Egyptian papyri or Mesopotamian **cuneiform**, and we can infer how they used the data. When reading such texts as the *Epic of Gilgamesh*, we feel we are getting into the minds of the people who wrote them—but they still seem alien: we cannot identify with them.

In a few centuries BCE, the advance of humankind into settled communities enabled writers to report their beliefs and experiences so well that we come to feel we share the culture we inherited from them (see pp. 46–47). In their alphabet and writing systems (first **boustrophedon**, then left to right), the Greeks developed the system we still use today, though now more often using the Roman alphabet developed in Italy.

The Book Trade and Libraries

With the increase in literacy came other changes. In the work of Sappho, women's voices could be heard. With literacy also came a trade in books, and libraries in which to keep them. In the great Alexandrian Library founded in the reign of Ptolemy I Soter (323–283 BCE) or by his son, the Greeks also moved toward punctuation and standardizing texts in the **papyrus** rolls they had to recopy (see pp. 48–49). Larger collections increased the library's needs for stock control: awareness of the idea of information overload is over 2,200 years old. The Alexandrian critic, librarian and bibliographer Callimachus, c. 305–240 BCE, developed library cataloging and the compilation of bibliographies: his 120-volume *Pinakes* is the best guide to some early Greek writing. Later librarians may share his belief that a big book is a big evil.

Alexandria was not the only city in which there was a major Greek library. There was another in Athens, the Lyceum. Under the Romans, libraries spread in Italy and elsewhere in the empire, such as the famous Celsus Library in Ephesus, erected at the expense of the Greco-Roman Senator Tiberius Julius Celsus Polemaeanus and completed in 135 CE. (Its stock of 12,000 **scrolls** was destroyed by earthquake and fire in 282 CE.)

Possessing a large library was seen as a source of power for rulers. Another large rival library was developed by Eumenes II in Pergamon (now Bergama, in western Anatolia). The Ptolemys in Egypt stopped exporting papyrus, partly because of competition with Pergamon, and the tradition is that the Pergamenes developed a new surface to use in books, *pergaminus* or *pergamena* (**parchment**). The competition with Alexandria ceased when Rome took control of Pergamon: reputedly, Mark Antony gave the content of the Pergamon Library of 200,000 volumes as a wedding present to Cleopatra!

Destruction of Books

The building survives at Pergamon, but presumably all its books were destroyed when the Alexandrian Library itself came to an end. Parts were lost when accidentally destroyed by fire under Julius Caesar; other parts may have been destroyed in later wars— or by Christian fervor, on the order of Theophilus, Bishop of Alexandria, who ordered the destruction of the Serapeum in 391 CE. Another source blames the destruction on the Muslims, now in control of the city. A man asked to be able to take books from the library: "If those books are in agreement with the Koran," he was told, "we have no need of them; if they are opposed to the Koran, destroy them." Religion, all religion, is often an enemy to books.

Whether Muslim or Christian in charge, ancient (pagan) books were in great danger of destruction. It was fortunate that the old system of writing on papyrus scrolls was replaced by the use of parchment folded into **quires** to make codices. Quires could be sewn together, and codices could be bound in boards (see pp. 50–51), creating a convenient and manageable unit. The use of the **codex** is often associated with the spread of Christianity, and the continued storage and preservation of books in remote monasteries ensured the survival of books lost in city libraries.

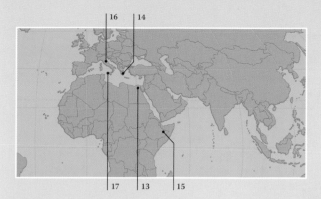

New Formats, Continuing Problems

With good longevity of the newer format (especially since they were written onto sturdy **vellum**), when they were in languages and scripts that could be read, and if they interested potential readers, texts stood a chance of being copied from scrolls onto codices. Easy reference to parts of the text was important for frequently consulted books such as cookbooks, and the codex was a more handy format than scrolls (see pp. 52–53). Books regarded as heretical or that aroused religious fervor would seldom be copied onto parchment, and sometimes, when on parchment, their texts were erased, leaving blank volumes that could be used again (**palimpsests**). Sometimes the only known surviving copy of a particular text was on one of these (see pp. 54–55).

We shall never know how many thousands of texts were copied from decaying papyrus to other scrolls, nor how many lost texts were never transferred to the new medium of parchment. Librarians and private owners had to pay rewriting costs and it was a significant expense. Nobody had to ensure that, for the sake of posterity, what ought to be copied was copied. As Callimachus was both a librarian and an esteemed poet, one would expect plenty of copies to be made of his work. A later Byzantine encyclopedia, the *Suda*, stated that Callimachus wrote some 800 works; but we now have only parts of a couple of long books, plus 64 epigrams, six hymns and some fragments. Probably less than 10 percent of Callimachus' output has survived.

This is an instance of the truism that, when switching from one recording medium to another, there is *always* a considerable data loss. As the Roman empire declined, continuing preservation of early texts would be dependent on the efforts of the book copyists in the Middle Ages—and good luck. Are there any resemblances to our current digitization concerns?

Origins of a Childrens' Classic

For well over 2,000 years, children around the world have enjoyed Aesop's fables. But who wrote them? Did Aesop really exist?

Aesop's fables are so widely known that we can casually mention a wolf in sheep's clothing, or sour grapes, for the reference to be recognized in almost every culture. For example, the fables were translated into Japanese and compiled into a single volume, entitled *Esopo no Fabulas*, by Portuguese missionaries in 1593, and the book was so well assimilated there that it remained the only European book allowed to be printed in Japan after Westerners were expelled.

Yet are the fables really of European descent? As well as Greek sources, there are parallels with Indian writing; and some similar stories were also included in the Talmud. In the Greek-speaking world, it seems clear that many Aesopian fables were circulating in oral tradition by the fifth century BCE, or even earlier. The "real" fabulist lived about 620–564 BCE and his work is mentioned by Herodotus, Aristophanes, Socrates and Plato. Everyone knew his fables; yet his very existence remains uncertain—and some scholars

have found Aesopian fables in Sumerian and Akkadian **cuneiform**, as ancient as the third millenium BCE.

Some of Aesop's fables were rewritten as *Aisopeia* by Demetrius Phalereus (c. 350–280 BCE), famous for his part in the founding of the Alexandrian Library under Ptolemy I Soter. But Demetrius' version of the fables perished; today, we rely instead on a text by Valerius Babrius, who lived some time before 200 CE. The earliest fragments of Greek **papyrus** manuscripts of the fables were rapidly followed by other manuscripts, in Latin and many other languages. Editions of Aesop's fables have been printed frequently, from the earliest days after Gutenberg's printing press to today.

A quarry in which many translators and poets have mined their texts, the visual attractiveness of the fables has also made the work of Aesop particularly appealing to illustrators and publishers, in the production of *livres d'artistes* and volumes designed for young children.

LEFT **A 17th century Aesop**
A bear overturns a beehive and is attacked by bees, in this 17th-century version of an Aesop fable. Etching by James Kirk after Francis Barlow.

Connections

For other books of fables and legends, see

Epic of Gilgamesh, *pp. 18–19*

Indian Panchatantra, *pp. 84–85*

For other books for children, see

Newbery's Little Pretty Pocket-Book, *pp. 156–157*

Aikin's Robinson Crusoe, *pp. 194–195*

Hoffman's Struwwelpeter, *pp. 196–197*

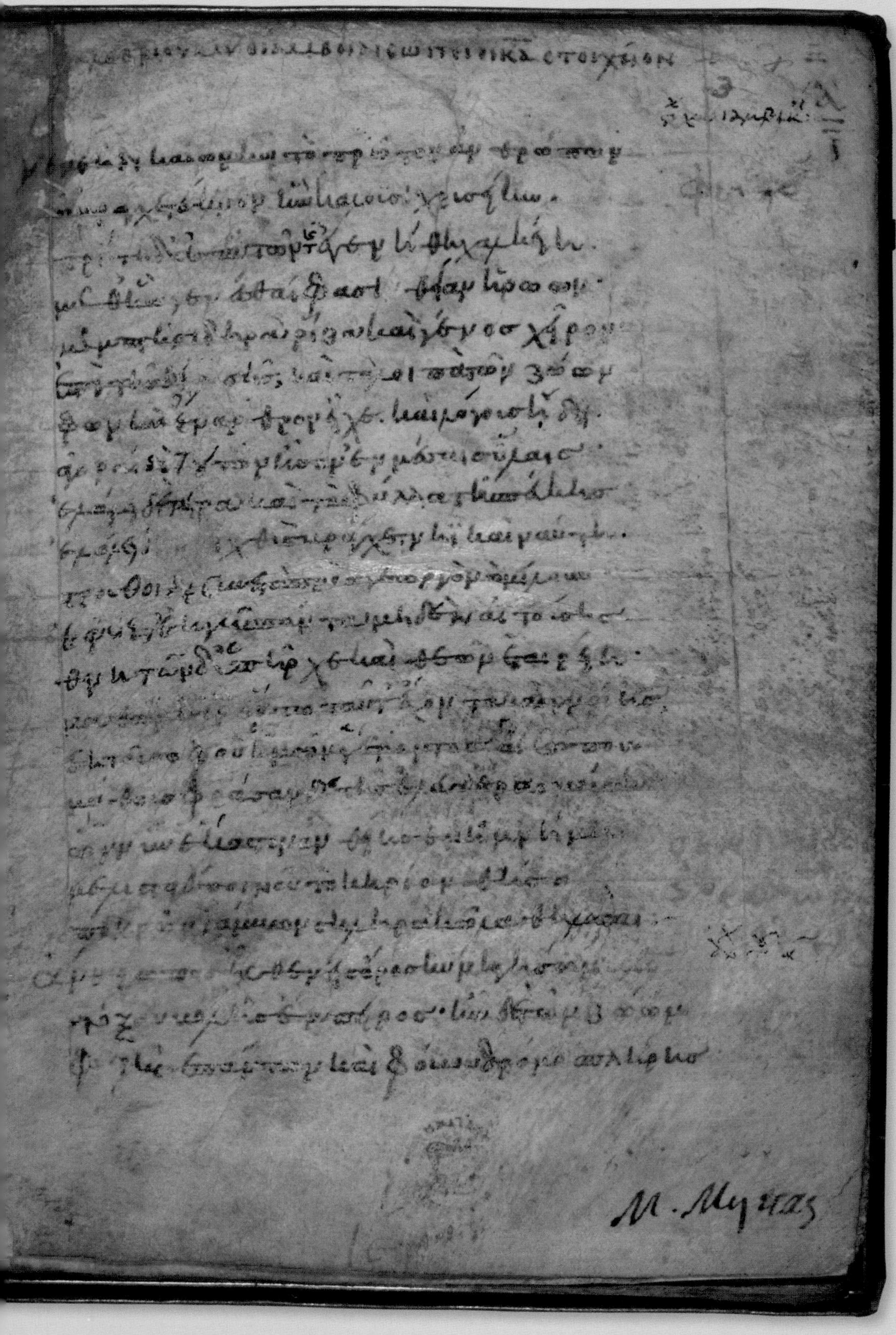

LEFT Aesop's fables This
11th-century parchment
manuscript of *Mythiambi
Aesopici*, bound in goatskin,
comes from Mount Athos.
Its **choliambic** Greek verse
betrays a Latin influence,
echoing the mongrel origins
of the fables. The Hellenized
Roman author, Babrius,
dedicates the verses to the
child "Branchus," causing
debate as to the identity
of himself and the child.

A Timeless Epic

Homer's Iliad *is one of the everlasting literary successes, for more than 2,000 years it has been restudied, translated and published. Yet the earliest days of its production are lost in history and the versions we use come from manuscripts a mere 1,000 years old.*

If asked to name the most important literary work of all time, many people would name Homer's *Iliad*. Or possibly the *Odyssey*, also attributed to Homer: although the survival rate of Egyptian **papyrus** fragments of them (454 bits of the *Iliad* preserved against about 140 of the *Odyssey*) suggests that the *Iliad*'s Iron Age reminiscence of Bronze Age combat was always favored.

Homer's epic was believed to have been composed between 750–650 BCE, though some authorities date it much earlier to the 12th century BCE; but it is accepted that the texts of the *Iliad* and the *Odyssey* were standardized in processes that have continued ever since. The role of the Alexandrian Library was important in this. The division of the text of the parts of the *Iliad* are attributed to its first librarian, Zenodotus of Ephesus (fl. 280 BCE); the best text was established by another of the librarians, Aristarchus of Samothrace (c. 220–c. 143 BCE).

Almost miraculously, the content of Aristarchus' commentaries have been preserved in a manuscript in Venice, known as "Venetus A." Written in Greece in the ninth century CE, it was imported to Italy by an Italian scholar who took back Greek manuscripts to Italy. It passed into possession of Cardinal Bessarion (1403–1472), a scholar largely responsible for the Italian Renaissance revival of Greek studies. In 1468, he presented his manuscripts to the Senate of Venice, and they remain the nucleus of the Biblioteca Marciana.

The fame of Venetus A always attracted scholars; but the manuscript was showing its age, with ink fading and other deterioration, making continuing scholarly use impossible. A triumph of modern technical enterprise has enabled the Marciana and the Center for Hellenic Studies at Harvard to prepare a digital version in the Homer Multitext project. It presents the textual transmission of the *Iliad* and *Odyssey* in a historical framework, and echoes the enthusiasm of the first Homerian scholars who worked to preserve it in Alexandria.

LEFT **Homer's *Iliad*** This 10th-century illustration, from the Venetus A manuscript, depicts the Spartan queen Helen with Paris (son of Trojan king Priam) setting sail for Troy, with Aphrodite, who has brought the couple together. Paris cuckolds Menelaus, Helen's husband, and the Greek attempts to retrieve her were the basis for their famous siege of Troy.

Connections

For other epics, see

Epic of Gilgamesh, *pp. 18–19*

Aldine Virgil, *pp. 108–109*

For other books with serious conservation problems, see

Archimedes Palimpsest, *pp. 54–55*

Book of Kells, *pp. 60–61*

Electronic Beowulf, *pp. 242–243*

An Early Masterpiece of Ethiopian Art

Only recently known to the wider world, the Garima Gospels are far older than almost any Bible manuscripts. Written when Christianity was first introduced to Africa, they have been kept in the Garima library for over 1,600 years.

This is an outstanding example of Ethiopian Bible illustration and the oldest known Bible to have been written in this early center of Christianity. Held in the Monastery of Abuna Garima in the mountains of northern Ethiopia, this **parchment** manuscript was hardly known in the West until a British art historian saw it when visiting the abbey in 1950. At first, experts believed it to be about 1,000 years old, but recent radiocarbon dating of the goatskin parchment used for the volumes reveals that one was made about 390–570 CE

and the second about 550–660 CE. The binding of Garima I is believed to be the oldest known still attached to a manuscript. For over 1,600 years, these volumes have been preserved in the monastery.

According to tradition, Saint Abba Garima, one of the nine Ethiopian saints, arrived in Ethiopia in 494 CE and evangelized the country. These volumes were written soon after that. The dating has excited art and Bible historians, because these volumes are some of the earliest to have survived. All ancient manuscripts are vulnerable, and some damage has resulted from inept repairs undertaken in the past, but this Ethiopian treasure's future has been assured by conservation work commissioned by the Ethiopian Heritage Fund.

Most countries produce versions of their sacred texts, such as the Torah and the Koran, which typify the spiritual and artistic nature of the nation. Ethiopia separated from Catholicism and orthodoxy in the middle of the fifth century CE, and this Bible is written in the Ge'ez language. The script, **Amharic**, was related to Hebrew, but written from left to right, using reed pens and locally prepared pigments. The two volumes were written by different scribes, each needing many months to complete their labor. The illumination is thought to be more similar to Byzantine work than to most later Ethiopian Bibles, but it possesses the same vigor and energy of Ethiopian manuscripts written many centuries later.

LEFT **Garima Gospels** Radiocarbon analysis dates these to between 330 and 650 CE; as such, they are probably the earliest surviving illustrated Christian manuscripts. Comprising three vividly decorated manuscripts in two volumes, they are written in the Aksumite Ethiopic language, formerly known only from coins or stelae.

Connections

For other ancient books with conservation problems, see
Book of the Dead of Ani, *pp. 22–23*
Archimedes Palimpsest, *pp.54–55*
Electronic Beowulf, *pp. 242–243*

For other Bible texts, see
Book of Kells, *pp. 60–61*
Chludov Psalter, *pp. 62–63*
T'oros Roslin Gospels, *pp. 66–67*

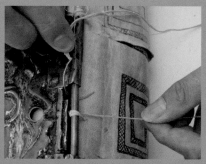

ABOVE **Garima binding** The metal covers are believed to be contemporary with the manuscripts themselves; that of Garima I, of gilded copper with holes that would have once held precious stones, is the oldest known binding still attached to its manuscript. The silver boards of Garima II are later, 10th to 12th century.

ABOVE **Repairing the Gospels** The vibrant decorative work is Byzantine in style, possibly from Syria or Jerusalem, though Garima II (shown here) bears some affinity with Coptic decoration. Some 20 species of birds of a Middle Eastern, not Ethiopian, type, occur throughout. The now-brittle parchment shows signs of past repairs, folds and insect damage.

ABOVE **Resewing the Gospels** The three parchment Gospel manuscripts were bound in two volumes, some, over the years, misbound into the wrong order. Expert conservator Lester Capon repaired and rebound the pages with fine linen threads (here, reattaching the front board in Garima I).

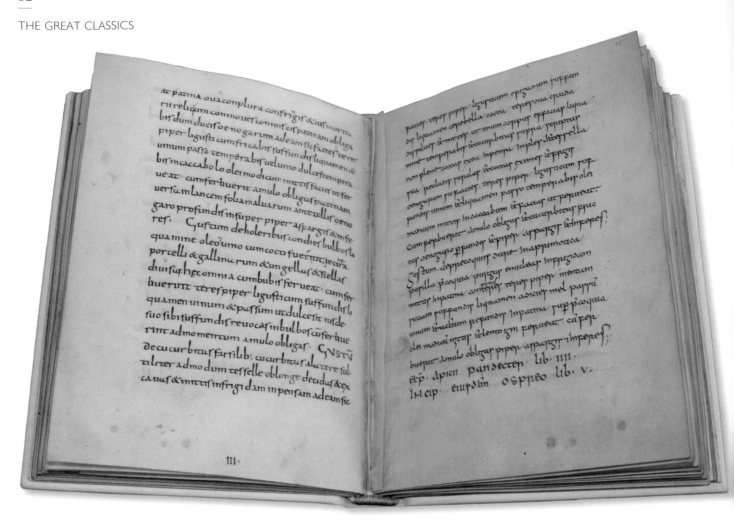

The First Cookbooks

The Egyptians, Babylonians and Greeks were all interested in the food they ate. But the earliest serious cookbook surviving is simply known as Apicius. *It conveys the excesses of the Roman empire about 2,000 years ago—but we still don't know much about its author.*

In 1498, about 45 years after Gutenberg first printed the Bible, the Milan printer Guillermus le Signerre published *Apicius de re quoquinaria* and a variant edition issued by Joannes de Legnano. Another pirated text was published in Venice about 1500. Cookbooks were already seen as sure sellers.

The earliest manuscript, in the Vatican Library, dates from the fourth or fifth century CE. It is ascribed to a famous Roman gourmand, Marcus Gavius Apicius, who lived in the reign of Tiberius. There were many mocking references to his gluttony by

ABOVE *Apicius* The New York Academy of Medicine owns one of the two earliest copies of this second-century cookbook, from the monastery of Fulda in Germany, where it was transcribed, c. 830. Its 57 pages contains some 500 recipes; while larks' tongues and boars' bottoms might be scarce at the butchers today, many ingredients, such as for the bean and apricot stews described here, are familiar and deliciously cookable.

RIGHT **Sprinkle on pepper and serve** This fresco fragment, 50–75 CE from a villa near Boscoreale, Naples, shows barefoot kitchen staff gutting an animal, probably a fawn. The metal tray, at left, holds garlic and some of the costly imported spices favored by wealthy Roman gourmands, and by Apicius, for their often elaborate cuisine.

such writers as Martial, Seneca, Athenaeus and Pliny. For example, Pliny reported that after he had seen how *foie gras* was made, Apicius devised a similar way of improving pork liver, by feeding his pigs with dried figs and then slaughtering them with an overdose of *mulsum* (honeyed wine).

As in so many cases when we think we know about Roman history, much is purely surmise. Marcus Gavius Apicius certainly existed, but the collection of recipes attributed to him was probably never written by him at all, in the way that the attribution of particular fables to Aesop is merely a guess. The collection of recipes was probably assembled in the fourth century CE, and several later manuscripts are known. The value of having a collection of recipes was clear to anyone who had to order or prepare meals; other such manuscript collections survived the same wear and tear of many practical manuals, and copies of cookbooks were often used to destruction (equally true later of printed editions). Pasta and tomatoes, so vital in modern Italian cooking, were unknown to the Romans, and we have only guesses at the taste of the (now extinct) plant silphium used widely in Roman cooking, or whether their commercially produced liquamen was something like Worcestershire sauce.

Plenty of later people have been interested in the recipes given by Apicius, and we can now read heated arguments in online discussion groups and in learned journals about how this or that dish was spiced. Access to the text of Apicius is far better today than at any earlier period, and this cookbook is the ancestor of the many thousands produced since.

Connections

For a more practical how-to cookbook, see:

Soyer's Modern Housewife, *pp. 202–203*

A Mathematical Miracle

Archimedes is one of the most important mathematicians of all times, but many of his written works disappeared during the Middle Ages. Then, in 1906, a vellum manuscript with some of his texts was found, but unfortunately its text was almost unreadable.

BELOW Archimedes Palimpsest On 174 scraped-back parchment leaves, this Byzantine Prayer Book, 1229, overwrites a 10th-century copy of texts by ancient writers, including seven treatises by Archimedes and speeches by the orator Hypereides. These are now barely but tantalizingly discernible, often at right angles or in the margins, beneath the 13th-century texts.

LEFT **Imaging the palimpsest** Conservation and complex imaging processes were undertaken to reveal the hidden texts and diagrams. In this example, the "true-color" image (far left) carries only faint clues of what lies beneath; the diagram is revealed much more clearly in the grayscale image (left).

Archimedes discovered many theorems that were later used by Galileo, Leibniz and Newton: modern mathematics came from his work. Archimedes was also the inventor of the screw pump, still widely used today; and reputedly he was the key figure in the defence of his home-city Syracuse when it was attacked by the Romans in 282 BCE. Archimedes' fame lasted, but his mathematical texts were difficult and so not widely recopied.

By the fifth century CE, **vellum** or **parchment** had become the usual writing surface used in Europe. It was expensive to buy and lasted for centuries, often long after the manuscript's owner was interested in the text. Scraping the text off or washing away the ink left a book with pages that could be used again; this was so common in the seventh century that there was a synodal decree forbidding the cleaning of religious texts.

If the text was not completely cleaned off, the hidden texts could sometimes be read. Such recycled manuscripts (or **palimpsests**) excited later classical scholars, who often used heat or chemicals to make the text readable but also damaged the manuscript and accelerated their decay rapidly. (Palimpsests cause many problems for conservators.)

The history of the Archimedes Palimpsest reads like the plot of a bad thriller. In the 1840s a section of the manuscript was "borrowed" from the library of the Jerusalem Holy Sepulchre in Constantinople. Mysteriously, when the Turkish government was in disarray after World War I, the Greek government organized the secret (and illegal) removal of the content of the library in Constantinople to Athens. The Archimedes manuscript then disappeared, apparently to Paris where it was "augmented" with some forged illustrations, and finally ended up in an auction sale in the 1990s.

There was considerable fuss about the legal ownership of the manuscript before possession passed to the Walters Art Museum in Baltimore. On a cursory glance the Walters acquisition was just a fragile and decayed Christian prayer book, written in 1229 in Jerusalem; but underneath the prayers (and the forged illustrations) was the text of several books by Archimedes, which were totally unknown. Photographing the palimpsest pages to make the texts available in a digital form presented numerous novel difficulties, but means that scientists around the world can now read Archimedes' hidden texts.

Connections

For other ancient vellum codices, see

Homer's Iliad, **pp. 48–49**

Garima Gospels, **pp. 50–51**

For other mathematical books, see

Euclid's Elementa Geometriae, **pp. 106–107**

Newton's Principia, **pp. 138–139**

For use of innovative imaging techniques, see

Book of the Dead of Ani, **pp. 22–23**

Electronic Beowulf, **pp. 242–243**

Technion Nano Bible, **pp. 246–247**

RIGHT **St. Matthew at his Gospel** Armenian priest T'oros Roslin decorated his Gospels with exquisitely painted miniatures, using ink, colored pigments and gold leaf. This full-page portrait shows the evangelist author at work dipping his brush into an inkwell. See pp. 66–67.

CHAPTER

4

Medieval Worlds & the Book

Though bookselling and literacy declined in Europe during the Middle Ages, monks working in scriptoria preserved many classical works. And with the coming of the Renaissance, scribes and artists produced some books whose beauty has never been equaled.

From the end of the classic European civilizations to the coming of printing was like the passing of the seasons: a long autumnal decline, a harsh winter in which little grew except in a few sheltered spots, followed by a spring in which fresh signs of life and the coming of flowers moved on to the rich warm and fruitful summer of the Renaissance. Thomas Hobbes described primitive life as having, "no account of time; no arts; no letters; no society; and … the life of man, solitary, poor, nasty, brutish and short." Of course, the medieval world was not altogether like this. The onset and severity of the seasons varied in different places, and in the eastern Byzantine empire, it sometimes seemed that the fall would last for ever. In the Far East, and in areas that came under control of Islam, the climate was also more propitious.

In the West, literacy declined drastically: no commercial copying of texts or trade in books; libraries and their stocks decaying or disappearing. Three things saved knowledge of the older world: first, the spread of the use of **parchment** as the normal writing surface; second, the general adoption of the **codex** form led to new ways of protecting texts (bookbindings), which improved the chances of books' survival; third, the reverence for holy books, which led to the establishment of scriptoria in monasteries and the encouragement for clergy to be able to read.

THE COMING OF SCRIPTORIA

Many monasteries were famous for their scriptoria. Marmoutier near Tours, founded by St. Martin about 372 CE, produced many manuscripts of great value before being pillaged by the Normans in 853 CE and was then destroyed in the French Revolution. It was reported that, "No art was practiced there, except that of transcribers"; and Marmoutier manuscripts were famous for the clarity of their calligraphy. A later Abbot, the great English scholar Alcuin (c. 735–804 CE), worked for Charlemagne and developed the style of writing known as the **Carolingian minuscule**, which was the model for the scripts and **typefaces** that we call **roman** and use today.

THE IRISH INFLUENCE

Ireland and Northumbria were other great centers of monastic scriptoria, particularly under the influence of St. Columba (521–597 CE; see pp. 60–61). Legend has it that in about 561 CE Columba got into a dispute about a copy he made of a **psalter** owned by St. Finnian, who apparently believed the copy should become his, and some monks were killed. Not totally disastrous: Columba went into exile and founded another abbey in Iona (Scotland), from which for several centuries Irish monks moved to other scriptoria in Germany, Austria and Switzerland. Though it was also attacked, the later monastery in St. Gallen still owns manuscripts copied in its scriptorium 1,000 years earlier.

These Irish monks continued to decorate their manuscripts in the same **Insular** style as in the *Book of Kells*, but they did not always lead a totally austere life: one scribe at St. Paul's Abbey in Lavanttal (Carinthia) wrote in the margin of a book a short poem in Irish:

> *I and Pangur Ban, my cat,*
> *'Tis a like task we are at;*
> *Hunting mice is his delight,*
> *Hunting words I sit all night.*

At the other end of Europe, in Constantinople, religious discords were sometimes revealed in the illuminated manuscripts produced there (see pp. 62–63). The copying of important ancient Greek manuscripts still continued, and surviving reputations of ancient Greek physicians and scientists ensured that their books would be recopied—and read (see pp. 64–65). But sometimes old texts in these manuscripts were not wanted, or could not be read. Their parchment leaves were then used to make palimpsests (see pp. 54–55).

Farther east was the kingdom of Armenia, which, like the Byzantines, and Georgians or Ethiopians and other distinctive and often inward-looking societies, developed its own traditions in bookmaking (see pp. 66–67).

THE CAROLINGIAN REVIVAL

In the West, the Carolingian renaissance of the eighth and ninth centuries CE was in some ways an attempt to recreate the previous culture of the Roman Empire, though its effect was greatest on the clergy, not the laity. The rediscovery of old documents was usually beneficial, but it also had a downside: it encouraged attempts at forgery. The so-called "false decretals," for example, were used as ammunition in the struggle between centralized and decentralized authority in the Roman church. The genuine manuscripts among the forgeries are still tainted.

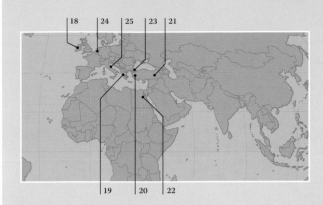

Forgery is still extensively used as a weapon in propaganda. It is currently also a curse for those working with manuscripts—partly because of the astronomical prices of manuscripts, partly also because of the frequency of looting and theft. The manuscript market was recently described as "not only full of dubious material, but full of untruthfulness and deceit of every kind." The production of facsimiles and digital surrogates ought to alleviate that, but it also increases the temptations for the unscrupulous who want to own the real thing.

As the spring of the Middle Ages progressed, the revival of interest in manuscripts and learning generally accelerated the development of humanism. People were becoming aware of the wider world (see pp. 68–69 and 70–71).

UNIVERSITIES AND BOOK COLLECTING

The emergence of universities—starting with Bologna in 1088, Paris by 1150 and Oxford by 1167—increased the demand for books at a time when library provision was pitiful. Students needed access to good-quality texts, and the universities organized **pecia** systems, whereby stationers would provide copies of texts in parts (or pieces) at approved rates. Academic libraries increased in size, slowly. The fashion of collecting a personal library became increasingly common. The English Benedictine Richard de Bury (1287–1345) is remembered mainly as a book collector, and his *Philobiblon* (completed 1345) is often regarded as the first book on library management. De Bury planned to establish an Oxford hall to maintain the collection, but his books were dispersed when he died, and only two volumes from his library are now known.

Lavishly prepared illuminated manuscripts were fashionable with the aristocracy, and some were written long after Gutenberg's inventions. The taste for luxury continued to ensure that *de luxe* books would continue to be produced; not to be read, but to be admired—a taste mocked by Sebastian Brandt in his *Das Narrenschiff* (*The Ship of Fools*, 1494) and by many others since. Many of these beautiful books prepared in Flanders and Italy survive (see pp. 72–73 and 74–75)—and how much we still admire them!

RIGHT *Book of Kells* This Chi-Rho, one of the most beautiful pages in the manuscript, uses the christogram as the template for its glorious interlace design. It is the largest and most lavish surviving monogram of any Insular Gospel book, with heavenly and earthly creatures interwoven within its intricate knotwork.

Ireland's Greatest Treasure

The superb manuscript known as the Book of Kells (Leabhar Cheanannais) *is one of the cornerstones of Irish identity. Its survival after Viking raids (and later attacks) was almost miraculous.*

In our primary schools we learned that St. Patrick brought Christianity to Ireland, and that later his follower St. Columba and other monks went to Iona in 563 CE to convert the pagan Picts. We read that later Irish monks settled on Lindisfarne island, to bring the religion to the Anglo-Saxons in northern England. Irish missionary zeal continued and was not limited to the British Isles: over several centuries, the Irish were active in setting up abbeys in parts of continental Europe.

The style of art known as **Insular** (or Hiberno-Saxon) Art developed from Irish and Anglo-Saxon traditions, as well as from the vestiges of Mediterranean styles, and is particularly noticeable in the decoration of illuminated manuscripts in these abbeys. The *Lindisfarne Gospels*, prepared about 715 CE, is the finest surviving in the United Kingdom. There are other manuscripts in Insular style, prepared under one of Columba's followers, St. Gall, (c. 550–646 CE), who established the Abbey of St. Gall (Switzerland), with a famous scriptorium.

The most famous manuscript of all in Insular style is the *Book of Kells*, written at the end of the eighth century and named from the abbey in County Meath (founded by St. Columba about 554 CE). Some experts believe that the *Book of Kells* was written and illuminated at Iona, but because of increasing Viking attacks on Iona it was evacuated to Kells; others believe that it was produced by the monks in Kells. Despite further Viking attacks on Kells, the manuscript

survived and fortunately its local fame kept it in the church safely until 1654. Cromwell's cavalry was then quartered in the church at Kells; for its safekeeping, Protestant clergy passed the manuscript to Trinity College in Dublin in 1661. It remains there to this day.

The beauty of the illumination, and the importance of the manuscript in Irish history, secured its survival. But the cultural and patriotic importance of the *Book of Kells* means that *every* tourist visiting Dublin wants to see it: not a facsimile, not a digital surrogate, but the real thing itself. Display brings income for the library, but it also increases the rate of decay—a challenge for conservators.

Connections

For other brilliant illuminated manuscripts, see

Chludov Psalter, pp. 62–63

T'oros Roslin Gospels, pp. 66–67

Cristoforo's Liber Insularum Archipelagi, pp. 70–71

Farnese Hours, pp. 74–75

For a much more puritanical religious manuscript, see

Boke van Bonang, pp. 92–93

bgeneratio

RIGHT **Chludov Psalter** "They gave me also gall for my meat; and in my thirst they gave me vinegar to drink": in this extraordinary manuscript, stored in Mount Athos until 1847, the miniaturist illustrates Psalm 69. Below, the iconoclast John VII, originally an icon painter himself, is satirically depicted in a mirroring action whitewashing the portrait of Christ.

Schism and Discord

Illuminated manuscripts often portray the power and importance of rulers. Is this a deliberately subversive one?

The history of every religion includes many instances of competition, intrigue and sometimes bloodshed between one group and another. Whether Sunnis or Shiites, Catholics or Protestants, the groups feel passionately about their cause. Looking at the illuminated manuscripts produced in the long years of Byzantine Orthodox Christianity, we can forget that there were strong advocates or opponents of any particular belief. In the Catholic churches, some grew into anti-image groups in the Protestant movements; in Orthodoxy, the battles raged between the iconoclasts (like the Armenian emperor, Leo V) who wished to destroy all icons, and the iconophiles, who venerated them. In the end the iconophiles, under the new Empress Theodora, triumphed.

It is rare to find manuscripts whose decoration provides evidence of the struggle between the two groups. At first glance, the Chludov Psalter is a typical Orthodox **psalter** written in Constantinople in the middle of the ninth century CE and following the liturgy of Hagia Sophia. It was produced in the Imperial workshops soon after the return of the iconophiles to power in 843 CE. As so often happened, the scribes wrote their texts leaving wide margins, so that decorations could be added by others, in this case using a small **uncial** script (with much of it crudely rewritten several hundred years later, in a **minuscule** script).

The decoration is different from the ordinary formulaic pictures of Bible scenes. In the crucifixion scheme, as well as the Roman soldier offering Christ a sponge with vinegar on a pole, there is a picture of a figure erasing a picture of Christ in the same way. This was a reference to John the Grammarian, Patriarch of Constantinople (and the last Iconoclast Patriarch). On several pages John is illustrated to appear ridiculous, an uncouth man with wild hair. The decoration would probably date from about 843 CE, at the time John was deposed from his patriarchate.

Marxist historians see the iconoclast/iconophile disputes as being a medieval instance of class struggle. If true, is the Chludov Psalter an instance of a subversive publication? Its style is rare in Byzantine art.

Connections

For other Greek/Byzantine manuscripts, see

Homer's Iliad, **pp. 48–49**

Dioscorides' De Materia Medica, **pp. 64–65**

Ptolemy's Geographia, **pp. 68–69**

For a tourist's visit to Constantinople, see

Cristoforo's Liber Insularum Archipelagi, **pp. 70–71**

καὶ τὴν ταλαιπωρίαν ημου καὶ τὴν ἐμ τρο
πιμμου· ἐμαρτιομοσυπομτεσοιθλι
βορτεσμε·

+ Ο ρει δε μόμ τα ρ σεδοκισερικ ψυχλιω·
καὶ ταλαιπωριαμ· καὶ ὑπεκμφαϲου
λιπουμεμον καὶ ου χὺτορε· καὶ
παρακαλουμ τας καιου χευρον·

+ Καὶ εδωκαμ εἰς τὸ ιρομαμου χολημ·
καὶ ἐστὴμ διψαμμου ἐποτισαμμεοζος·

+ Γερηθη τω ι τραπεζασαυπομεμοπὴ
ομωμπαι εἰς παιδωκαι εσαυτατο
δωστρκαιεσ οκομ δεκαμ·

+ Σκοτισθη τω οδμοιοφθαλμοι αυτωμ
του μλικλεπειμ· καὶ τομμωτομαυ

+ Τωμ δια τα σεμ τρεσουγκαλομε·

+ Εκ χεομε παυτοις τημ ορ γημσου· καὶ
ὁ θυμος τασοργημεσου κατα λα
βοι αυτοις·

+ Γερηθη τω η επαυ λιϲ αυτωμ ηρημω
μεμη· καὶ ερι ποις κημεσθαυτωμ αυ
τωμ μη εστωοκ ατοικεμ·

+ Ο τιϲ ου επα ταξασαυτικαλοι εξαμ
και επιτο ναλγεσ τωμτραυμω μω προι μω

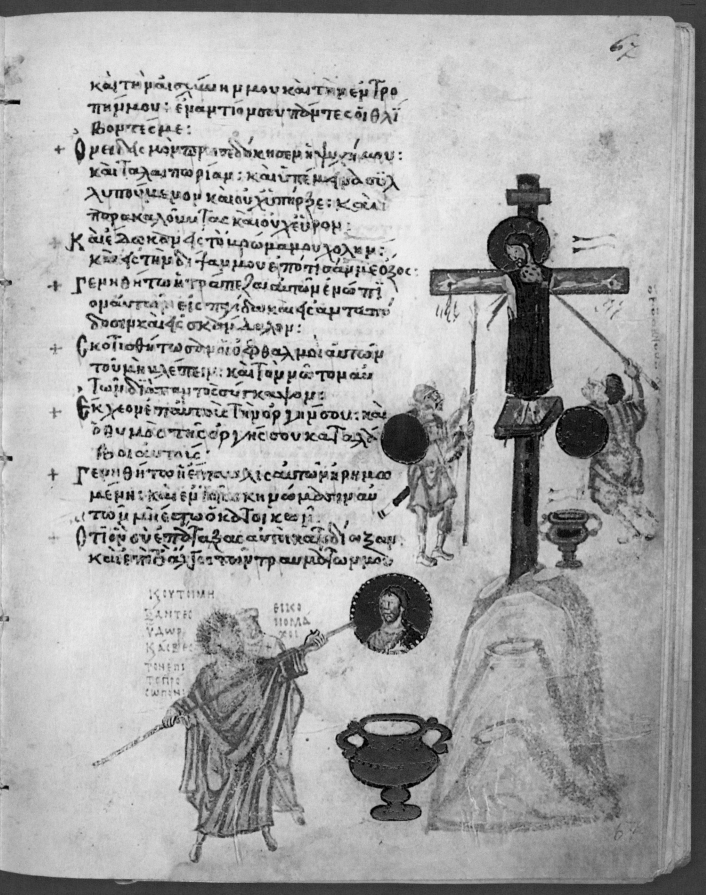

RIGHT *De Materia Medica*
Made by Yusuf al-Mawsili for
Shams ad-Din in Northern
Iraq or in Syria, 1229, this
loosely inserted page in
Dioscorides' manuscript is the
single known copy of a nature
print in the Islamic world.

طبع

نكه كرفش جبلي له قضبان تعلو شبر واحد مرا صل غلط مستدير به
قضبان صغار وله راس كراس الشوكران وله ثمره طويله جرعينه طيبه تشبه
الكمون تنبت في الصخور والمواضع الجبلية لثمرته قوة اذا شرب الجزر ادرا البول
واحد الطمث وبلطان في المعالجبر والابازير الحار

The Foundation of Pharmacology

Until the 17th century, medicines were herbal remedies based on extracts from plants. The Greek Dioscorides remains the most important figure in the development of modern medicine.

With the Hippocratic Oath, the history of medicine is conventionally held to start with Hippocrates of Cos (c. 460–370 BCE). Medical practice depended largely on preparations made from plants, and knowing which plants could cure (or kill) was vital. In prehistory, such knowledge was passed orally, but Pedanus Dioscorides systematized this information in his book known as *De Materia Medica*, written about 30–50 CE. An army surgeon attached to Roman forces in Nero's time, Dioscorides traveled widely in the Middle East. He identified the pharmacological properties and remedial effects of over 100 plants previously unknown to Roman and Greek physicians, and he also discussed over 500 other plants that were probably used earlier during Alexander the Great's conquests.

De Materia Medica became a standard text used by herb gatherers and pharmacists for over 1,500 years, spawning many manuscripts (and later printed versions) created all over the Western world—and in Arab lands even more than in Europe. Many manuscripts had such stylized representations of plants that they would not be useful for plant identification; but the best manuscripts had illustrations by artists who had enough knowledge to portray the roots, stems, stalks and flowers from the plant in front of them. This was always a slow business, but it was executed with skill in early manuscripts such as the famous *Codex Vindobonensis* (now in Vienna), prepared in Constantinople about 512 CE for the Byzantine princess Juliana Anicia.

The manuscript illustrated here is a later one, copied about 1228 in Anatolia or Syria by a scribe known as Bihnam the Christian and based on another Arabic manuscript now in Paris. Bihnam had the bright idea of inking the leaves of a plant and pressing them onto paper, to transfer an image that then could be colored and completed quickly and easily—and

ABOVE **Dioscorides** In an illustration from Bihnam's version of the *De Materia Medica*, Dioscorides is seen with a male disciple (perhaps personifying Heuresis, or Learning, more usually shown as a woman), holding a mandrake.

with complete accuracy. Such **nature printing** became commonly used by Italian botanists in the 15th century, but Bihnam's innovation was not followed in the Arab world, although Dioscorides' book continued to be copied.

Connections

For another herbal manuscript, see

Blackwell's Curious Herball, pp. 144–145

For other botanical books, see:

Linnaeus' Species Plantarum, pp. 160–161

For further medical development, see

Mansur's Anatomy, pp. 90–91

Vesalius' De humani corporis fabrica, pp. 134–135

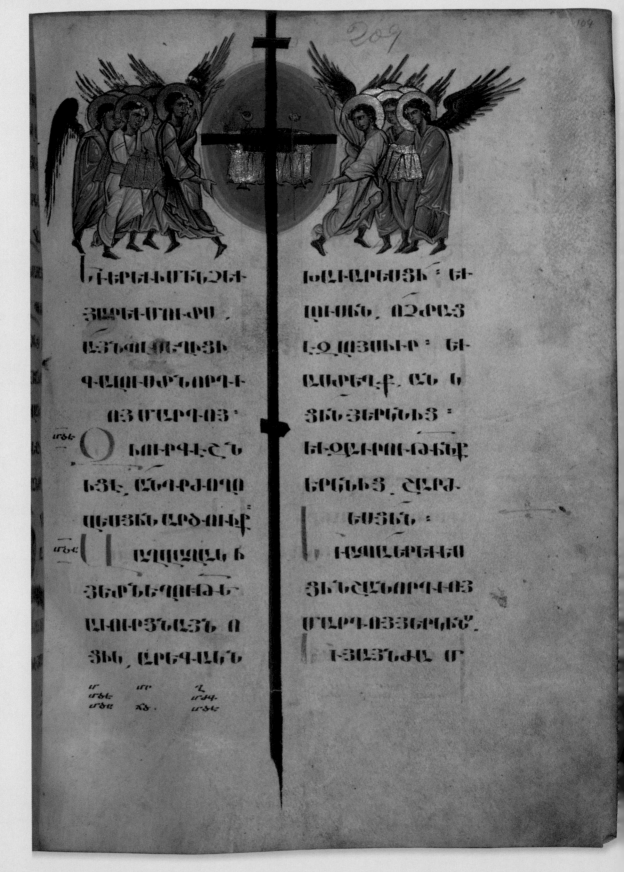

A Masterpiece of Armenian Illumination

Like Ethiopia and Ireland, the ancient culture of Armenia produced some books very different from other countries, and particularly those of the famous artist, T'oros Roslin.

From the days of Assyrian, Greek and Roman empires to times of Mongolian, Persian and Turkish control, the Armenians, despite all odds, doggedly maintained themselves as a cultivated people with their own language, scripts and cultural traditions. Because of its geographical location, Armenia was influenced by other countries as far east as China, while its religious connections with Byzantium and other Christian countries meant that its writers and artists would normally look west.

Armenian manuscript illumination dates from the sixth or seventh centuries CE and, as in the markedly different Ethiopian tradition, it was largely limited to sumptuous manuscripts of the Gospels. The oldest dated and illuminated is the Gospel of Queen Mlké of 862 CE. Many of these were produced for rulers and senior church officials. The Armenian kingdom of Cilicia (in the area now in Turkey, south of the Taurus Mountains and north of Aleppo) had an important center in the east called Hromkla, where the most important manuscript artists worked. The best known was T'oros Roslin (fl. 1256–68), believed to have been a priest. Some claim he was of mixed Crusader and Armenian descent: Roslin is not an Armenian name.

Most Armenian Bible manuscripts were produced to a convention using 10 full-page pictures with portraits of the four evangelists and the major events in Christ's life. With the headpieces and marginal decoration also used, the originality in treatment distinguishes these Bibles from other Byzantine and Western illumination. The materials used by the Armenian artists were very good: they used a deep crimson ink made from Ararat cochineal insects (also used as a dye in Turkish and Persian rugs). The Armenian brown, green and blue pigments were famous in the Middle East.

Good white **parchment**, these colors and a sophisticated use of gold leaf enabled Roslin and others to create memorable manuscripts. Seven made by Roslin still survive, but because of the diaspora of the Armenians in the early 20th century, many such manuscripts have migrated (often in highly questionable circumstances) to European and American museums.

LEFT **T'oros Roslin Gospels** This "Sign of the Son of Man appearing in Heaven," applied in ink, paints and gold leaf to the parchment, shows the sensitive work for which Roslin, the scribe and illustrator, was renowned. It was produced in 1262 at the Hronkla scriptorium under the patronage of Constantine I.

RIGHT **The Blind Men of Jericho** The T'oros Roslin Gospels is rich with finely painted marginal illustrations. This, fo. 88v, is from Matthew 20.30, depicting the men whose eyes, and then hearts, were opened by Christ.

Connections		
For other illuminated Bibles, see		
Garima Gospels, *pp. 50–51*		
Book of Kells, *pp. 60–61*		
Gutenberg's 42-Line Bible, *pp. 98–99*		
For another manuscript written in Anatolia, see		
Dioscorides' De Materia Medica, *pp. 64–65*		

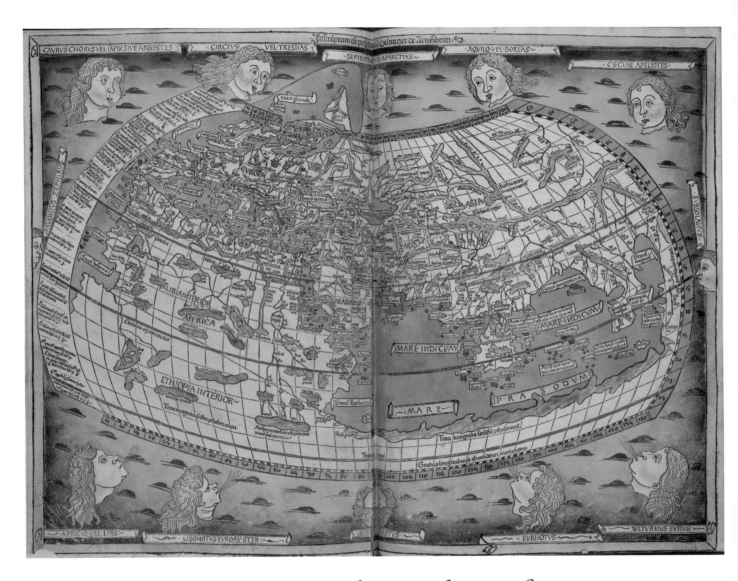

ABOVE **Ptolemy's world map** Twelve named wind-heads surround Ptolemy's world vision, from the *Cosmographia* of 1482, describing the known world. As Ptolemy worked in Alexandria, most of the detail is around the Mediterranean, but the map contains some modern updates (for example, on Scandinavia), while omitting the Portuguese discoveries in Africa. The Indian Ocean is closed and an unknown Southern Continent connects Asia and Africa.

The Father of Mapping

In presenting for the first time the idea of latitude and longitude, Ptolemy's Geographia *was the basis of all modern mapping—but for centuries it was forgotten in the West.*

Born in Alexandria, Ptolemy (Claudius Ptolemaeus c. 90–168 CE) was one of the most important Greek scientists, whose work on astronomy was to control European thought for over 1,500 years. Ptolemy's work in astronomy and geography deeply influenced Arabic

scholarship, in the work of the geographer al-Masudi (d. 956 CE) and others. It was largely because of their work that Ptolemy's manuscripts survived.

The *Geographia* was in several parts, the first dealing with the problems of mapping our spherical globe on a flat surface. Ptolemy invented the concepts of latitude and longitude, and his careful and detailed records of 8,000 places allowed later cartographers to plot these on their own maps. His collection of place names and their coordinates reveals the geographic knowledge of the Roman Empire in the second century. Apparently, a large-scale Ptolemean map was displayed in Autun (France) in the fourth century.

Knowledge of Ptolemy's *Geographia* was rediscovered in Constantinople about 1300 by a Greek monk, Maximus Planudes. Taken to Italy by the Byzantine humanist Manuel Chrysoloras about 1400, and translated into Latin by Jacopo Angelo da Scarperia as *Cosmographia* 1406–09, the manuscript was dedicated to Pope Alexander VI. It was very popular and many manuscript copies were produced; printed editions started to appear from 1477. Ptolemy's projections and careful data enabled other cartographers, particularly the Benedictine monk Nicolaus Germanus (c. 1420–90), to provide more accurate maps.

The maps illustrate how wide was Ptolemy's knowledge of the globe—for instance, in showing recognizable mapping of the Malay peninsula and the areas around the Mediterranean and Middle East. Seeming distorted when compared with modern maps, their weaknesses come from the inaccurate data Ptolemy collected from earlier sources: crude time measurements made accurate calculation of latitude impossible, and he underestimated the size of the globe by one-sixth. But his methodology was impeccable and his maps form the basis of all modern mapping.

ABOVE **The Psalter map**
This tiny 13th-century map anchors the world firmly in the Christian tradition, with Christ as overseer and Jerusalem at its center. It depicts Biblical events, like Moses' crossing of the Red Sea, top right, and "monstrous" races—strange figures, some headless—in Africa, depicted on the right-hand edge.

Connections

For other geographical and travel books, see

Cristoforo's Liber Insularum Archipelagi, *pp. 70–71*

Schedel's Nuremberg Chronicle, *pp. 100–101*

Linschoten's Itinerario, *pp. 132–133*

For mapping of the stars, see

Al-Sufi's Book of Fixed Stars, *pp. 86–87*

Brahe's Astronomiae, *pp. 136–137*

A Sailor's Guide to Byzantium

In the middle of the 15th century, a Florentine noble explored the Greek islands and Byzantium. His manuscript was a guide still used long after the city fell to the Turks in 1453.

In classical Greece, *periplus* was the name used for written maritime navigation aids. ***Portolans**, **rutters*** and *isolarios* were names used for the later European books of sailing directions. This book was one of the first isolarios produced, concentrating on the Mediterranean. It records the journeys of a young Florentine noble, Cristoforo Buondelmonti (1386–c. 1430), a monk and pioneer in spreading first-hand knowledge of Greece and its antiquities. With a friend, the famous Renaissance humanist Niccolò de Niccoli (1364–1437)—a scribe credited with the development of **italic** lettering—Cristoforo started to travel in the Greek islands in about 1414, moving on to Byzantium (Constantinople) a few years later.

RIGHT *Liber Insularum Archipelagi* A magnificent manuscript using Flemish **bastarda** script. In his text the author includes a hidden compliment to flatter the dedicatee: the initial letters of the chapters of the book spell out *Christofus Bondelmonti de Florencia. Presbiter, nunc misit Cardinal Iordano de Ursinio. MCDXX* (Cristoforo Buondelmonti of Florence, priest, now sends this to Cardinal Giordano of Orsini. 1570).

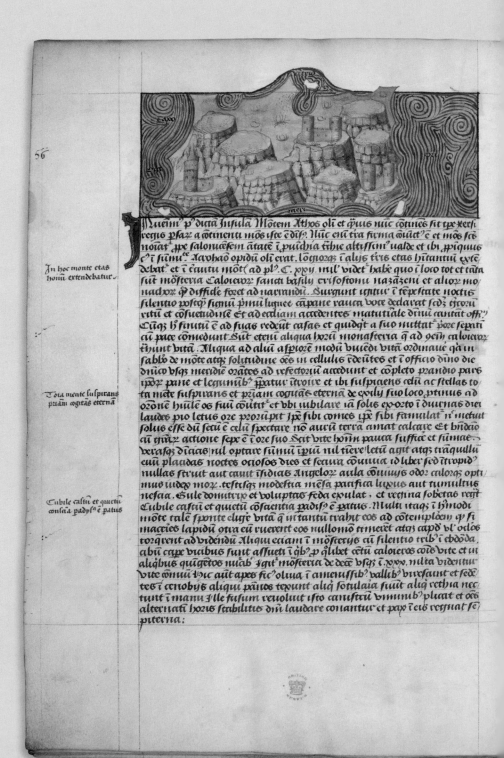

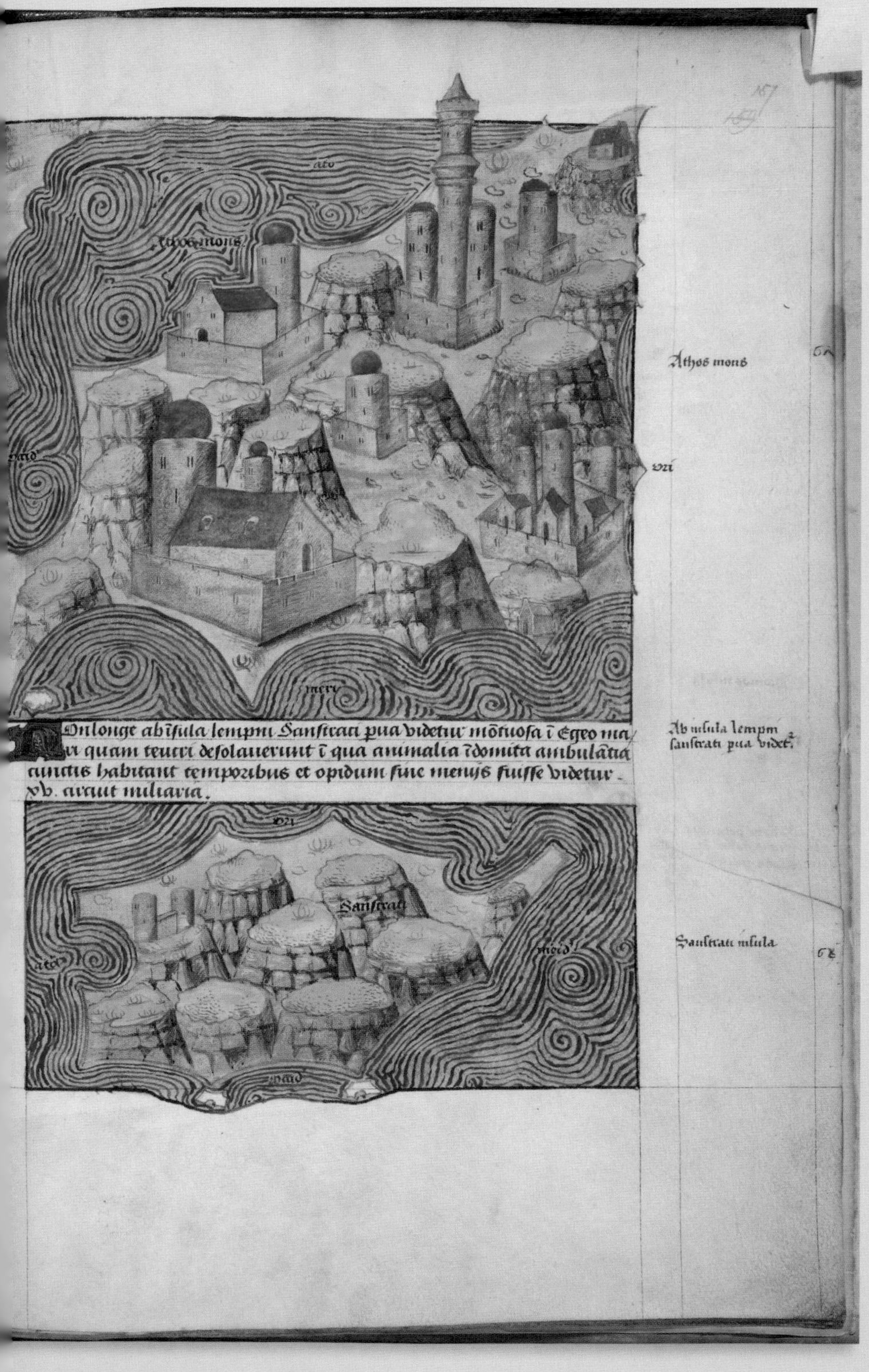

The text of his *Liber Insularum Archipelagi* was completed about 1420 and dedicated to Cardinal Giordano Orsini (d. 1438), a major patron of the arts who was the center of an early circle of humanist culture. Cristoforo's text included careful descriptions of the antiquities in the places he visited and provided maps of the cities and islands. It became recognized as a useful guidebook and many manuscript copies were made in Venice and elsewhere. Heinrich Hammer (Henricus Martellus), a German cartographer working in Florence, used Cristoforo's *Liber Insularum Archipelagi* as the basis for his own 1474 book; and the maps were also copied in an isolario printed in Venice in 1485, written by Bartolommeo "Dalli Sonetti"—so nicknamed because he wrote his text in verse. (Some experts identify him as Bartolomeo Zamberti, a translator of Euclid into Latin.)

The text of Cristoforo Buondelmonti's book remained unpublished until a German scholar edited it in 1824, but those who knew the manuscripts valued them greatly—as nowadays. (One was sold at auction in 2012 for nearly US$2,000,000.) The copy illustrated here was probably prepared in Burgundy for a patron who also valued the content of Cristoforo's work, Raphael de Marcatellis (1437–c. 1508), abbot of St. Bavon's in Ghent. The illegitimate son of Philip the Good, Duke of Burgundy, Marcatellis was a traditionalist who preferred manuscripts over printed books and could afford to buy the best: this came from the hands of master scribes and illuminators.

Connections

For another brilliant Burgundian manuscript, see

Bruges Roman de la Rose, **pp. 72–73**

For another voyage of discovery, see

Linschoten's Itinerario, **pp. 132–133**

Illumination by the Master of the Prayer Book

A superb example of sophisticated illumination by the Master of the Prayer Books, produced in Bruges about 1500, this book still causes controversy.

ABOVE **The voice of Reason** Also written and illuminated in Bruges, in 1475, was this Dutch *Die Lof der Vrou* (or *Cité des Dames*), by the celebrated author Christine de Pisan. This illustration, in the manner of the popular Books of Hours, which often depicted people at their labors, shows Christine with the figure of Reason, who instructs her in clearing the Field of Letters of misogynist opinion.

In the late Middle Ages, there were several varieties of manuscripts luxuriously decorated for the sophisticated courtiers, and particularly for women. One was for piety: the Books of Hours. The other was for emotional entertainment: **romances**.

The *Roman de la Rose* (the *Romance of the Rose*) was an allegorical dream vision written about 1230; in this French poem of some 4,000 lines, Guillaume de Lorris described the attempts of a courtier to woo his beloved. In about 1275, Jean de Meun extended the poem to nearly 18,000 lines—and Meun's language was far more sensual. Sometimes regarded almost as a sex manual, his *Roman* rapidly became a bestseller in the late Middle Ages and was used by Chaucer in his own writings. It was attacked strongly by Christine de Pisan (1364–c. 1430), an early feminist and successful writer.

The *Roman de la Rose* continued to be popular well after the invention of printing in the West, with seven editions of it published before 1500. Several hundred manuscript copies of de Meun's poem survive today, many with elaborate miniatures. This manuscript is a late one, prepared in Bruges about 1500, and commissioned by Count Englebert II of Nassau from a master Burgundian illuminator. Known as the Master of the Prayer Books, the artist worked with great skill on courtly books like this one. The text was written by an unknown scribe in an accomplished **bastarda** hand and was copied from a printed edition. The Master painted 92 large illuminations for this manuscript.

Because of the continuing scholarly interest in the *Roman* and the dispersal of its many manuscripts, the *Roman de la Rose* Digital Library has been established as a joint venture of the Johns Hopkins University and the Bibliothèque Nationale de France. Through its work, over 150 of the manuscripts have been digitized and can freely be accessed throughout the world.

RIGHT **Roman de la Rose** A lutenist and singers in a garden, from the Bruges manuscript, c. 1490–1500. As well as an idealized picture of aristocratic pleasures, the illumination is enriched by naturalistic borders of flowers and birds, which present another aspect of the *Roman*.

Connections

For other sex guides of a different kind, see

Cleland's Fanny Hill, **pp. 168–169**

Stopes' Married Love, **pp. 230–231**

For similarly brilliant illumination, see

Farnese Hours, **pp. 74–75**

For another book produced in Bruges, see

Caxton's Chesse Moralysed, **pp. 102–103**

Ssez y fery et   front reluisant souraz voustie
surtay.   Lontreoeul si nestoit pas vne
Et maintesfoie   Amesut assez mais y mesme
le escoutay   Lenez eut bien fait a droiture
Se le veroye seane mille ame   Lee voulx eut vrie come faulsone
Le guichet qui estoit de charme   Pour faire enuie a toute some
Ille ouurit vne pucellette   Doulse alaine eut et sauouree
Qui masse estoit comte et nette   La face blanche et consouree
Lenaulx eut blone come vng bassi La bouche petite et esroffette
La char plus tendre qunng poussin Et au menton vne fossette

A Giant Among Giants

Books of Hours were among the most popular of all kinds of Renaissance manuscripts. This, by a Croatian master, is one of dozens of this quality produced in Italy.

In the period in which rulers commissioned great artists working in the styles harking back to antiquity—the Renaissance in Italy—there was a flourishing trade in the production of illuminated manuscripts, particularly in northern Italy. Such cities as Bologna, Florence, Ferrara, Mantua, Milan and Siena, as well as Venice and Rome, supported artists of consummate ability in preparing miniatures in manuscripts like this.

Giulio Clovio (Julije Klović, 1498–1578) was a Croatian who, at 18, moved to Rome and the household of Cardinal Marino Grimani, where he was trained as a painter. He also studied under Giulio Romano (a former pupil of Raphael) and with Girolamo dai Libri, a Veronese member of a dynasty of illuminators. The earlier King Matthias Corvinus of Hungary was a famous book collector and patron of illuminators, and Clovio moved to Hungary, where his career would probably have continued as a painter—but the death of the Hungarian King Louis II in a major defeat by the Turkish army, and the decline of the kingdom of Hungary, forced Clovio to leave.

In 1534 Clovio returned to the household of the Venetian Cardinal Marino Grimani and produced several major works, including his miniatures

Farnese *Hours* A glorious example of High Renaissance illumination. Described by his contemporary Vasari as a "rare painter of little things" and a "new, if smaller Michelangelo" (whose influence may be seen in the border decoration), Clovio's superb *Fall of Man* also recalls the engraving by another Renaissance master, Albrecht Dürer.

for Grimani's Epistle of St. Paul (1537). Thereafter his career was largely in Rome, from the 1540s working for Cardinal Alessandro Farnese (1520–89), another famous patron and collector of the arts. Farnese commissioned Clovio to prepare this Book of Hours, completed in 1546—nearly a century after Gutenberg began printing.

The beauty of the **italic** script in the text, allied to Clovio's superb miniatures, created a book that was quickly recognized as a masterpiece. Clovio was highly praised in Vasari's *Lives of the Painters* (1568), with Vasari writing, "never [was] a more rare painter of little things." El Greco also honored Clovio by painting his portrait with his *Book of Hours* and also another painting that showed him with three other masters, Titian, Raphael and Michelangelo.

Connections

For other Italian Renaissance illuminated books, see

Euclid's Elementa Geometriae, **pp.** *106–107*

Aldine Virgil, **pp.** *108–109*

For similarly brilliant illumination, see

Cristoforo's Liber Insularum Archipelagi, **pp.** *70–71*

Bruges Roman de la Rose, **pp.** *72–73*

CHAPTER

5

Light from the East

RIGHT **The traveling monk**
This drawing from Dunhuang, 851–900 CE, now in the British Museum, probably depicts the celebrated Chinese monk Xuanzang, carrying on his back the Buddhist scriptures he collected on his travels in India. The tiger and small Buddha form part of Xuanzang's mythology. See pp. 80–81.

Impetus in literary and scientific work was even more important in several centers in the East, long before European cultures were re-established in the Renaissance. The amazing Islamic developments foreshadowed later European work; Chinese, Japanese and Indian literary writings were equally inventive.

The Chinese invented many things absolutely crucial to the development of the book. The ingenuity and intelligence of its peoples enabled even poor, remote and unsophisticated groups (like the Naxi in Yunnan) to develop ways of making **paper** and cutting woodblocks for printing the artifacts needed in their cultures.

BOOK TRADE GROWS

In centralized government and cultural groups with respect for the written and printed word (to be found in many parts of China), it was almost inevitable that a trade in books would develop. In Buddhist training, it was believed that the best way to comprehend a sutra was to copy it (a practice still followed in Buddhist monasteries in Southeast Asia): it is fitting that the oldest surviving printed book should be a sutra (see pp. 80–81). Copying encouraged the development of printing as well as teaching calligraphy. The availability of a large and skilled Chinese workforce of woodcutters and engravers enabled the development of printed editions using hand-inking and burnishing paper sheets.

Printed editions were thought inferior, and in the 12th century the stock of the Imperial Library in Hangzhou was still three-quarters filled with manuscripts. But printing advanced rapidly in China, and **colophons** in southern Sung books revealed publication of a wide range of storybooks, almanacs and practical handbooks for the semi-literate, as well as serious books for the Mandarin classes—and by the time of the Sung dynasty, unauthorized (pirated) editions were already plaguing the book trade.

With the development of printing came the emergence of fiction. Some Chinese classics were lengthy: *The Water Margin* from the 14th century, *The Golden Lotus* (first printed in 1610 and, for centuries, censored), or in the 18th century *The Dream of the Red Chamber*—all now regarded internationally as masterpieces.

In Japan, there was a similar flowering of courtly novels, of which Murasaki Shikibu's the *The Tale of Genji* is the best known (see pp. 82–83). Her contemporary Sei Shonagon's *The Pillow Book* is of similar quality. Japanese book production, however, took a different path from that of China. The aesthetic qualities of the *kana* style of script, as used in *The Tale of Genji*, was better represented by woodcut blocks. Although the use of printing **types** was introduced by the Jesuits in the 1590s at the same time it was also being introduced from Korea, it dropped out of use: the Japanese concept of the book was not hospitable to the more modern technology. However a commercial book trade started to emerge in Kyoto, Edo and Osaka in the early 17th century, and books aimed directly at a female readership appeared. Censorship (on moral grounds) emerged, and after the expulsion of the Jesuits from Japan, any reference to Christianity was forbidden and only Dutch books were allowed in.

In South Asia, typography was slow to be accepted. In the Moghul realms, the skills of scribes (and the beauty of the miniature paintings in their work) lasted for centuries, and handwritten news-sheets remained common, until the 19th-century development of **lithography** enabled the scribal skills to be reproduced better than using printing type.

ADVENT OF ISLAM

The use of paper (and the **codex** format) was much greater in Muslim areas than elsewhere, which was still faithful to **lontar** manuscripts. It is impossible to gauge how many palm-leaf manuscripts from India survive: estimates range from five million to 39 million, just a small proportion of those originally written. Manuscripts such as the *Ramayana* were often recopied, as were the ever-popular folk tales of the *Fables of Bidpai* (see pp. 84–85). These stories re-appeared in Mughal miniatures, via the Persian and Arabic translations, as *Kalilah wa Dimnah*.

In the Middle East and North Africa, the introduction of Islam led to some welcome developments. Taking over the ownership of many earlier Greek manuscripts made Islamic scholars develop new centers of learning. In Baghdad the *Bayt al-Hikma* (House of Wisdom), set up by Caliph Harun al-Rashid in the ninth century, was the largest library, research center and observatory, only earlier equalled at Alexandria (see pp. 86–87 and 88–89). The cultural centers of Cordoba and Cairo were almost equally eminent, and Isfahan and even Timbuktu were also

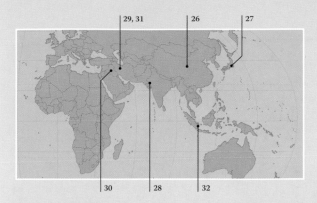

famed (see pp. 90–91). But the pattern of Islamic learning was destroyed by religious wars and reckless looting, as with the fall of Cordoba to Christian Spain. Even more disastrous were the Mongol attacks by Hulagu Khan (c. 1218–65), grandson of Genghis Khan. In 1258, Baghdad was sieged and looted by Hulagu's forces, and thousands of the population killed. The total destruction of the *Bayt al-Hikma* was disastrous for the future of Islamic science and Baghdad never recovered its eminence.

Books in Indonesia

In Indonesia, though there were earlier great cultures, they were not known for great scientific investigation. The late introduction of Islam through the Indonesian islands was insidious, rather than cataclysmic. For Islamic books, the format used in Arab books was seen as preferable, even when written in local scripts as well as in Arabic. Using **dluwang** (a paper-like material thought to be from Java) as a substitute for the paper made in the Middle East enabled local scribes to produce books of a distinctively Javanese style (see pp. 92–93).

By the time Islamic books were being written in Java, there were other influences. European missionary and colonizing activities were becoming pervasive. Jesuits took Islamic astronomical work to China, and the Dutch took their European knowledge to Japan and Indonesia. New ideas and methods were becoming adopted in the East Indies long before Gutenberg's innovations changed the book world forever.

The Oldest Printed Book of All

One of the great treasures of the British Library, this innocent-looking book was purchased as a result of the imperialistic rivalry between Russia and Britain.

The *Diamond Sutra* is one of the key religious books of the sayings of the Buddha. It was first translated from Sanskrit to Chinese in 401 CE. The sutra's name came from an Indian term, a symbolic ritual object that symbolizes the indestructibility of a diamond and the force of a thunderbolt. Believers thought they gained merit by copying the text; and this copy was made by Wang Jie on May 11, 868 CE. It is the oldest surviving dated book, printed nearly 600 years before Gutenberg started printing in Europe.

In time, colonial powers bought (or looted) manuscripts from Egypt and other countries, and particularly from China. Such book acquisition was often part of archaeological expeditions. Frequently the expeditions served as cover for empire-building maneuvers between Russia and Britain. France, Germany and Russia sought similar collections, causing enterprising forgers (such as Islam Akhun, an Uyghur con man from Khotan) to attempt to market their products.

Archaeological expeditions along the Silk Route took Aurel Stein (a Hungarian archaeologist working for Britain) to the Mogao caves at Dunhuang (in Gansu, northwest China). A Daoist priest, Wáng Yuánlù, discovered a blocked-off cavern that contained many ancient books, untouched since the 11th century. Stein bought a collection of these (40,000 **scrolls**, including the *Diamond Sutra*) and in 1907 shipped them off to London. A French Sinologist, Paul Pelliot, went to Dunhuang in 1908, subsidized by the Russian government and accompanied by Carl Gustav Mannerheim (a Finn serving in the Russian army). Pelliot bought another equally valuable collection for Paris, paying 500 *taels* (=US$120 in 1908). The Chinese still regard these purchases by Stein and Pelliot as great robberies of their cultural heritage.

These collections, and the other Dunhuang manuscripts that have been moved to Beijing and elsewhere, have been well maintained. Based in the British Library, a major research program, the International Dunhuang Project, is providing freely available digitized images of all the Dunhuang manuscripts.

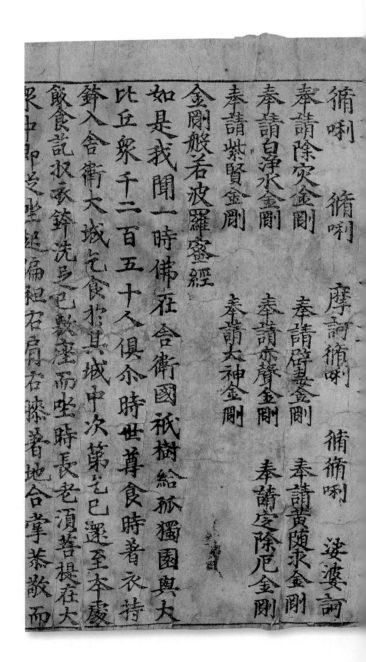

BELOW ***Diamond Sutra*** Found in a sealed-up
cave of Dunhuang, northwest China, this—
the earliest surviving dated printed book
(868 CE) and one of the most important sacred
Buddhist texts—comprises seven strips of
yellow-stained block-printed paper, pasted
together to form a scroll over 16 feet
(5 meters) long.

Connections

For other early Asian printing, see

Shôtoku's Dharani, pp. 30–31

Tripitaka Koreana, *pp. 32–33*

For other rare books "bought" (looted/stolen), see

Caral Khipu, pp. 20–21

Codex Mendoza, *pp. 130–131*

LEFT *The Tale of Genji*
This narrative **scroll**, c. 1130,
showing court ladies with
their maidservants, is the
earliest surviving version
of Lady Murasaki's tale.
Originally 450 feet
(137 meters) long, it now
exists only in fragments,
and is a fine example of the
tsukuri-e (manufactured)
style of court painting from
the Heian period.

A Literary and Artistic Masterpiece

Over 1,000 years ago, a lady-in-waiting at the Japanese imperial court
wrote what is often claimed to be the first modern novel, at a time when
it was rare for women to write, or for men to take them seriously.

The classic verse epics of the *Iliad* and *Odyssey*, Petronius' *Satyricon* or Apuleius' *The Golden Ass*— or even the medieval *Beowulf*—are often described as the ancestors of the novel. But the first prose book, often regarded as the earliest psychological novel, is *The Tale of Genji* by Murasaki Shikibu (in English, Lady Murasaki), born in 978 CE and died c. 1014 or 1025.

Murasaki was a member of a minor aristocratic Japanese family: her great-grandfather and grandfather were poets, and her father was a functionary in the Ministry of Ceremonials and also a poet. In those days Japanese families were usually divided, with daughters living with their mothers: girls were not educated to learn Chinese because women were thought incapable of serious study. Unusually, Murasaki grew up in her father's household and, like her brother, was grounded in classical Chinese. She had an unusually liberal education and accompanied her father on some of his official travels, something very rare in Japan. Her exposure to the secretive court life enabled her to understand the complexities of this inward-looking microcosm of Japanese life.

In her twenties she started work on *The Tale of Genji*, a long, three-part novel in 54 chapters, which may have taken her a decade to complete. Even at the time, Murasaki's literary style (like her personality) was complex: her work demanded careful concentration. But it received detailed, respectful and continuing attention. Soon after she wrote it, many manuscript copies were made. So many varying versions of the text were created (several hundred) that, as early as the 12th century, serious attempts were being made to produce the authoritative text. Illustrating Murasaki's tales fascinated Japanese artists even then, and numerous illustrated versions were made.

The Japanese language has changed a lot since Murasaki's time, and her archaic text is hard for the modern reader to understand. Today, *The Tale of Genji* is always read in translation, either in modern Japanese or in other languages, and this clever and unhappy woman's insights into an ancient curtained-off culture continue to fascinate readers and artists.

ABOVE **Courtly discretion**
In the manuscript, the ladies' faces remain oblique, as in this wedding scene. This may be to protect the real-life identities of Murasaki's courtly ladies, or a device to invite readers to insert their own imaginary characters into the scene.

Connections

For even earlier Japanese work, see

Shōtoku's Dharani, *pp. 30–31*

For scholarly books by other gifted women, see

Bruges Roman de la Rose, *pp. 72–73*

Blackwell's Curious Herball, *pp. 144–145*

Atkins' Photographs of British Algae, *pp. 184–185*

The "Indian Aesop"

The Fables of Bidpai *was one of only two books known to have survived the burning of the Alexandria Library—but the stories were thousands of years older.*

All societies need myths and fables to enable humankind to understand the world we live in. The need is so old and so strong that many of the fables we still use today can be traced back thousands of years. Many of them personify animals (such as Br'er Rabbit or Anansi) who are sometimes tricksters. The fables all have a strong didactic element, and in their earliest Asian forms were probably designed for the instruction of children in powerful families, serving as "mirrors for princes." (Machiavelli's *The Prince* had the same purpose.)

Scholars trace back some of these fables to the Buddhist *Jakatas*, stories telling about previous lives of the Buddha, in human and animal form, which first appeared in central India about 400 BCE. Many of the same fables appeared in the *Panchatantra* (often known as the *Fables of Bidpai*) after the *Panchatantra* was written in Sanskrit by Vishnu Sharman in the third century BCE, but there is little consensus on the actual date of the composition.

The *Panchatantra* (*Five Principles*) is probably the best known of all Indian literary creations and

LEFT *Panchatantra* This rare manuscript, c. 1754–55, of the *Panchatantra* (*Five Principles*) illustrates Sanskrit moral tales—animal fables intended to educate young princes in good Hindu principles of political science. The 49 delightful miniatures are in a style typical of provincial southern Rajasthan.

RIGHT **Kalilah and Dimna** Two moralizing jackals are the key players in this Persian version of the didactic animal fables. In this illustration of ink, colors and gold on paper, possibly from Baghdad, c. 1460, the jackal persuades the lion to stop his ferocious devouring of the ass and to devote himself instead to pious acts.

translations of it spread widely, first to Persia around 570 CE. From Persian these fables were then translated into literary Arabic as *Kalilah wa Dimnah* in 750 CE by Abdullah Ibn al-Muqaffa; the quality of Abdullah's text was so high that his book is still taken as a model of Arabic literary style.

Most later translations were made from the Arabic text and many such manuscripts exist. It was translated from Arabic into Latin in Toledo in 1251. A 12th-century translation into Hebrew was retranslated into Latin; and this version, by John of Capua, was among the first books printed in Europe, with 11 editions of it published before 1500. Nonetheless, the greater popularity of Aesop in Europe has never been matched by the Bidpai fables (though **incunabula** of both often have woodcut illustrations, attractive in their naiveté). The large number of Indian, Persian and Turkish illuminated manuscripts of Kalīlah wa Dimnah are often exquisite.

Connections

For a very different Indian manuscript, see

Nalanda Perfection of Wisdom Sutra, *pp. 34–35*

For other books written with didactic intent, see

Aesop's Fables, *pp. 46–47*

Newbery's Little Pretty Pocket-Book, *pp. 156–157*

Aikin's Robinson Crusoe, *pp. 194–195*

The Standard Islamic Book of Astronomy

One of the important books in the development of astronomy was written by a Persian, long before the invention of the telescope.

The Persian Abd-al-Rahman al-Sufi (903–986 CE) was the court astronomer in Isfahan when the Shi'ite Buyid dynasty controlled most of Persia and Mesopotamia. Astrology was taken seriously in Persia, and astronomical observations even more seriously. Al-Sufi's depiction of the visible stars became the standard book consulted in all Islamic countries, and continued to be copied for centuries, as far east as Samarkand where the ruler, Uleg Beg, commissioned a copy in 1417. In 1429, Uleg Beg also inaugurated an astronomical observatory built at Samarkand, many years before astronomical research developed in Europe.

Al-Sufi's *Book of Fixed Stars* was based on earlier work carried out by other Islamic scholars working in North Africa and al-Andalus (Moorish Spain), as well as in the Middle East. Ptolemy's astronomical book, the *Almagest*, which was translated from Greek into Arabic in the ninth century, was the main source used by al-Sufi. At that time, Western knowledge of the *Almagest* had disappeared: it was only in the middle of the 12th century that Ptolemy's work became available, through a translation from Greek to Latin made under the Norman kings of Sicily, with another translation from Arabic being made about 1160 in Toledo by Gerard of Cremona. (Gerard was one of the bridge builders so important in introducing Islamic thought to the West.)

The earliest surviving manuscript of al-Sufi's astronomical book, written in 1009 CE, is held by the Bodleian Library, Oxford; it was bequeathed to the Bodleian by Narcissus Marsh in 1713. (Bought at a sale in Leiden in 1696, the manuscript was probably found some years earlier in Turkey by book hunter Christian Ravis.) Known as Marsh 144, this manuscript displays the combination of scientific exactitude and the relaxed, casual painting style typical of Persian art. Other later manuscripts in Western European libraries, and in Turkey, were modeled closely on al-Sufi's treatment of ways of representing the constellations of stars.

ABOVE **Al-Sufi's influence** This is seen in this description of the constellation of Ursa Major in a Persian manuscript, of the late 17th or early 18th century.

Connections

For other Islamic discoveries and inventions, see

Al-Jazari's Mechanical Arts, *pp. 88–89*

Mansur's Anatomy, *pp. 90–91*

For other astronomical books, see

Brahe's Astronomiae, *pp. 136–137*

For proselytizing in Islam, see

Boke van Bonang, *pp. 92–93*

Gregorio's Book of Hours, *pp. 110–111*

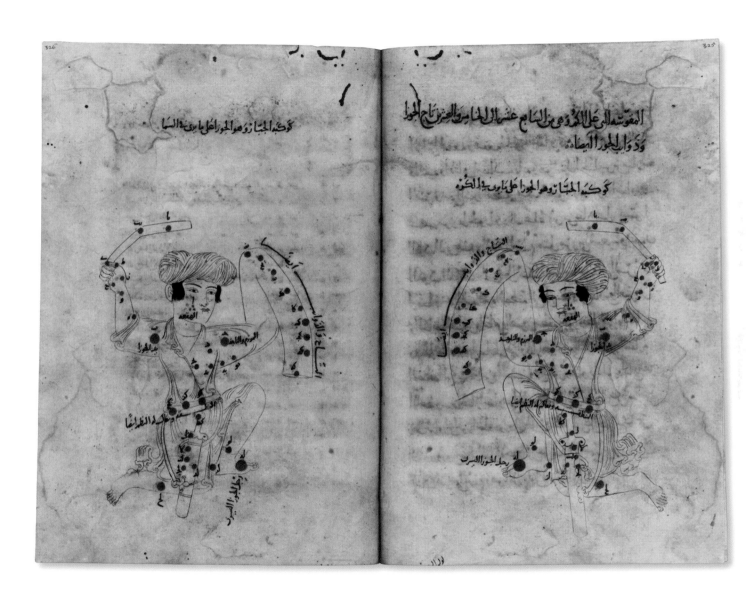

ABOVE *Book of Fixed Stars* The Persian astronomer al-Sufi described the stars—positions, brightness, color—by constellation: here, Orion (*al-jannâr*), the giant. For each, he drew the outside and inside of the celestial globe. This Bodleian manuscript (the oldest surviving version) was made by his son in 1009–1010.

A Forgotten Precursor of Leonardo da Vinci

In European and American schooling, we learn about ancient Greek engineers and the inventive work of Leonardo da Vinci in the Renaissance. The Islamic world had equally inventive engineers—and the West is only now recognizing the importance of al-Jazari.

From the time of Hero of Alexandria, in the first century CE, people were interested in automata, self-operating machines. Greek work of this sort became known in the Islamic world and methods developed so much that, in the 10th century, Baghdad was reported to have silver singing birds perched in an artificial tree in the palace gardens.

As the advances in Islamic astronomy owed much to the skills of artificers, so the development of all sorts of other engineering processes came from engineers particularly interested in automata. The work of one, known to us only as Pseudo-Archimedes, was used by a 12th-century engineer, al-Shaykh Ra'is al-A'mal Badi' al-Zaman Abu al-'Izz ibn Isma'il ibn al-Razaz al-Jazari. Al-Jazari's first interests were in the application of waterpower, used for pumping irrigation water or powering water clocks; one of his inventions was a valve that essentially is still used in toilet cisterns.

Al-Jazari was as prolific an inventor as Leonardo da Vinci (who probably knew of and used al-Jazari's work), or Thomas Edison in the 19th century. His inventions included the camshaft, crankshaft, segmental gears, the use of escape mechanisms and mechanical controls—all essential for modern engineering and unknown in Europe for some time after al-Jazari's death in 1206.

Al-Jazari might have been forgotten (like the Pseudo-Archimedes) had he not written a summary of his work in *A Compendium on the Theory and Practice of Mechanical Arts*, completed a few months before his death in 1206. The engineer wrote it at the request of the Artuqid Sultan, Nasir al-Din Mahmud (1200–22). Al-Jazari's brilliant, clear illustrations were as good and useful as those published in modern home-improvement manuals, and several of his plans have been used by modern museums to recreate working models of his machines.

Al-Jazari's manuscript was frequently copied, and these copies are to be found in many libraries in Turkey, Europe and America. Fortunately, copyists followed al-Jazari's drawings closely, and the surviving manuscripts give us a good idea of what his machines looked like at a time when Baghdad led the world in engineering innovation.

RIGHT *Compendium on the Mechanical Arts* This text of al-Jazari, master engineer at the affluent Artuqid court, is full of delightful and detailed drawings of 50 monumental water clocks, fountains and other intriguing automaton devices—here, a wash basin in the form of a peacock, for performing one's ritual ablutions.

Connections

The First Anatomical "Atlas"

For centuries, all important medical research was undertaken in Islamic countries, not in Europe. This remarkable Persian book came at the end of the surge of medical research there.

In the Islamic world, many branches of study flourished. This was particularly true in medicine, which was at a low ebb in Europe in the Middle Ages. The Islamic advance was evidence-based, derived from the work (in Greek) of Galen of Pergamon (131–201 CE). Galen was an experienced medical man, the surgeon to the gladiators and later physician to the emperor Marcus Aurelius. In Western European societies the work of Galen dropped out of view, until the 11th century when a Carthage-born physician, Constantine the African, started medical teaching and writing in Salerno. Until then, European medical practice was poor.

In the eighth century, the Caliph Harun al-Rashid established a Baghdad teaching hospital where doctors and their students made daily rounds—a precedent used in medical schools ever since. Similar teaching hospitals were set up in Marrakesh and elsewhere. Observation and experimentation continued normally in Islamic medicine, and under physicians such as Ibn Sina (Avicenna) and Ibn Zakaria Razi (Rhazes) medical knowledge advanced considerably, particularly in the Persian territories.

One late pioneering surgeon in the 14th century was Mansūr Ibn Ilyās, who came from a long dynasty of physicians working in Shiraz. His illustrated anatomical text, known as the *Tašrīh-e mansūrī* (or *Mansur's Anatomy*), was dedicated to Pir Muhammad Bahadur, ruler of Fars and grandson of Tamerlane. It is unique in being devoted only to anatomy: its text seems to have been based on work done by Galen, but Mansur's illustrations were his own work, showing schematized human figures in a frog-like, squatting stance, used to display nerves, bones, arteries, muscles and organs. (In some manuscript copies, a pregnant woman and fetus are also shown.) In Islam, making images of people was firmly discouraged; Mansur's work was bold.

Tašrīh-e mansūrī was frequently copied, and manuscripts are now spread around the world. Mansur's use of the squatting posture spread to the East and became used for a variety of purposes, from massage manuals in Thailand to tattooing instructions in Burma. Later Persian manuscripts showed little advance on Mansur's own discoveries; medical research was thereafter undertaken in Europe.

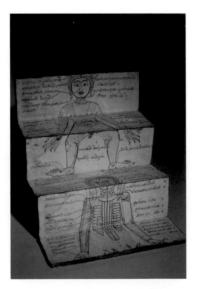

ABOVE **A Buddhist anatomy** This medical text on topical ailments, from Thailand or Cambodia, c. 1830–50, comprises 40 concertina pages in a **parabaik**-style manuscript, and appears stylistically to reflect the influence of the Persian Mansur. The anatomical lines of descent for both, however, are from even earlier Chinese and Indian anatomies.

Connections

For earlier medical works, see

Dioscorides' De Materia Medica, pp. 64–65

For later and more gruesome illustrations, see

Vesalius' De humani corporis fabrica, pp. 134–135

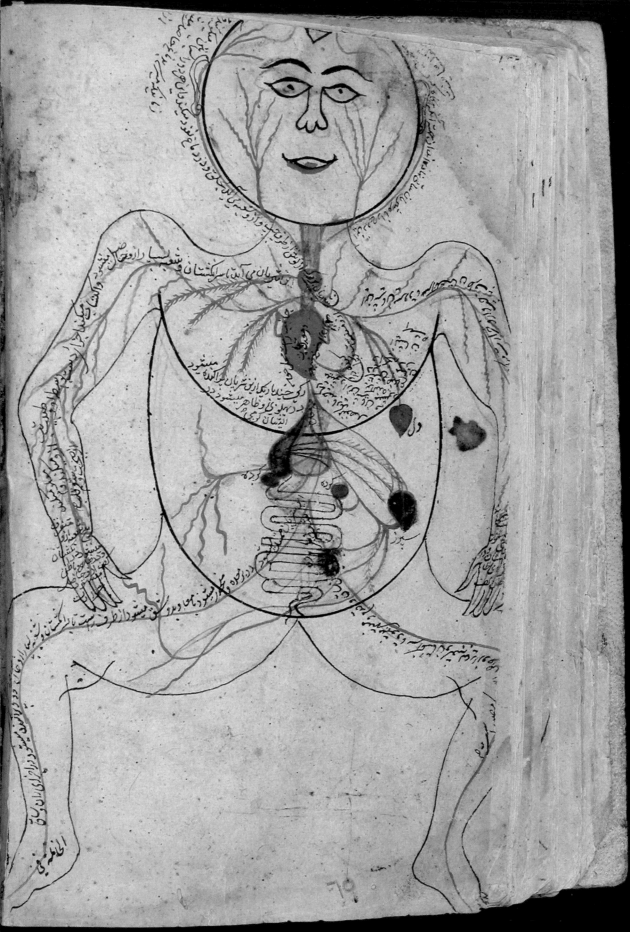

An Early Islamic Book Produced in Java

At first sight, visitors to Java might have overlooked this plain-looking book. In fact, it was important for its author, its subject and the way it was produced—and for its introduction to Europe.

The Islamic faith spread more slowly into the Far East and Indonesia than it did into North Africa and up into Europe. By the 15th century, it had spread through Java. The author of this book, Sunan Bonang (1465–1525) is revered in Java as one of the *wali sanga* (trusted ones), much as St. Columba is remembered for the spread of Christianity in Britain. Many other Islamic missionaries in Indonesia came from the Middle East, but Bonang was a local man of mixed Chinese and Javanese blood. His cultural background was influential in his proselytizing.

Most other Islamic missionaries believed that as the Koran was revealed in Arabic, all believers should learn the language and use it. Bonang's book on an aspect of Muslim mysticism and theology, *al-Bâri* (the One who creates form out of nothing), was instead written in Javanese, using the old Javanese script, making it more accessible to other local readers. He also proselytized in a subtle way, composing Javanese songs of a traditional kind but with an Islamic message in them. One for a gamelan orchestra, *Tombo Ati* (*Cures of the Heart*), is still taught in Islamic schools and often performed.

Bonang used traditional means to persuade Java to accept Islam. His book was written on a familiar proto-**paper**, *dluwang*, beaten out of the inner bark of the paper mulberry and produced in Java until its use was wiped out by Dutch importations of European papers in colonial times. (The colonists had no name for it, but simply described it as Javanese paper.)

This volume attracted one of the first Dutch navigators visiting Java, who took it back to the Netherlands. By 1600 its ownership passed to a scholar who could recognize the importance of a manuscript, even if he could not read it. This was Bonaventura

Vulcanius (1538–1614) a leading Dutch humanist and editor of several ancient texts, including the earliest surviving Gothic Gospels, the *Codex Argenteus* (one of the precious manuscripts later passed as booty from one side to another in 17th-century wars).

Professor of Greek at the new University of Leiden, Vulcanius ensured that his own personal collection went to the university library in 1614. Thanks to its careful maintenance in Leiden, the *Boke van Bonang* is the oldest known surviving Javanese dluwang book, one that was written when Islamic expansion and European colonization reached Java.

RIGHT **Making bark paper**
A Dayak tribeswoman pounding bast (sub-bark) in her long-house in the Kalimantan Barat Province of Indonesia, c. 1910–20. Similar methods, using heavy stone, ivory, wood or metal beaters, were employed for making **tapa** and *dluwang* throughout the region; such beaters have been found dating back to Neolithic times.

LEFT **Boke van Bonang** This treatise on Muhammadan theology, written in Javanese, in the ancient quadratic script, is the oldest known manuscript on dluwang paper, collected on the north Java coast before 1600 by a Dutch navigator. This opening page, with its Islamic decoration, is incised with a stylus, perhaps a quill or a bamboo reed.

Connections

For other attempts to understand colonized peoples, see

Caral Khipu, **pp. 20–21**

Codex Mendoza, **pp. 130–131**

For other use of non-roman scripts, see

Batak Pustaha, **pp. 38–39**

Garima Gospels, **pp. 50–51**

T'oros Roslin Gospels, **pp. 66–67**

Sulawesi Lontar, **pp. 252–253**

CHAPTER

6

Wheels of Change

RIGHT **A strange *Weltchronik***
There are several maps in
Schedel's world chronicle.
Bordering one page are
illustrations of the feared
"Other"—strange creatures
such as dog-headed creatures,
cyclops and folk with faces
in their stomachs, who
were popularly supposed
to inhabit the distant lands.
See pp. 100–101.

The modern world can be said to have been created by Gutenberg's inventions that enabled him to print from movable types—but this was not done by Gutenberg alone, and over a long period other people helped (and hindered) its advance.

Oe homib⁹ diuerſaꝝ foꝛmaꝝ dicit ꝑli.li. vij. ca. ij. Et Aug.li. xvi. de ci. dei. ca. viij. Et Iſidoꝛus Ethi.li. xi. ca. iij. oîa q̄ ſequitur in india. Cenocephali homines ſunt canina capita habētes cū latratu loquitur aucupio viuūt. vt dicit ꝑli. qui omnes veſcūtur pellibus animaliū.

Cicoples in India vnū oculum bn̄t in fronte ſup naſum bn̄ ſolas feraꝝ carnes comedūt. Ideo agrioſa gite vocātur ſupꝛa naſomonas confineſꝗ̃ illoꝛū boȝ mines eſſe: vtriuſꝗ̃ nature inter ſe vicibus coeitus.

Calliphanes tradit Areſtotiles adijcit dextram māmam ijs virilem leuam muliebꝛem eſſe quo hermofroditas appellamus.

Ferunt certi ab oꝛiētis pte intima eſſe homines ſine naribus: facie plana eq̄li totius corpis planicie. Alios ſupioꝛe labꝛo oꝛbas. alios ſine linguis ꝛ alijs cō creta oꝛa eſſe modico foꝛamine calamis auenaꝝ potū haurietes.

Item homines habentes labiū inferius. ita magnū vt totam faciem contegant labio doꝛmientes.

Item alij ſine linguis nutu loq̄ntes ſiue motu vt monachi.

Pannothi in ſcithia aures tam magnas bn̄t. vt con tegant totum corpus.

Artabꝛite in ethiopia pn̄i ambulāt vt pecoꝛa. ꝛ aliqui viuūt ꝑ annos. xl. quē nullus ſupꝛgreditur.

Satiri homūciones ſunt aduncis naribus coꝛnua i frontibus bn̄t ꝛ capꝛaꝝ pedibus ſimiles qualē in ſolitudine ſanctus Antonius abbas vidit.

In ethiopia occidentali ſunt vnipedes vno pede latiſſimo tam veloces vt beſtias inſequantur.

In Scithia Ipopedes ſunt humanā foꝛmaꝝ eq̄nos pedes habentes.

In affrica familias quaſdā effaſcinātiū Iſigonus ꝛ Memphodoꝛus tradūt quaꝝ laudatōne intereāt pꝛ bata. areſcāt arboꝛes: emoꝛiātur infantes. eſſe eiuſdem generis in tribalis et illirijs adijcit Iſogon q̄ viſu quoꝗ̃ effaſtinent iratis pꝛcipue oculis: quod eoꝛū malū facilius ſentire puberes notabiliⁱ eſſe ꝗ pupillas binas in oculis ſingulis habeant.

Item boies. v. cubitoꝛ nūꝗ infirmi vſꝗ ad moꝛtez Hec oîa ſcribūt ꝑli. Aug. Iſi. pꝛeterea legitᵉ i geſtⁱ Alexādri ꝗ i india ſunt aliȝ boies ſex manⁱⁱ bn̄tes. Ite boies nudi ꝛ piloſi in flumine moꝛātes. Ite boies manib⁹ ꝛ pedib⁹ ſex digitos habentes. Ite apothami i aꝗs moꝛantes medij boies ꝛ medij caballi.

Item mulieres cū barbis vſꝗ ad pect⁹ ſ capite plano ſine crinibus.

In ethiopia occidētali ſūt ethiopeſ. iiij. ocłos bn̄tes. In Eripia ſunt boies foꝛmoſi ꝛ collo gruino cū roſtris aialium boîmꝗ effigies mōſtriferas circa extremitates gigni mime mirū. Artifici ad foꝛmanda coꝛpora effigieſꝗ celandas mobilitate ignea.

Antipodes.āt eē .i. boies a ꝫria pte terre vbi ſol oꝛit qn̄ occidit nob aduerſa pedib⁹ n̄ris calcare veſtigia nulla rōe credendū e vt ait Aug.16. de ci. dei. c. 9. Ingēs tn̄ b pugꝶ lr̄aꝝ ꝑtracꝗ vulgi opioes circūfundi terre boies vndiꝗ couerſiſꝗ iter ſe pedib⁹ ſtare et cūctſilem eē celt vticē. Ac ſiłi mō ex q̄cūꝗ pte mediā calcari. Cur āt n̄ decidāt: mirēf ꝛ illi nos n̄ decidere: nā em repugnāte: ꝛ quo cadāt negāte vt poſſint cadere. Nā ſic ignis ſedes nō e niſi i ignib⁹: aꝗrū niſi i aꝗs. ſpūs niſi in ſpū. Ita terre arcentibus cūctis niſi in ſe locus non eſt.

t is convenient to attribute the revolution in printing to Gutenberg's advances in the middle of the 15th century. However, events a couple of centuries earlier (including the effects of the Black Death) laid the foundations for Gutenberg's developments, and his inventions successfully combined already existing skills and techniques. To succeed, printing had some special requirements: a demand for books, the ready availability of **paper** and **parchment**, an advanced metal technology to allow the successful cheap casting of **type**, and skilled literate craftsmen to compose the type into pages. Then, using a suitable ink and a press, the workmen could print as many copies as customers required, and at a price they would pay. After printing, the pages of type had to be "**dissed**" (broken up), and the type thus made available for the printers to compose fresh texts for new publications.

Many of these needs could already be met. After papermaking was introduced in Europe, at Xativa in Spain in the 12th century and at Fabriano in Italy in the 13th century, the supply of good-quality paper made from linen rags ensured its continuing availability, at a low cost. (For this, the development of water-powered paper mills in Germany was vital.) **Vellum** was always expensive, and there were limits to providing vellum and parchment in quantity, but the skins remained available—at a price. (Every vellum copy of Gutenberg's first Bible required a full 170 calfskins to make the volume—see pp. 98–99.)

Goldsmiths and other metallurgical workers already had the skills necessary for making types. But even after an effective casting method was developed, the process was complicated and obtaining **fonts** remained expensive. Setting-up costs for a printer were high, and there was a long time lapse before these costs could be recouped through sales. A wealthy patron (often a ruler or of the Church) or investors could provide funding, and success in securing these was vital (see pp. 100–101). The development of banking and the emergence of capitalism enabled such investors, who anticipated (and often gained) good profits from publishing. The downside was that poor publishing decisions often caused business failures: prudent printers (like the earliest in England) chose to take no risks, and print only books they knew would sell (see pp. 102–103 and 104–105).

Today, it is generally accepted that it was Johannes Gutenberg who invented the tools (the adjustable mold) that made printing possible in the West; the long period of his experiments in Strasbourg and in Mainz, and widespread attempts to develop the means of multiplying books, led to many claims for others. They included a Czech goldsmith working in Avignon in the 1440s, Procopius Waldfoghel, who was certainly experimenting; Johannes Mentelin of Strasbourg, an early independent printer (issuing his Bible in German in 1460); and Laurens Janszoon Koster of Haarlem who (as a statue in Haarlem shows) was for centuries claimed as the Dutch inventor of printing.

Another early in the field was Nicolas Jenson (1420–60), a French engraver working in the royal mint at Tours who, in 1458, was sent (perhaps as an industrial spy) to study Gutenberg's early printing in Mainz. It has been suggested that Jenson was responsible for improvements in the techniques of typecasting, and later, when working in Venice as an early printer, Jenson cut a **roman** typeface that is still regarded as one of the best ever made. Changes in type design and improvements to the printing press in Italy in the late 15th century enabled local printers to produce books whose typographic quality was superb; the roman faces used by Erhard Ratdolt and Aldus Manutius showed Jenson's influence (see pp. 106–107 and 108–109) and are still inviting and readable.

The German books of the same period were also carefully and competently produced, like the *Nuremberg Chronicle* (see pp. 100–101), one of the well-funded and profitable publications of the time. Its production, though, illustrates the increasing problems of piracy by other printers, who had no editorial costs and bore no risks but cut into the profitability of the original publication.

PROS AND CONS OF PRINTING

Gutenberg's invention had unexpected and unwelcome consequences, discussed in Chapter 7. In the short term, almost all his contemporaries writing about printing praised it as a divine benefit to mankind. One of the shrewder commentators slightly later was Johannes Trithemius (1462–1516), Abbot of Sponheim. Trithemius was an erudite man who wrote on a wide range of subjects, including an early bibliography. (His *Steganographia*, the first ever book on cryptography, remained in manuscript for over 100 years, but when published in 1606 was promptly put on the *Index Librorum Prohibitorum*—the *Index of Prohibited Books* of the Catholic Church).

Recognizing the advantage of printing, Trithemius built up his abbey library by offering other libraries new books (bought directly from the printers by

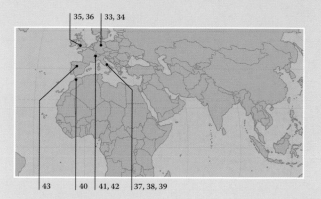

Trithemius) in exchange for their manuscripts. He obtained over 1,500 volumes in this way, making his one of the largest collections of the time. By acquiring these manuscripts, Trithemius showed that he was not just a firm believer in the new technology: in 1494 he published his *De Laude Scriptorum* (*In Praise of Scribes*). In this he urged scribes to continue to copy manuscripts, questioning whether printing ink would prove to be corrosive and eat holes in the pages. Trithemius' concern for conservation was rare, indeed, and is a lesson to modern library managers who discard printed volumes, believing that e-books are the only way of the future.

New Needs, New Typefaces

Gutenberg's invention did not eliminate the continuing need for scribes: the typewriter would do that. Passages written in unfamiliar alphabets still had to be written into printed books by hand, until types for them were cut; which came quickly for Greek, and rather more slowly for Hebrew and Arabic (see pp. 110–111 and 112–113).

Typefaces for other purposes were also prepared for other needs such as music (see pp. 114–115 and 116–117), but production of music in manuscript form also remained in wide use for many years.

Printing outside the mainstream of printing had its own patterns. Jewish tenacity enabled Hebrew printing to survive, and (for Biblical studies) Hebrew typefaces were widely available in Europe. The Islamic resistance to printing delayed the production of Arabic types, and almost all early books in Arabic produced were the fruit of Christian missionary activities, or, later, emerged in response to academic developments. (The bookbinding art that developed in Moorish Spain and in the Middle East is not considered in this book.)

Once university presses came into being, the production of such massive and expensive works as **polyglot** Bibles could be expected to trickle from them, but in the first century of printing such work had to be produced with the help of a very wealthy and determined man, such as Cardinal Ximénes and his Complutensian Polyglot Bible, the last book included in this chapter (see pp. 118–119).

Gutenberg's Revolution

Everybody learns at school about Gutenberg's invention. Since the early 16th century, printers, bibliographers and librarians have celebrated his work, but most people are a bit hazy about what he actually invented.

By the early 15th century, the European demand for books had increased enormously. This made several people in Germany, France, Italy and the Netherlands consider how they could produce books faster or more cheaply. The first masterpiece of printing is Gutenberg's 42-Line Bible, produced in Mainz and completed in the mid-1450s.

The success of Gutenberg (c. 1395–1468) was in seeing how various existing skills and technologies could be put together to make books by mass-production methods. In earlier times, a single manuscript would be written and completed, and any further copies had to be handmade from scratch. In Europe, the production of **woodcut block books** was also starting. Gutenberg realized that if you could

cast letters, numbers and punctuation, these could be assembled and reassembled to create pages; the face of the letters could be inked and a sheet of **vellum** or **paper** pressed onto the **type**-block to take a print of the whole page. Repeating the inking and pressing processes would create second and subsequent printed pages quickly and cheaply.

It was never as simple as this suggests, and much experiment and expenditure was needed to enable the inventor to create a book that looked as good as a manuscript. Gutenberg seems to have started work experimenting in Strasbourg in the 1430s; back in his native city of Mainz his method was promising enough for a wealthy local man of burgher stock, Johann Fust (c. 1400–66), to back him. Their more important co-worker was Peter Schöffer (c. 1425–c. 1503), who had trained as a scribe in Paris.

It seems that Gutenberg, Fust and Schöffer decided that their first publication should be as good as the best manuscripts, and their choice of the best **parchment** and great care in printing produced the best book they could. The 42-Line Bible was a fine specimen of north German letter styles and **formats**. An historian later said, "it is the only art in which no progress has been made: that the first example of printing is the best."

Copies of their Bible, offered for sale at the Frankfurt Fair in 1454, created a sensation and all copies were sold quickly, despite the high price. Printing was a success—but not an economic success for Gutenberg: Fust demanded repayment of his loans and took over the business with Schöffer as its manager. (Later, Schöffer prudently married Fust's daughter, a tried-and-true method of getting job security.) Knowledge of the techniques of printing spread rapidly to other cities in Germany.

Instantly famous, the 42-Line Bible (so named from the number of lines printed on each page) has always been highly valued. About 50 copies survive from the edition estimated at 180 copies, an exceptionally high survival rate.

BELOW **Göttingen model book** This fascinating scribes' pattern book, *c.* 1450, originally belonged to a monastery and included instruction on ornament and the making of pigments. The floral motifs described in this manuscript were closely copied in several of the earliest Gutenberg Bibles, including the Göttingen copy.

LEFT **Gutenberg's 42-Line Bible** Jerome's Epistle, in this British Library paper copy, is handsomely illuminated, probably at Erfurt by Eberhard König: the initial F, in colored inks highlighted with gold, extends down the margin to a floriated border. Printers at first attempted to print the **rubric** (in red at top), but it proved too difficult and was instead penned by scribes.

A Blockbuster Among Early Printed Books

The Nuremberg Chronicle *was a well-financed book famous for its copious and elaborately designed illustrations. Remarkably, the documentation on its production has survived far better than for its contemporaries.*

Many printers depended on support from a patron or the (unreliable) income from sale of their books. The *Nuremberg Chronicle*, known also as the *Liber Chronicarum* or *Die Schedelsche Weltchronik* (*Schedel's World History*) was one of the best financed and most sumptuous of all 15th-century books.

Two wealthy Nuremberg merchants commissioned a German historian, Hartmann Schedel, to write a Latin world history and engaged another Nuremberg government official, George Allt, to translate Schedel's text into German. Parallel editions were published, using different **typefaces** and sometimes altering the text between the two editions. Both were illustrated with a huge range of **woodcut** illustrations, designed and cut by Michael Wolgemut and Wilhelm Pleydenwurff, who ran the most important **atelier** in Nuremberg. (Albrecht Dürer was one of their pupils.) The printing of the book was entrusted to Anton Koberger (c. 1440/1445–1513), a former goldsmith who, in 1471, turned to publishing in Nuremberg, building a business that was the biggest in Europe. (Koberger had agents from Paris to Budapest and Venice, and reputedly had 24 printing presses at work on his books.)

The *Nuremberg Chronicle* was a major success. Nearly 2,000 copies were printed of the two 1493 editions, and nearly 700 copies still survive, making it one of the commonest surviving 15th-century books. Containing over 1,800

woodcut illustrations, the production was of great complexity and the results remarkably successful. In many copies, the illustrations were colored by hand.

The financiers made substantial profits from their venture, but not without piracy from other unscrupulous printers: the enterprising Augsburg printer Johann Schönsperger (c. 1455–before 1521) produced three cheaper and more compact editions. Schönsperger followed the Wolgemut/Pleydenwurff woodcuts, sometimes simplifying their designs to suit the smaller **format**. In those days before copyright, the production of these cheaper versions deterred the original Nuremberg publishers from printing new editions of this remarkable book.

Tercia etas mundi   Foliũ   XLIIII

Connections

For other early publishing enterprises, see

Aldine Virgil, **pp. 108–109**

Complutensian Polyglot Bible, **pp. 118–119**

Diderot's Encyclopédie, **pp. 158–159**

For other outstanding woodcut illustrations, see

Vesalius' De humani corporis fabrica, **pp. 134–135**

Bewick's British Birds, **pp. 172–173**

Cranach-Presse's Hamlet, **pp. 214–215**

ABOVE ***Nuremberg Chronicle***
Hartmann Schedel's ambitious work was illustrated throughout with lively hand-colored woodcuts. Many were designed afresh, but several were "stock" images; this view of Venice is singular in being adapted from an earlier woodcut, by Erhard Reuwich, in the first illustrated printed travel book, Breydenbach's *Sanctae Perigrinationes* (Mainz, 1486). This volume of the Chronicle belonged to the 19th-century designer William Morris.

RIGHT **God the Father** A pen-and-ink design for the frontispiece of the *Weltchronik*, depicting God, overseer of all, seated on his throne. It was executed in 1490 by Michael Wolgemut. Albrecht Dürer, apprenticed to Wolgemut and godson of Koberger, may have had a hand in some of the illustrations.

A Book from the First English Printer

Many early printers attempted to produce perfect texts of important classical books—and failed in business. England's first publisher aimed at printing books that would be wanted and bought by English readers.

Printing in England started in 1476, at the same time that Erhard Ratdolt began printing in Venice, but it is hard to find commonalities. England was late to commence printing, and its printers deliberately selected to print middlebrow books. Technically its production was mediocre, and the number printed in England remained only a small part of the total book market. To get what they wanted, serious book collectors in England had to import continental books.

Two things about English printing made it notable. The English book trade was largely of books issued in English—few in Latin or other tongues—and the literary importance of Geoffrey Chaucer enabled English printers to crystalize their language and eventually make it the most successful in the world.

William Caxton (c. 1424–91) was a mercer trained in London. In about 1446 he moved to Bruges, at that time at the height of its commercial importance. His import–export business there (which may have included importing manuscripts to London) was successful, and he became Governor of the English merchants in Bruges. He established close links with patrons, and seemed to work successfully as translator for them, which led to his work as a printer.

Caxton learned about printing in Cologne, and in about 1473 set up as a printer in Bruges with Colard Mansion, a long-established Flemish scribe and agent commissioning manuscripts. Mansion and Caxton effectively courted patrons, and many of the editions they printed were commissioned by the aristocracy. Caxton's translations were often commissioned like this, as was his Bruges edition of *The Game and Playe of Chesse* (1474) by a 13th-century Piedmontese, Jacobus de Cessolis (c. 1250–c. 1322). Despite its title, it was not a manual on chess playing, but a morality volume teaching roles in society and the duties of nobles.

Caxton moved his business from Bruges to Westminster in 1476 and his Cessolis book was successful enough for him to print a new illustrated edition of it in 1483. Caxton's printing is most famous for his edition of Chaucer's *Canterbury Tales* (1476), of which he later printed an illustrated edition in 1483. Caxton's successor running his English printing business, Wynkyn de Worde, also reprinted Chaucer, but with a difference: de Worde's later edition was based on a comparison of several manuscript copies. Scholarly editing was becoming common with continental printers of the classics, but was unusual for more popular books.

ABOVE **Sarum Pye** Printed by Caxton at Westminster in 1476–77, this is the earliest surviving printed advertisement in English, promoting the printer's *Sarum Ordinale* (or *Sarum Pye*), a priest's manual of liturgical ritual during the ecclesiastical year. The Red Pale in the Almonry, Westminster, was Caxton's printshop.

Connections

For other books published for the common reader, see

Wynkyn's Demaundes Joyous, pp. 104–105

Markham's Cavelarice, pp. 140–141

For other (better) use of bastarda scripts, see

Cristoforo's Liber Insularum Archipelagi, pp. 70–71

Bruges Roman de la Rose, pp. 72–73

This first chappitre of the first tractate shelweth vn~
der what kyng the playe of the Chesse was founden andy
maady .   Capitulo primo

Monge alle the euyl condicions & signes that may
    a   be in a man the first and the grettest is . Whan he fe~
reth not ne dredeth to displese & make wroth god by synne
& the peple by lyuyng disordonatly / Whan he rccheth not ·
nor takoth hede vnto them that rcprcue hym and his vy~
ces , But sleeth them · In suche wyse as did the emprour
nero · Whiche did do slee his mayster seneque · for as moche
as he myght not suffre to be rcprcuyd & taught of hym · in
like wise was sotyme a kyng in babilon that was named
                                         a   iiij

LEFT *The Chesse Moralysed* Caxton's English translation of *De ludo scachorum*, printed at Bruges in March 1474 (two years before a French version), was the first printed book to achieve a second edition. This 1482 reprint, from his new press at Westminster, which refers to the game "moralysed," prudently omits the first edition dedication to the "false, fleeting, perjured Clarence," recently beheaded for treason.

The first word of the text (below the **woodcut** illustration) is "Amonge." The printer has left a two-line blank space for the "A" to be added by hand and added a guide letter ("a") to show the artist what letter to draw in.

The First Joke Book

Some early printed books are important for their beauty. Others, like this book of riddles, are equally important— and much rarer.

Often galleries and museums exhibit important books like the *Nuremberg Chronicle*, but it is much rarer for them to display small, unassuming books whose sales enabled printers to undertake more ambitious work. We shall never know how many of these incidental early publications are now lost because for centuries librarians, booksellers and book collectors thought they were beneath interest. This undergrowth of publishing includes publications that were often read to pieces, like *The Boke of Cokery*, 1500, a collection of recipes of which only a single copy survives. It was printed by a successful Norman printer, Richard Pynson, who in 1506 was appointed King's Printer to Henry VII and later to Henry VIII, a post that brought him great prestige and a lot of official printing as well.

One of Pynson's greatest rivals was Wynkyn de Worde, who took over Caxton's printing business in Westminster, and in 1500–01 moved to London, where he settled at the Sign of the Sun on Fleet Street. By 1509 he also had a shop at St. Paul's Churchyard, later the center of the book trade. Wynkyn sought commercial success through the production of books that would become steady sellers, including poetry, school textbooks, romances, medicine and guides to leading a good life. But for other sorts of customers, in 1511 Wynkyn published the first English adult-jokes book, *Demaundes Joyous*, of which only a single copy survives. Wynkyn collaborated with other booksellers and printers outside London, and no doubt copies of *Demaundes Joyous* were also distributed through them.

Though the intellectual content of Wynkyn's publications was not always high, his business sense was excellent. The quality of his book production was often better than that of Caxton, using **paper** from the mill of John Tate, the first papermaker in England. While Wynkyn often preferred the familiar **blackletter type** for his books, he was also the first English printer to adopt **italic** and to use Arabic and Hebrew types; in 1495 he also became the first to use music types.

Connections

For another under-the-counter book, see
*Cleland's Fanny Hill, **pp.** 168–169*

For other books for popular sale, see
*Powell's Old Grizzly Adams, **pp.** 192–193*
*Nadozie's Beware of Harlots, **pp.** 222–223*

The Earliest Scientific Texts

Venice became the center of the book trade in Italy, but when Renaissance design was in full flower,
one of its most innovative printers was not an Italian, but a young man from Augsburg, in Bavaria.

Among the most interesting and important printers working in the 15th century, the Augsburg-born Erhard Ratdolt (1442–1528) is most significant for the books he printed in Venice from 1476–86.

Ratdolt was by no means the first German printer to work in Venice: over 50 Germans worked there before 1500. Ratdolt had possibly been a worker in Nuremberg for the astronomer Regiomontanus, who had a private printing office to produce his own books. Ratdolt's first Venetian publication was of the astronomer's work, and at first, working with two other German printers, he produced several astronomical books translated from Islamic authors. In addition, Ratdolt printed some superbly designed and printed editions of classical authors, using a handsome roman **typeface** that was one of the best ever produced in Venice.

Ratdolt's edition of Euclid's mathematical work has seldom been equaled for the skill with which he solved the problem of showing geometrical diagrams in a typographical, efficient way. Evidently proud of his work on this book, Ratdolt sought recognition by including a dedication to the Doge of Venice, printed in gold.

Ratdolt's volumes were not printed books pretending to be manuscripts; they were self-assured, typographic volumes. His other innovations were in improving ways of printing in several colors, printing the first title page, publishing the first type specimen and issuing the earliest-known list of publisher's books for sale. Such innovation should have led to commercial success, but the competition in the Venetian book trade was strong. When Count Friedrich von Hohenzollern (newly appointed Bishop of Augsburg) invited Ratdolt to go back to Augsburg, to take charge of printing for the diocese, he left Venice for good. He printed profitably in Augsburg for over 30 years more, but seldom with the panache and flair he showed in Venice.

Centuries after his death, the superb quality of Ratdolt's books continued to be recognized, and the influence of his designs on figures such as William Morris is palpable.

Connections

ABOVE **Ratdolt's dedication**
In this ornamented **vellum** copy in the British Library (and in a handful of others), Ratdolt's dedicatory letter to the Doge Giovanni Mocenigo, bearing the latter's arms, was printed in gold in a variant typesetting.

LEFT *Elementa Geometriae* Euclid's great work, translated from Arabic into Latin by the 12th-century scholar Adelard of Bath, was printed by Erhard Ratdolt at Venice in 1482. This handsome, ornamented edition was illustrated with more than 400 geometrical figures, demonstrating the printer's expertise in his new technique.

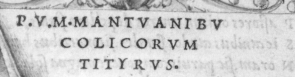

P·V·M·MANTVANIBV COLICORVM TITYRVS.

Melibœus. Tityrus.

Ityre tu patulæ recubâs sub   Me.
te gmine fagi
Siluestrem tenui musam meditaris
auena.
Nos patriæ fines, et dulcia linqui
mus arua,
Nos patriam fugimus, tu Tityre lentus in umbra
Formosam resonare doces Amaryllida syluas.
O Melibœe, deus nobis hæc ocia fecit.   Ti.
Namq; erit ille mihi semper deus, illius aram
Sæpe tener nostris ab ouilibus imbuet agnus.
Ille meas errare boues, ut cernis, et ipsum
Ludere, quæ uellem, calamo permisit agresti.
Non equidem inuideo, miror magis, undiq; totis   Me.
Vsque adeo turbatur agris. en ipse capellas
Protinus æger ago, hanc etiam uix Tityre duco.
Hic inter densas corylos modo nanq; gemellos,
Spem gregis ah silice in nuda connixa reliquit.
Sæpe malum hoc nobis, si mens non leua fuisset,
De cœlo tactas memini prædicere quercus.
Sæpe sinistra caua prædixit ab ilice cornix.
Sed tamen, iste deus quis sit, da Tityre nobis.
Vrbem, quam dicunt Romam, Melibœe putaui   Ti.
Stultus ego huic nostræ similem, quo sæpe solemus

A Model for Future Book Design

Small, reliable, legible and inexpensive: a model for most later
printers to emulate. Few publishers were more successful than
Aldus Manutius.

The Republic of Venice was at the height of its powers by the 1490s, and the city was the center of world publishing. With its trading connections with the East and with Austria and Germany to its north, it was well positioned for business, as many German printers had already discovered.

Many early printers had a background as scribes, bookbinders or booksellers. Aldus Pius Manutius (or Aldo Manuzio, 1449–1515) came to printing from a scholarly background, educated in humanistic studies and as a close friend of a contemporary scholar, Pico della Mirandola. Aldus spent much time working as a tutor for Pico's nephew Alberto Pio, Prince of Carpi. Alberto Pio was inspired by Aldus's vision for scholarly publishing, and in the mid-1490s he provided funds for Aldus to set up a printing office and an academy, creating something like an early university press.

Aldus was fortunate in his patrons, friends and workers at his printing business. He employed men such as Cardinal Bembo as an author/editor; Bartolomeo Sanvito (1435–1518), a brilliant scribe who developed small **formats**; and the gifted punch-cutter Francesco Griffo, who designed the range of Greek, **roman** and other **typefaces** used at the Aldine Press (as it was known). Aldus' innovations included some refinements in punctuation and the use of a small pocket format for the modestly priced large editions of his books, many set in **italic** types that he inaugurated.

Almost all Aldine editions were well-designed, desirable volumes; his edition of the most famous Roman author, Virgil, is characteristic of his work. Aldine editions remained famous for their good editing and the clarity of their typography. Their influence on modern book design is still strong—and beneficial.

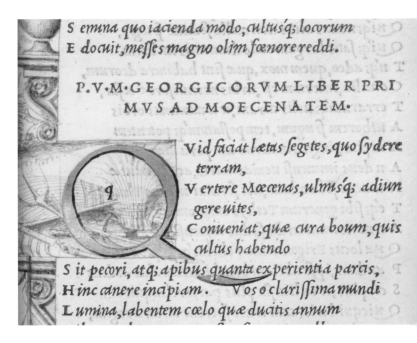

ABOVE **Pastoral initials** The Rylands Collection in Manchester owns the most nearly complete collection of Aldine editions. In this copy, printed on **vellum**, Aldus incorporated beautifully hand-decorated initials; their pastoral nature, like this Q with its wheatsheaf, reflects the content of the *Georgics*, for which this page is the opener.

LEFT **The Aldine Virgil** This exquisite first page of the *Aeneid*, Book I, was published by Aldus in 1501. It was the first work to be printed in Aldine Type; what we now know as italics, developed by his punchcutter Francesco Griffo, and the first in the new **octavo** pocket format.

Connections

For other skilled cutting of typefaces, see

*Euclid's Elementa Geometriae, **pp.** 106–107*

*Boucher's Molière, **pp.** 152–153*

*Cranach-Presse's Hamlet, **pp.** 214–215*

For a tour de force of bookmaking, see

*Hunter's Old Papermaking, **pp.** 238–239*

For Venetian printing for export, see

*Gregorio's Book of Hours, **pp.** 110–111*

Printing in Arabic

The first book printed in Arabic came a full half century after Gutenberg's printing with movable type—but it was a Christian work, and printed in Italy.

In many ways, the Ottoman Sultan Bayazit II (1481–1512) was a wise and humane Islamic ruler, who allowed his subjects considerable liberty. When, in the 1490s, the Spanish rulers expelled all Jews and Muslims from Spain, the Sultan organized their evacuation to North Africa and helped them settle in parts of European Turkey. Indeed, the first printer to work in Constantinople (in 1493) was Jewish, printing in Hebrew.

Bayazit, a connoisseur of calligraphy, was strongly opposed to the introduction of printing in Arabic, though printing by Jews, Greeks and Armenians was tolerated in the Ottoman Empire. It was centuries before printing in Arabic **types** was accepted in the Islamic world; and all attempts to produce Arabic books for export from Venice or other European cities were consequently surreptitious.

The earliest-known surviving book printed in Arabic, the *Kitab Salat al-Sawa'i*, a Book of Hours intended for the use of Arabic-speaking Christians or potential converts from Islam, would not have been approved by Bayazit or any sultan. It was produced about 1514–17;

RIGHT ***Book of Hours*** Gregorio's *Kitab Salat al-Sawa'i*, a book of Christian prayers printed at Fano in Italy in 1514, is recognized as the earliest surviving Arabic book to be printed from movable type. It was probably printed for export to the Christian communities of Syria.

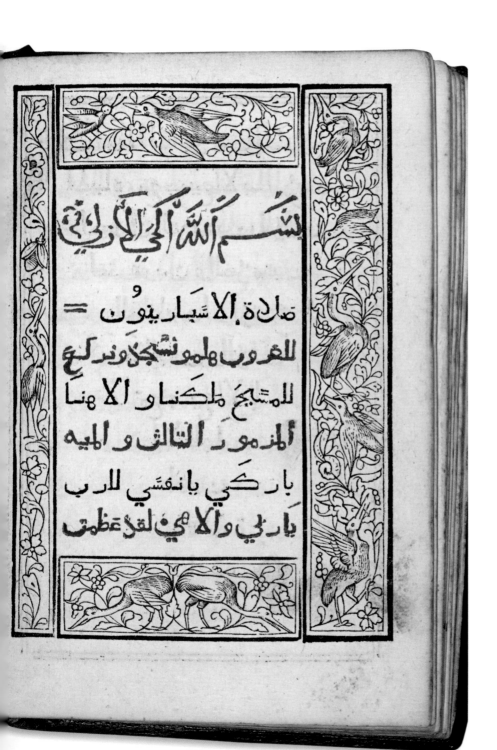

some experts claim it was for use of the Melchite (Christian) communities in Syria, though others believe it was for missionary activities. The production of the book may have been funded by Pope Julius II, who commissioned it; what is certain is that it was printed by one of the many gifted and versatile Venetian printers, Gregorio de Gregorii—but without a Venetian imprint. Instead, it was stated as having been printed at Fano, a town close to Venice but outside the Venetian territories. (One explanation is that Venice was one of the rare states that was developing effective copyright restrictions, and the exclusive Venetian rights to print books in Armenian and Arabic had already been granted to Democrito Terracina, lasting for 25 years.)

The *Kitab Salat al-Sawa'i* showed the **arabesque woodcut** decorations common in northern Italian work. The design of its Arabic type itself was rather clumsy, and Islamic scribes would have condemned it; but the *Kitab Salat al-Sawa'i* pointed to an ideal and unrealized future—if only Islam had seized printing as other cultures did.

Connections

45

רבותי מזרחי ויקיף כדרכו עד שינטע למזרחי
נטעת ואחריה צפונית מערבית ואחריה מערב
רבומיית ובא לו לכבא וירד ויסוד רבותי דתניא
בברייא ואת רינו ושפוך על יסוד מזבח העולה
זה יסוד דרומי או איכו אלא יסוד מערבי אמרת
ילמד ירידתו מן הכבש מיציאתו מן ההיכל מיד
יציאתו מן ההיכל איכו מותן אלא בסמוך אף ירידתו
מן הכבש איכו מותן אלא בסמוך והטעים מצא ראין
מערבין על העצות ומאכלן לפניו מן הקקולעיס
שמצער נחטאת בצקוס קרום יאכל כחבר אכ דל
מוער יאכלוה והועמבן הין קלעיס סמבכות החבר
וכבית עולמים הין חומות העזרה לוכר כמוכד
שמ הכהן המיחטא אותה יאכלוה למפוקי כאיס
שאיכן רחויות לטעו וכתל כל וכר בכהנים יאכל
אותה וכל מאכל תמצוס רקתע נב פסח איס נאכל
אלא צלי תנא וכלהו בכל מיאלו אכו מאכון הן צלי הן
מקה שירה וצוב ראמרי מתפות כהום איו נאכל
אלא צלי שמא למצחה בהם לעולם כדרך שהעלים
אוכלן חיום אלא מעלם בעולם שיערו למס אכילה
יפה אכלאס רגה לאכל איום מועאל יתר תלל
קרשות כבדו לעם ועלה רילפוקן בפך רובחיס ובטר
זבח קודיס שלמיו למרכו הירה שנאכלת לעוס
ועלה אחר חטאת וחמס מעון הל וכחי וכקרשיס
עלה הוכך אחר היום שלא לא ימח ימעזו עד בקר
עד יחצות סייג עשו כדי להרחיק את האדם מן
העצירה כדינן בפך רברבות כל נבאל לאס אחד
יתנהן עד שיעלה עמוד השחר ולמה אתרו חכמים
עד יחצות כדי להרחיק את האדם מן העבירה
ר העולה קרס קרשיס לאפס ביתא
ועד ל ייס ומיחסר כפריס
ואסי רבקדתי בה קרם קרשיס ולא קתנ יהי בכלהן
תסוס רלא כתיבכה קרס קרשיס אסיועיכן תנא
ראמי הכי הכי קרם קרשיס היו ריחו כלה ונוה שלק
שחיטתה בצטן שמצ בה על ירך העזבח הימוכה נטוה

וקבל רימה וכן כיאו שפירשכו למעלה ורימה מעטן
שתי מיתכות שהן ארבע אלא מבאמו שנכתב בעולם
קרבות המזבח אלא נאמ כתוריקתבדימה וזרקו את
הדס על המזבח סביב ומעיה שאין קביב את הקרן
שנריכה ארבע מהמות והן בקרן מזרחית נעומית
וכקרן מערבית דרומית שנכגרה בהלכסון והיד
זורק על הקרן והרס הוך הוך וחוך וגעשה כמין
גס וזהו שתי מיתכות שהן ארבע בעשין שירא
הדס בארבע רוחות והרי לא מעכחתלה אלא בשתי
קרכות זו בלכסונה רחי בשתים עבריה אחת אל
הוי הרס אלא בשלם רוחית המזבח ולא קריכן בירך
סביב וההי הבן בעסקת המיד בא לו לקרן מזרחי
צפטית כותן מזריחה נעומה מערבית דרומיית כותן
מערבה דרומיה והטעם מעב שעורקית דרומי
לא היה לה יסור וחי איעמר שיהחיל תמנה מעמ
שהעולה תחלת מיהן רימה טעון נג יסוד ראמר ל
עקיבא קו ורימה שאיי מעכפרין ואין בלין
לכפריה טע עין יסוד ירלוכדדיס עולה שמכפרת
ובא לכפריה איכו בין עולה שטעונה יסוד

והנה אציר לך מול רבוע המזבח והרס על הדרך
שאתרמון וכי קרן דרומיית מזרחית לא היה לה יסוד
רס

The First Printing in Africa

The first book printed in Morocco was from Jewish immigrants. Its production illustrates the tenacity with which the widely persecuted Jews held on to their right to print.

ABOVE ***Sefer Kol Bo*** Gershom Soncino (the wandering printer), was one of the most important early Hebrew printers. From 1488 to 1534, he printed some 200 works—roughly half in Hebrew and half in Latin or Italian. This title page, printed in Rimini in 1526, displays the printer's **device**.

LEFT ***Sefer Abudarham*** This important book, the first ever to be printed in Africa (Fez, 1516), instructs in Sephardic Jewish customs. Page 47, here, illustrates the altar in the Temple at Jerusalem. Directions pertain to the ritual slaughter of animals, replaced by prayer after the destruction of the Temple.

Islam was resistant to typography, but Jewish printers embraced the new techniques with enthusiasm. When driven out of Spain, some Spanish Jews moved to Portugal and set up presses. One of their early books was the *Sefer Abudarham*, a religious text still important for the rituals used in the synagogue, which had been written by Rabbi David Abudarham, a religious leader and tax collector under King Sancho the Great (1258–95) in Seville. His volume was first printed in Lisbon in 1489 by Eliezer Toledano, whose name (from Toledo) shows that he came from Spain.

Printing in Hebrew became impossible in Portugal after forced apostasy started under King Manuel. Like the Spanish Jews, many in Portugal preferred to face the hardships of exile in Morocco or elsewhere in the Islamic world. Among these exiles was Samuel ben Isaac Nedivot, who had worked for Eliezer Toledano at his press in Lisbon. With his son Isaac, and now settled in the thriving Moroccan city of Fez, in 1516 Samuel Nedivot printed another edition of the *Sefer Abudarham*, following closely the text of the earlier Lisbon edition.

They had great difficulty in obtaining **paper**, which had to be imported from Spain (where papermaking was introduced in the 12th century at Xativa, near Valencia), but the Nedivots obtained enough stock to print 15 books over the next decade.

Their book, printed in Fez, was by no means the first Jewish printing anywhere: the Nedivots had been preceded by printers in Italy, particularly by the Soncino family who printed in many Italian cities in the 15th century, and later in Constantinople, Salonica and eventually Egypt. The Soncino editions were famous for their typography and the accuracy of their texts, in Greek, Latin and Italian, as well as Hebrew.

The numbers of books printed in Hebrew amounted to less than one percent of all **incunabula**, and all early Jewish books are rare indeed. The *Sefer Abudarham* typifies the problems faced by Jewish communities everywhere, but is also notable as the first book printed anywhere in the African continent. Apart from later Jewish printing in Egypt, for nearly 300 years there was no printing in Africa until the craft was introduced by British colonization in Sierra Leone and by the Dutch at the Cape of Good Hope at the end of the 18th century.

Connections

For other Hebrew books, see

Complutensian Polyglot Bible, **pp.** *118–119*

Technion Nano Bible, **pp.** *246–247*

Heavenly Voices

The invention of the alphabet and later of printing was concentrated on words. Different skills and techniques, including music notation, were essential for other ways to record sounds.

St. Isidore of Seville, described as the last scholar of the ancient world (and now celebrated as the patron saint of computing and the Internet) said, in his *Etymologiae*, "Unless sounds are held by the memory of man, they perish, because they cannot be written down." It was a task for musicians to find ways of recording sounds, in the way the invention of the alphabet allowed mankind to remember words.

Methods of recording sounds were developed in the classical world: surviving manuscripts show how it was done in classical Greece. In Western Europe, a system for writing Gregorian chant using **neumes** in *campo aperto* (without staff lines) was inspired by Charlemagne and created at Metz around 800 CE.

Manuscripts of music were naturally produced in the **scriptoria** of abbeys, transcribed by monks like the Irishman at St. Paul's, Lavanttal, who wrote the poem to his cat, Pangur Ban (see page 58). The manuscript shown here was written at the Abbey of St. Gall (Switzerland) about 922–25 CE, and it is the oldest known use of neumes, with an elaborate binding and container also dating from this time. It seems likely that one scribe wrote out the text and another scribe inserted the neumes later.

When **type** for music notation developed later, the large size needed for books for shared use by choirs made printing impracticable. Monastic manuscript production of large antiphonaries and other liturgical works continued for centuries, and leaves taken from these are common in the antique trade. Later production sometimes employed stenciling for parts of the text, though the staves and notes were still laboriously written out by scribes.

RIGHT **St. Gall *Cantatorium***
This 10th-century *Antiphonarium Missae*, or Gradual, in Gregorian Plainchant (here, the Alleluia verses) is lettered in **Carolingian minuscule** with gold decoration and neumes. Liturgical song books were used as early as 430 CE, as described by North African bishop Victor Vitensis in the fifth century. In practice, cantors usually sang from memory.

Connections

For another book of religious music, see

Constance Gradual, *pp. 116–117*

For frivolous secular music, see

Tomlinson's Art of Dancing, *pp. 146–147*

For other books created by monks, see

Garima Gospels, *pp. 50–51*

Book of Kells, *pp. 60–61*

Chludov Psalter, *pp. 62–63*

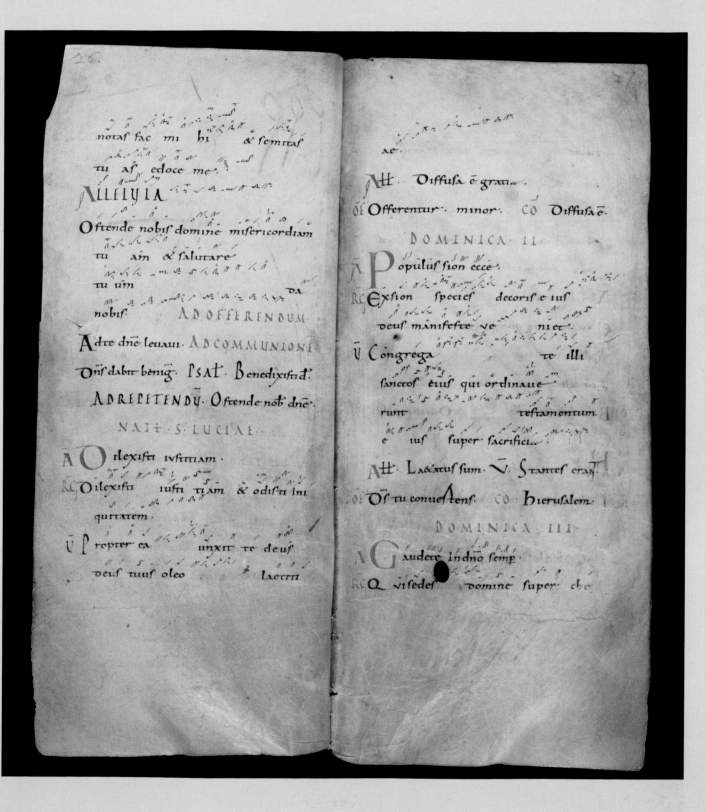

26.

notas fac mi hi & semitas

tu as edoce me.

ALLELVIA

Ostende nobis domine misericordiam

tu am & salutare

tu um DA

nobis. AD OFFERENDUM.

Ad te dne leuaui. AD COMMUNIONE

Dns dabit benig. PSAL. Benedixisti d.

AD REPETENDV. Ostende nob dne.

NATL. S. LUCIAE.

A Dilexisti iustitiam.

RG Dilexisti iusti tiam & odisti ini

quitatem.

U Propter ea unxit te deus

deus tuus oleo laetti

ae.

Att. Diffusa e gratia.

Of Offerentur minor. CO Diffusa e.

DOMINICA. II

A Populus sion ecce.

RG Ex sion species decoris e ius

deus manifeste ve niet.

U Congrega te illi

sanctos eius qui ordinaue

runt testamentum

e ius super sacrificia.

Att. Laetatus sum. V. Stantes erat.

Of tu conuertens. CO Hierusalem.

DOMINICA. III

A Gaudete Indno semp.

RG Q ui sedes domine super che

A Gutenberg Problem Solved

Many experts thought that the undated Constance Gradual *was printed before Gutenberg's books.*
Modern technology enabled paper experts to establish that it was printed many years later.

For centuries, bibliographers and historians tried to establish who printed what, when and where—rather like assembling a jigsaw, but with no picture to guide them. Relatively simple when the volume contains details of author and title and an imprint; much harder when any of these is missing or the volume is incomplete.

Modern techniques include analysis of the **typefaces**, particularly helpful for **incunabula** when printers had their typefaces cut for themselves. Another method is the examination of **watermarks**: for example, an unidentifiable volume on 15th-century **paper** made in Spain is unlikely to have been printed in Germany in the 16th century. One difficulty with watermark identification is that, when pages are closely printed, it's hard to see or photograph the watermark covered with ink.

Even with such aids, accurate identification was a serious problem. One group of publications was the **block books** (or **xylographica**), such as the Paupers' Bibles, in which text and picture were cut in wood, as in Chinese printing. (These block books were long believed to have been produced in the 1420s or 1430s, before Gutenberg created printing from movable type.)

Another problem book was the *Missale Speciale Constantiense* (or *Constance Gradual*), a rare (one of just three copies) and undated book printed, rather crudely, in an unpolished version of the typeface used by Gutenberg and his partners Fust and Schöffer, in the famous and beautiful Mainz Psalter of 1457. Was the *Constance Gradual* produced much earlier than the 42-Line Bible, as some experts thought?

Hans P. Kraus, a New York book dealer, believed it was; so did the Pierpont Morgan Library, which bought it. Subsequent examination by a paper expert using new techniques revealed that both the block books and the *Constance Gradual* were on German paper made in the early 1470s, so printed long after Gutenberg's work. (The development of beta-radiography about 1960 as a tool in paper identification is now a standard tool used by art galleries and libraries.) Re-dating the *Constance Gradual* to about 1473 answered one question, but opens others. Was the typeface sold by Gutenberg or Fust to another novice printer? The *Constance Gradual* is not as early as previously thought, but it remains important as rare evidence on early printing methods, and how new technology still provides fresh information.

RIGHT Constance Gradual Title page of the Morgan Library's **missal**, probably printed in Basel c. 1473. This rare typographical treasure came into the American book-dealer's hands in 1953. Wrapped in an old newspaper, it was purchased from a Capuchin monastery in Romont, Switzerland, where, one story has it, the monastery cat had bedded down on it.

LEFT Block book This super block book is the *Ars memorandi per figuras Evangelistarum*, printed in Germany in 1470 as an aid to memorizing the Gospels, using symbols. Each page is printed in brown ink on one side only, **versos** and **rectos** alternately (one of text, one illustrated), so that each printed opening is followed by the blank reverses.

Connections

For other very early Western printing, see

Gutenberg's 42-Line Bible, **pp. 98–99**

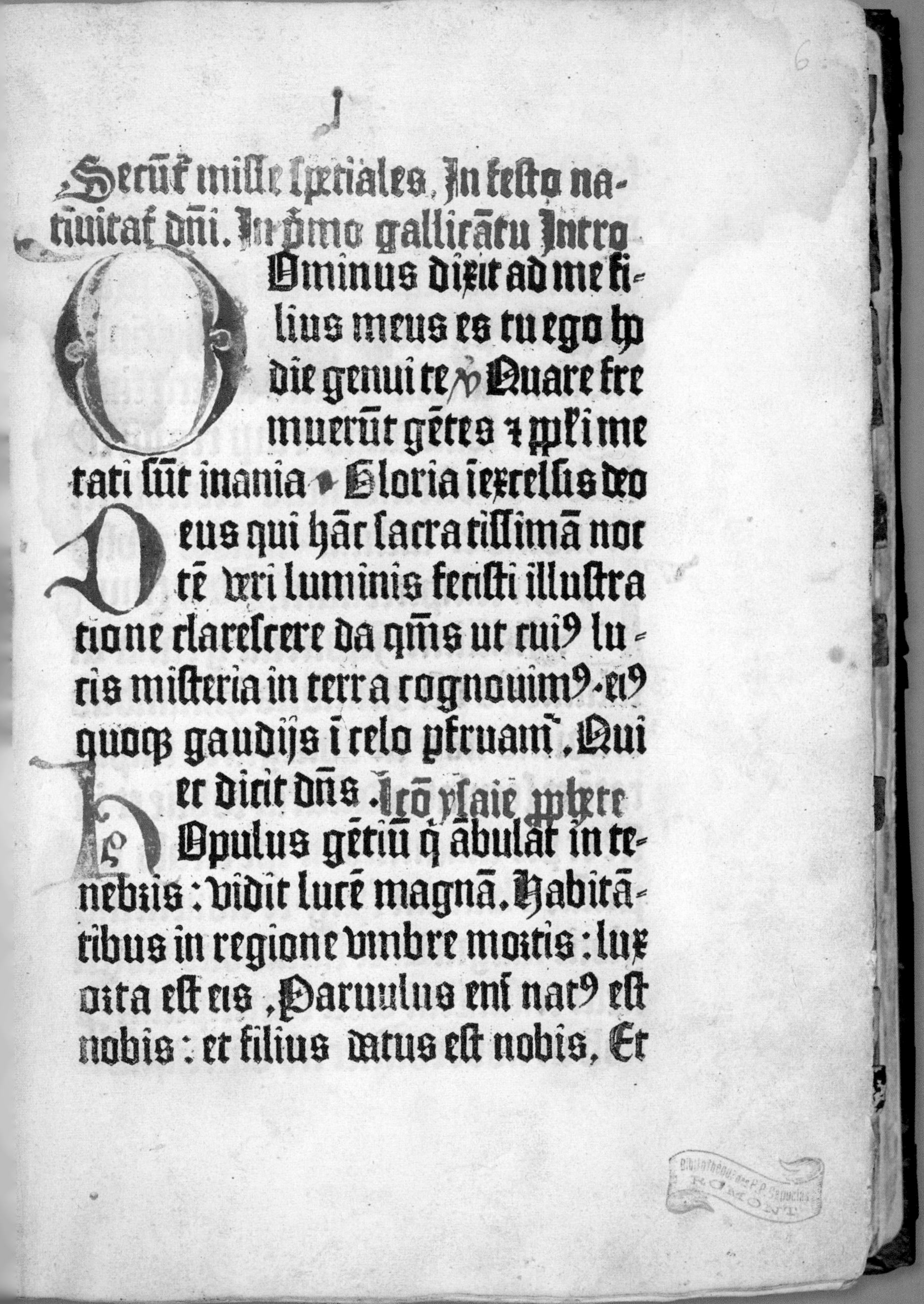

Secuntur misse spetiales. In festo na-
tiuitas dni. In pmo gallicātu Intro

Ominus dixit ad me fi-
lius meus es tu ego hp
die genui te. Quare fre
muerūt gētes ⁊ ppli me
tati sūt inania. Gloria iexcelsis deo

eus qui hāc sacra tissimā noc
tē veri luminis fecisti illustra
tione clarescere da qñs ut cui⁹ lu-
cis misteria in terra cognouim⁹ ei⁹
quoqꝫ gaudijs i celo pfruamꝰ. Qui
et dicit dñs. lcō ysaie ꝓphete

Opulus gētiū q̄ ābulāt in te-
nebris: vidit lucē magnā. Habitā-
tibus in regione vmbre mortis: lux
orta est eis. Paruulus eni nat⁹ est
nobis: et filius datus est nobis. Et

RIGHT **Complutensian Polyglot Bible** The multilingual Bible proposed "to revive the languishing study of the Sacred Scriptures." Here, verses from Deuteronomy XXXII, given in Hebrew, Vulgate and Greek Septuagint in the three main columns at top, left to right; in the lower section, Chaldaic, with a Latin translation. In the left margin are the Hebrew and Chaldaic roots.

A Major Work of Biblical Scholarship

The first of many polyglot Bibles, this one is noted for its success in solving design problems—and for the beauty of its typefaces.

The illustration of this multilingual (**polyglot**) Bible from the early 16th century shows how much the techniques of scholarly printing changed in the first 50 years of printing since Gutenberg's 42-Line Bible. The complexity of setting the **types** in five different languages was solved successfully by this polyglot's printer, Arnao Guillén de Brocar (c. 1460–1523), a Frenchman who had trained in Toulouse and moved as a printer to Logroño in northern Spain.

The main impetus for this major work was the extraordinary and energetic statesman and ascetic,

Cardinal Ximénes (Francisco Jiménez de Cisneros, 1436–1517). In 1500 he founded and financed the new university of Alcalá de Henares (in Latin, Complutum). Ximénes' plan was to produce a multilingual edition of the Bible; he engaged Diego López de Zúñiga (d. 1531) as editor, assisted by other eminent scholars, to work with Guillén de Brocar in printing the polyglot. Work started about 1502; the completed Bible, in six volumes (estimated as having cost Ximénes 50,000 gold ducats), was produced between 1514 and 1517, but Ximénes died before it was completed. The sixth and final volume contained Hebrew, Aramaic and Greek dictionaries, and various study aids.

The knowledge that the polyglot was in preparation drove Erasmus of Rotterdam to hurry publication of his own Greek–Latin New Testament, issued in 1516,

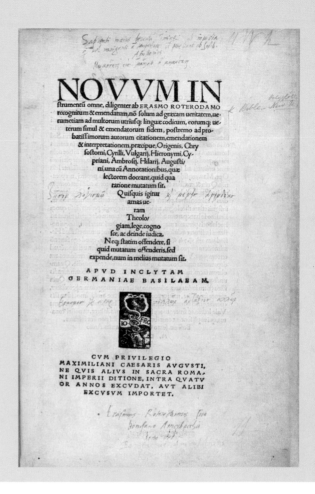

ABOVE Erasmian New Testament The handsome title page of Erasmus' bilingual edition. In the dedication he wrote: "I perceived that that teaching which is our salvation was to be had in a much purer and more lively form if sought at the fountain-head and drawn from the actual sources than from pools and runnels."

for which he gained a four-year exclusive privilege from Rome for its distribution. Printing of the Complutensian Polyglot Bible was completed by 1517, but distribution of its first edition, of 600 copies, was delayed until Pope Leo X authorized it in 1520. By misfortune, a large number of copies were then lost at sea while being exported to Italy: only 123 copies now survive.

Described as "the single most important scholarly publication of the Spanish Renaissance," the Complutensian Polyglot Bible is famed for its editing, the success of its design and the beauty of its Greek typeface, which has been influential on type designers since the late 19th century.

Connections

For other early collaborative books, see

Schedel's Nuremberg Chronicle, pp. *100–101*

Aldine Virgil, pp. *108–109*

For a later and different joint effort, see

Diderot's Encyclopédie, pp. *158–159*

For other Bible printing, see

Gustav Vasa Bible, pp. *124–125*

Bay Psalm Book, pp. *128–129*

CHAPTER

7

A Dangerous Invention

New interests, new methods and new problems emerged in the 16th and 17th centuries. Some of these issues, including quality control and copyright, continue to cause concerns today.

RIGHT *De humani corporis fabrica* Vesalius had access to human bodies, usually of executed criminals. In 1543 he described chancing on and stealing a corpse left hanging for a year by the roadside "for the benefit of the rustics": "This skeleton was completely dry and completely clean, and I examined it carefully, determined not to lose such an unexpected and long-sought opportunity." See pp. 134–135.

SEPTIMA
MVSCVLO-
RVM TABV-
LA.

I n the earliest days of printing, there was a widespread reverence for books and a keen appreciation of what we gain from being literate. In the 16th century, as literacy increased and books proliferated, attitudes changed. One aspect of the Reformation was the greater urge for people to be able to read Scriptures, as the range of Bible translations increased (see pp. 118–119, 124–125, and 128–129). However, translating could be dangerous work: William Tyndale was burned at the stake.

Even printers with official support were not trouble-free. For the Anglican Great Bible of 1538 printed in Paris, its publisher Richard Grafton had to flee from the Inquisition; he then had it printed in London, but was jailed for having done so. Nonetheless, Bible printing was a profitable business. Rulers could subsidize printing; just as King James I required every parish to have a copy of the Authorized Version of the Bible, so the King's Printers profited substantially. Until recently, a form of subsidy continued to the Royal Printers and the two university presses of Oxford and Cambridge. All three benefited greatly and so were more likely to follow government policies.

There were other ways for those who believed they knew the Truth: censorship. In almost every society, prepublication censorship (and often self-censorship) came to be used and to have value—for example, the peer reviewing of scientific literature, still used for the best of reasons. Officially sponsored lists of banned publications started to appear as early as the 15th century. The Roman *Index Librorum Prohibitorum* was first issued in 1559: one effect of the ban on Erasmus is shown vividly (see pp. 126–127).

Although the Puritans emigrated to British America partly to seek freedom to worship in their chosen ways, censorship was tight in Massachusetts. No Bibles were printed in North America until 1782, except one produced purely for missionary work. Like the more famous Bay Psalm Book of 1640, the Eliot Indian Bible was produced in Cambridge, Massachusetts, at a printing office set up in the home of the President of Harvard, where interference with the freedom of the press was muted (see pp. 128–129).

Missionary work was an important role for preachers in Spanish America, too. Though the Spanish role in dealing with the peoples of Mexico sometimes seems more like their part in the conquest of Moorish Spain, there were serious and sincere attempts to publish books in local languages. But even these approaches were often made by knowers of the Truth, like the Bishop of Yucatan, Diego de Landa Calderón, who destroyed as much as he preserved. Conveying information about the New World to the Old was often difficult; one of the most important documents, the *Codex Mendoza*, sent to Spain from Mexico never arrived, but instead ended up in the possession of Spain's enemies (see pp. 130–131).

Later books describing remote lands and civilizations often took a different form, more like the ancient **periplus**. Exploration was also undertaken by French, British and Dutch travelers, who came seeking the treasures of Cathay or the Indies, but through eastern trade rather than conquest. The 17th-century accounts by Hakluyt and others are still remarkably readable: the Dutch book by Jan van Linschoten typifies the best of such books (see pp. 132–133).

SCHOLARLY PUBLISHING

Two centuries after Gutenberg's invention, different styles of books became more easily recognizable. The earliest were scientific publications, all related to the earlier periods of study in the Islamic world and Renaissance enquiry in Europe, and increasingly from specialist publishers and booksellers known for their scholarly work. This did not necessarily free them from worries about state control (the checkered careers of Oporinus in Basle or the Estiennes in France demonstrate that clearly), but the publication of the great anatomical work by Vesalius (see pp. 134–135) marked a watershed in medical publication.

In Denmark in the mid-16th century, accuracy in scientific printing was problematic. Much earlier, Cardinal Ximénes created the organization needed to produce the Complutensian Polyglot Bible (see pp. 118–119), and King Frederick II of Denmark funded the research of the great astronomer Tycho Brahe (see pp. 136–137). Taking printing in-house for quality control worked for Tycho; and was later used by some other scholars. Increasingly, however, publishers relied on the expertise of regular and trained proofreaders, like those recommended by Hieronymus Hornschuch in his *Orthotypographia* (1608), the earliest technical manual for printers.

By the middle of the 17th century, production of bibliographies and the emergence of book auctions simplified distribution. The professionalization of scientific research and publication was coming to completion. The emergence of the research journal is outside the scope of this book, but the formation

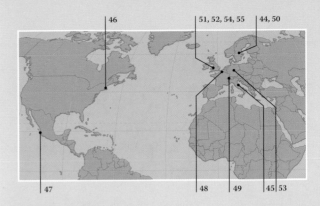

of scientific and linguistic societies and academies is almost as old as printing itself. Modern science can sometimes be dated from the start of the Royal Society in London in 1660 or the Académie Royale des Sciences in France in 1669. Their members were learning new ways of organizing their information and systematizing their results in publications. Isaac Newton's *Principia Mathematica* of 1687 (see pp. 138–139) was an outstanding book. The speed with which its brilliance was recognized shows how good the dissemination of information was.

Just as the presentation of text changed, so did the styles and content of book illustration. **Woodcut** illustration (as in Vesalius) could be superb, but copper-engraving and etching became more common. These methods had drawbacks: as they had to be printed separately from text, they were more expensive to produce. But they were modish and over the years these **intaglio** prints became commonly used.

EMERGING WRITERS

It would be possible to fill this book with reproductions from important Elizabethan and Jacobean literary works, including Shakespeare's poems or plays, or nonfiction such as Burton's *Anatomy of Melancholy* (1621). But instead, it is instructive to look at inferior or nearly forgotten writers because they illustrate the amazing exuberance and inventiveness of the period. The books of Gervase Markham (see pp. 140–141), a minor playwright and hack writer, had flashes of gold in a lot of dross. Markham foreshadowed the increasing compilation of a series of detailed descriptions of crafts and skills, often written by craftsmen proud of their trade. One, Joseph Moxon, became the first tradesman elected to the Royal Society, and his *Mechanick Exercises or the Doctrine of Handy-works* (1678–83) remains one of the most important studies of printing and other technologies. Such books were not written by master tradesmen only; increasingly, these were books intended for women, sometimes written by women (see pp. 142–143), and sometimes for a male readership as well (see pp. 144–145). Developments in the book trade encouraged more speculative book production through **subscription publishing**, which increased the range of illustrated books whose authors could (with luck) earn a profit from their books (see pp. 146–147).

Developing the Swedish Language

Most European countries published Bibles in the 15th and 16th centuries, and their production helped solidify their national identity—particularly in Scandinavia.

Because of the religious controversies that fed the Reformation and Counter-Reformation in Western Europe, and the increased pressure for people to read the texts for themselves, many rulers and churches commissioned printers to produce new editions. Many of the early translations into local languages were made from the Vulgate versions, and the early printing of any dialect tended to fix and preserve that language for future use.

With the growth of the Protestant Reformation and the wish to avoid using the Vulgate came the demand for fresh translations for the various Lutheran, Calvinist and other groups. Martin Luther's German translation in 1522 was followed by a Dutch version issued by Jacob van Liesveldt (Antwerp, 1526).

The growth of the Lutheran churches in Scandinavia led the local rulers to have Bibles prepared in their own languages. They had them printed in formal styles, just as in England with the Great Bible (1539) and the later King James Bible (1611)—which, in the 16th century predicated using **blackletter types** and a **folio format**. In Denmark, King Christian III organized the production of a Danish Bible (1550–51), which was the basis for the Icelandic Bible supervised in 1584 by the local Bishop of Hólar.

The history of Bible printing in Sweden was similar. A Swedish New Testament was published in 1528, and the complete Bible (based on Luther's texts) was completed at

LEFT **Gustav Vasa Bible** Vadstena monastery, founded by St. Birgitta at Lake Vättern in 1346, led the way in translating religious texts into the Swedish vernacular. Following this tradition, the Bible's widespread distribution, read from the pulpit in every parish, played a unique role in forging a uniformity of the Swedish language.

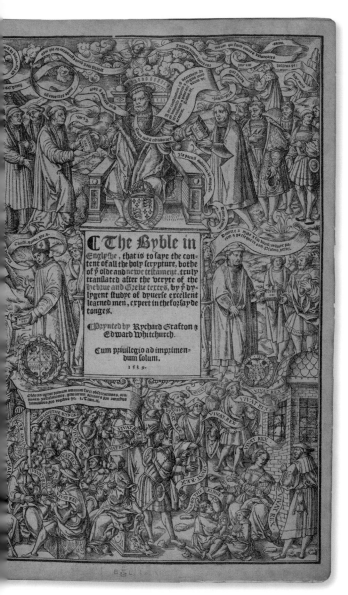

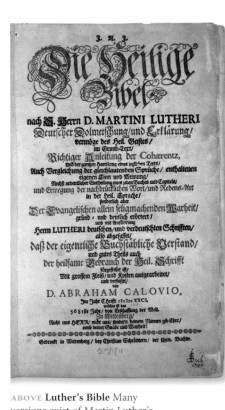

LEFT **Cromwell's Great Bible** *The Byble in Englyshe* is sometimes known after Thomas Cromwell, the Vicar General who commissioned this first authorized translation. Printing began in Paris but, seized for heresy, it was completed in London in April 1539. Its densely ornate title page depicts Lord Cromwell's employer, Henry VIII, with his clergy.

ABOVE **Luther's Bible** Many versions exist of Martin Luther's Bible. This three-volume edition, by 17th-century theologian Abraham Calovius, was published in Wittenberg in 1681–82. This particular copy, now in the Concordia Seminary, St. Louis, belonged to the great composer J.S. Bach, who made some 25 annotations in the margins; his monogram is inscribed bottom right.

Uppsala in 1541. Known as the Gustav Vasa Bible, after the King who commissioned it, its production closely followed the styles and typography developed by the Germans, using their **Fraktur** faces. (The Finns also used Fraktur.) The Gustav Vasa Bible was a handsome book; the language and literary style of the translation helped to form the modern Swedish language, and the orthography and use of accents made its difference from Danish more distinctive.

Since the King James Bible was published, the English language has changed; similarly, the Swedes feel that their Bible's language is old-fashioned. But the Swedish abandonment of Fraktur has caused another problem: modern Swedes find that typeface almost unreadable, and so the original is now seldom read.

Practical Censorship at Work

*Destroying books is commonplace enough in many periods
and countries. This technique of burning words out of the page
is much less common—and equally ineffective in destroying
interest in the text.*

Censorship was present almost as soon as printing was developed by Gutenberg in the mid-15th century. Ironically, the first attempt was made in 1471 by the scholar Niccolò Perotti, who proposed a system of centralized control to ensure that texts were well edited; but his Utopian proposal was not accepted.

Instead, control of the press was directed at political or religious publications. The attempts to preserve morality came much later, particularly in the 18th century (see pp. 168–169).

The most famous of the attempts to control reading through censorship was the production of the Catholic

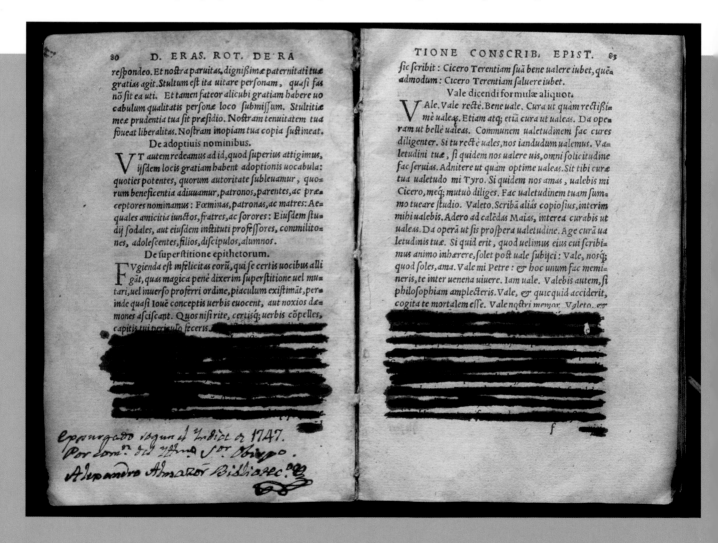

Index Librorum Prohibitorum (*Index of Prohibited Books*) promulgated in 1559 by Pope Paul IV. It forbade Catholics to read books on the Index, unless given specific permission, and it listed individual books and, frequently, the complete works of banned writers. The lists, of course, changed over the centuries; the last edition was published in 1948, and the Index was formally abolished under Paul VI in 1966.

One of the banned authors was Desiderius Erasmus (1466–1536), author of the satire *Moriae Encomium* (*The Praise of Folly*), published 1511. His translation of the Greek New Testament appeared in 1516. Though he remained a Catholic, Erasmus was blamed for giving opportunities for Lutherism to develop, and so his work was later put on the Index.

Some zealots interpreted the prohibition all too literally. The Italian Andrea Alciati's *Emblematum liber* (1531) set a fashion for **emblem books** popular for several centuries. Alciati's work was not banned, but Erasmus' was, and mentioned in *Emblematum liber*. One owner of Alciati's book burned out Erasmus's name every time it appeared in the text. The 1747 owner of this copy of Erasmus' *Epistolas*, printed by Froben at Basle in 1522—the censor for the Inquisition—was more careful, and blotted out every offensive passage, but his redaction simply attracts readers' curiosity. Censorship almost always creates a counter-reaction.

Connections

For control for political/governmental reasons, see

Diderot's Encyclopédie, pp. 158–159

For censorship for moral reasons, see

Cleland's Fanny Hill, pp. 168–169

Stopes' Married Love, pp. 230–231

LEFT **Expurgated epistles** In this copy of *De ratione conscribendi epistolas*, published by Erasmus in Basle in 1522 (now in the Episcopal Library of the Seminary of Barcelona), the censor for the Inquisition in 1747 saw fit to obliterate large passages of the offending text, clearly marking it "expurgado."

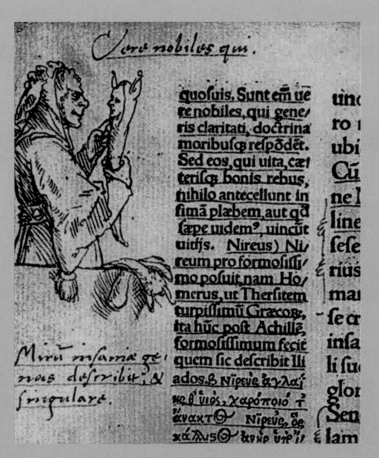

LEFT *The Praise of Folly* This biting satire on the Catholic Church was written by Erasmus in 1509 while visiting his friend Sir Thomas More, and became instrumental in the Reformation. Hans Holbein, a friend of both, drew this witty portrait of Erasmus as Folly in the author's own copy of the book: these marginalia formed the basis for engravings in a later illustrated edition.

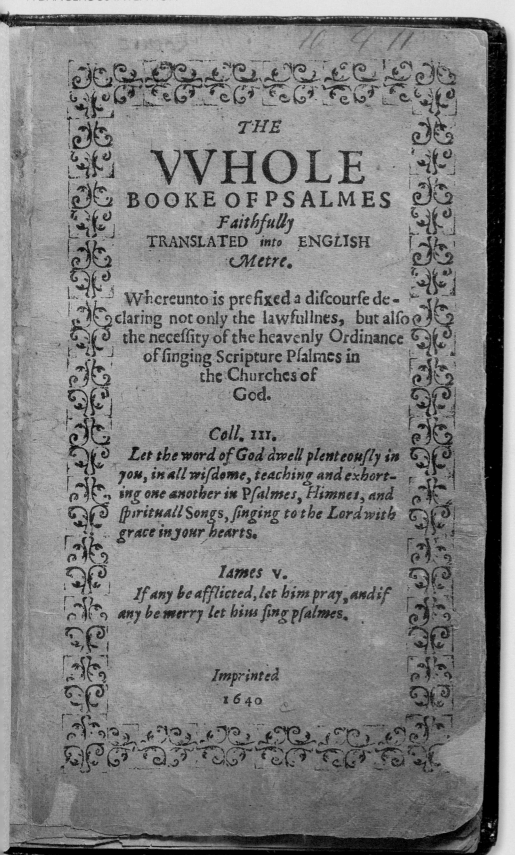

THE
VVHOLE
BOOKE OF PSALMES
Faithfully
TRANSLATED into ENGLISH
Metre.

Whereunto is prefixed a difcourfe de-
claring not only the lawfullnes, but alfo
the neceffity of the heavenly Ordinance
of finging Scripture Pfalmes in
the Churches of
God.

Coll. III.
*Let the word of God dwell plenteoufly in
you, in all wifdome, teaching and exhort-
ing one another in Pfalmes, Himnes, and
fpirituall Songs, finging to the Lord with
grace in your hearts.*

Iames v.
*If any be afflicted, let him pray, and if
any be merry let him fing pfalmes.*

Imprinted
1640

LEFT Bay Psalm Book
Produced in Massachusetts
Bay Colony by newly
immigrant Congregationalist
Puritans, *The Whole Booke
of Psalmes* was the first book
to be printed in America.
Stephen Daye, an indentured
locksmith, sent the press from
England, together with paper
and type. Just 11 copies
survive of an edition of 1,700.

**TOP RIGHT "When as I with
my voice doe cry"**
The Whole Booke of Psalmes,
its poetical form intended
to express the Hebrew
original more closely than
its antecedents, was a new
translation for a New World,
by "thirty pious and learned
Ministers"—leading New
England scholars such as John
Cotton, Richard Mather and
John Eliot.

**BOTTOM RIGHT Algonquin
Bible** Puritan emigré John
Eliot believed that Native
American conversion to
Christianity would be more
successful if the Bible was
printed in the native language.
After studying Algonquin
(then a spoken language only)
from native speaker John
Sassamon, Eliot, minister
for Natick (one of the key
Algonquian praying towns),
set about translating the
Catechism and then the
Bible into their own Natick
vernacular (1653). His
translated Bible was the first
Bible to be printed in America.

The First Printing in British America

*The first steps in the American printing and publishing trade were taken
at Harvard in the early Puritan colony in Massachusetts.*

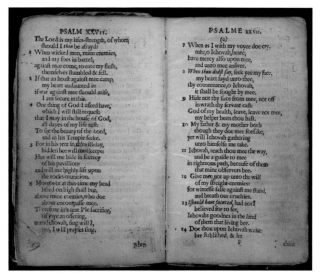

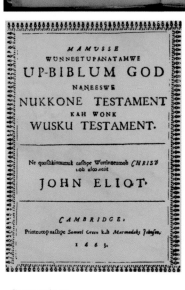

Much early printing in Spanish America was for religious purposes, and often directed by Jesuit missionaries. In the middle of the 17th century, at the time of the English Civil War and the Restoration, the authorities in Virginia were strongly opposed to the introduction of printing. In 1671 Sir William Berkeley, then Governor of Virginia, wrote, "I thank God that there are no free schools, nor printing, and I hope we shall not have, these hundred years"—but in Massachusetts, printing had already started in Cambridge in 1639.

The first substantial book was *The Whole Book of Psalms*, printed by Stephen Daye in 1640. Daye was not a printer by trade (he was a locksmith), nor did he own the printing equipment. It had been shipped to Massachusetts by the Reverend Henry Glover, who died on the voyage, and by contract Daye was obliged to set up and run the press for the widowed Mrs. Glover. When she then married the President of Harvard College, Henry Dunster, the press was moved into Dunster's house—and gained a degree of protection against others who shared Berkeley's views. (There were further attempts to restrict printing in Massachusetts in 1649, 1662 and 1690, when publication of a newspaper was undertaken.) The press at Cambridge was also used later for printing a Bible. But not for settlers' use: a translation was made by the missionary John Eliot, one of the Psalm Book editors, into the native dialect used by the local Algonquin tribes. One thousand copies of the Eliot Indian Bible were printed in 1660–63. One of its printers was a Native American, a Nipmuc man named James Printer, a student at the Indian College at Harvard.

The Bay Psalm Book (as it is often known) was probably printed largely by Daye's son Matthew, and sold by Hezekiah Usher, the first bookseller in British America. For inexperienced printers, it was a good production. Eleven copies now survive; one was auctioned in November 2013 for US$14.2 million: less than the pre-auction estimates of US$15 million to $30 million, but still making it one of the most expensive printed books ever sold.

Connections

An Aztec View of Pre-Columbian Life

Few written records survive from Amerindian life before the Spanish conquest: the destruction of Aztec and Mayan books was part of it. But a few of them have survived....

All wars are horrible; colonial aggression often illustrates the ugliness of the aggressors, but can sometimes produce its own enlightened heroes. The Spanish conquest of Mexico in 1519 included the brutality of Hernán Cortés, and Nuño de Guzmán who destroyed books and peoples. This was followed in Mexico by the more humane Bartolomé de las Casas and Vasco de Quiroga. More typical was the cleric Diego de Landa Calderón, working with the Maya in Yucatan, who had an intense interest in the Maya and their language (his writing about them has enabled modern scholars to interpret the Maya **syllabary**)—but believing that their survival would delay successful Christian missionary work, he ordered the destruction of all Maya manuscripts that could be found.

It was difficult for the Spanish kings to grasp what was happening in their colonies: the Amerindian cultures were different from the conquered Muslims in Spain and totally alien. To help remove this ignorance, the enlightened viceroy, Antonio de Mendoza (who introduced printing to Mexico in 1539), commissioned the preparation of a manuscript. The *Codex Mendoza*, as it is now known, gave an outline history of the Aztec rulers and their conquests, details of tributes paid to the Spanish, plus a description of contemporary Aztec life, using traditional Aztec **pictograms** with Spanish commentary.

This invaluable text was shipped to Spain intended for Charles V, to give him some guidance. The **provenance** of the manuscript is romantic. Seized by French privateers, it came into the hands of André Thévet, an important French explorer and writer who was involved in the unsuccessful French attempt to found a colony near Rio de Janeiro. The manuscript was then bought in Paris by the English writer on exploration, Richard Hakluyt; it was later used by another English writer on exploration, Samuel Purchas, who regarded it as the jewel of his collection, reproducing several illustrations in his famous *Purchas his Pilgrimes*. Then bought by the historian and book collector John Selden (described by Milton as "the chief of learned men reputed in this land"), the manuscript passed in 1654 to the Bodleian Library in Oxford and is prized as one of its most important books.

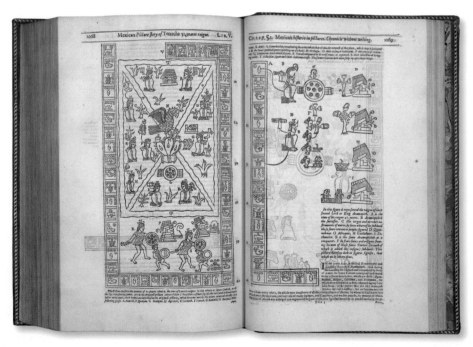

LEFT *Purchas his Pilgrimes*
The chapter on New Spain in Book IV of *Hakluytus posthumus* (as *Purchas his Pilgrimes* is otherwise known; 1625) reproduces illustrations from the *Codex Mendoza*— here, the 10 Tenuch lords. This copy comes from the Library of Congress Kraus collection, relating to the travels of Francis Drake, whose voyages are also described within.

Connections

For other views of pre-Columbian life, see

For other trophies from European colonizing, see

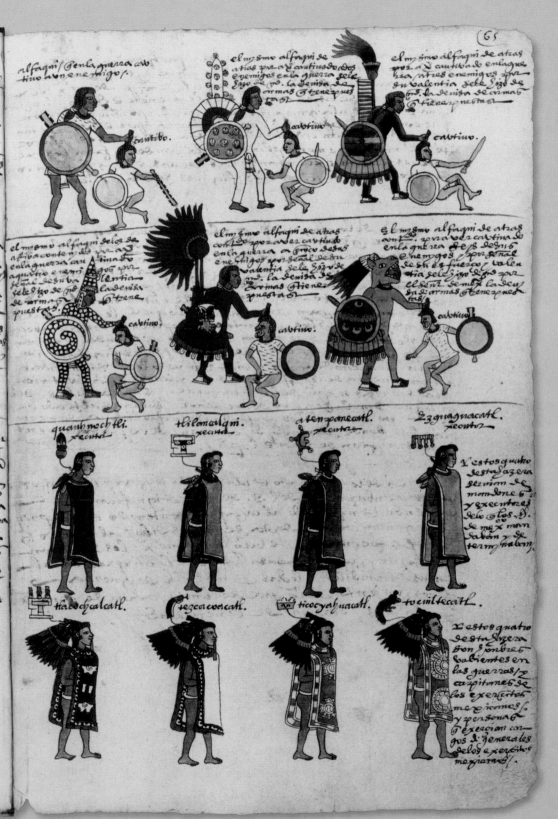

LEFT *Codex Mendoza* Folio
65r of this intriguing codex,
created in Mexico City in the
1640s, illustrates six stages in
the career of successful priest-
warrior (*calmecac*) and below,
two sets of imperial officers.
Other pictograms illustrate
Moctezuma's palace, tributes,
the duties of priests, the
education of children
and other lively scenes
of Aztec civilization.

Searching for Pepper and Nutmeg

An important Dutch sailing manual, this book led to developing
European colonialism in East Asia.

The quest for spices and precious materials from the East goes back almost to prehistory. The first-century CE Greek *Periplus of the Erythraean Sea* and the ninth-century travels of the Arab Al-Mas'udi show that this was no new thing. But the Portuguese explorations to India and farther east enabled Europe to get oriental spices more easily than older land routes through the Islamic world to Venice.

The profitable Portuguese imports of spices arrived in Lisbon. For many years, Antwerp was the distributor to the Netherlands, until the division of the Catholic south and the newly independent Protestant north made this impossible. The Dutch wanted spices, and the chance to import for themselves; but the Portuguese prevented foreign vessels from getting to the spice islands.

A resourceful Dutchman, Jan Huygen van Linschoten (1563–1611), found a solution. He had worked for the Portuguese Archbishop in Goa, and kept copious notes of what he saw, adding what he learned from other Dutch travelers who went farther east. It was many years before he eventually returned to Holland, having joined Willem Barentsz on voyages in search of the Northeast Passage, north of Siberia, and on another voyage seeking spices in the East.

Working with the cartographer Petrus Plancius, Linschoten compiled an extensive **rutter** to enable vessels to navigate to the Far East, by-passing the Portuguese forts at Malacca. Not unlike Cristoforo Buondelmonti's earlier *isolario* (see pp. 70–71), Linschoten's *Itinerario* (1596) was packed with detailed sailing directions and information about the peoples living in parts of Asia still little-known in Europe. His book was widely reprinted and translated, and his work provided the easy access that eventually led to the Dutch expelling the Portuguese from most of their Asian colonies. The opening of trade led to the formation of the Dutch, English, French, Danish and Swedish East India Companies, which for centuries would then dominate trade with Asia.

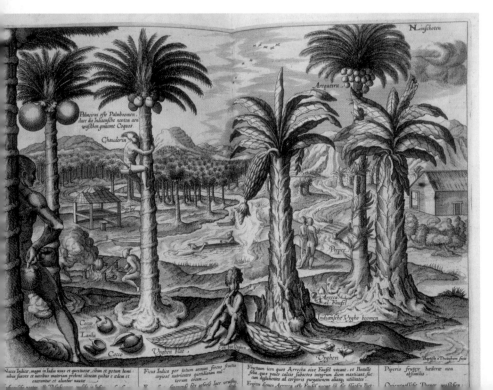

LEFT **Collecting coconuts** In this semi-naturalistic setting, mohawk-wearing natives collect coconuts growing among other tropical plants such as peppers and bananas. Although some details, like the open-sided building, are probably based on direct observation, the **provenance** of others is clearly European—notably the classical cherub, center foreground, happily munching a banana.

Connections

ITINERARIO,

Voyage ofte Schipvaert / van Jan Huygen van Linschoten naer Oost ofte Portugaels Indien,

inhoudende een corte beschryvinghe der selver Landen ende Zee-custen / met aenwysinge van alle de voornaemde principale Havens / Revieren / hoecken ende plaetsen / tot noch toe vande Portugesen ontdeckt ende bekent: Waer by ghevoecht zijn / niet alleen die Conterfeytsels vande habyten / drachten ende wesen / so vande Portugesen aldaer residerende / als vande ingeboornen Indianen / ende huere Tempels / Afgoden / Huysinge / met die voornaemste Boomen / Vruchten / kruyden / Specerye / ende diergelijcke materialen / als ooc die manieren des selfden Volckes / so in hunnen Godts-diensten / als in Politie en Huijs-houdinghe: maer ooc een corte verhalinge van de Coophandelingen / hoe en waer die ghedreven en ghevonden worden / met die ghedenckweerdichste geschiedenissen / voorghevallen den tijt zijnder residentie aldaer.

Alles beschreven ende by een vergadert, door den selfden, seer nut, oorbaer, ende oock vermakelijcken voor alle curieuse ende Liefhebbers van vreemdigheden.

t'AMSTELREDAM.

By Cornelis Claesz. op't VVater, in't Schrijf-boeck, by de oude Brugghe.
Anno CIƆ. IƆ. XCVI.

RIGHT **An anatomy lesson**
The title page of the *De humani corporis fabrica* illustrates a dissection taking place. Unlike Galen, Vesalius was able to base his work on direct observation and referred scornfully to "Galen and his apes," to whom the figure with the monkey, lower left, seems to makes reference.

The First Modern Study of Anatomy

Before the Renaissance, medical education looked backward to the faulty work of Galen. From the dissecting theater at Padua, the brilliant anatomist Vesalius changed this, with the publication of his brilliantly illustrated book.

The anatomical studies of the Greek Galen (129– c. 200 CE) were for centuries the foundation of all medical work, throughout the Islamic world and later in Italy. Galen's fame was so great that anatomists taught from his texts, not from first-hand dissection— not realizing that when Galen was denied access to human cadavers, he used the bodies of Barbary apes, believing that the human body was the same. The mistakes were perpetuated because of Galen's high reputation.

This erratic understanding was overthrown in the 16th century by the brilliant Brabantian, Andreas Vesalius (Andries van Wezel, 1514–64), who became professor of surgery and anatomy (*explicator chirurgiae*) at Padua in 1537. Padua, in the Venetian territories, was safe from interference from the Inquisition, which was important because Vesalius carried out his autopsies in front of students and visitors—a significant advance in medical teaching.

To make his anatomical research more widely available, Vesalius prepared his amazing *De humani corporis fabrica* (*On the Fabric of the Human Body*), printed in 1543. The obvious course was to have his book printed in Venice; instead he went to the scholar-printer Johannes Oporinus in Basle. Oporinus had a reputation for publishing advanced books—he got into

difficulties for publishing a Latin translation of the Koran—but he was also admired for the design of his publications.

De humani corporis fabrica was a masterpiece, for the importance of Vesalius' research and for the superb **woodcut** illustrations in it. The artist believed to have prepared the drawings was Jan Steven van Calcar (c. 1499–1546), who had been one of Titian's pupils. According to Vasari and others, he was a brilliant imitator of Giorgione and Raphael, and his skill in making close and accurate copies of what he saw in the Padua dissecting theater was unequaled.

Vesalius' book is regarded as one of the most brilliant anatomies and can now be accessed online. The style of its illustrations was influential on contemporary anatomists, such as Vesalius' pupil Jan Valverde de Hamusco; and it cast a long shadow on later books such as Govard Bidloo's *Anatomia humani corporis* (1685) or William Cheselden's *Osteographia* (1733). These also had striking illustrations, but they hardly match the brilliance of those in Oporinus' book.

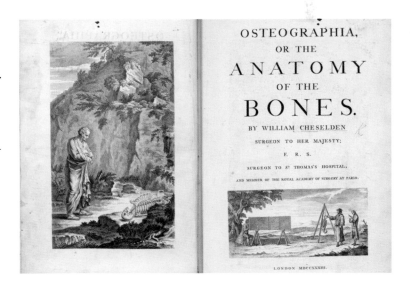

ABOVE **Cheselden's *Osteographia*** For the drawings for his *Anatomy of Bones*, 1733, Cheselden made use of the **camera obscura**, as shown in the title-page vignette. The human and animal skeletons throughout are shown often in semi-naturalistic settings, like the one on the frontispiece, facing, which depicts Galen, perhaps in acknowledgment of the anatomist's debt.

Connections

For other books using pop-ups or flaps, see

Repton's Red Books, pp. 174–175

Meggendorfer's Grand Circus, pp. 198–199

For earlier anatomical research, see

Mansur's Anatomy, pp. 90–91

An Amazing Amateur Astronomer

For centuries, the impetus for astronomical research and publication came from the Islamic world. It took a stubborn and single-minded Dane to develop the foundations for modern astronomy.

Astronomy figured largely in scientific work in classical Greece, as in the Islamic world. When printing came into use in Europe, the production of astronomical books was always problematic: absolute accuracy in reporting data was as vital as it was in making astronomical observations, and for some purposes paper-based "computers" (**volvelles**) were used. Several early European astronomers such as Regiomontanus and Hevelius tried to achieve accuracy in their texts by setting up personal presses to print their work.

This was even more important for the remarkable Danish mathematician, astronomer and astrologer Tycho Brahe (1546–1601) because he had an almost pathological fear of having his scientific results stolen by others. Fortunately for him, Brahe had high-placed family connections; and Brahe's precocious astronomical skills impressed King Frederick II of Denmark so much that the King granted ownership of the island of Hveen (in Äresund) to Brahe, with enough money to build an observatory there. (Today, the Danes speak of *Tycho Brahes dage*—unlucky days for undertaking anything important—but obviously Brahe himself experienced very lucky days.)

Work on his new observatory, Uraniborg (or Castle of the Heavens), started in 1572. Brahe installed papermakers and a printer (recruited from Germany) as well as the assistants who helped to construct his astronomical instruments. Printing work on his first astronomical book from Uraniborg started in 1588, but that year King Frederick II died. His successor Christian IV was much less willing to continue to finance such research and discontinued his subsidies. In 1597, Brahe abandoned Uraniborg and moved instead to Bohemia where, in 1598, he was appointed Imperial Mathematician to Emperor Rudolf II. He died suddenly and unexpectedly in 1601; his demise is now thought by some to have been from mercury poisoning through his alchemical experiments.

Brahe's calculations gave much better and more accurate data than available before. His work as an astronomer was remarkable, but also disappointing. So much promise, so much attempted, but so much left unfinished: his assistant Johannes Kepler was to complete Brahe's books, and Kepler would develop a new and better understanding of the planetary motion that underpins modern astronomical work.

Connections

For an earlier astronomical book, see

Al-Sufi's Book of Fixed Stars, **pp. 86–87**

For other wealthy and eccentric bookmakers, see

Repton's Red Books, **pp. 174–175**

Cranach-Presse's Hamlet, **pp. 214–215**

Hunter's Old Papermaking, **pp. 238–239**

RIGHT **Tycho Brahe** The *Astronomiae* title page depicts the astronomer in his observatory with some of the instruments he built between the 1570s and his death in 1601. After his death these were kept in a cellar in Prague, and destroyed during the uprisings there of 1619. Renowned cartographer Jean Blaeu (Brahe's pupil) later illustrated Brahe's instruments in his own *Grande Atlas*.

QVADRANS MVRALIS
SIVE TICHONICVS.

A Foundation Stone of Modern Science

Newton's work was crucial for the development of science, but the difficult and secretive genius who wrote the Principia *was embroiled in many disputes about who was the first in the field.*

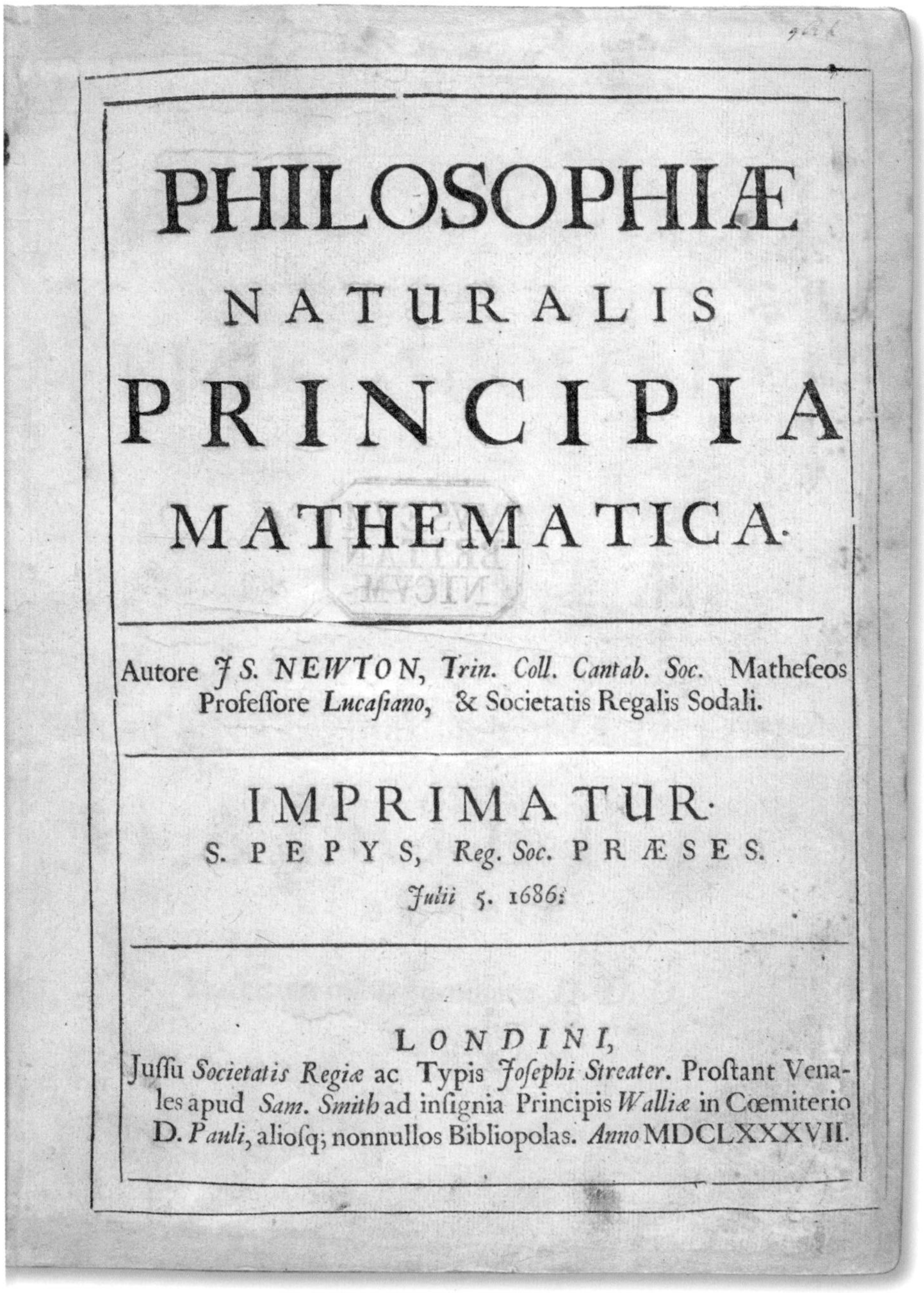

PHILOSOPHIÆ

NATURALIS

PRINCIPIA

MATHEMATICA.

Autore *JS. NEWTON, Trin. Coll. Cantab. Soc.* Matheseos Professore *Lucasiano,* & Societatis Regalis Sodali.

IMPRIMATUR.

S. PEPYS, *Reg. Soc.* PRÆSES.

Julii 5. 1686:

LONDINI,

Jussu *Societatis Regiæ* ac Typis *Josephi Streater.* Prostant Venales apud *Sam. Smith* ad insignia Principis *Walliæ* in Cœmeterio D. *Pauli,* aliosq; nonnullos Bibliopolas. *Anno* MDCLXXXVII.

LEFT Newton's *Principia*
Newton's great work, of monumental importance to the development of modern physics and astronomy, was published by the Royal Society in London in 1687. The President of the Society who signed the Imprimatur ("let it be printed") was the diarist Samuel Pepys—his correspondence with Newton over the rolling of dice resulted in the naming of the probability puzzle the Newton–Pepys Problem.

TOP RIGHT *Principia* revised
Despite his book's significance, Newton was criticized for failing to fully explain why gravity occurred. The copy in Cambridge University Library is the author's own, annotated by himself, in preparation for a further edition, which he eventually published in 1713.

BOTTOM RIGHT *Newtonianism for Ladies* Francesco Algarotti, the Italian scientist and member of the Royal Society, made Newtonianism popular with his 1737 bestseller. A series of lively and deceptively light-hearted dialogs between a *cavaliero* and a *marchesa*, it offered a considered study of Newton's experiments, in particular on the nature of light and colors, and helped to promote natural philosophy as a literary genre.

If you were seeking a scientist who was the most important in the modern scientific revolution, Isaac Newton would be close to the top of your list, even if all you can remember is the apocryphal story of the apple falling on his head, which led him to discover the laws of gravity.

Newton (1642–1727) was undoubtedly a genius. After an unpromising start (his widowed mother wanted him to farm in Lincolnshire), in 1661 he started university study at Trinity College Cambridge, rising to become a Fellow of the College in 1667. Having unorthodox views on religion, he was much influenced by the mathematician Isaac Barrow, the first Lucasian Professor at Cambridge. Newton succeeded him as second Lucasian Professor in 1669—a fortunate appointment since, thanks to the support of King Charles II, Newton was not required to become a clergyman, as most academics were. He became a Fellow of the Royal Society in 1672, and was to be a long-term President of the Society from 1703 to his death. He was also for many years the Warden and Master of the Mint, and took an active and effective role in pursuing counterfeiters.

Newton carried out his official roles successfully, but his reputation came from his published work. Drawing on earlier work by Tycho Brahe and Kepler, Newton laid the foundations of classical mechanics, and his laws of gravitation, in his *Philosophiae Naturalis Principia Mathematica* (*Mathematical Principles of Natural Philosophy*), first published in three volumes in 1687. It is regarded as one of the masterpieces in the history of science.

Undoubtedly Newton was a difficult man, getting on poor terms with Robert Hooke about optics, and there was a long and acrimonious dispute about whether the invention of calculus was by the brilliant German Gottfried Leibniz or Newton. This foreshadowed later scientific disputes between Britain and Germany: in England, the *Philosophical Transactions of the Royal Society* supported Newton; in most places on the continent, the important Leipzig journal *Acta Eruditorum* believed Leibniz. Scientific literature is by no means always impartial or neutral.

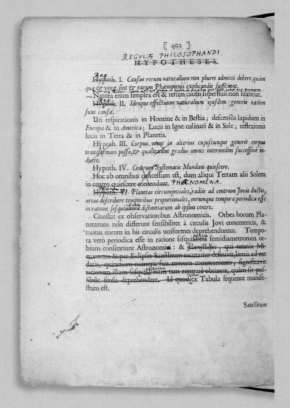

Connections

Everyman His Own Expert

If, 400 years ago, you needed a recipe, or to know how to design a garden, clip a poodle or train a colt, then prolific hack writer Gervase Markham provided such information in his how-to manuals.

If you tried to invent a Hollywood Elizabethan drama, the career of Gervase Markham (c. 1568–1637) would seem over the top. A younger son of a landowner in Nottinghamshire, Gervase started his career as a retainer to the Earl of Rutland. After seeing military service in the Netherlands and Ireland under the Earl of Essex, he was probably lucky to escape arrest himself when, in 1601, Essex was executed for treason.

Markham had literary yearnings, translating Ariosto and writing his own poetry and plays, and he was also an actor. He was a dramatist, dismissed as "a base fellow" by Ben Jonson; and some critics think that in the character of Don Adriano de Armado in *Love's Labour's Lost*, Shakespeare was mocking Markham.

An enthusiastic and capable horse breeder (who reputedly brought the first Arabian horse to England), Markham spent many years farming and in rural pursuits, becoming expert in many aspects of rural life. And he was subject to logorrhea—books on a wide range of subjects poured from him: *Hobsons horse-load of letters* (a guide to letter writing), *The English Husbandman* (on kitchen gardens and orchards) and *Countrey Contentments* or *The English Huswife* (full of recipes for cooking and domestic management). Covering aspects of daily life in Elizabethan and Jacobean times, many of these popular guides were extensively reprinted and are still enjoyed today. But Markham's real love was horses. His first book on horses was published in 1593, but the most important was *Cavelarice* (*English Horseman*), published in 1607. In it, Markham included eight carefully worded dedications to different eminent men, each expected to win the author some reward from the dedicatees. *Cavelarice* went into many editions, revealing his remarkably extensive knowledge and enthusiasm for horses— and also his understanding of human nature.

Markham went on to write many more such manuals, to such an extent that the booksellers felt it was becoming counter-productive. In 1617, the Stationers Company (the powerful London trade guild of printers and booksellers) forced him to sign an unprecedented agreement:

> *Never to write any more book or bookes to be printed, of the Deseases or cures of any Cattle, as Horse, Oxe, Cowe, sheepe, Swine and Goates &c.*

Few publishers have tried like this to dissuade successful authors from writing. With Gervase Markham, they failed.

Connections

For other self-help books, see

Soyer's Modern Housewife, pp. 202–203

Stopes' Married Love, pp. 230–231

RIGHT *Cavelarice* The flamboyant title page of Gervase Markham's 1607 manual, which contained the substance of the author's earlier writings on "all the Arte of Horsemanship," including "how to teach them to doe trickes."

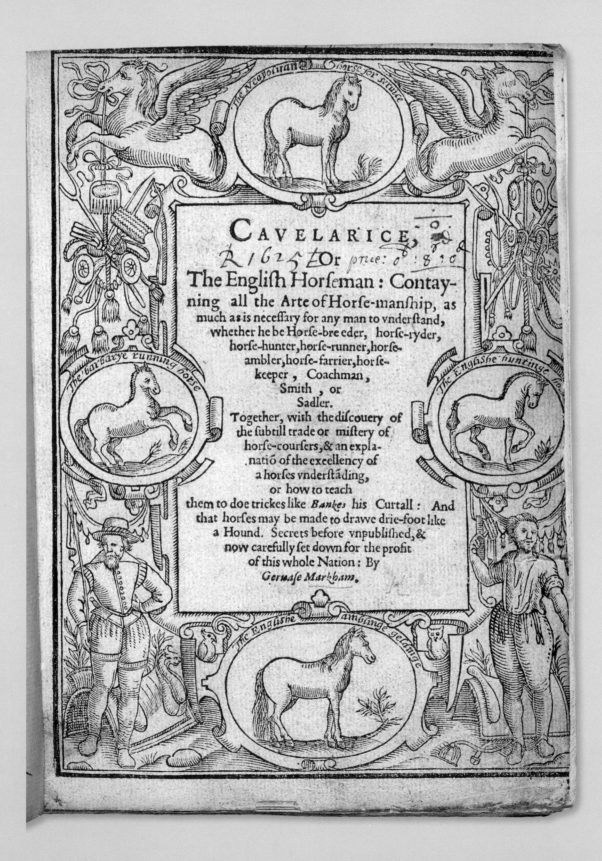

The Neapolitan Horse for seruice

The barbarye running horse

The Englishe huntinge horse

CAVELARICE,

Or

The English Horseman : Contay-

ning all the Arte of Horse-manship, as
much as is necessary for any man to vnderstand,
whether he be Horse-breeder, horse-ryder,
horse-hunter, horse-runner, horse-
ambler, horse-farrier, horse-
keeper , Coachman ,
Smith , or
Sadler.
Together, with the discouery of
the subtill trade or mistery of
horse-coursers, & an expla-
natió of the exeellency of
a horses vnderstáding,
or how to teach
them to doe trickes like *Bankes* his Curtall : And
that horses may be made to drawe drie-foot like
a Hound. Secrets before vnpublished, &
now carefully set down for the profit
of this whole Nation : By
Geruase Markham.

The Englishe amblinge geldinge

Fashion in Clothing

Fashion plates of ladies' dresses were commonplace in the 19th century, but earlier how-to books written by and for women marked the start of major changes in publishing.

Until the 18th century, books written by women on the arts and crafts were rare, and those written for a female readership were rarer still. Artists such as the great Dutch flower painter Maria Sybilla Meriam or the Scotswoman Elizabeth Blackwell (see pp. 144–145) were remarkable.

Female interest in embroidery was long-standing and highly approved: "to work neatly and skillfully at fancy work is one of the attributes of good female society," wrote a Victorian lady, and all young middle-class women were taught how to embroider. But where to find their designs? A French writer recommended using **nature printing** from leaves to create patterns to embroider, but most women in Britain, France and Germany preferred to buy patterns for themselves.

Earlier books published in London or Paris were written by men. But in about 1725, a Nuremberg woman published the first volume of her book on embroidery, *Kunst-und Fleiss-übende Nadel-ergötzungen* (*Art and Industry in the Practice of the Needle*), in which she laid out her patterns on a squared background, simplifying the task of copying the designs onto fabric. The author, Margaretha Helm, wife of the cantor of a local church, taught embroidery

as well as being an expert embroiderer and engraver herself. In her book she gave advice on the materials, threads and colors to be used. Professional mantua-makers (as well as amateur dressmakers) could use Helm's informative book to create clothes to impress.

Helm's publisher Christoph Weigel was an eminent and respected engraver, as well as being a publisher (some of Johann Sebastian Bach's music was engraved and published by the family's firm). Weigel was well known for his illustrated instructional books and issued two other books of patterns, emphasizing that they were of original designs. In Margaretha Helm's book, he wrote a short preface, recommending needlework as being the most seemly occupation for aristocratic and *bürgerliche* (middle-class) ladies. Over the years, further patterns were published, the last in 1742, the year Margaretha Helm died. Being **intaglio** work, her beautiful book would always have been expensive and printed in relatively small editions, and is now very rare indeed.

LEFT *Kunst-und Fleiss-übende Nadel-ergötzungen* Title page of Margaretha Helm's "newly invented Sewing and Embroidery Book," *Kunst-und Fleiss-übende Nadel-ergötzungen* (*Art and Industry in the Practice of the Needle*). The Nuremberg seamstress taught embroidery and also worked as a copperplate engraver, both occupations of skilled "closework."

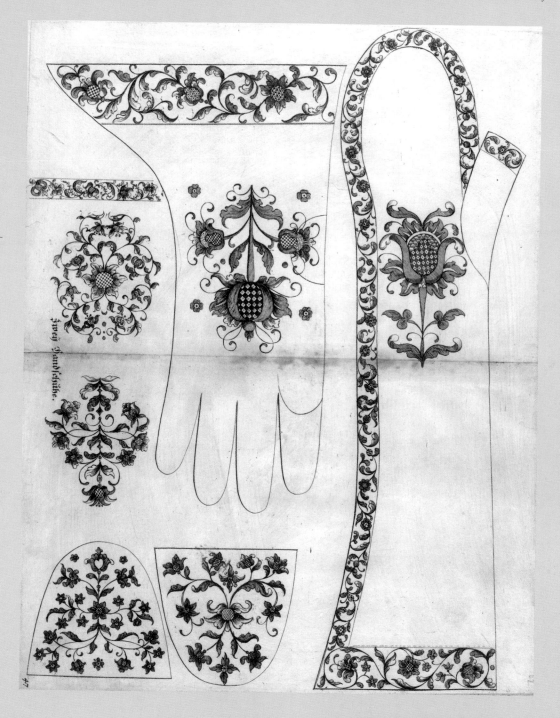

Connections

For other books by women, see

Blackwell's Curious Herball, *pp. 144–145*

Atkins' Photographs of British Algae, *pp. 184–185*

Aikin's Robinson Crusoe, *pp. 194–195*

For a more modern feminist viewpoint, see

Stopes' Married Love, *pp. 230–231*

ABOVE **"Two Gloves"** Plate 47 includes this etched design for embroidering mitts and gloves. Such fine work was often undertaken on silks, taffeta or velvet, using silver or gold metal threads. Elsewhere in the book are floral motifs for fine linens and wearing apparel.

An Outstanding British Contribution to Botany

Elizabeth Blackwell's book A Curious Herball *was noteworthy for its contribution to botanical illustration— but most curious are the conditions under which she wrote and illustrated this remarkable book.*

Like Maria Sybilla Meriam, or Margaretha Helm (see pp. 142–143), the botanical artist Elizabeth Blackwell (c. 1700–1758) was an extraordinary woman at a time when the occupations of botanizing, writing and illustration for publishing were usually a male preserve. Yet we know very little about some aspects of her life and her background.

Born to a prosperous Aberdeen merchant's family, in about 1730 she secretly eloped with a cousin, Alexander Blackwell. A plausible ne'er-do-well, he claimed to have studied at Leiden with the eminent doctor and botanist Herman Boerhaave. In the early 1730s they were living in London, where Alexander worked for the printer William Wilkins as a corrector to the press. Alexander tried to set up in business as a printer himself, oblivious to the fact that only freemen of the Stationers Company were allowed to print in London: as a result Alexander lost his business, and a heavy fine to the Stationers got him into a debtors' prison.

To try to earn his freedom, with the assistance of such friends as Hans Sloane and Richard Miller at the Chelsea Physic Garden, the indomitable Mrs. Blackwell worked on producing *A Curious Herball*, collecting the data, engraving the plates, coloring the copies by hand and preparing all the accounts for purchasers. The book with its 500 plates was published in 125 weekly parts from 1737 to 1739 and, despite pirated copies sold by other engravers, it earned enough money to get Alexander Blackwell out of jail and for them to live modestly in Chelsea.

Alexander got into further scrapes in London, and in 1742 moved to Sweden. Ending up as court physician to King Frederick I, he was found guilty of treason and was beheaded in 1747. As far as is known, the widowed Elizabeth stayed in Chelsea drawing flowers until her death in 1758.

Later editions were reprinted from her plates, and the Nuremberg publisher Christoph Jacob Trew issued an expanded version (with re-engraved plates) as *Herbarium Blackwellianum*, 1750–73. Digitized versions of both editions of this remarkable book are available on the Internet.

Acanthus Spinosus

ABOVE Mary Delany's papercuts Blackwell's near contemporary, Delany turned to papercuts at age 72. The famous botanist Joseph Banks declared her exquisite flower **collages** as "the only imitations of nature that he had ever seen from which he could venture to describe botanically any plant without the least fear of committing an error."

RIGHT Elizabeth Blackwell's *Curious Herball* Many of the "500 cuts" were meticulously recorded by the author at Chelsea Physic Garden, where many exotic species from the New World were cultivated. Engraving and hand-coloring the illustrations herself, Blackwell interspersed the plates with descriptions of the plants, outlining their common uses.

Connections

Plate 1.

Dandelion

Eliz. Blackwell delin. sculp. et Pinx.

1 Flower
2 Root
3 Seed

Dens Leonis
Taraxacum

RIGHT *The Art of Dancing*
Kellom Tomlinson's 1735
manual included 37 finely
engraved plates by Jan
van der Gucht and others.
Combining mapping and
perspectival illustration
(somewhat like 3D-
sketching programs today),
Tomlinson placed figures
within the tracks of
Feuillet's complex notation
to convey a sense of gesture
and movement, as well
as the footwork, of the
Baroque dance.

Connections

A Baroque Dance to the Music of Time

Polite society in the 18th century saw many advances in its material comforts. Expert training in dancing was one aspect, but it could be costly.

"Let us read, and let us dance; these amusements will never do any harm to the world," wrote Voltaire. In the courtly circles about Louis XIV and other European rulers, being an accomplished dancer was of great importance for one's prestige. Dancing masters flourished in capitals and other important cities.

According to legend, Louis XIV instructed his court dancing master to create a system of dance notation. The notation was developed and published by Raoul-Auger Feuillet in 1700 with the title *Chorégraphie*, and was widely adopted in other countries, including England. The system was rather complex, comprising the music, guidance on the floor patterns to be followed, as well as the steps and positions to be held by the dancers. The books showing the system were normally used more by dance masters than their pupils, who would learn by rote from their teacher.

This book, *The Art of Dancing*, by a famous London dance master Kellom Tomlinson (c. 1690– c. 1753), was an ambitious attempt to provide a sumptuous book, much of which was worked out in manuscript form. Engraved **intaglio** plates were essential for the illustrations. Copperplate printing was expensive, demanding an up-front outlay that would be more than a dance master could risk for books requiring a high price, so Tomlinson resorted to **subscription publishing**.

Subscription was fashionable and reduced risks of financial loss, but it had two serious disadvantages: production might be slow, and potential competing authors and publishers might get there first. Both happened: a rival translation of a French manual was rushed out, and it took Tomlinson a full 10 years to achieve publication of his seminal work in 1735. His subscribers were largely drawn from the aristocracy and gentry, as well as dance masters, theater managers, musicians, booksellers and printers. Priced at two and a half guineas, the book was an expensive publication—in modern terms at least US$600—but it stands as the most important book on the subject, and a handsome example from the best period of English book production.

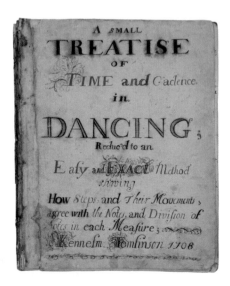
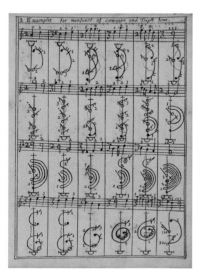

ABOVE **A small treatise...** Recently discovered in a private collection is this fascinating workbook, compiled by Kellom Tomlinson between 1708 and c. 1721. The dance master cribs from European dance texts, recording the notation for existing dances, and working out some fresh compositions. The complex notation shown here is from Raoul Auger Feuillet's "Traite de la Cadance," prefacing Louis Pécour's *Recüeil de dances* (Paris, 1704). Pécour choreographed the "Saraband for two" for the Paris Opera's *Tancrède*, 1704, while Tomlinson's version, 1716, performed at Lincoln's Inn Fields, was a one-man composition.

CHAPTER

8

Printing & the Enlightenment

RIGHT *A Dictionary of the English Language* Published on April 15, 1755, and written largely singlehandedly by Samuel Johnson, the *Dictionary* was first published in two folio volumes (later editions, from 1818, were published in four volumes). See pp. 154–155.

Almost all forms of publication that are commonplace today were becoming established in the 18th century; and publishing and reading among Enlightenment thinkers led to the belief in scientific and rational thought that underpinned the ideas leading to the French Revolution.

A
DICTIONARY
OF THE
ENGLISH LANGUAGE:
IN WHICH
The WORDS are deduced from their ORIGINALS,
AND
ILLUSTRATED in their DIFFERENT SIGNIFICATIONS
BY
EXAMPLES from the best WRITERS.
TO WHICH ARE PREFIXED,
A HISTORY of the LANGUAGE,
AND
An ENGLISH GRAMMAR.

By SAMUEL JOHNSON, A.M.

IN TWO VOLUMES.

VOL. I.

THE SECOND EDITION.

Cum tabulis animum censoris sumet honesti :
Audebit quæcunque parum splendoris habebunt,
Et sine pondere erunt, et honore indigna ferentur.
Verba movere loco ; quamvis invita recedant,
Et versentur adhuc intra penetralia Vestæ :
Obscurata diu populo bonus eruet, atque
Proferet in lucem speciosa vocabula rerum,
Quæ priscis memorata Catonibus atque Cethegis,
Nunc situs informis premit et deserta vetustas.   HOR.

LONDON,
Printed by W. STRAHAN,
For J. and P. KNAPTON; T. and T. LONGMAN; C. HITCH and L. HAWES;
A. MILLAR; and R. and J. DODSLEY.
MDCCLV.

I n the long 18th century—the period from about 1688 in Britain to the French Revolution, or even the downfall of Napoleon in 1815—printing and book production and marketing changed into a form we still recognize today. It was a period of steadily increasing prosperity for the upper and middle classes, despite the antagonism and conflict between France and Britain.

At the start of this period, the French were (or were thought to be) the dominant force in science and technology. The 17th-century establishment of the *Imprimerie du Roi* (the King's Printers) was one way of advancing taste. The cutting of special **typefaces** (the *romain du roi*), was organized by the Académie Royale des Sciences, also involved in preparing the *Descriptions des Arts et Métiers*, published much later. The *romain du roi*, first used in 1702, was a rationalized family of typefaces that moved away from the traditional **old-face** letterforms. This way of designing was followed by the Parisian type designer Pierre-Simon Fournier, who in 1737 perfected a system of measuring type, eventually leading to international standardization—though the difference between the **Didot** system (in France) and the traditional **Pica** system (in Britain and America) reflects the typographical differences between the countries.

French taste and types were superbly matched to the skills of engravers (see pp. 152–153). The large books from the *Imprimerie Royale* were impressive, as King Louis XIV intended. What prevented them from being altogether superb was the **paper** and presswork. Most French paper was still prepared in stamping mills; but by the late 17th century the windmill-powered **hollander** beaters were developed, and had spread in general use in Europe. Allied to the improvements in bleaching, the use of wove molds and **hot-pressing** (or **calendering**), developed in England by James Whatman and the typefounder/printer John Baskerville, from about 1750, made production of delicate and better-looking books easier.

Influences on British book design were largely from the Netherlands, which supplied paper, printing presses and typefaces (as for the reconstituted Oxford University Press in the 1660s). The Dutch typefaces were solid, no-nonsense, old faces; and in about 1720, long after the French theorizing about ideal type-designs, the London typefounder William Caslon issued a range of old-face designs that became the standard face in Britain and British America; the first printed US Declaration of Independence was printed in Caslon types. In Britain, too, the Statute of Anne (chapter 19) of 1710 was the first copyright law recognizing authors ownership rights in their books. Admittedly, enforcement of the statute was ineffective in Ireland and British America, but the British law enabled writers to make money from their craft (see pp. 154–155). In time, through copyright conventions between countries, in the days before the Internet, copyright worked as originally intended.

Scientific Publishing

The development of bookselling and publishing, on both sides of the English Channel, enabled firms to specialize in particular fields, such as John Newbery (1713–67) in books for children (see pp. 156–157); in France, Charles-Joseph Panckoucke (1736–98) was equally important for spreading the ideas of the Enlightenment.

The development of scientific or philosophical thought was by no means limited to France and Britain (see pp. 158–159). There was a European-wide endeavor to spread knowledge through the proceedings of learned societies (such as the *Acta Eruditorum, Journal des Savants*, or the *Philosophical Transactions of the Royal Society*). Their work was facilitated by more informal means, through correspondence. It is hard to imagine that the work of the great Swedish naturalist Carl Linnaeus (1707–78) could have been achieved without these means—and the links spread to others (like Benjamin Franklin) much farther away (see pp. 160–161). These informal means of communication were by no means limited to the scientific fields: much of the information on aspects of history, art, music and literature was circulated in the handwritten newsletters by Melchior Grimm (1723–1807). (Such handwritten letters were not subjected to censorship, as was all printed work.)

Rather different from these men, John Baskerville's career almost typifies the English approach to the Enlightenment. Baskerville started as a writing-master. Closely associated with the Birmingham-based Lunar Society (whose members were involved in developing the industrial revolution), Baskerville turned to type design, printing and publishing. With the use of smooth paper, improved ink and presses (and the new types cut for him), Baskerville's books were elegant and much admired. The impressario Beaumarchais used Baskerville's types for the Kehl edition of Voltaire (1784–89). It was not an idle whim, but secretly bankrolled by the Parisian publisher Panckoucke

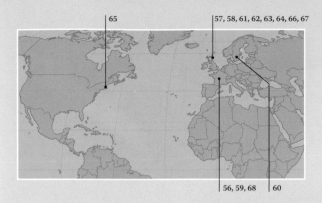

(connected with Diderot's *Encyclopédie*). Based in Kehl (in Baden), Beaumarchais and Panckoucke avoided the dangers of French censorship, and Baskerville's influence was Europe-wide. Another largely forgotten man associated with the Lunar Society was a dangerous man to work with: the inventor of graphs and pie-charts, William Playfair, who also worked in Paris trying to advance the Industrial Revolution in the Ancien Régime (see pp. 162–163).

New Publishing Forms

In the 18th century, some forms of publication became commonplace, including sensational literature in such publications such as the *Newgate Calendar* (see pp. 164–165). The emergence of the novel came in Britain as on the Continent, and such books as Voltaire's *Candide* and Laurence Sterne's *Tristram Shandy* were widely admired, and acted as catalysts for other novelists' work (see pp. 166–167 and 168–169).

With the spread of printing throughout the Western world, many publishers added the annual production of almanacs to their range of publications. Perhaps most noticeable in North America, where from 1732 Benjamin Franklin published *Poor Richard's Almanack*. Very few almanac publishers had such good sales, but *Poor Richard's Almanack* was a model, including one of the earliest manifestations of Negritude (see pp. 170–171).

Natural history books had long been popular, but the expense of engraving and printing the plates limited the wide spread of such books. One beneficial effect of Baskerville's better presses, ink and smooth paper was to allow the genius of the wood-engraver Thomas Bewick to make popular this method of illustration worldwide. The use of wood engraving became the most common method of illustration well into Victorian times (see pp. 172–173).

In the late 18th century came a series of remarkable manuscript books aimed at the top of the British social scale: Humphry Repton's Red Books, altering garden design (see pp. 174–175). Just before the French Revolution changed everything, attempts were first made to produce books intended to help the blind learn (see pp. 176–177).

Rococo Dress for Classical Drama

Racine, Corneille and Molière were the greatest French dramatists of the 17th and 18th centuries. In 1734, at the height of Parisian book production and with the support of the French royal court, a deluxe edition of Molière's work was published to display French pre-eminence in the arts.

For much of the 18th century, French art and literature were at their peak. English artists such as Hogarth showed great ability in graphic work, and the Bickhams their technical competence, but the books coming from Paris excelled in typographic design and illustration and in bookbinding. The technical excellence of French **intaglio** engravers was recognized, and it took the French artist Gravelot (who had studied with Boucher, worked in London with the Bickhams, and in turn taught Gainsborough) to mold English work to equal or surpass French book illustration.

One artist who was even more successful was Gravelot's old master, François Boucher (1703–70), an artist who had the good fortune to attract the favor of the French King Louis XV; later, teaching the king's powerful mistress, Madame de Pompadour, how to etch was also useful. (She engraved the illustrations for an edition of Corneille's *Rodogune*, printed at her personal press at

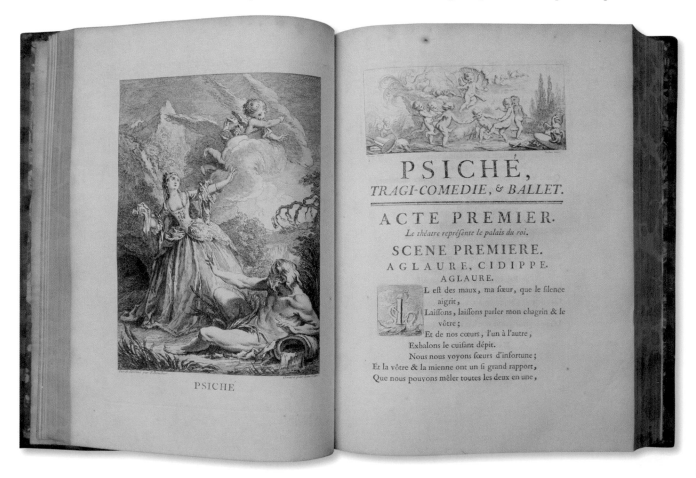

RIGHT **Boucher's *Molière*****
A master of the French rococo
style, François Boucher also
designed sets and costumes
for the theater, which he
attended regularly in his
preparation for illustrating
the great French dramatist's
works. This is the frontispiece
from Pierre Prault's 1734
six-volume edition, with 33
drawings by Boucher—perhaps
one of the most beautiful of
18th-century publications.

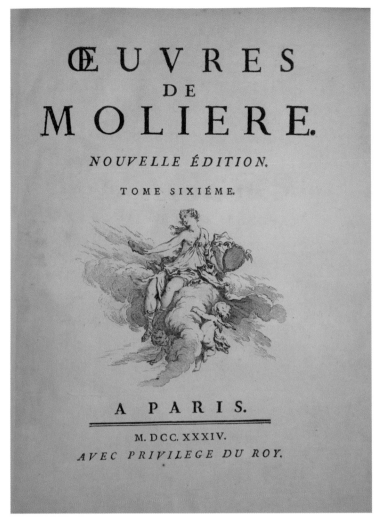

Versailles, 1770.) Boucher is remembered mostly for his
charming (and often daring) pictures of aristocratic life in
the Ancien Régime as well as for his decoration at Versailles.

As with the other great French tapestry designers and
book illustrators, Jean-Baptiste Oudry (whose sketches for
his *Fables de La Fontaine* were re-interpreted by Charles-
Nicholas Cochin for a sumptuous edition published in 1755),
Boucher's drawings were engraved by others. His most
famous book illustration, with most of the pictures engraved
by Laurent Cars, was this 1734 collected edition of the plays
of the dramatist Molière, probably the most famous
French writer of comedies. The production is said to have
been financed in part by Louis XV, and its publication
was facilitated by state censors and editors.

Modern readers of Molière prefer to turn back to
the original 17th-century editions, or a modern edition.
The importance of the 1734 Molière is not its text, but
the *mise-en-page*, the typographical style, the rococo
decoration and the engravings, which make it perhaps
the best French illustrated book of the century.

LEFT ***Psyche*** This tragi-comic ballet is a
cleaned-up version of Apuleius' ribald tale of
Psyche and Cupid in *The Golden Ass*. Early in
his career Boucher studied with Jean-François
Cars, whose son Laurent (with François Joullain)
engraved the plates.

Connections

For other monumental editions, see

*Cranach-Presse's Hamlet, **pp. 214–215***

*Whitman's Leaves of Grass, **pp. 216–217***

The Greatest Dictionary of the English Language

Two great 18th-century works—Johnson's Dictionary *and the* Encyclopédie *of Diderot and d'Alembert— typify the conservative, bluff, traditionalist British scholarship and the sparkling, innovative approaches from the French Enlightenment. But there are remarkable parallels in the preparation of these books.*

Other European countries had their own "official" language dictionaries—the *Vocabolario dell' Accademia della Crusca* in Italy in 1612 and the *Dictionnaire de l'Académie française* in 1694. In 18th-century England, the best dictionary available was an unofficial one by Nathaniel Bailey (1721), which was insufficiently comprehensive, so in 1746 a consortium of publishers engaged Samuel Johnson (1709–84) as compiler for a new one. Johnson had a reputation as an essayist and poet, but his only relevant expertise had been in assisting Dr. Robert James with entries for his successful three-volume *Medicinal Dictionary* (1743–45), which was then being translated by Denis Diderot and others for a French version.

Johnson and Diderot were, in a sense, both hack writers starving in garrets who cut their editorial teeth on the same book, but there the similarities cease. Johnson's *A Dictionary of the English Language* (1755) was largely conceived and executed by a man working alone, with some inept clerical assistance from six English and Scottish destitutes (possibly appointed more out of compassion than need because Johnson cared for people less fortunate than himself). In the garret of his house at Gough Square (off Fleet Street in London), Johnson and his assistants toiled to produce one of the greatest reference books ever written.

For preparing his *Dictionary*, Johnson read extensively to gather examples of word usage

Connections

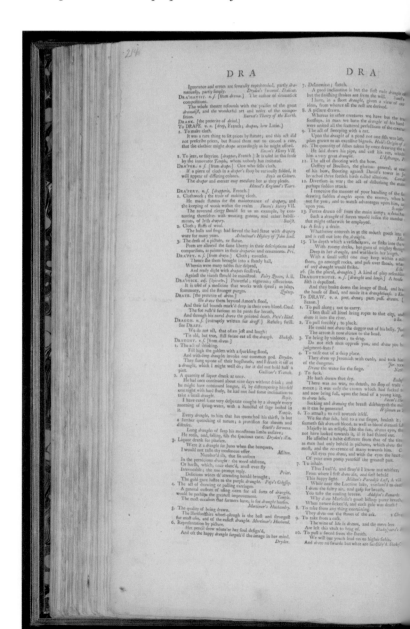

BELOW ***Dictionary of the English Language*** Published on April 15, 1755 and written largely singlehandedly by Samuel Johnson, the *Dictionary* was first published in two folio volumes (later editions were published in four volumes). Image shows pages 214–15 of the first edition, annotated in Dr. Johnson's own hand.

RIGHT **Bandog, may be a dog of bad omen** An elaboration on the definition of an unwelcome dog, made by Samuel Johnson in his own copy of the *Dictionary*. He presented a copy of his *Dictionary* to his good friend Hester Thrale (later Hester Thrale Piozzi), who also annotated her copy with her own recommendations.

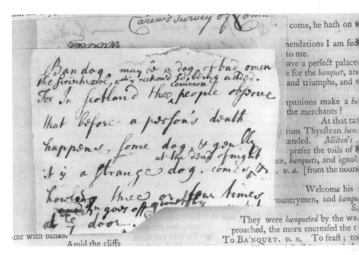

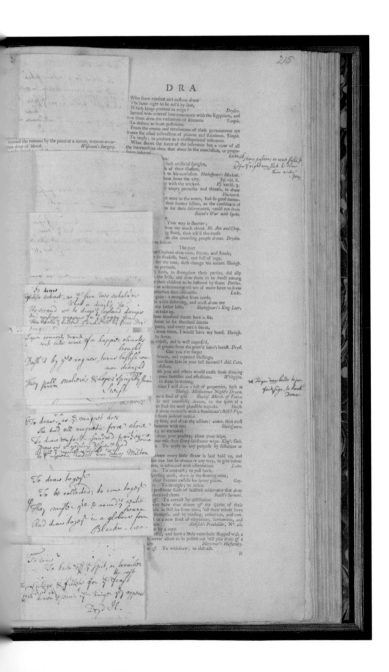

from a wide range of literature. Having collected enough samples, he prepared definitions, nowadays famous for the dry humor in his wording:

> EXCISE: *a hateful tax levied upon commodities and adjudged not by the common judges of property but wretches hired by those to whom excise is paid.*
> MONSIEUR: *a term of reproach for a Frenchman.*
> OATS: *a grain which in England is generally given to horses, but in Scotland supports the people.*

Johnson's *Dictionary* was quickly recognized by his contemporaries as the pre-eminent English-language lexicon, though it had its detractors: "I cannot imagine that Dr. Johnson's reputation will be very lasting," wrote Horace Walpole. Recent critics are more generous: "one of the greatest single achievements of scholarship" (from the *Oxford English Dictionary* editor). Johnson's method for preparing his *Dictionary* was followed in Victorian times when the collaborative *Oxford English Dictionary* was prepared (first published in parts 1884–1933). The Internet has made Johnson's *Dictionary* readily available, and many readers savor the insight it gives into the mind of this extraordinary man who described his own profession of lexicographer as, "a writer of dictionaries; a harmless drudge."

A Very Early Book for Children

Chapbooks and other books intended for children were often used until they fell to pieces. In the English and American editions, the publishers had the brilliant idea of adding value by providing toys.

BELOW *A Curious Hieroglyphick Bible*
Another landmark of 18th-century children's literature is this Bible published by the Boston printer Isaiah Thomas in 1788. It contains nearly 500 **woodcuts** by American artists, and his use of "Hieroglyphicks" is another example of trying to educate and entertain.

It's possible to think that writing and publishing books for children was something developed in the Enlightenment period. It's certainly true that successful production of children's books was inaugurated in London by John Newbery in the 1740s, but the earlier deliberate creation of books for children was by the great Moravian educationalist, Jan Amos Komenský (Comenius, 1592–1670), whose *Orbis Sensualium Pictus* (*Visible World in Pictures*) of 1658 was widely adopted and translated throughout Europe.

Comenius' book was didactic, but many of the small books published 1737–67 by the energetic and versatile John Newbery were as much for amusement as for instruction. His first London book, *A Little Pretty Pocket-Book* (1744), attempted to teach children the alphabet "by way of diversion." Parents were lured by its promise to "infallibly make Tommy a good boy, and

Polly a good girl." The book came with either a free pincushion or a ball, and a letter from Jack the Giant-Killer within describing the correct use of these toys. It was enormously successful, and over his career Newbery issued well over 100 children's books, which he sold widely in Britain and the British American colonies. A good Samaritan to writers such as Christopher Smart and Oliver Goldsmith, and a close friend of Samuel Johnson, Newbery made much of his fortune as the sales agent for Dr. James's Fever Powder, for which he pushed sales through advertising and puffs in books that he published.

One of the North American readers of Newbery's books was Isaiah Thomas (1749–1831), who was perhaps the most important patriot printer during the American War of Independence and ultimately the founder of the American Antiquarian Society at Worcester, Massachusetts.

Thomas was no friend of Britain, and he blithely disregarded British copyright law (Statute of Anne, chapter 19), which automatically vested authors with the ownership of their texts. The contemporary Massachusetts theologian Jonathan Edwards was troubled that Thomas never paid Newbery for the books imported from London. Thomas adapted and reprinted *A Little Pretty Pocket-Book* in Worcester 1787, again with ball and pincushion. This edition is much more common than the many London editions issued by Newbery but, as the first American book to mention baseball, Thomas's edition is much coveted by libraries and collectors.

TOP RIGHT **"Instruction with Delight"** The free toys issued with the *Pocket-Book* (the pincushion for the girls and ball for the boys,) was an effective early example of gender-targeted sales, though such marketing was most successful with their parents, who perhaps, then as now, anticipated respite from hyperactive or unruly children.

BOTTOM RIGHT **"Away flies the Boy"** *A Little Pretty Pocket-Book* contains the first-known reference to the game of "Base-Ball"—albeit with a moral aim. (In fact it probably depicts rounders, from which baseball developed.) A landmark in children's literature, Newbery's book has been used by social historians researching the history of games.

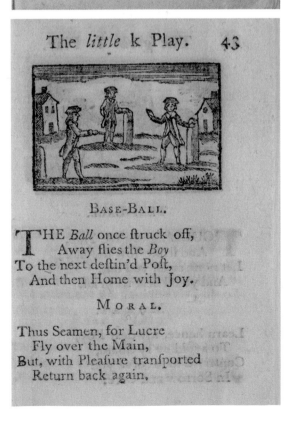

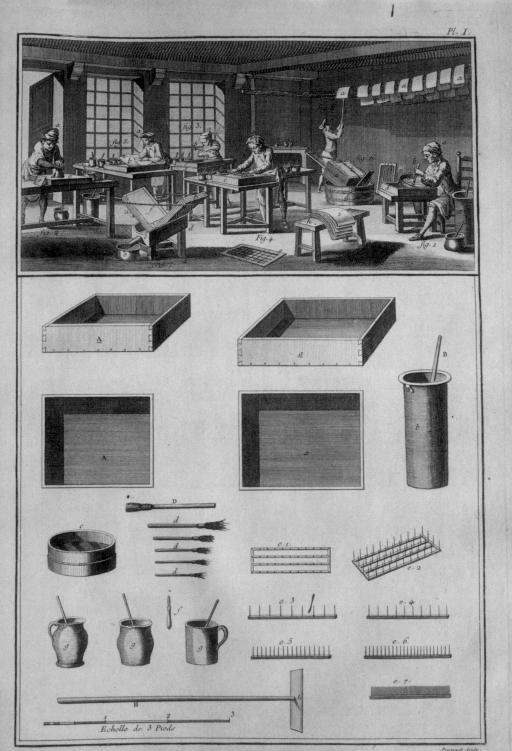

Pl. I.

Prevost Sculp.

Marbreur de Papier.

The Lodestone for the Enlightenment

This enterprise nearly failed—the English and German editors for a French encyclopedia were not up to the task. Replacing them, the publisher appointed Denis Diderot as editor, and European culture was changed forever.

The first half of the 18th century was a great period for the publication of reference books. One of these was the *Dictionnaire Historique et Critique* (*Historical and Critical Dictionary*) by Pierre Bayle (1695), which was important as a model on which other encyclopedias were based; another was the English *Cyclopaedia* of Ephraim Chambers (1728), which dealt with topics in science and technology absent from Bayle. Parisian publishers wanted to produce a French version. The English and German scholars engaged as translators were sacked for incompetence, but in a lucky moment the publishers selected Denis Diderot (1713–84) as chief editor, with Jean d'Alembert as co-editor until 1759. Both were brilliant writers and essayists; but in the witty, assiduous but unreliable and dangerous Diderot, there was a touch of genius rare in such scholars.

Diderot and the publishers brought in many other eminent writers, including Montesquieu, Quesnay, Rousseau, Turgot and Voltaire, who contributed some particularly memorable and influential essays. The most productive writer was Louis de Jaucourt, whose 18,000 articles comprised a quarter of the encyclopedia, but the brilliance in Diderot's encyclopedia articles (and in his remarkable novels and tales) overshadowed his colleagues. From Bayle, Diderot had learned the technique of using "see also" cross references to link articles, and to use irony to provide for alert readers ideas not immediately obvious to the censors. It was a dangerous method; the alarmed printer André le Breton surreptitiously toned down the wording of some articles. Even so, it took the support of Madame de Pompadour (the king's mistress) and the censor Malesherbes to save the work from being banned.

Originally planned as a two-volume work, the *Encyclopédie, ou Dictionnaire raisonné des sciences, des arts et des métiers* was published in 17 volumes between 1751 and 1765, with 11 volumes of illustrations issued between 1762 and 1772. These were partly copied from the splendid plates prepared earlier for the *Descriptions des Arts et Métiers* (*Description of Arts and Crafts*), which had been planned for publication by the *Académie Royale des Sciences* three-quarters of a century earlier. The importance of the Diderot/d'Alembert *Encyclopédie* would have been lessened had the earlier work been issued quickly, but the *Descriptions* volumes were not published until 1761–88.

The *Encyclopédie* was enormously successful, with editions of over 4,000 copies sold. The publishers made a good income, despite their worries. Whether its publication led to the French Revolution—because of its emphasis on Enlightenment political theories— is still debated, but its production changed European thought forever.

RIGHT **A systematic dictionary** Title page of Diderot and d'Alembert's *Encyclopédie* (*Systematic Dictionary of the Sciences, Arts and Crafts*), 1751.

LEFT **Diderot's *Encyclopédie*** Diderot's 28-volume work contained some 3,129 full-page and detailed illustrations, like this one depicting the techniques and equipment for paper marbling, engraved by Bonaventure-Louis Prévost.

Connections

For another encyclopedia, see

Yongle Dadian, *pp. 36–37*

For other technological work, see

Al-Jazari's Mechanical Arts, *pp. 88–89*

For other subversive publications, see

Kamiński's Stones for the Rampart, *pp. 226–227*

Bulgakov's Master and Margarita, *pp. 228–229*

A Pioneer in Information Retrieval

From the earliest times, physicians, herbalists and plant gatherers tried to find ways of arranging the huge range of plants into a sensible, rational order. In the 18th century, an ambitious Swedish scientist found a method that is still crucial for our thinking about animal and plant life.

No one has been a greater Botanist or Zoologist. No one has written more books, more correctly, more methodically, from his own experience. No one has more completely changed a whole science and initiated a new epoch.

This self-assessment by the Swedish scientist Carl Linnaeus (1707–78) sounds like an absurdly over-confident job application, but his self-praise was similar to comments made by other important figures in the Enlightenment period. Goethe reported that only Shakespeare and Spinoza had influenced him more; and Rousseau (not given to praising others) said, "Tell him I know no greater man on earth."

Linnaeus, who spent most of his career as Professor of Medicine and Botany at the University of Uppsala (Sweden), earned these plaudits for his work in systematizing plant and animal life, using binomial names such as *Homo sapiens* for mankind. An earlier attempt had been made by Gaspard Bauhin at Basel in

1596, in *Pinax Theatri Botanici* (*Illustrated Exposition of Plants*), but Bauhin's method had not been fully developed. A workable scheme of taxonomy was not completely realized until Linnaeus' *Systema Naturae*, a work first published in just 12 pages in 1735, whose plan for classifying and naming plants was elaborated in his *Species Plantarum* (1753), which remains the prime authority for plant names.

By 1758, natural historians throughout the world had already adopted Linnaeus' methods, and new versions of their books were prepared using the Linnaean names used in the 10th edition of his book, which classified 7,700 species of plants and 4,400 species of animals. Gathering, arranging and rearranging data on this scale called for close collaboration with other botanists and the accurate use of sophisticated information-handling techniques, ranging from the use of spreadsheets to the (re)invention of card indexes.

Linnaeus' methods for classifying plants were easily taught, described by an historian as making "botany into a party-game for any young lady who could count up to twelve." It looked as though nature was being brought under control, using rational thought and observation—the methods that philosophers believed could bring about the better world sought in the Enlightenment.

LEFT **On the "wedding of plants"** The "Praeludia Sponsaliorum Plantarum," a 1729 paper written by Linnaeus when he was 21, which describes the sex life of plants. As well as praise, it attracted some criticism for its "blasphemous" notion that plants might reproduce sexually.

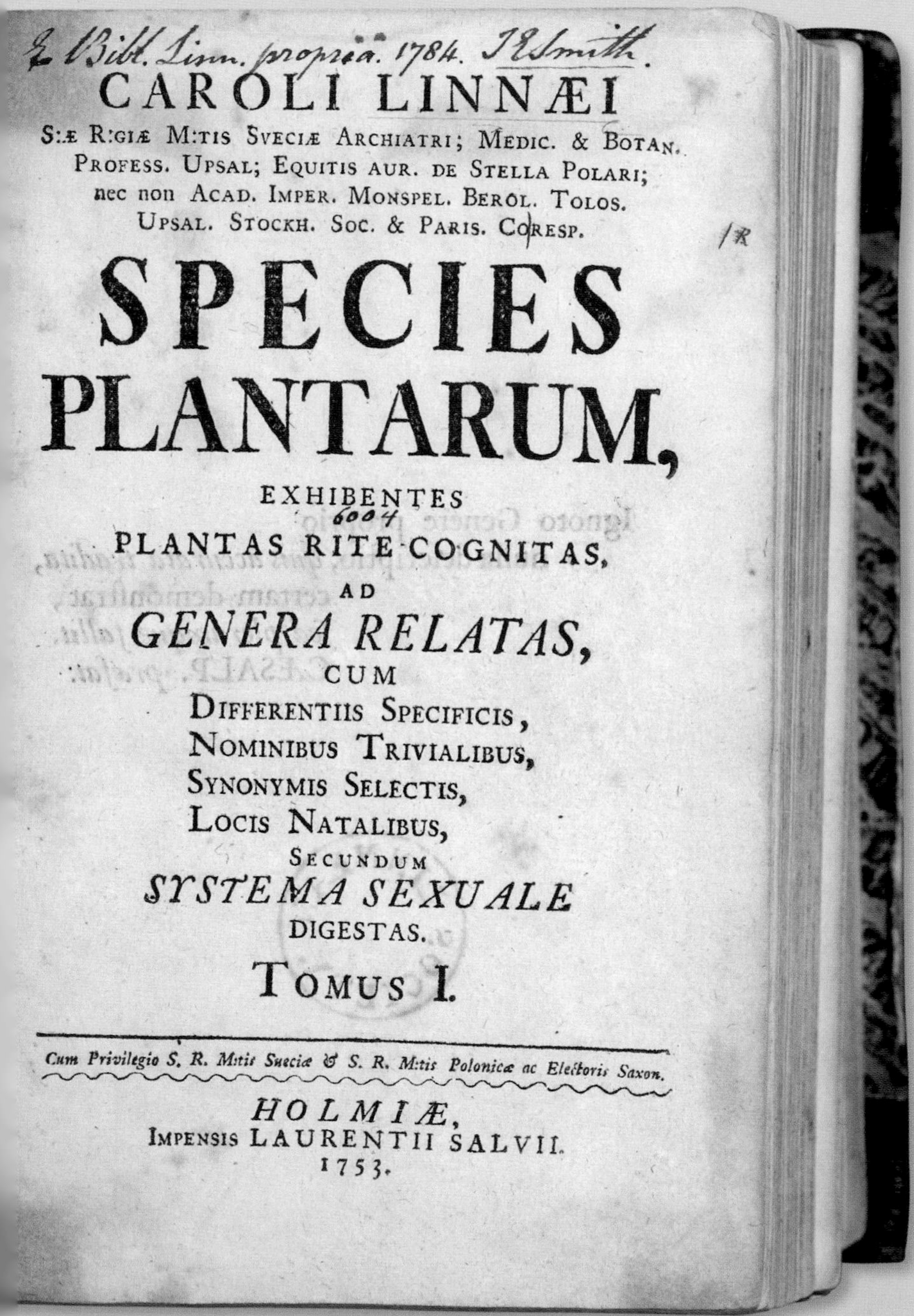

E Bibl. Linn. propriâ. 1784. JESmith.

CAROLI LINNÆI

S:æ R:giæ M:tis Sveciæ Archiatri; Medic. & Botan.
Profess. Upsal; Equitis Aur. de Stella Polari;
nec non Acad. Imper. Monspel. Berol. Tolos.
Upsal. Stockh. Soc. & Paris. Coresp.

IR

SPECIES PLANTARUM,

EXHIBENTES
6004
PLANTAS RITE COGNITAS,

AD

GENERA RELATAS,

CUM

DIFFERENTIIS SPECIFICIS,
NOMINIBUS TRIVIALIBUS,
SYNONYMIS SELECTIS,
LOCIS NATALIBUS,
SECUNDUM
SYSTEMA SEXUALE
DIGESTAS.

TOMUS I.

Cum Privilegio S. R. M:tis Sueciæ & S. R. M:tis Polonicæ ac Electoris Saxon.

HOLMIÆ,
IMPENSIS LAURENTII SALVII.
1753.

LEFT Annotated *Species Plantarum* Linnaeus' *Species Plantarum* was annotated by himself, often in Latin. He often wrote different annotations in several copies of the same book.

BELOW Genus and species Linnaeus introduced his two name principle, or binary nomenclature, in his *Species Plantarum*. This page of his 1753 edition includes his revisions for *Polygynia* (many styles) for the *Rosa eglanteria*, the sweet briar or Eglantine rose.

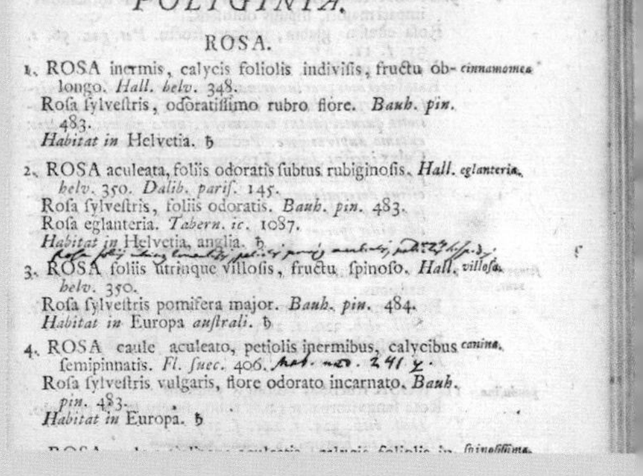

POLYGYNIA.

ROSA.

1. ROSA inermis, calycis foliolis indivisis, fructu ob- *cinnamomea* longo. *Hall. helv.* 348.
Rosa sylvestris, odoratissimo rubro flore. *Bauh. pin.* 483.
Habitat in Helvetia.

2. ROSA aculeata, foliis odoratis subtus rubiginosis. *Hall. eglanteria. helv.* 350. *Dalib. paris.* 145.
Rosa sylvestris, foliis odoratis. *Bauh. pin.* 483.
Rosa eglanteria. *Tabern. ic.* 1087.
Habitat in Helvetia, anglia.

3. ROSA foliis utrinque villosis, fructu spinoso. *Hall. villosa. helv.* 350.
Rosa sylvestris pomifera major. *Bauh. pin.* 484.
Habitat in Europa australi.

4. ROSA caule aculeato, petiolis inermibus, calycibus *canina,* semipinnatis. *Fl. suec.* 406.
Rosa sylvestris vulgaris, flore odorato incarnato. *Bauh. pin.* 483.
Habitat in Europa.

Connections

For earlier botanical books, see

Dioscorides' De Materia Medica, **pp. 64–65**

Blackwell's Curious Herball, **pp. 144–145**

For books using Linnaeus' classification, see

Atkins' Photographs of British Algae, **pp. 184–185**

Using Graphs to Convey Information

One might expect that an inventor of statistical graphs would have led a safe, humdrum life, but he was an embezzler and a blackmailer forced to leave Paris in a hurry during the French Revolution.

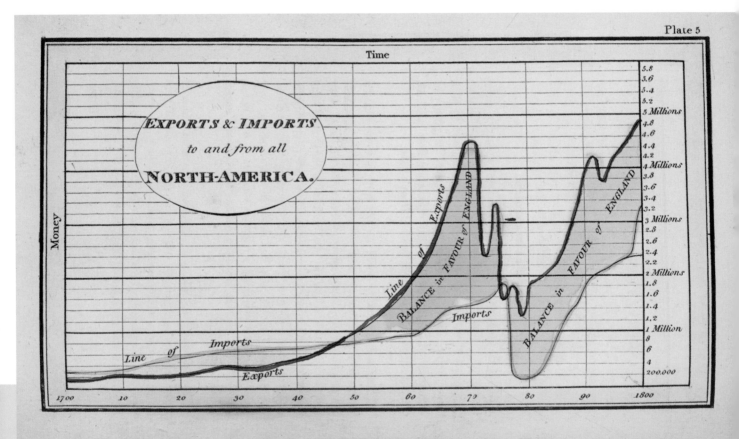

ABOVE **Playfair's *Commercial and Political Atlas*** Playfair's 1786 atlas was the first publication to contain statistical charts and the first—and beautifully clear—bar and line graphs (though, despite its title, no maps), illustrating his astute observations on international trade and economics. The copperplate chart shown here dramatically describes the effect of the American Revolution on trade between England and its former colonies.

Connections

For other engineering innovations, see

Perkins' Patent, pp. 182–183

For earlier graphic ways to present data, see

Mansur's Anatomy, pp. 90–91

William Playfair (1759–1823) was one of the bright young Scottish men who went to England to seek their fortunes. Educated with support of an older brother (who later became a professor of mathematics at Edinburgh University), William was apprenticed as an engineer. He moved to Birmingham to work at the great Boulton & Watt engineering company, working with James Watt on the inventor's steam engines. In Birmingham, Playfair came to know James Keir and Joseph Priestley and others in the Lunar Society, important in advances in scientific thought in the Enlightenment period. Playfair then worked with James Keir on the development of Watt's office-copying process, but Keir suspected Playfair of having "borrowed" some of his ideas for several metalworking patents and they parted company.

For a few years Playfair worked in London as a partner in a silversmithing firm, making plate. It failed, and this was to be a pattern in his life: grand visions; disputes with colleagues; possible fraud. But for a while he succeeded well with his publications, in which he developed new and easily comprehensible graphic ways of expressing statistical data, inventing the pie-chart, the time-series line graph and the bar chart; three methods still in everyday use. His *Commercial and Political Atlas* (1786) was the first to use these. On the Continent the book was warmly regarded by such different men as Humboldt and King Louis XVI.

Playfair's statistical publications earned little money or reputation in Britain. In France, during the Revolutionary period, Playfair became involved in a dishonest land-sale company to settle French immigrants in the US. He was suspected of embezzlement and had to flee to England. His later life in France and England continued as a series of frauds, lawsuits, attempted blackmail and death in destitution—a sad end for a man whose skills and acute mind promised so much. In France, the brilliant engineer Charles Joseph Minard was to develop even more effective graphic representation of data, but it was only after the work of these later followers that the importance of Playfair's innovations was recognized in Britain.

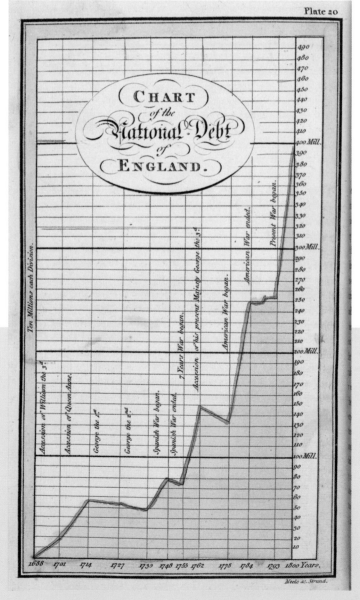

RIGHT "**The National Debt of England**" This chart in *The Commercial and Political Atlas* is strikingly relevant to our times. It shows national debt on the up, with the clear implication that war (in this case with North America) increases such debt, and commenting that heavy taxation will result in the "general penury of the middle and lower classes."

Records of Crime and Punishment

To learn of criminals getting their just desserts is still popular with many people. In the earlier harsher controls of crime, it excited people who read about thieves' "cant," and about the "breakfast of hartichoke and caper sauce" (hanging) given to prisoners at public executions.

Improving literature takes many forms. In the average 18th-century British household, there was always a Bible, and often John Bunyan's *The Pilgrim's Progress*, first published in 1678. The third book said to be often found is more surprising: *The Newgate Calendar*.

Originally based on broadsheets hawked by peddlers at public executions and fairs, these were alarming and sensationally written accounts of the crimes, trials and punishments of notorious criminals, often executed at Tyburn or Newgate Prison. Popular for anyone interested in the London underworld, the reports had a morbid fascination for many readers, then as now. The collection started recording crimes committed in 1700, and was continued through the 18th century, taking a strong patriotic tone about Catholicism, the French, and crime and punishment in general.

Far more important but less sensational in tone were *The Proceedings of the Old Bailey*, issued from 1674 until 1913, which recorded all criminal trials in London. Overall, there were (often lengthy) reports on nearly 200,000 trials, using a much more neutral and impartial tone than *The Newgate Calendar*. *The Proceedings of the Old Bailey* formed an unequaled picture of the London underworld.

Sets of these reports survived in printed volumes, but easy access to much of the material important for social history was difficult and limited in the period before computer-based information services. In 2003, a fully indexed and digitized version was first issued as Old Bailey Online, funded by state and university organizations in Britain. Freely available, its sophisticated indexing covers names of witnesses, lawyers and all other people involved with the court procedures, as well as those being charged. It enables extensive and comprehensive analysis, which is resulting in better and well-informed historical and social research being published. *The Newgate Calendar*—arguably more sensational, astonishing and entertaining—has also been digitized as a private venture.

Engraved for The Malefactor's Register.

Dodd delin.   *Pollard sculp.*

The CONVICTS *taking Water near Black-Friars Bridge, (in order for their being conveyed to* WOOLWICH.

LEFT ***The Newgate and Tyburn Calendar*** This 1779 illustration depicts convicts making their way by Blackfriars Bridge in London, to be conveyed to the hulks at Woolwich, before deportation to Australia was introduced. This is one of the less bloody images; the engravers delighted in scenes of often painful retribution for those who stepped out of line.

Connections

For another book aimed at popular taste, see

Wynkyn's Demaundes Joyous, **pp.** *104–105*

For earlier and more gruesome pictures of hangings, see

Vesalius' De humani corporis fabrica, **pp.** *134–135*

For other tales of crime and adventure, see

Powell's Old Grizzly Adams, **pp.** *192–193*

Boldrewood's Robbery Under Arms, **pp.** *204–205*

THE

NEWGATE CALENDAR;

COMPRISING

INTERESTING MEMOIRS

OF

THE MOST NOTORIOUS CHARACTERS

WHO HAVE BEEN CONVICTED OF OUTRAGES ON

𝕿𝖍𝖊 𝕷𝖆𝖜𝖘 𝖔𝖋 𝕰𝖓𝖌𝖑𝖆𝖓𝖉

SINCE THE COMMENCEMENT OF THE EIGHTEENTH CENTURY;

WITH

OCCASIONAL ANECDOTES AND OBSERVATIONS,

SPEECHES, CONFESSIONS, AND LAST EXCLAMATIONS OF SUFFERERS.

BY

ANDREW KNAPP AND WILLIAM BALDWIN,

ATTORNEYS AT LAW.

The Tower of London.

VOL. IV.

𝕷𝖔𝖓𝖉𝖔𝖓:

J. ROBINS AND CO. IVY LANE, PATERNOSTER ROW.

1826.

The Literary Oddity that Entranced Europe

Sometimes, published books change the whole way in which we think about life.
Laurence Sterne led novel writing into fresh ways that are still significant today.

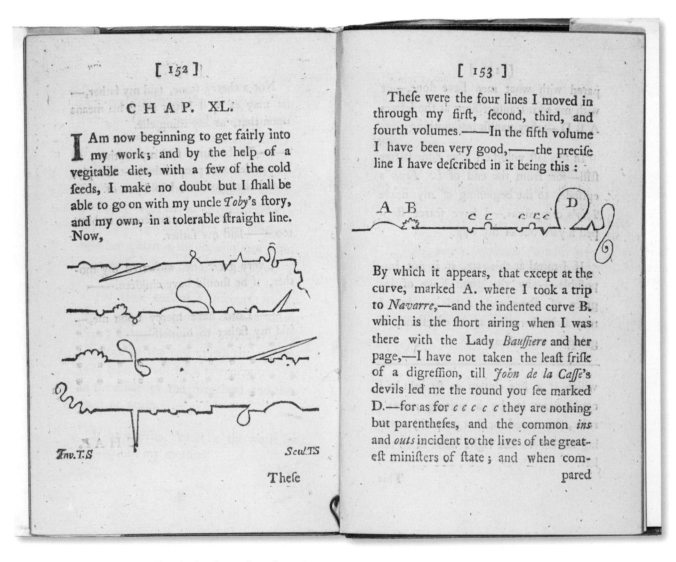

ABOVE **Tristram Shandy, Gentleman** Sterne's erratic text, sometimes described as postmodern for its subversion of narrative, is filled with allusions to leading 17th- and 18th-century writers such as Rabelais and Robert Burton, whose work he pastiches in a playful manner. The audacious typography is no less skittish, as seen in the opening pages of chapter XL above, and this 18th-century novel is still influential today.

However fantastic or satirical in content, the 18th-century English novel frequently painted a realistic portrait of contemporary life. Such writers as Daniel Defoe (with *Robinson Crusoe*, 1719) or Jonathan Swift (*Gulliver's Travels*, 1726) had great success with continental readers, and Samuel Richardson's *Pamela* (1740) was to be the model for Rousseau's *Julie ou la Nouvelle Héloïse* (1761).

The long rivalry and hostility between France and Britain did not apply to literature: French novels were widely read and (like Paris fashion) admired in Britain. However immoral and wicked its author was thought to be, Voltaire's glittering *Candide* (1759) came to typify French writing for the British.

An English writer who was well aware of *Candide* was Laurence Sterne (1713–68), and his novel *The Life and Opinions of Tristram Shandy, Gentleman* (1759–67) became widely and wildly popular on the continent. Voltaire said his work was "clearly superior to Rabelais," and Goethe also praised him highly. Yet *Tristram Shandy* was a long, rambling, inconsequential, allusive and often derivative joke, summarized by a modern critic as "the greatest shaggy dog story in the language."

"Nothing odd will do long. *Tristram Shandy* did not last," Samuel Johnson said sternly, but his judgment was vastly wrong. The Rabelaisian humor that percolated through the nine volumes of *Tristram Shandy* was certainly enough to make Victorian readers wary of this obscure Anglican clergyman; but in his own time and again from the beginning of the 20th century onward, Sterne's novel has been celebrated. In writing his *Jacques the Fatalist*, Diderot was inspired by him; and such disparate writers as Virginia Woolf, James Joyce, Machado de Assis, Georges Perec and Italo Calvino also drew inspiration from this extraordinary book. Remarkable in the 18th century, Sterne's typographical tricks, like his text, are still influential today. Could his methods be used for e-books?

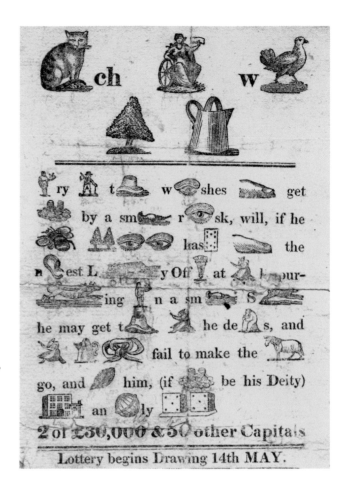

ABOVE **A rebus puzzle** This State National lottery advertisement in the form of **pictogram** puzzle, dating from the start of the 19th century (around 1805), reflects the rise in popularity of playful typography in Sterne's age, an era marked for its fondness for satire. Such pictograms became popular in correspondence, and were often used in political satires.

Connections

For later typographical tricks, see

Kamensky's Tango with Cows, *pp. 218–219*

For contemporary British typography, see

Johnson's Dictionary, *pp. 154–155*

Cleland's Fanny Hill, *pp. 168–169*

For one of Sterne's followers and imitators, see

Diderot's Encyclopédie, *pp. 158–159*

Mighty Lewd or Literary Classic?

Literary censorship has existed since the invention of printing, and there are current serious worries about pornography. Through the swing of fashion, a major book banned in the 18th century as pornographic is now regarded as a literary classic.

In his diary for January 13, 1668, Samuel Pepys reported that he had bought a "French book for my wife to translate, called *L'eschole des filles*, but when I come to look in it, it is the most bawdy, lewd book that ever I saw." (After reading this famous book, first published in Paris in 1655, Pepys then burned it.) His reaction was characteristic of the large group of readers—women as well as men—who enjoyed lubricious writing. Frequently authors, publishers and distributors of pornography were punished, but this seldom resulted in the disappearance of the books: they just went underground. Pepys' bawdy lewd book had been banned in Paris, but he had bought a pirated Dutch reprint.

In England, the market for pornography was usually in books translated from Italian or French writers. The most famous English book of frank celebration of sexuality was *Memoirs of a Woman of Pleasure*, often called for its heroine, *Fanny Hill*. Written by John Cleland (c. 1710–89) in Bombay in the 1730s, it was originally drafted to prove to a colleague that a novel about whores could be written without using vulgar language. Later, in prison for debt in London in 1748, Cleland completed the book and it was published in 1748–49. It was a complete success, a stylistic tour-de-force, frequently translated into other languages. Though banned then (even in an expurgated form), it has remained quietly available ever since. In 1789 an obituary of Cleland claimed the author received a government pension of £100 (US$165) per year to dissuade him from writing similar books; if true, it is an uncommon means of censorship.

Victorian censorship banned *Fanny Hill*, in the way public mores forced publishers and libraries (and such major novelists as Thackeray, Trollope and Dickens) to censor the most innocent of texts. Nonetheless, in Victorian times *Fanny Hill* was still available in illicit editions (often printed abroad with false imprints)—how different from today, when changing fashions and tastes of 40 years ago allowed Oxford University Press and others to add the book to their series of classics.

LEFT **The book that made Pepys blush**
Translated as the *School of Venus* or *Ladies' Delights*, this 1855 sex manual took the form of a dialog between a young virgin and her more experienced female cousin. Pepys, famously keen on the ladies, skipped church to read it, protesting, "it was not amiss for a sober man once to read over to inform himself in the villainy of the world."

Connections

MEMOIRS

OF A

WOMAN

OF

PLEASURE.

VOL. I.

LONDON:

Printed for G. FENTON in the Strand.

ABOVE **Selling a woman of pleasure** Rabelais, himself a writer of bawdy humor, might have been amused by his proximity to "vice in its gayest colours" in this advertisement for *Fanny Hill* in the *London Intelligencer*, on the day it was published.

LEFT *Fanny Hill* The demure and rather elegant typography in the title page of this early edition with a false imprint, c. 1765, belies the book's licentious content—so regarded that even 200 years later, in Massachusetts and California, the book itself was put on trial. The Californian court found that "Obscene material in book form is not entitled to any First Amendment protection merely because it has no pictorial content."

RIGHT **Banneker's *Almanack*** A freeman born to slave parentage, Benjamin Banneker published six of these Farmers' Almanacs between 1792 and 1797. He sent the first to Thomas Jefferson, urging him to reconsider slavery, as the one "Universal Father... afforded us all the same sensations and endowed us all with the same faculties."

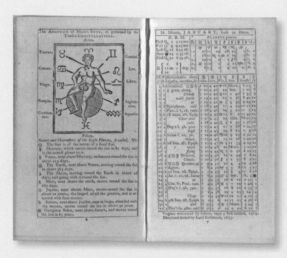

ABOVE **Man of signs** Though he received some education from the Quakers, Banneker was largely self taught. His almanacs contained medical information, astronomical and tidal information all largely calculated by himself. This diagram from his almanac shows the 12 constellations governing the human body, which were typical of many such booklets.

Connections

For earlier American books, see

Bay Psalm Book, *pp. 128–129*

Newbery's Little Pretty Pocket-Book, *pp. 156–157*

For views of post-emancipation West Indies, see

Duperly's Daguerian Excursions in Jamaica, *pp. 186–187*

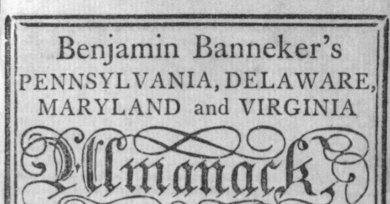

Benjamin Banneker's
PENNSYLVANIA, DELAWARE,
MARYLAND and VIRGINIA
Almanack
AND
EPHEMERIS,
FOR THE YEAR OF OUR LORD,
1 7 9 2;
Being BISSEXTILE, or LEAP-YEAR, and the SIX-TEENTH YEAR of AMERICAN INDEPENDENCE, which commenced *July* 4, 1776.

CONTAINING, the Motions of the Sun and Moon, the true Places and Aspects of the Planets, the Rising and Setting of the Sun, and the Rising, Setting and Southing, Place and Age of the Moon, &c.—The Lunations, Conjunctions, Eclipses, Judgment of the Weather, Festivals, and other remarkable Days; Days for holding the Supreme and Circuit Courts of the *United States,* as also the usual Courts in *Pennsylvania, Delaware, Maryland,* and *Virginia.*—ALSO, several useful Tables, and valuable Receipts.—Various Selections from the Commonplace-Book of the *Kentucky Philosopher,* an *American Sage;* with interesting and entertaining Essays, in Prose and Verse—the whole comprising a greater, more pleasing, and useful Variety, than any Work of the *Kind* and *Price* in *North-America.*

BALTIMORE: Printed and Sold, Wholesale and Retail, by WILLIAM GODDARD and JAMES ANGELL, at their Printing-Office, in *Market-Street.*—Sold, also, by Mr. JOSEPH CRUKSHANK, Printer, in *Market-Street,* and Mr. DANIEL HUMPHREYS, Printer, in *South-Front-Street, Philadelphia*—and by Messrs. HANSON and BOND, Printers, in *Alexandria.*

An African-American Work in an Ancient Field

Almanacs are so commonplace that we easily forget how useful they were for consciousness-raising. This work by a free African American attempting to persuade Jefferson to change his views was very unusual.

Almanacs—periodic publications detailing the movements of the moon and tides and seasons— were some of the earliest forms of book production. In Egypt and Babylonia, some were produced as early as the second millennium BCE; in China, their production can be attributed to the reign of the great sage emperor Yao (c. 2356–2255 BCE), and the annual publication of the *Tung Shing* (*Victorious in All Things Almanac*) remains regularly consulted by Chinese communities everywhere.

In Europe, publication of almanacs came with the introduction of printing, and the book trade in every country relied on their sales as a source of income. (In England, in the 18th century, it was believed that almost every household owned an almanac as well as a Bible.) The production of almanacs became so commonplace in North America that their significance is now almost forgotten. Benjamin Banneker's (1753–84) *Almanack*, published annually from 1792 to 1797, was one. What was important about it was that it was calculated, written and published by a free African American, who disputed with Jefferson. Only the amazing Senegal-born poet Phillis Wheatley (1731–1806) preceded Banneker as a published African-American writer.

Writers and scholars argue about many aspects of Banneker's life and achievements, some claiming he was of purely African descent and others that his mother was a white indentured servant. The Bannekers owned a farm in Maryland, and the young Banneker was taught to write and to develop mathematical and surveying skills by neighboring Quakers, particularly the Ellicott family, who enabled Banneker to work on the surveys laying out the District of Columbia.

Using the editorial opportunities from his *Almanack*, Banneker wrote to Thomas Jefferson urging that the continuation of slavery was in contradiction of the US Declaration of Independence, which Jefferson had drafted. The statesman's position was equivocal, but his response was superficially encouraging: he said

he was going to forward Banneker's almanac to the Marquis de Condorcet, a fellow Enlightenment figure active in the emancipationist *Société des Amis des Noirs* (the Society of the Friends of the Blacks) in Paris.

The times were unpropitious: Condorcet's arrest and death during the French Revolution (1789–99), and the Haitian Revolution (1791–1804), brought immediate hopes of emancipation to an end. Emancipation in France (1848) and the US (1861) was delayed until many years after the slave trade was abolished in Britain (1807) and British colonies (1834), and Banneker's remonstrance still resonates today.

Published according to Act of Parliament, Sept.ʳ 1.1773 by Archᵈ Bell.

Bookseller Nº 8 near the Saracens Head Aldgate.

LEFT **The slave-poet**
Banneker's junior, Phillis Wheatley, was a West African sold into slavery in 1760 at the age of seven. Her Boston slave masters taught her to read and encouraged her poetry. Praised by George Washington himself, among others, she wrote *Poems on Various Subjects* (1773), of which this is the frontispiece. It was the first to be published by an African-American woman.

The Master of Black and White

In the second half of the 18th century, and as the British surpassed the French in book illustration, a new method of printing wood engravings was developed by an artist in Northumberland, in the north of England.

For most of the 18th century, **intaglio** illustrations were the chosen medium for book illustration. The days of Dürer and Jan Steven van Calcar (whose **woodcuts** were the most accomplished and sophisticated illustrations) were long over. The wood-cutting techniques slipped down the social and artistic scales until few publishers or artists chose to employ them—except in such crude publications as *The Newgate Calendar* (see pp. 164–165).

The technique was revived in France by the engraver Jean-Michel Papillon, who wrote about engraving for Diderot's *Encyclopédie*; his methodical manual *Traité historique et pratique de la gravure en bois*, published in Paris (1766), was the first to describe the white-line method of engraving on the endgrain of boxwood blocks. Papillon's work was competent, but the technique was perfected by Thomas Bewick (1753–1828), whose work was rapidly received as near miraculous. His small, finely engraved boxwood blocks seldom exceeded 1 x 2 inches (2.5 x 5 centimeters), but he developed a method of

miniaturizing a view of an animal that caught every nuance of the subject. His real fame came from his work for the *History of British Birds* (1797–1804), of which eight editions were published in his lifetime.

Son of a Northumberland farmer, Bewick early on developed a love of the countryside, and with his painterly eye he became a graphic equivalent of the poet John Clare, partly because of what he learned when he was apprenticed to an engraver at Newcastle upon Tyne. Apart from walking tours in Scotland and a short sojourn in London (which he disliked intensely) he spent his life in and around Newcastle upon Tyne. Many of the talented later engravers in English book illustration through to mid-Victorian times were Bewick's apprentices, and through Bewick's example the whole approach to wood engraving changed forever. As the American artist Audubon put it, Bewick should "be considered in the art of engraving on wood what Linnaeus will ever be in natural history, though not the founder, yet the enlightened improver and illustrious promoter."

RIGHT **"The fiend pinning down the thief's pack behind him..."** "I passed over quickly: it was an object of terror." This uncaptioned tailpiece in *British Birds* is described by Charlotte Brontë in the first chapter of *Jane Eyre*, where, sitting "cross-legged, like a Turk" in her window seat, unhappy 10-year-old Jane escapes into Bewick's world.

HISTORY

OF

BRITISH BIRDS.

THE FIGURES ENGRAVED ON WOOD BY T. BEWICK.

VOL. II.

CONTAINING THE

HISTORY AND DESCRIPTION OF WATER BIRDS.

NEWCASTLE:

PRINTED BY EDWARD WALKER, FOR T. BEWICK: SOLD BY HIM, AND
LONGMAN AND REES, LONDON.

[Price ⸱⸱ in Boards.]

1804.

FAR LEFT "The nightingale" Bewick's 1797 engraving of the nightingale (*Luscinia megarhynchos*). The bird was much loved by poets, especially Wordsworth, who the following year wrote in his poem "The Two Thieves:" "O now that the genius of Bewick were mine, And the skill which he learned on the banks of the Tyne."

LEFT Bewick's *History of British Birds* This title page, with its charming vignette of boys boating at a pool with the spire of St. Nicholas' Cathedral, Newcastle, in the background, drawn and cut by Thomas Bewick, is of volume II of the first 1804 edition, *Water Birds*. Bewick produced the engravings and text of this second volume.

ABOVE **Repton's Red Books** Employing his before-and-after
flap device, are Humphry Repton's 1801 proposed modifications
for Wimpole Hall, a house built in 1640 in a 200-acre deer park
in Cambridgeshire, England. Here the modifications include the
reinstatement of a small garden on the north side of the Hall,
improving on existing landscaping by "Capability" Brown and
William Emes.

Landscape Design at Its Best

By the time that English ideas of gardening and landscape design had diverged completely from the formal designs of the French, "Capability" Brown and Humphry Repton transformed the English landscape—and Repton was also a skillful self-promoter.

The most important and famous of landscape gardeners, "Capability" Brown (1716–83) designed the grounds of over 170 great houses in Britain. His career was closely followed by Humphry Repton (1752–1818), with the difference being that while Brown had been trained as a gardener, Repton taught himself. Gardening was being gentrified.

As a young man, Repton was confidential secretary to the Secretary of the Viceroy of Ireland, and through these connections he was able to mix on easy terms with politicians and landowners. When he turned to the designing of estates, he used these acquaintances to develop an uncommon and effective way of peddling for business: Repton's Red Books. These oblong volumes, almost always bound in red morocco leather, included Repton's suggestions for ways to make clients' estates even more beautiful; with a hill removed here, a lake created there, a clump of trees artfully placed.... The books were not printed but were manuscripts, with the texts, maps and drawings done by experts at the height of their professions. Each book included a before and after—a watercolor view of the chosen scene after proposed changes had been made, overlaid by a hinged cutout turning the picture back to the original view.

The Red Books formed handsome albums of views for display in the patron's library, to serve as plans or to record work in progress. But Repton's work was very expensive; some clients commissioned their surveys for social prestige, but never attempted to put his recommendations into practice. Done as one-off commissions, the books are individual and Repton's beliefs caused marked reactions in other fashionable writers: authors such as Sir Uvedale Price and Richard Payne Knight on the picturesque and the sublime. Their aesthetic disputes were reflected in the work of novelists such as Jane Austen (*Northanger Abbey*) and Thomas Love Peacock (*Headlong Hall*), who were alert to the fact that readers were expected to have views about garden design.

As a reflection of confident taste in a time of growing prosperity, Repton's work was remarkable. The Red Books are desperately rare, highly sought after by libraries and collectors—and still expensive.

How Tactile Writing Began

Until the 18th century, very few attempts were made to educate the blind. The biggest advances came first in France, through the efforts of a Parisian philanthropist.

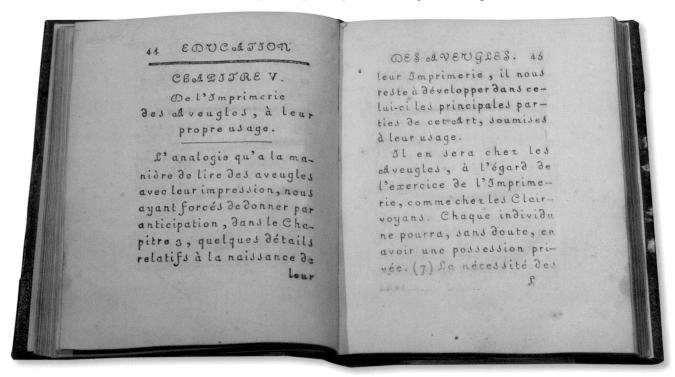

ABOVE *Education of the Blind* The school where Louis Braille would spend his life was founded by Valentine Haüy 2 years before Haüy's 1786 publication of a revolutionary book for the blind, using an embossing process to produce raised letterforms for reading by touch. It was printed by blind children in the workshop of Jean-Gabriel Clousier, printer to the King.

Learning how to read normally demands sight; how could sightless people be taught how to read? In the 16th century, the Italian mathematician Girolamo Cardano suggested that touch could be used to teach blind people to recognize the alphabet, but he did not develop this idea.

By the 18th century, there were famous instances of blind prodigies: in the *Journal des Savants* the Swiss mathematician Jacob Bernoulli reported how he taught the musician Esther Elizabeth Waldkirch to learn to read by tracing the shapes of the letters cut out of a stencil. Another blind musician, the well-connected Austrian Maria-Theresia von Paradis, learned by pin-pricking letters into paper—and at a concert put on by Queen Marie-Antoinette at Versailles in 1784, she met Valentin Haüy (1745–1822), who was already interested in helping with education for the blind. His school for educating blind children, the Institution des Jeunes Aveugles, the first ever, was started in 1785. It received royal approbation from a demonstration in the royal court at Christmas, 1786, when the blind children presented a book they had printed under the direction of Jacques-Gabriel Clousier, a Parisian trade printer.

The style of raised lettering used by Haüy was decorative, being closely based on French scripts of the period, and found to be not easy for children to read. In the late 1820s its use at the Institution des Jeunes Aveugles was replaced by the more scientific system now widely used, the method that Louis Braille (1809–52) developed from a military system of "night writing" invented by Charles Barbier, with a pattern of raised dots to stand for each letter.

The Braille letters were easier read through touch than the scripts of Haüy and his successor Sebastien

ABOVE **Dr. Moon's Alphabet for the Blind** The already partially sighted William Moon became fully blind aged 21. Finding no existing touch-reading systems satisfactory, he set about creating a method of his own. The Moon letters, shown in this alphabet card printed at his Brighton workshop, bear a resemblance to sighted letterforms.

ABOVE **A blind *Pilgrim's Progress*** Bunyan's classic tale of good overcoming obstacles was published in 1860 by the London Society for Teaching the Blind to Read. It was embossed in Lucas Type, another tactile system of reading devised by a teacher of shorthand, Thomas Lucas, of Bristol, around 1835.

Guillié, but at first had less favor in Britain. Other philanthropists working in Bristol, Edinburgh and other cities as well as London, devised different ways of printing for the blind. Technically successful, their methods eventually failed because of the difficulty of producing a sufficient range of reading to meet the needs of blind learners. One longer-lived system, the only serious challenger to Braille, was introduced in Brighton by another blind man, William Moon (1818–94), using embossed alphabets that were thought to be easier to learn than Braille. With Moon's efforts and the support of a rich blind benefactor, the Moon Printing Works continued this brave endeavor until 1960, when it succumbed to the French invention.

Connections

For other ways of teaching reading, see

Newbery's Little Pretty Pocket-Book, pp. 156–157

Aikin's Robinson Crusoe, pp. 194–195

For other technical advances in printing, see

Perkins' Patent, pp. 182–183

CHAPTER

9

Print & Steam

RIGHT *Robinson Crusoe In Words of One Syllable* Published by the McLoughlin Brothers in 1882, the text by Mary Godolphin (Lucy Aikin) had a colorful cover, with a young-looking Crusoe in snazzily striped drawers. With six full-color plates inside, it appealed strongly to a younger readership. This much battered copy bears witness to years of use. See pp. 194–195.

In the 19th century, the publishing stream burst its banks.

The flood of new, different kinds of books was seen as both

a blessing, by increasing literacy, and a curse, by those who

feared it would encourage revolution.

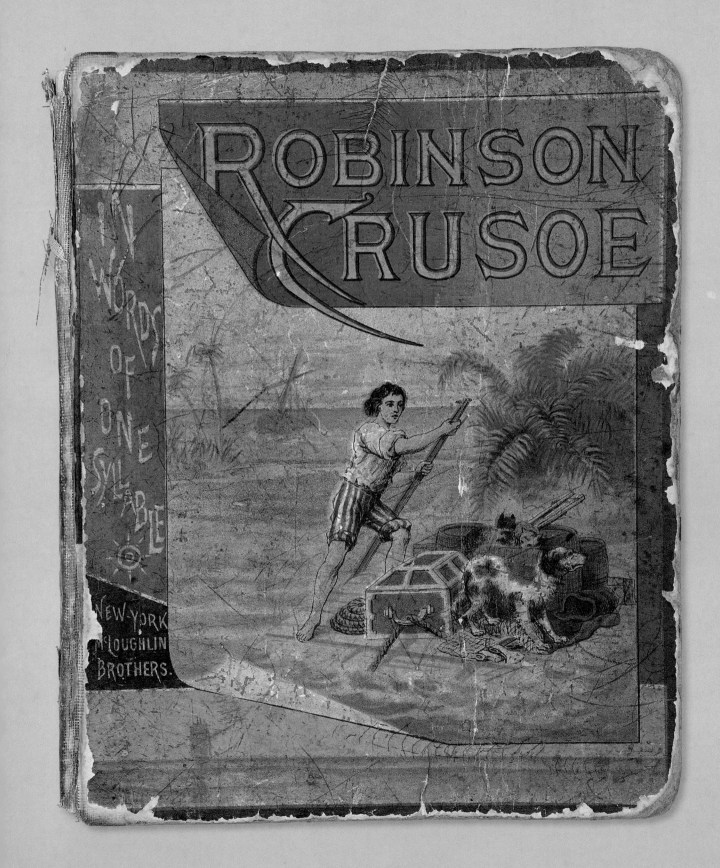

nnovation and invention were essential parts of the industrial revolutions. Many aspects of the 19th-century book trade—new papermaking, improved typefounding and the introduction of new illustration methods—had also started to change before 1800. One of the most significant was **stereotyping**, a way of making cast copies of full pages of **type**. Originally developed by William Ged in 1725, this facilitated reprinting easily; and stereotype plates became valuable assets to publishers. Using them for new editions (or selling the plates to others for reprint series) was a mainstay for the book trade because the plates could be used for decades. The typesetting (also becoming cheaper) and using stereotyping meant significant gain, driving down the cost of books.

As with other advances, there were downsides. The cheapness and convenience of stereotyping prompted publishers to continue reprinting, rather than commissioning revised and improved editions. The development in papermaking machinery enabled Europe to produce enough **paper** to satisfy the growing demand, and industrial scientists found ways to exploit other vegetable fibers to supplement the linen rags traditionally used. It was at the cost of longevity: rag paper from traditional paper mills lasted well, whereas machine-made paper using wood pulp decays rapidly. (Even by the 1820s, the instability of papers was commented on.) Papermaking from esparto (in Britain) or maize (in the German states) provided good paper. Everywhere after about 1875, the cheapest books, magazines and newspapers were on wood-fiber pulp, often condemned, for good reason, as sheeted sawdust.

One of the greatest changes was in book illustration. Steel engraving was aided by Jacob Perkins' **siderography** (see pp. 182–183), and other patents introduced by other inventors. The use of wood engraving (see pp. 172–173) was greatly facilitated by the use of stereotype and, from about 1840, **electrotype**. Advances in **lithography** and in photography were paralleled by other long-forgotten methods, like **daguerreotypes** and **cyanotypes** (see pp. 184–185). Their use was not limited to the great printing centers such as London, Paris or Leipzig; colonial initiative in Jamaica used daguerreotyping early (see pp. 186–187), and many other nascent centers attempted ambitious work. In India and the British colonies, publishing could (as in Jamaica) take unexpected forms: even Mission Presses in Canada produced **nature prints** (see pp. 188–189).

SPREAD OF RECREATIONAL READING

The development of book production was really a circular process: reader demand driving fresh publishing; publishers seeking fresh, cheaper, printing methods; the increasing production of printed matter in turn reaching new readers. Publishers and subscription library managers, and innovative authors such as Charles Dickens (see pp. 190–191), established conventions, including serial publication. These were profitable—the three-volume novel became the normal form for most novelists. New media demanded different functions from writers, and the extended plots in the novels of writers such as Dickens, Thackeray, Trollope and Mrs. Gaskell were the result.

Lower in the social hierarchy, increased reading by those becoming literate was sometimes regarded with fear. In his *A Spelling-Book* (1831), written for the working classes, the radical William Cobbett claimed that novels "are the gin and whiskey of literature: they besot, without enlivening, the mind." Corrupted minds in the working classes were the cause of many ills, it was believed, as glances at **penny dreadfuls** seemed to reveal (see pp. 192–193). There were many sincere and serious attempts to enrich peoples' minds with improving literature, including encouraging mechanics institutes and supporting the establishment of free public libraries, which started to spring up in the middle of the century. Books for children had an important role to play (see pp. 194–199).

BIBLIOGRAPHICAL CONTROL

With the increasing volume of publications and the increased range of distribution, society needed new ways of dealing with the information explosion. In the 18th century, it was often enough for publishers to announce, "This day is published." Now they had to find ways of enabling booksellers and potential readers to know what was being published. Reviewing journals helped; the publication of trade lists and advertising were also essential. In 1840 (say), an author could pay the relatively low cost of having a small edition printed, and there was enough market for vanity publishers to encourage putative authors to go to them. As still is true today, getting booksellers to stock their books, journals to review them or libraries to buy them was difficult.

In Britain, the only libraries routinely acquiring every book produced in the UK were the six legal deposit libraries. By law, publishers were obliged

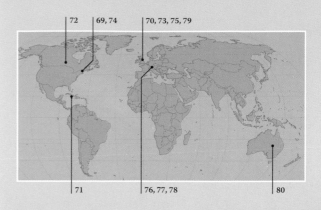

to deposit on request. The laws did not call for
the deposit of every reprint or new impression—
fortunately for the libraries receiving publications
(penny bloods, children's books and the like) in which
they saw no value for their own readers. The scarcity
of many of these unvalued publications today perhaps
foreshadows future problems in accessing forgotten
self-published titles and e-books.

National libraries set mechanisms in place to
control their accessions. The British Museum's famous
91 rules of 1841 were the first of many codes and
systems created by other national libraries. Later,
professional associations of librarians (formed in the
US in 1876 and the UK in 1877) and commercial
services were among groups seeking bibliographical
control. In the scientific and medical fields, the start
of abstracting and indexing services made the
increasing task of keeping abreast more possible.
At the same time, improvements in printing,
particularly typesetting machines from the US,
such as the **Linotype** (1886) and **Monotype** (1887),
made more rapid production simpler and cheaper.

Low prices encouraged the purchase of books
for personal use. For the expanding travel trade,
guidebooks like those issued by Bradshaw or Baedecker
and in Murray's Handbooks were so profitable that
guidebook publishing became a separate branch (see
pp. 200–201). By serving the growing market for books
on cookery and household management, some astute
authors (such as Mrs. Beeton) became bywords. One
of the most important was the larger-than-life Alexis
Soyer (see pp. 202–203).

Toward the end of the 19th century, cheap editions
had replaced the three-volume novel (see pp. 204–205)
and it was possible to buy serviceable editions for a
shilling or less. But there were many dissatisfactions.
Technical advances outstripped aesthetic sensibilities,
and gutter journalism alarmed some, with a comment
about "the penny dreadful being replaced by the half-
penny dreadfuller." Critics such as William Morris
could see that Venetian books of 1520 were far better
in design than English books of 1885. Others in France,
Spain, Holland and Germany noted similar failings:
their conservative or radical solutions are discussed
in Chapter 10.

Patently Brilliant Yankee Inventiveness

The advance of the Industrial Revolution was fueled by the patent system, on both sides of the Atlantic. One of the most important inventors, Jacob Perkins, was successful on both.

Though rulers often granted privileges to inventors (as they did to printers), the modern system of patent law had its origin in England, in the Statute of Monopolies (1623); from the reign of Queen Anne (1702–14), inventors were required to provide written descriptions of their inventions, which had to be registered by a range of law offices (this system was streamlined after the Great Exhibition of 1851). These printed patent specifications enabled the faster development of the Industrial Revolution, and—though seldom widely gathered in libraries, sold in auction houses or preserved by book collectors—they have been vital for the modern world.

Most inventors wanted to profit from their patent rights, and some, like Boulton & Watt, gained riches from their licenses. It was the motivation for Jacob Perkins (1766–1849) to leave Massachusetts for the richer rewards of Britain. A versatile inventor, Perkins created the rotary printing press and machines for making nails that were highly successful in the US. He thought his new process of engraving hardened steel—**siderography**—could enable the printing of

unforgeable banknotes, for which the Bank of England offered the enormous award of £20,000 (in current terms, well over a million dollars).

In 1819, Perkins moved to England to lobby for his process. He failed at first to persuade the Bank of England, which preferred an English inventor, but Perkins' process became crucial for the development of steel engraving in England, and thus for book history. His firm of Perkins & Bacon printed many securities and banknotes for provincial banks, and from 1840–61 produced the highly profitable postage stamps for Britain and the British colonies (including the short-lived "Penny Black").

As well as Perkins' siderography, he invented many other things: a steam-powered gun (rejected by Wellington as too destructive), steam engines, ship propulsion. But what was, in the long term, the most life-changing was his British Patent GB 6662/1835, "Apparatus and means for producing ice and in cooling fluids." This was used by Alexis Soyer in his Reform Club kitchens in 1838 (see pp. 202–203). The refrigeration industry was born.

LEFT Specimen banknote
Front view of the very first specimen pound note engraved on hardened steel, by Perkins, Fairman & Heath, c. 1821, in pursuit of a Bank of England commission. Although the Bank did not take them up, many others did.

Connections

For other inventors, see

Al-Jazari's Mechanical Arts, **pp. 88–89**

Gutenberg's 42-Line Bible, **pp. 98–99**

Playfair's Commercial and Political Atlas, **pp. 162–163**

For a later American inventor, see

Carlson's Lab Book, **pp. 212–213**

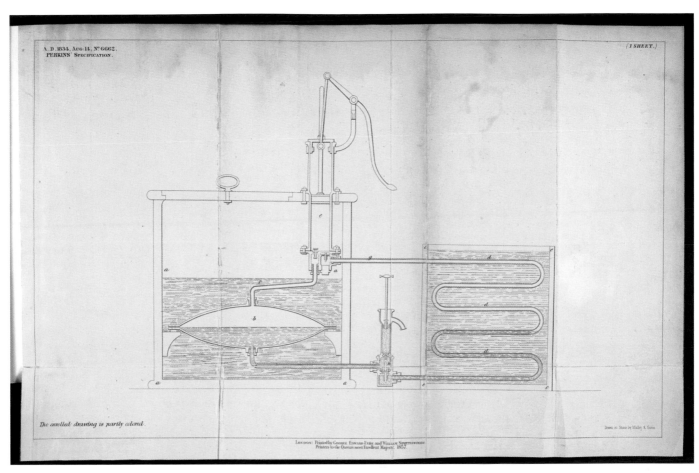

LEFT *The Pleasures of Hope*
Thomas Campbell's 1799 book was reprinted by Longman in 1821 with new illustrations by Richard Westall. This 1821 edition, with the illustrations engraved by Charles Heath and printed by Perkins, Fairman & Heath, was the first to use hardened steel plates, which outlasted the softer copper used until then.

ABOVE **Perkins' patent**
Jacob Perkins' patent for an "Apparatus and means for producing ice and in cooling fluids," August 14, 1835. Constructed by John Hague in London, this used ethyl ether to produce ice. The printing and publication of patents themselves is a significant part of publishing history, without which many of the industry's own inventions wouldn't be around today.

The First Book Illustrated Photographically

The development of modern photography descends from the work of French and English experimenters. Remarkably, the first (and beautiful) book with photographic images was produced by a third process by an amateur, a woman working alone.

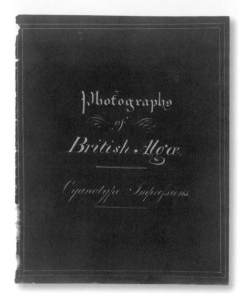

ABOVE **Cyanotype** The title leaf of Atkins' book of cyanotypes featured reversed-out lettering.

From the mid-17th century onward (some art historians claim much earlier), artists used a **camera obscura** to assist in their drawing. The device had limitations, and the English inventor of photography, William Fox Talbot, reported that his own failures, using one when sketching on Lake Como, persuaded him to search for chemical methods for copying images.

In fact, the first successful photographic process was French, invented by the ingenious Nicéphore Niépce (1765–1833) and Louis Daguerre (1787–1851). The **daguerreotype** process was eventually replaced by processes developed by Talbot, but another beautiful process, **cyanotype**, was invented by Sir John Herschel in 1842. This process was used by an amateur for the first book published with photographic illustrations.

Anna Atkins (1799–1871) was the unusually well-educated daughter of a distinguished scientist, John Childers, whose translation of Lamarck's *Genera of Shells* (1824) was illustrated by Anna. Both Childers and the Atkins knew Talbot and Herschel. Intended as a companion to William Harvey's unillustrated *Manual of British Algae* (1841), in October 1843 Atkins issued the first **fascicle** of *Photographs of British Algae: Cyanotype Impressions* in October 1843.

The cyanotype provided images that were far more long lasting than the other photographic methods then used. For every copy of the nearly 400 plates in her book, Atkins had to mix the chemicals, prepare the photographic paper, arrange the specimens of seaweeds, expose each photogram in sunlight, and then develop the 8,000 plus images. (One hates to think of the number of spoiled prints in the production.)

Apart from some encouragement from the family and a little assistance from a friend, Anna Dixon, all the work was done by Atkins alone. The process was ideal for seaweeds, but the effective production depended on the printer's taste as well as on her skill—and patience. Her edition of *Photographs of British Algae* was naturally very small, but on the rare occasions her cyanotype prints come up for sale they are much sought after: at a 2004 auction, a copy of her book sold for US$406,460.

RIGHT **British algae** A photogram of one of the brown algae seaweeds, in Anna Atkins' book *Photographs of British Algae: Cyanotype Impressions*, 1843–53—the world's first photographic book, preceding Fox Talbot's *Pencil of Nature* by some eight months. These photographic impressions were contact printed, without the use of the camera, by placing specimens directly on the sensitized paper and exposing them to sunlight.

Connections

For another book using photography, see

Duperly's Daguerian Excursions in Jamaica, pp. 186–187

For other female enterprise in book-making, see

Helm's Art and Industry, pp. 142–143

Blackwell's Curious Herball, pp. 144–145

Dictyota dichotoma
in the young state, and
in fruit.

Photography Moves to the Third World

From the 1840s onward, travelers started to try to record views of places they visited using photography. One of the earliest successful attempts came from Jamaica, a book produced by a French immigrant.

BELOW *Daguerian Excursions in Jamaica* Title page and (right) "A View of the Court House at Kingston, Taken on the Day of an Election," from Duperly's book published in Kingston in 1840. The daguerreotypes from which the lithographs are drawn are perhaps the earliest known photographic views of the island.

Adolphe Duperly (1801–65) was a Parisian-trained engraver, lithographer and printer, who in the early 1820s sought fame and fortune in Haiti and perhaps also in Cuba. Failing to find either, he then moved to Kingston and set up as a lithographer just at the period when slavery was ending in Jamaica. In 1833 he published a **lithograph** depicting the 1831 Christmas Rebellion, and in 1838 a lithograph of emancipation celebrations in Kingston.

Duperly's Jamaican fame depends largely on his lithographic illustrations for Isaac Mendes Belisario's *Sketches of Character in Illustration... of the Negro Population of Jamaica* (1837–38). Duperly's modest fortune came from his early adoption of Louis Daguerre's method of photography, establishing his own photographic firm in Jamaica in 1840–42. The first Jamaican photographic company, later Adolphe Duperly & Son, survived into the 1920s, with the production of portraits, *cartes de visite* and later picture postcards intended for tourists being the core of the business.

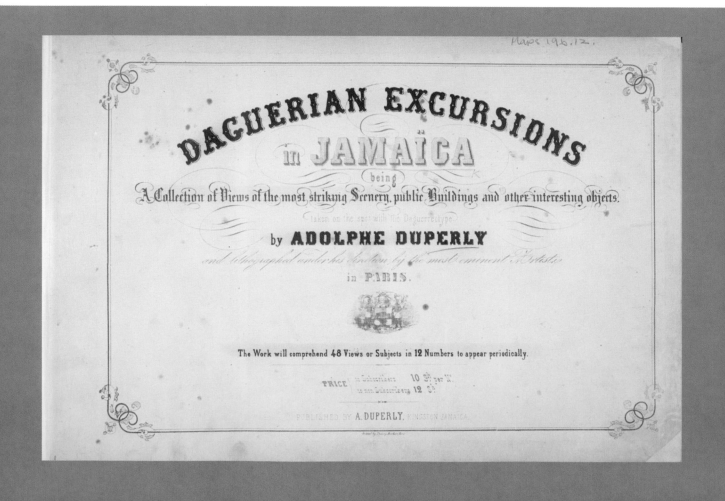

In the mid-1840s, Duperly published a series of lithographs made from his own **daguerreotypes** of Jamaican scenes. Like many other French lithographers, he recognized the usefulness of the process as a tool to simplify lithographic drafting. In the earliest French daguerreotypes, exposure times were too long to record movement, and yet in *Daguerian* [sic] *Excursions in Jamaica*, published in installments in the early 1840s, Duperly's book records some lively street scenes, with none of the images out of focus. This was not achieved by photography alone: Duperly sent his images to J. Jacottet, one of the competent Parisian topographic lithographers of the time. He added value to Duperly's work by drawing in many aspects of the picture so skillfully that many people believe the images are exact reproductions of what was caught in Duperly's lens. Doctored prints became common.

On seeing one of Daguerre's plates, the artist Paul Delaroche declared, "Painting is dead from this day!"— but nonetheless continued painting himself. Duperly

had grasped how well photographic methods could be combined with lithography to produce better books. His *Daguerian Excursions in Jamaica* was one of the finest topographical books ever produced in the West Indies or other British colonies.

Connections

For post-emancipation writing from Brazil, see
Nnadozie's Beware of Harlots, *pp. 222–223*

For a plea for American emancipation, see
Banneker's Almanack, *pp. 170–171*

For another book using photography, see
Atkins' Photographs of British Algae, *pp. 184–185*

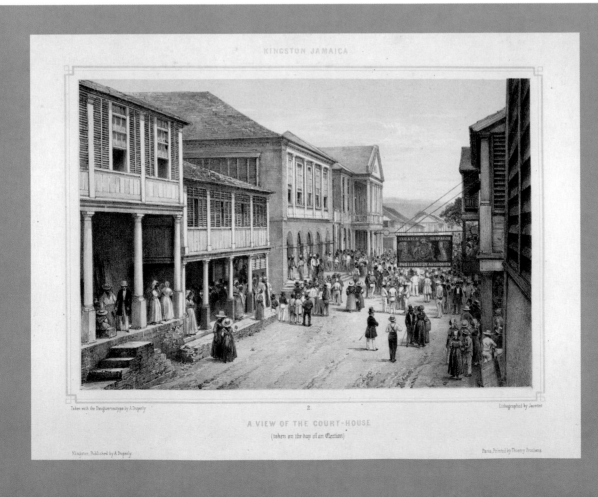

KINGSTON JAMAICA

Taken with the Daguerreotype by A Duperly   2.   Lithographed by Jacottet

A VIEW OF THE COURT-HOUSE
(taken on the day of an Election)

Kingston, Published by A Duperly.   Paris, Printed by Thierry Brothers.

Missionary Printing in Canada

Books printed by missionaries are rare and were seldom collected by libraries.
For his work teaching First Nations people, a Canadian printer abandoned
the alphabet and instead used a syllabary for the Cree languages.

ABOVE **A syllabic hymnbook** James Evans' 23-page hymnbook, published at Norway House in 1841, was simply bound in an elk-skin wrapper with a syllabary printed on the front and back. With neither press nor type available, he constructed the letter molds from oak wood, type metal from scraps of lead from musket balls and the lining of tea-chests, his ink from lampblack (or soot) mixed with fish oil, and for printing he appropriated a jackscrew press—more commonly used by the fur trade to compress animal hides for shipment.

Soon after Europeans started colonizing other continents, they tried to convert the indigenous population to Christianity, and (usually) to try to win converts to a particular sect, with Catholic missions competing against stations set up by Anglicans or Nonconformists. Learning new languages, which had often never been written down, was difficult, and providing suitable texts for new converts always challenged the missionaries' enterprise.

The first printing in Canada was in 1751, at Halifax, Nova Scotia. Sending religious manuscripts back to Europe for printing created serious logistical problems. The alternative, setting up presses in remote (and often hostile) places, was theoretically easier; the iron presses introduced in the 19th century were transportable and sturdy. Groups like the London Missionary Society introduced printing to many parts of Africa, Asia, and the Pacific area—and to peoples of the First Nations in Canada.

Missionaries had to be resilient, resourceful and determined to satisfy needs. One of the most interesting was James Evans (1801–46), who immigrated to Canada from Kingston upon Hull, England, with his parents in 1820. After working as a teacher, in 1833 Evans was ordained as a Wesleyan minister, and in 1840 was put in charge of the Norway House area, north of Lake Winnipeg—an important point for the Hudson's Bay Company's routes to the fur-seeking areas in the west. The area was also a center for the Cree people, so it was natural that Evans concentrated on teaching them to read.

Many missionaries elsewhere (for example, in Fiji or New Zealand) struggled to use the **roman** alphabet to represent different languages and their unfamiliar sounds. In societies that had been purely oral, the complexities of the 26 letters made the teaching of reading very difficult. Already conversant with the Ojibwa language, Evans decided that for Cree as well as Ojibwa it was better to use a syllabary.

At first Evans wrote the characters on pieces of birch bark; these worked so well in teaching the Cree to read, that he decided to have **type** made of them. The Hudson's Bay Company was hostile and unhelpful

ABOVE *Nature's Self-Printing* A title page displaying a contact-printed **nature print** of *Lycopodium cernuum*, from Jacob Hunziker's book, subtitled *Useful and Ornamental Plants of the South India Flora*. The text is in the Kannada language of South India, as used in Mangalore where the book was printed by the Basle Mission Press.

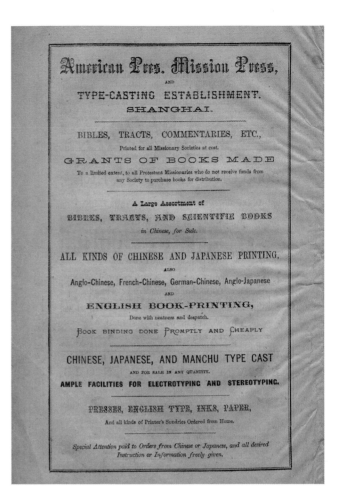

ABOVE **American Presbyterian Mission Press** This pleasing advertisement for the Shanghai Mission Press in the *Chinese Recorder and Missionary Journal*, 1875, shows how apparently well set up some of the mission presses were: multilingual texts, a wide selection of types and bookbinding, all done "promptly and cheaply"!

(Evans had already annoyed the company officials by struggling to persuade the Crees not to work on the Sabbath) and refused him a press and type. Undeterred, Evans built a simple press, found a way of casting his characters (using lead musket balls to provide the metal for the type) and compounded ink from soot and oil. With these contrived tools, Evans printed 100 copies of his syllabary and some gospel texts in Cree—and this was enough to persuade the Missionary Society to adopt his method. Evans' syllabary was adopted by rival mission groups (the Church Missionary Society and the Missionary Oblates of Mary Immaculate). If you visit areas to the south of Hudson's Bay and notice signs in an unfamiliar script, as well as in French and English, you are seeing Evans' characters in use today.

Connections

For other use of syllabaries, see

Garima Gospels, pp. 50–51

For other missionary printing in North America, see

Bay Psalm Book, pp. 128–129

For other homemade type and presses, see

Hunter's Old Papermaking, pp. 238–239

The Development of Serial Publishing

What is the right length for novels? In the 1830s the length, production methods and publicity for novels were dictated by the brilliant Charles Dickens—and his publishers. It was a profitable time for them.

In the 18th century, some novels such as Voltaire's *Candide* were very short; others, such as Richardson's *Pamela* and Sterne's *Tristram Shandy*, ran to many volumes. By the 1820s a length of three volumes became the normal highly priced format for novels, too expensive for individuals, who turned to borrowing instead through **subscription libraries** that obtained massive discounts from publishers. For publishers, business was simplified by the guaranteed purchases by these libraries. Without this practice, publishers had to sink a lot of capital up front, but could earn no profit until the third volume was published. Authors were unpaid until they received royalties.

Becoming the most successful and prosperous writer in England, Charles Dickens and his publishers Chapman & Hall devised a brilliant new marketing strategy. Alongside the three-volume form, books were published in 20 fortnightly parts, each at 2 shillings, in paper wrappers carrying advertising. The last issue, a double number, also had the title page and illustrations, so that customers could have their set bound.

This method suited printers, authors (who could start to receive payment quickly) and the publishers, who received the advertising revenue and profit from early sales. This system proved so successful that other authors and publishers adopted the method. Cheaper one-volume editions were published after the sets in parts had been completed. The market for novels was now under control, supplying editions that most people could afford.

This brilliant formula had its problems. As with writing for soap operas, authors needed to end the first part at an exciting point. Prudent writers, such as Trollope and Thackeray, completed and planned their whole books before printing started; Dickens did not, and his unfinished *Edwin Drood* was the consequence. He sometimes altered parts of his novels in response to readers' comments, making it hard for future editors to produce the authoritative texts.

Dickens' work had no copyright protection outside Britain, but Chapman & Hall made contracts by which American publishers who paid a modest fee received advance proofs. In Europe, the publisher Bernhard Tauchnitz paid fees to British and American authors, forming close friendships with Dickens and others. This ensured that their well-printed volumes in Tauchnitz Edition could be found for sale everywhere on the continent, and the methods used in Britain made Dickens by far the most famous of all writers. Readers gained, and the English publishers—and Dickens—became very wealthy.

LEFT Tauchnitz magazine
This "English monthly miscellany" was published at Leipzig in August 1892 for "continental readers." In a letter to Tauchnitz in 1860, Dickens expressed "perfect confidence" in his German publisher.

RIGHT The Pickwick Papers Serialized by Chapman & Hall in 20 monthly parts from April 1836 to November 1837, this first edition of *The Posthumous Papers of the Pickwick Club* featured 43 original and 25 duplicate plates by Robert Seymour, R.W. Buss and "Phiz" (H.K. Browne).

Connections

For other worries about pirated editions, see

Boldrewood's Robbery Under Arms, pp. 204–205

For other publishers' profitable series, see

Lehmann's Invitation to the Waltz, pp. 224–225

No. XIV.] [PRICE 1s.

THE

POSTHUMOUS PAPERS

OF THE

PICKWICK CLUB

CONTAINING A FAITHFUL RECORD OF THE

PERAMBULATIONS, PERILS, TRAVELS, ADVENTURES

AND

Sporting Transactions

OF THE CORRESPONDING MEMBERS.

EDITED BY "BOZ."

WITH ILLUSTRATIONS.

LONDON: CHAPMAN & HALL, 186, STRAND.

MDCCCXXXVI

No. 23. *Published Every Week.* **M. J. IVERS & CO., Publishers,** (James Sullivan, Proprietor,) **379 Pearl Street, New York.** *Price 5 Cents.* $2.50 a Year. Vol. II.

OLD GRIZZLY ADAMS, THE BEAR TAMER;

Or, "The Monarch of the Mountains."

BY DR. FRANK POWELL,

Pulp Fiction, Victorian Style

In the 19th century there was a major revolution in publishing popular reading. Beadle & Adams' Dime Novels were to be found everywhere.

Growing cities, faster communication, powered printing, cheap **paper** and mechanized bookbinding—and the increase of literacy in the working classes—all encouraged printers and publishers to seek new markets and to try to find different marketing strategies. Until late-Victorian times, first editions of novels normally cost a guinea and a half (or 31 shillings and 6 pence) in England—the equivalent of about three weeks' wages for an artisan. Publishing cheaper reprints encouraged more people to buy; and in Britain **yellowback** series such as Routledge's Railway Library (sold through station bookstalls) tapped a latent demand. But at 3 shillings and 6 pence each, these were still expensive for working men.

Issuing novels in parts made the books seem more affordable, as with Dickens' novels. As an extension of the idea, **penny dreadfuls** or penny bloods (smaller, unbound books of a sensational nature, sold, in the UK, at 1 penny each) proved affordable for many in Britain. They were so cheap that they sold in thousands, providing the publishers and writers a comfortable living.

In the US, the equivalent were the **dime novels**. Particularly associated with the New York publishers Beadle & Adams, their series from 1860 had wide appeal, particularly with male readers. These received a boost from sales to Union soldiers in the Civil War. By giving each new volume a series number and claiming they were periodicals, Beadle & Adams distributed the dime novels cheaply by mail, cash on delivery—until the United States Postal Service closed that loophole. From 1861 to 1866 the firm had a branch in London, and sold their books at 6 pence each, until the rights were bought out by Routledge.

Frank Powell's *Old Grizzly Adams, the Bear Tamer* (1884) is typical of the rattling yarns that Beadle & Adams published, in an efficient and effective production line of pulp literature. Naturally, their success spawned imitators, such as the Canadian George P. Munro, a former employee of Beadle who, from 1865 to 1893, pioneered dime novels for a female readership. In 1894, Erastus Beadle died a wealthy man, and his firm disappeared soon after. One of the most interesting followers was in the Bandarlog Press, where two Chicago newspaper men, Frank Holme and George Ade, printed several volumes tongue-in-cheek in their "Strenuous Lads Library" series, such as *Handsome Cyril, or the Messenger Boy with the Warm Feet*. Alas, no e-book versions have appeared.

LEFT *Old Grizzly Adams, the Bear Tamer* The cover of Frank Powell's version of the Old Grizzly story from 1899 promised the type of thrilling adventures boys had come to expect from Beadle's Boy's Library series. Many versions of this story seem to exist, ascribed to various authors.

RIGHT *The Indian Queen's Revenge* Munro, a Canadian and former employee of Beadle & Adams, quickly set himself up as a rival. Many of his titles, such as this tale of the Mohawk Valley in revolutionary times, 1865, involved Native American tribes, of perennial appeal to their young readership.

Connections

For other books aimed at a mass market, see

Newgate Calendar, pp. 164–165

Dickens' Pickwick Papers, pp. 190–191

Lehmann's Invitation to the Waltz, pp. 224–225

For other stereotyped editions, see

Baedeker's Switzerland, pp. 200–201

Innovative Books for Young Readers

Writing and illustrations intended for children emerged in the 18th century. New methods of printing and fresh ideas about how to teach reading took different courses in Victorian times.

In the 1740s, publishers like John Newbery in London (see pp. 156–157) laid the foundations for a trade in publishing for children. In the increased piety noticeable in the early 19th century, there were well-intentioned and serious attempts to produce books that would instruct as well as amuse. Many of these were written or printed by dissenters who believed they should do this—and their status gave their books a guarantee that they were wholesome for people to buy.

Instruction was not enough: the books should divert children while they were learning to read. Many of these texts were published by Darnton & Harvey, Quaker printers who bought Newbery's copyrights. They were active in London, producing many cheap improving books from the 1790s until they closed about 1870. Two of their best-known authors/engravers were sisters, Jane Taylor (1783–1824) and Ann Taylor (1782–1866), remembered for

80   ROBINSON CRUSOE

should do. And as they knew that the most safe way was to hide and lie in wait, they first of all took down the huts which were built for the two good men, and drove their goats to the cave, for they thought the wild men would go straight there as soon as it was day, and play the old game.

The next day they took up their post with all their force at the wood, near the home of the two men, to wait for the foe. They gave no guns to the slaves, but each of them had a long staff with a spike at the end of it, and by his side an axe. There were two of the wives who could not be kept back, but would go out and fight with bows and darts.

The wild men came on with a bold and fierce mien, not in a line, but all in crowds here and there, to the point were our men lay in wait for them. When they were so near as to be in range of the guns, our men shot at them right and left, with five or six balls in each charge. As the foe came up in close crowds, they fell dead on all sides, and most of those that they did not kill were much hurt, so that great fear and dread came on them all.

Our men then fell on them from three points with the butt end of their guns, swords, and staves, and did their work so well that the wild men set up a loud shriek, and flew for their lives to the woods and hills, with all the speed that fear and swift feet could help them to do. As our men did not care to chase them,

Crusoe's trip through China.

such poems as "Twinkle, Twinkle, Little Star" and "Dance Little Baby, Dance Up High," which are still read to infants today. Ann Taylor's charming *Rural Scenes, or a Peep into the Country* was steadily reprinted for the first 40 years of the 19th century.

A later toiler in the same field was Lucy Aikin (1781–1864), another privately educated dissenter, whose life was passed in writing books intended for women and children. Often of an historical kind, her books also had a considerable feminist slant, which makes her interesting in the development of women's writing. Always interested in teaching the young, in the last years of her life she devoted her time to producing adaptations of famous books written in words of one syllable, which she published under the pseudonym Mary Godolphin. Her versions of such books as *Robinson Crusoe*, *The Swiss Family Robinson* and *Aesop's Fables* sold steadily for the rest of the century.

Another publisher seized her idea for providing simple reading and writing exercises, and editions of *Robinson Crusoe in Words in One Syllable* in shorthand were also published by Isaac Pitman, to help office staff to learn his system of shorthand.

Connections

For another book for children, see

Newbery's Little Pretty Pocket-Book, pp. 156–157

For more scary reading for children, see

Hoffman's Struwwelpeter, pp. 196–197

For another book to help teach reading, see

Haüy's Education of the Blind, pp. 176–177

LEFT **Crusoe's trip through China** One of six full-page plates, this episode is drawn from *The Farther Adventures of Robinson Crusoe*, the second part of the Crusoe novels, published in 1719–20. Unlike the first, inspired by true-life castaway Alexander Selkirk, this second installment was apparently inspired by the Moscow embassy's journey to Peking from 1693–95.

RIGHT **Rural scenes, or, A Peep into the Country** This literary collaboration between sisters Anne and Jane Taylor, 1805, found, like the Mary Godolphin books, a loyal readership among the young. *The Monthly Review*, writing in 1806, commented on the prints which "please the eye and fancy" and the "moral hints which they impart... may contribute to farther edification and permanent benefit." This copy is from 1825.

Moral Education through Pictures

In the early Victorian period, it was becoming recognized that pure moralizing repelled children. A brilliant German found that a mixture of fright and merriment was much more effective in teaching good behavior.

The stories included about shock-headed Peter and other naughty children have delighted many generations. Some people more sensitive to notions of political correctness, however, find the volume quite shocking—some going to the lengths of stating that the notions in it foreshadow the mindset of Hitler and National Socialism.

In fact, the text was written by a very un-Hitlerian German, Heinrich Hoffman (1809–94). He was a doctor who devoted his medical career to caring for paupers, and then became an unusually enlightened head of a psychiatric hospital, devoting his energies to successful campaigning for a new clinic providing gardens available to the patients—very different from the old grimmer lunatic asylums. The other side of Hoffman's life was spent with his wife and children,

whom he entertained with his comic drawings and pictures. In 1845 he was persuaded by a friend to publish some of his moral tales in a volume called *Lustige Geschichten und drollige Bilder ... für Kinder von 3–6 Jahren (Funny Stories and Whimsical Pictures ... for Children Aged 3 to 6)*, but now always called *Struwwelpeter* or *Shock-headed Peter*. The volume was an instant success, and was translated and printed in many European countries and in the US. Over 50 English editions were published in the first 50 years of its publication, a tribute to the author and the efficient marketing by the German publishers.

It was probably part of the charm of Hoffman's book that he had tried and tested the verses on his own children, who needed to be taught not to play with matches, or refuse to eat, or suck their thumbs. Lessons taught without overt preaching were welcomed by parents reading the books and by the children listening. Earlier instructional books often only moralized; the hint of wickedness in *Struwwelpeter* attracts children much more. Some of Hoffman's characters (such as the long-legged scissor-man) were potentially frightening to children and might cause nightmares; but with the book in a parent's hands, it was still safe.

As with many children's books, Hoffman's masterpiece tempts other writers and artists. Gentler, kinder books, such as Belloc's *The Bad Child's Book of Beasts* or Gorey's *Gashlycrumb Tinies*, recognized that the hints of disobedience or fright in Hoffman's tales can be a powerful way of transmitting a message.

The door flew open, in he ran,
The great, long, red-legged scissor-man.
Oh! children, see! the tailor's come
And caught out little Suck-a-Thumb.
Snip! Snap! Snip! the scissors go;
And Conrad cries out "Oh! Oh! Oh!"
Snip! Snap! Snip! They go so fast,
That both his thumbs are off at last.

Mamma comes home: there Conrad stands,
And looks quite sad, and shows his hands;
"Ah!" said Mamma, "I knew he'd come
To naughty little Suck-a-Thumb."

LEFT **The great long red-legged scissor-man** Alack! Hoffmann's terrifyingly scissor-happy visitor was just one of the many calamities in store for the disobedient child.

Connections

For other books for children, see

Newbery's Little Pretty Pocket-Book, pp. 156–157

Meggendorfer's Grand Circus, pp. 198–199

For another book with scary pictures, see

Ernst's Une Semaine de Bonté, pp. 220–221

LEFT *Struwwelpeter, Merry Stories & Funny Pictures* Blackie & Sons, of Glasgow, produced the English translation of this book, first written by Heinrich Hoffmann for his young son. Its dark humor so delighted readers that *Struwwelpeter* has been translated into more than 35 languages and parodied many times, such as *Swollen-headed William* and *Struwwelhitler* in the two World Wars, *Struwwel-Leise* (a girl counterpart) and even, in 1885, a *Short Gynaecological Struwwelpeter*!

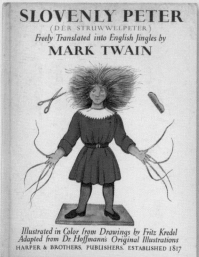

ABOVE *Slovenly Peter* Mark Twain's free translation of Hoffman's classic was written in 1891, but not published until after Twain's death due to copyright issues.

From Medieval Mysticism to Paper Engineering

First devised centuries before Western printing developed, paper-engineered books have become commonest in work for children, as writers and designers have found ways to turn sheets of paper to new uses.

We will probably never learn who invented the use of paper cuts to extend the possibilities of a flat sheet of paper. Both Catalan Ramon Llull (c. 1232–c. 1315) and the English monk Matthew Paris (c. 1200–1259) are known to have used rotating disks (**volvelles**) and the occasional pop-up, and folded pages appeared in scientific books such as by Vesalius (see pp. 134–135). But the real impetus in England for the modern development of books with moving parts came from 17th-century manuscript copies, which were made popular for children's reading about 1765 by the London publisher Robert Sayer.

These **metamorphoses, flap-books** or **harlequinades** were widely produced in Britain and the US until well into the 19th century. They were probably the source for the idea of pop-up or movable books; again, the earliest use of folded pop-ups came from London, from the miniature painter William Grimaldi in *The Toilet* (1821) and in another popular book, *A Suit of Armour for Youth* (1823). But the Regency delicacy of these little books was soon overshadowed by the exuberance and ingenuity of German printers and publishers, particularly those created by the Munich artist Lothar Meggendorfer (1847–1925) in his creative paper engineering. First working for the satirical/humorous magazine *Fliegende Blätter*, Meggendorfer started a huge range of books with carefully planned use of tabs to be pulled, to activate a hidden array of multiple levers, which then animate several features in each picture.

ABOVE **Llull's volvelle** The astronomical volvelle is one of the earliest examples; shown here is a facsimile of one made by Ramón Llull's in his *Ars Magna* (*The Great Art*), c. 1305. Resembling an astrolabe, it probably reached Europe via the Arab world and the Far East.

The technique called for very careful handling by readers, and no doubt clumsy children were soon in disgrace.

Meggendorfer's images repel some readers by their vulgarity, but their complexity and innovation (and the assiduous marketing) made his books very successful, with editions in German, English, French and other languages. From 1878 (when he first prepared one for his son), Meggendorfer completed more than 200 such books: though frequently emulated by other artists and publishers, his work has seldom been surpassed.

ABOVE **Adam and Eve Harlequinade** London publisher Robert Sayer called his mobile flap-books, produced around 1765 to illustrate children's stories, "Harlequinades," after the pantomime character who often featured in them. Enormously popular, they sold widely, inspiring many pirated editions. This American version, drawn by James Poupard (1788) after Sayer, has text, *The Beginning, Progress and End of Man*, after Benjamin Sands.

Connections

For earlier pop-up books, see

Vesalius' De humani corporis fabrica, pp. 134–135

Repton's Red Books, pp. 174–175

For other books for children, see

Newbery's Little Pretty Pocket-Book, pp. 156–157

Aikin's Robinson Crusoe, pp. 194–195

Have Guidebook, Will Travel

The development of tourism in the 19th century created a new publishing genre—the guidebook. One of the most successful and innovative firms was the German Baedeker company, who came to dominate the trade.

After the Napoleonic wars, German and British travelers flocked to the Continent and, owing to steamships and railways, the possibilities of brief and cheap holidays enabled the tourist industry to boom. An Englishwoman, Mariana Starke, started the trend for guidebooks; in his novel *Le Chartreuse de Parme* (1838), Stendhal mocked an English traveler who:

> ... *never paid for the smallest trifle without first looking up its price in the Travels of a certain Mrs Starke, a book which... indicates to the prudent Englishman the cost of a turkey, an apple, a glass of milk, and so forth.*

Mariana Starke's travel books, published in London by John Murray, gave exact information of this kind, and simplified travel for timorous tourists—and Starke invented a code for showing excellence, using !!!!!, where modern guide-writers use *****.

Murray recognized the potential market, and in 1836 published the first of his *Handbooks for Travellers*, which developed coverage of many regions, extending from Western European countries (in the first volumes) to such remote countries as Algeria, India, Japan and Syria. The series was enormously successful, with many revised editions being issued; but apparently finding competition too

strong in the late 19th century, Murray sold the rights to others, who later continued them as the *Blue Guides*. There were many other forays into this growing market, ranging from much cheaper and down-market volumes by Bradshaws (the railway timetable publisher) to the erudite and beautifully illustrated books of a former Murray author, Augustus Hare, whose *Walks in Rome* (1871) appeared in many editions until the 1920s.

Partly because of the thoroughness and persistence of Karl Baedeker (1801–59) and his sons, Murray's eventually withdrew from producing guidebooks. Baedeker published a few earlier travel books, but his volume on Switzerland (1844) was an innovation, with full, detailed information on routes, accommodation and everything else a tourist might need, employing Starke's method (but using *****) and following many features of Murray's books, but also publishing in other languages. (Murray's *Handbooks* were in English only).

By the 1930s, after Karl Baedeker the younger took charge of the business, 39 editions of the German Switzerland version, 20 of the French text and 28 English editions had been issued. Baedeker's business was thoroughly professional and efficient, with editions updated regularly, and the quality of the German printing and cartography was excellent. By 1900, "Baedeker" was taken to mean any guidebook, and (like the Tauchnitz editions of English-language novels) they were to be found for sale in bookstalls throughout Europe.

In the 20th century, other competing guidebooks also became ubiquitous. One of the most famous and influential is the *Michelin Guides*, started in 1900 by the Michelin brothers trying to improve sales of their tires, by giving guides free to any motorist who wanted one. (They switched to selling their guides in the 1920s.) Such is the importance of these guides that gaining a Michelin star can make a fortune for a restaurateur.

LEFT *Egypt* One of Baedeker's popular pocket-sized red guidebooks. His 1928 guide to the land of the pyramids contains the first-ever description of the tomb of Tutankhamun, discovered by Howard Carter just six years earlier.

BELOW *Rhine Journey from Strasbourg to Düsseldorf* Printed in Koblenz in 1839, this is the first Baedeker to have the Biedermeier binding, which is pictorially printed with views and arms of the Rhine states. Its fold-out map, from Mainz to Cologne, distinguishes it from previous publications.

RIGHT Baedeker's *Switzerland* This first edition was published by Karl Baedeker in 1844. One of his most successful titles, he published 39 editions until 1937. This well-used copy is bound in the pictorial yellow Biedermeier boards used by Baedeker in the 1840–50s.

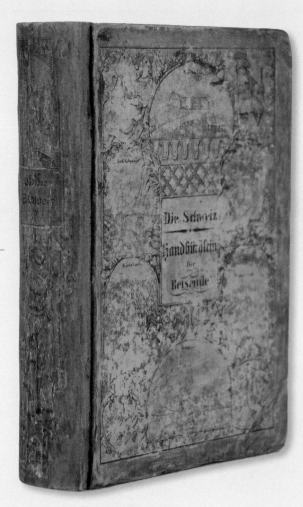

Connections

For earlier travel books, see

Cristoforo's Liber Insularum Archipelagi, pp. 70–71

Linschoten's Itinerario, pp. 132–133

For other books with international distribution, see

Meggendorfer's Grand Circus, pp. 198–199

Boldrewood's Robbery Under Arms, pp. 204–205

BELOW *The Modern Housewife* "Celebrity chef" Alexis Soyer had a sober side, working with Florence Nightingale in Crimea to improve military hospital food and creating a soup kitchen during the Irish Famine; his *Shilling Cookbook* aimed to help those on the "breadline" eat well. His popular housewife's manual, 1849, contains "nearly one thousand receipts, for the economic and judicious preparation of every meal."

RIGHT **Sauce for the ladies** *The Modern Housewife* included plates, depicting such enviable items as "Soyer's Magic Stove" and advertisements for consumables by the celebrity chef that were available for purchase, like this gender-specific *sauce succulente* in its curvaceous bottle. Owing to its popularity, *Punch* declared in 1848, that "the aristocracy is on the verge of the sauceboat"!

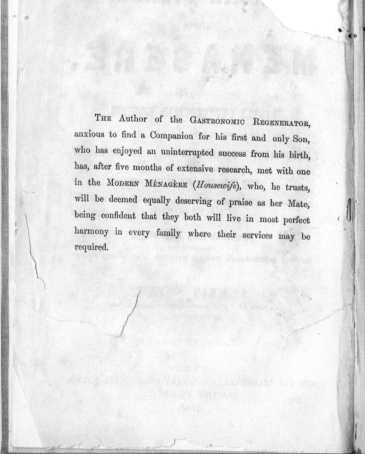

The First Celebrity Chef

Described as the Napoleon of the kitchens, this larger-than-life cook did
much to increase awareness of the importance of cooking, through his work
with soup kitchens and on the battlefield, as well as by his books.

Until well into the 19th century, cooks were not highly regarded in British society—if they were noticed at all. As a result of the greater contact between France and Britain after the Napoleonic wars, good French cooks could get well-paid posts in London. One of the most memorable was Alexis Soyer (1810–58), who had obtained a post as Second Chef to the Prince de Polignac at Versailles. Polignac's policies were part of the cause of the 1830 revolution in France, and like his employer, Soyer fled.

He landed on his feet in England, becoming chef in several great houses, and in 1837 was appointed to direct the kitchens of the new Reform Club, at the enormous salary of £1,000 (US$1,650) a year. He earned it: he introduced cooking on gas stoves, adjustable ovens, and (with the new dishes he created) made the Reform Club kitchens famous. A flamboyant, large-hearted man, Soyer realized early on that all publicity is useful, and he took every chance he had to make himself talked about. *Punch* regularly mocked him; Thackeray gently teased him in *The Book of Snobs* (1846); and the comic cook Alcide Mirobolant in Thackeray's *Pendennis* (1848–50) was based on Soyer.

Soyer's career was taken at a hectic pace. As well as running the Reform Club facilities and inventing and marketing various sauces and bottled drinks, Soyer was an inventor, patenting his portable stove. (It was so successful that versions of it were still being used by the military in the Gulf War, in 1990–91.) At his own expense, he set up soup kitchens for the poor in Spitalfields in the East End of London and in Dublin; he advised the British Admiralty on victualing the Navy's ships; and in 1855 he went to the Crimea to reorganize the Army's chaotic cooking facilities in the war there. (His work in the Crimea was much admired by Florence Nightingale, who described his untimely death as a great disaster.)

Soyer published many books on cooking—some written by assistants or ghostwriters—and all sold many copies. One could select several titles as appropriate: his *Charitable Cookery*, or, *The Poor Man's Regenerator* (1848); or his *Shilling Cookery for the People* (1855) of which 250,000 copies were sold. Instead, we show his *The Modern Housewife* (1849), written for the middle classes, and selling in thousands for many years.

M. SOYER'S CAMP AND BIVOUAC KITCHEN IN THE CRIMEA.—(SEE PRECEDING PAGE.)

LEFT **The military kitchen**
Soyer with Lord Rokeby and General Pelissier, beside the chef's bivouac kitchen in Crimea, from *The Illustrated London News*, September 1855.

Connections

For classical cookery, see

Apicius, **pp.** *52–53*

For other examples of inventiveness, see

Perkins' Patent, **pp.** *182–183*

Carlson's Lab Book, **pp.** *212–213*

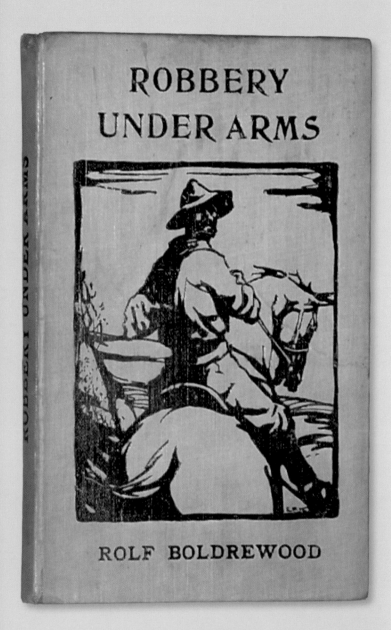

Marketing for the Colonies

Many successful books have their lives extended by the production of new editions. This series created new markets, and brought many colonial writers into the mainstream publishing world.

Widespread use of **stereotyping** in the 19th century enabled the development of cheap series of books, such as **yellowbacks** and **dime novels**. Publishers realized that there were untapped markets if they could find them.

Galignani in Paris had produced English-language books for sale to tourists; and in Leipzig in 1841 Bernhard Tauchnitz started his stereotyped volumes in his *Collection of British and American Authors*, distributed throughout Europe. Remarkably and scrupulously, Tauchnitz paid fees to British and American writers, although there was then no legal provision to enforce that.

Unrestricted piracy had afflicted publishers from the 15th century onward; in 1886, most European governments signed the Berne Convention (and in 1891 the US Chace Act) giving copyright protection to foreigners. A London publisher recognized that these new regulations would help his distribution of cheap books throughout the British Empire and America, without being undercut by American piracies.

In 1886, Macmillan started publication of his Colonial Library, for which the publisher had bought rights to produce cheap editions. As with Tauchnitz editions, the books were not available for sale in Britain: instead, they were aimed at sales in India and

LEFT *Robbery Under Arms* This tale of outback life was first serialized in the Sydney Mail in 1882–83. Added to Macmillan's Colonial Library in 1889, it quickly became one of the enduring classics of 19th-century Australian literature: by the 1920s, Macmillan had replaced its plain cloth cover for this more exciting pictorial version.

RIGHT A Colonial *Hound*
Sherlock Holmes is given
the export treatment in this
first colonial edition for the
London publisher Longman,
"intended for circulation
only in India and the British
Colonies." More elaborate
than the Colonial Library
edition by Macmillan, it
contained 16 plates as well
as its ornate binding.

Australia and other colonies, in clothbound and paper-
covered versions. It was an enormously successful
strategy: by 1913, Macmillan's Colonial Library
included over 600 titles, many strong sellers. The
publisher had anticipated good sales, and reviewers
(in such journals as the *South Australian Advertiser*
and the *Times of India*) commended the series, "The
individual book-buyer... in India, now, will get a great
deal more for his money than he ever got before."

One of the great successes, No. 94 in the Colonial
Library, was to become recognized as an Australian
classic. *Robbery Under Arms* was written by "Rolf
Boldrewood" (Thomas Alexander Browne, 1826–
1915, a New South Wales magistrate who had seen
pioneering lawlessness first hand). Still available
in print today, well over half a million copies of
Boldrewood's novel were sold in the first 50 years after
it was first published. This adventure story did much
to enable English readers to learn about the developing
colony, rather as they had consumed James Fenimore
Cooper's *The Last of the Mohicans*.

Connections

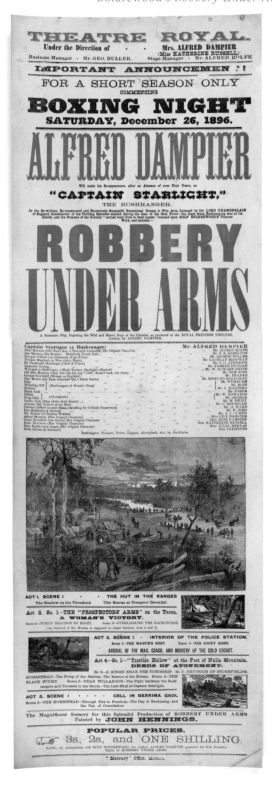

ABOVE A staged robbery A poster advertising a production based
on Boldrewood's tale, at the Theatre Royal, Hobart, in 1896.

RIGHT *Architecture at VKhUTEMAS* In the 1920s, the VKhUTEMAS (Higher State Artistic-Technical Workshop) was a center of experimentation and technical innovation in Moscow, akin to Weimar's Bauhaus. The design of this jacket by El Lissitzky, 1927, reflects its progressive, modernist intent. See pp. 218–219.

CHAPTER

10

The Book in the Turbulent 20th Century

Political, technological and cultural events, such as two World Wars and the advent of television and mass communication, could have destroyed the continuing production of books. The books of the 20th century were often very different to their precursors, but still full of life.

МОСКВА
1927

АРХИТЕКТУРА

АРХИТЕКТУРА

ВХУТЕМАС

The 20th century started offering many advances in the production of books, with the promise of an increase in their numbers, and that they be better printed, designed and illustrated. Availability was increased by improvements in education, and the spread of public libraries. First created about 1850, by the early 20th century public libraries were widely accessible, and the professionalization of librarians' work generally raised standards of library service. In the US Melvil Dewey and in Britain James Duff Brown were important for systemizing services and enabling open access to collections. In another library (the Pierpont Morgan), the memorable Belle da Costa Greene showed that good collection development was not limited to men. (In a very different way Nadezhda Krupskaya, Lenin's wife, enriched the content of Russian public libraries.)

THE COMING OF INFORMATION SCIENCE
The overabundance of books and other publications was becoming clear in Europe, as in America. One of the most significant developments came from Belgium, where two lawyers established the International Institute of Bibliography (IIB) in 1895, transformed in 1937 into the International Federation for Information and Documentation (FID); it was responsible for elaborating Dewey's classification into the Universal Decimal Classification. The IIB had grand plans for a universal bibliography, and by 1914 it had collected over 11 million entries for its Universal Bibliographic Repertory, kept on cards. As its name change suggests, the FID was much more interested in individual items of information than in books; their ways of trying to improve information service (including the use of microforms) were vital for the later development of computer-based systems.

The influence of the FID was marked and was behind many of the changes in what was coming to be called "Information Science." There was, however, a basic disagreement among the groups concerned with books in Britain: booksellers' and publishers' associations were not in the equation, and attempts by the Carnegie Trust to foster closer links between other groups ultimately failed. Documentalists set up their own professional association, the Institute of Information Scientists. For the provision of books in library service, these fault lines (which are not yet dormant) were a weakness.

Increasingly, those running libraries became managers rather than scholars or writers. Archibald MacLeish (Library of Congress) and Philip Larkin (University of Hull) were distinguished poets, but administrators tended to distrust creative librarians. In South America, however, writers were still honored and received state emoluments, the most significant and influential being Jorge Luis Borges in Buenos Aires (see pp. 210–211).

In the US, Fremont Rider, like the FID members, was concerned about the information explosion. In the 1940s he calculated that research libraries were doubling in size every 16 years—an overestimate, but still troubling. Rider devised a microform solution in the form of microcards, which would contain the full text of a publication and also serve as the catalog. Many millions of microcards were made of the content of large research libraries such as the American Antiquarian Society, but Rider's microcards have been superseded, the equipment to read them is obsolete, and microcards themselves are unreadable museum pieces—the same fate as other systems devised to replace print on paper (see pp. 212–213).

DEVELOPMENT OF BOOK DESIGN
In the pre-1914 years, the influence of the Kelmscott Press was still strong. Many owners of **private presses**, at that time and between the wars, wanted to create beautiful books, often produced irrespective of their marketability (see pp. 214–215 and 216–217). Such presses provided vehicles for artists who were rediscovering older illustration methods; but artists of a modernist kind often took radically different ways, which were slowly integrated into the normal ways of designing books (see pp. 218–219 and 220–221).

In third-world countries, the urge to publish and the urge to read caused the revival of older publishing forms. In India, Nigeria and Brazil (and other emergent countries), localized reading needs supported methods long since obsolete in Europe (see pp. 222–223).

TECHNOLOGICAL ADVANCES
Technical developments in Europe and America continued, mostly in the provision of more illustration methods (particularly gravure, half-tone and the relatively expensive collotype). Effective typographic education by such men as Stanley Morison (UK), W.A. Dwiggins (US) and Jan van Krimpen (Holland) strengthened classical approaches to design. Strangely

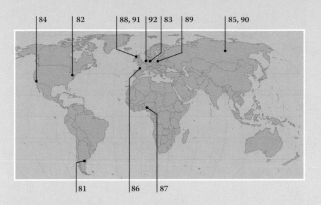

enough, World War II **paper** restrictions imposed in Britain helped to streamline book design, both those that were classic or modernist in approach. At that time book buyers were repelled by too much modernism—and the success of many paperback series reflected this (see pp. 224–225).

In the turmoils of revolution and the events of World War II, more books were destroyed than in the fall of Alexandria or the sack of Nalanda, and many irreplaceable manuscripts were destroyed. The total loss was alleviated because multiplication of copies (through printing and microtexts) spread the risk, and because legal deposit collections saved many. Some of the rarest 20th-century books were those printed in secret by clandestine presses (see pp. 226–227) or suppressed Russian books first issued in secret or in emasculated editions, such as Solzhenitsyn's *Gulag Archipelago* or Boris Pasternak's *Doctor Zhivago* (see pp. 228–229).

There is a variety of self-help books, which have appeared over a long period of time. Medical books touched on sexual matters, but very cautiously. In the 20th century, with the relaxing of Victorian mores, books on sex and sexual health started to appear openly and became widely available (see pp. 230–231).

Even wider was the distribution of books that fostered the cult of personality. The newer media that came in during the century changed the way people thought and behaved. They were responsible for some of the excesses, of course, but books were still vital as formers of opinion or belief. The sales of Hitler's *Mein Kampf* were colossal by the standards of the time.

In the first part of the 20th century, it was still relatively easy to set up as a publisher with limited financial resources. The variety of publishing was stronger than it was to be when previously independent publishers were absorbed into larger conglomerates, often run for profit rather than to publish important books. The replacement of independent bookstores by firms such as Barnes & Noble, Waterstones or Borders superficially provided a wide range of reading, but their policies further limited choice. Whether the effect of Amazon on publishing and book sales is good or bad cannot yet be determined.

The Blind Seer of Buenos Aires

Several librarians have become famous for their organizational or collection-building skills, but the Argentinian librarian Borges became well known for his extraordinary fictions, which foreshadowed changes in the modern information world.

Librarians of the past, such as Callimachus in Alexandria or Magliabechi in Florence, were often famous for their erudition. Modern librarians have also been erudite, but relatively few have become famous as creative writers, except for Jorge Luis Borges (1899–1986).

Borges, the director of the National Library in Buenos Aires, was most famous for his short stories. Educated in Switzerland, after living in Spain in the avant-garde Madrid literary circles, he returned to Argentina in 1921. Primarily a journalist, poet and essay writer, Borges was an intensive user of books and libraries, and in the early 1930s was appointed as First Assistant at the Buenos Aires Municipal Library, which left him ample time for writing and also for developing his own library-aware fiction. He also had political views, and in 1946 he was "promoted" by his enemy the dictator Juan Perón to become the Buenos Aires municipal market's Inspector of Rabbits and Poultry—an insult that the author did not forget. When Perón left office in 1955, Borges (by then almost totally blind) was appointed as Director of the National Library, resigning on Perón's return to power in 1973.

Borges' fictional writing was unusual, owing much to the surrealism of such artists as Max Ernst and Magritte. The earliest published collection of his stories, *El jardín de senderos que se bifurcan* (*The Garden of Forking Paths*, 1941) was soon reprinted in his *Ficciones* in 1944. Wide overseas recognition of his importance came thereafter, some critics assessing him as the most important writer in Spanish since Cervantes. His influence on Hispanic American writing has been great.

Partly because of his increasing blindness, Borges deliberately wrote short pieces. Describing himself as inept and lazy, he chose, he said, to write summaries or commentaries on imaginary books, rather than writing full books. Some pieces like "The Library of Babel" parallel Isaac Asimov's *Encyclopedia Galactica*; in his "Tlön, Uqbar, Orbis Tertius"(1940) Borges revealed an intimate knowledge of the *Encyclopedia Britannica*, as well as a brilliant ability for spoof writing. The title story, "The Garden of Forking Paths," has been seized on by those experimenting with **hypertext** fiction, and his influence is still increasing.

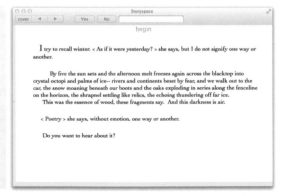

LEFT **Hypertext fiction** The formal experimentation of writers such as Borges and James Joyce influenced the development of hypertext fiction. This is Michael Joyce's *Afternoon, A Story*, first published in 1987 at a conference to demonstrate a hypertext writing system, and considered to be the first hypertext novel.

Connections

For other innovative fiction, see

Sterne's Tristram Shandy, **pp.** *166–167*

For other Central- and South-American publishing, see

Nnadozie's Beware of Harlots, **pp.** *222–223*

Prieto's Antibook, **pp.** *250–251*

JORGE LUIS BORGES

EL JARDIN DE SENDEROS QUE SE BIFURCAN

SUR

BUENOS AIRES

LEFT *The Garden of Forking Paths* An icon for gaming developers and programmers, Borges' novella is about a spy in England during World War I and his involvement in the legend of a lost labyrinth; as matters progress, the story itself becomes the labyrinth. Its alternative endings and interplay of time and plot resemble hypertext, foreshadowing interactive reading. The design is very close to that used in European publishing.

A Major Advance in Document Production

Chester Carlson's invention and the Xerox Corporation's development of electrostatic printing changed document production forever. Some people even claim that the success of xerography delayed the arrival of the paperless office.

When the Scottish inventor James Watt (1736–1819) found it burdensome to transcribe detailed documents for his partner Matthew Boulton, he invented an office-copying process. It was successful, and his machines were purchased by Benjamin Franklin, George Washington and others. Watt's invention was the ancestor of the many copying processes used in the 19th century, and mimeographed or spirit-duplicated processes remained in use until long after World War II. These all required planning, using special materials. For other written or printed documents only photography was suitable, and by the 1930s research libraries were already microfilming rare books and newspapers.

LEFT **The Xerox copier**
Chester Carlson with his first 1938 electro-photographic machine, a precursor of the Xerox photocopier—surprisingly, not much larger than a modern-day desktop scanner/printer.

There was also a need for ways of making single copies that could be read without equipment. There were various photocopying processes (such as thermofax), but these produced images that did not last well. The major breakthrough came from outside the printing and office-copying industries, in the unlikely hands of Chester Carlson (1906–1968). A largely self-driven inventor who was obsessed by the idea of making copies cheaply and easily, Carlson put himself through a Caltech Bachelor of Science degree in physics in 1930, just as the Depression was biting hard. While working for a patent attorney at Bell Telephone Laboratories, and later at home, he experimented with his ideas about ways of making copies, recording them in his laboratory notebooks. In October 1938, he included notes on his first successful attempts at electrostatic printing.

Not until the late 1950s did Carlson, the Battelle Institute and Haloid (later, the Xerox Corporation) manage to market a fully effective and reliable electrostatic printer, the Xerox 914. Earlier versions could catch fire, and office folklore (possibly fostered by business rivals) claimed using them made men impotent. Despite this the machine was an enormous success, and academic libraries and countless offices started to install them and other later models.

Carlson's invention facilitated publishing and scholarship as well as commerce. Instead of reading and then copying or summarizing, readers could now make copies easily and inexpensively (not an unmixed blessing). Firms like University Microfilms were soon marketing Xerox copies of academic dissertations. Though far from on-demand publishing, and the quality of early copies could be poor, Carlson's invention accelerated the information explosion and the emergence of the modern information society.

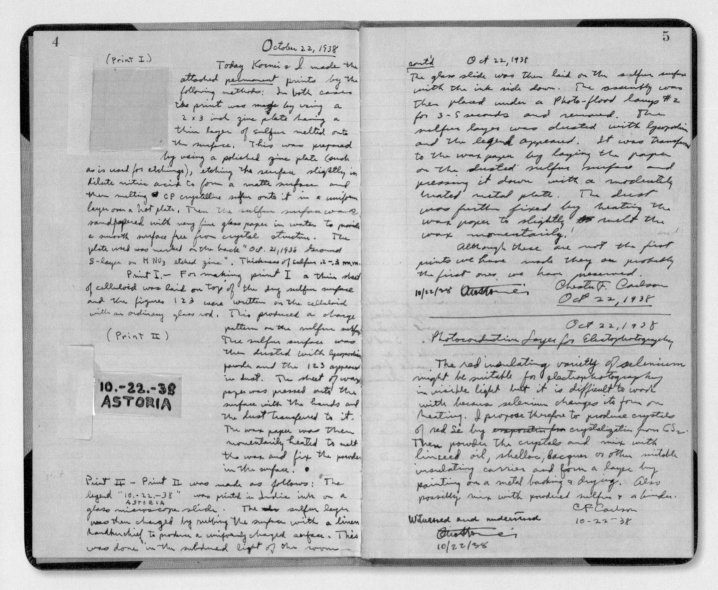

ABOVE **The lab book of Chester Carlson** Not a published book, but no less a book, Carlson's manuscript notebook, with his notes on electrostatic printing, has had a major impact on the history of book publishing.

Connections

For earlier developments in copying, see

Playfair's Commercial and Political Atlas, **pp. *162–163***

Atkins' Photographs of British Algae, **pp. *184–185***

For other attempts to replace printing, see

Ruiz's Mechanical Encyclopedia, **pp. *244–245***

Technion Nano Bible, **pp. *246–247***

Printing as a Performing Art

There have been many handsome editions of Shakespeare. One produced in Germany for a rich aesthete is possibly the most important example of 20th-century bookmaking.

By 1900, despite the many technical advances in printing and illustration, there was widespread dissatisfaction with the appearance of books. The European Art Nouveau (or Jugendstil) styles took a special form in Britain, as the Arts and Crafts movement, rejecting mechanization, returning to earlier forms and emphasizing truth to materials. The influence of William Morris' "little typographical adventure" at the Kelmscott Press was enormous in America and Europe.

Very different was the Cranach-Presse in Weimar, belonging to Harry Graf von Kessler (1868–1937). With an Anglo-Irish mother, he came from a rich and cultured German banking family (Kaiser Wilhelm I was his godfather). Interested in literature and the arts, he assembled a wide range of friends,

Hamlet
Act V. Sc. i.

Heer's a scull now hath lyen you i'th earth three & twenty yeeres.
Ham. Whose was it?
Clow. A whorson mad fellowes it was, whose do you think it was?
Ham. Nay I know not.
Clow. A pestilence on him for a madde rogue, a pourd a flagon of Renish on my head once; this same skull sir, was sir Yoricks skull, the Kings Iester.
Ham. This?
Clow. Een that.
Ham. Let me see. Alas poore Yoricke, I knew him, Horatio, a fellow of infinite iest, of most excellent fancie, hee hath bore mee on his backe a thousand times, and now how abhorred in my imagination it is: my gorge rises at it. Heere hung those lyppes that I haue kist I knowe not howe oft, where be your gibes now? your gamboles, your songs, your flashes of merriment, that were wont to set the table on a roare, not one now to mocke your owne grinning, quite chopfalne. Now get you to my Ladies table, & tell her, let her paint an inch thicke, to this fauour she must come, make her laugh at that. Prethee Horatio tell me one thing.
Hora. What's that my Lord?
Ham. Doost thou thinke Alexander lookt a this fashion i'th earth?
Hora. Een so.
Ham. And smelt so? pah.
138

including Bakst, Cocteau, Proust and Rodin; and he was the impresario behind the creation and production of Richard Strauss' opera *Der Rosenkavalier* (1911). Becoming aware of typography when he was working on the Jugendstil magazine *Pan* in the 1890s, Kessler decided in about 1911 to create his own press to bring together the best artists from Europe. With **typefaces** by English craftsmen, French papermakers, and British and French artists—plus a team of British and German printing experts—Kessler's Cranach-Presse at Weimar had enormous promise. Kessler's own close personal interest sometimes delayed things—his attempt to make the sculptors Aristide Maillol and Eric Gill work together was not productive—but he gave unstinting support to his artists.

Times were not propitious in 1914 for Anglo-German artistic cooperation: his typefaces remained unused and his book plans lay in abeyance until long after World War I. The most exciting and innovative were the editions of *Hamlet*, originally discussed with the brilliant English dramatic expert, artist and writer Edward Gordon Craig (1872–1966), who in 1911–12 was working with Constantin Stanislavski in the Moscow Arts Theater on a modernistic performance of *Hamlet*. Most exemplary editions from other **private presses** (like the Doves Press) treated *Hamlet* solely as a text to be read. Craig envisaged a book that reflected the drama being played, with ingenious ways of illustrating each opening of the book. As another cosmopolitan, Kessler was persuaded to put a great deal of money and personal attention into the small edition of this "bravest artistic adventure among all private press books." Types, paper, illustration, binding and execution produced a book whose real significance has only recently been recognized.

ACT IV SCENE V
LINES 56-74

THE TRAGICALL HISTORIE OF

Louange
d'Amleth tuans
le tyran.

mesme, puis que c'estoit par luy, que j'avois perdu ce qui me lioit à telle consanguinité et alliance. Homme pour vray hardy et courageux, et digne d'eternelle louange, qui s'armant d'une folie cauteleuse, et dissimulant accortement un grand desvoyement de sens, trompa souz telle simplicité les plus sages, fins, et rusez: conservant non seulement sa vie des efforts et embusches du tyran, ains qui plus est, vengeant avec un nouveau genre de punition, et non excogité supplice la mort de son pere, plusieurs annees apres l'execution: de sorte que conduisant ses affaires avec telle prudence, et effectuant ses desseins avec une si grande hardiesse, et constance, il laisse un jugement indecis entre les hommes de bon esprit, lequel est le plus recommandable en luy, ou sa constance et magnanimité, ou la sagesse, en desseignant, et accortise, en mettant ses desseins au parfaict accomplissement de

King. Pretty Ophelia.
Ophe. Indeede la, without an oath Ile make an end on't,
By gis and by Saint Charitie,
Alack and fie for shame,
Young men will doo't if they come to't,
By Cock they are to blame.
Quoth she, Before you tumbled me,
You promis'd me to wed,
(He answers.) So would I a done by yonder sunne
And thou hadst not come to my bed.
King. How long hath she beene thus?
Ophe. I hope all will be well, we must be patient, but I cannot chuse but weepe to thinke they would lap him i'th' cold ground, my brother shall know of it, and so I thanke you for your good counsaile. Come my Coach, God night Ladies, god night, sweet Ladyes god night, god night.

Vengeance juste,
ou est ce que doit
estre consideree.

Intention
de David
commandant
ceste vengeance.

son oeuvre de long temps premedité. Si jamais la vengeance sembla avoir quelque face et forme de justice, il est hors de doute, que la pieté et affection qui nous lie à la souvenance de nos peres, poursuivis injustement, est celle qui nous dispense à cherher les moyens de ne laisser impunie une trahison et effort outrageux et proditoire: veu que jaçoit que David fut un sainct, et juste Roy, homme simple, et courtois, et debonnaire, si est-ce que mourant il enchargea à son fils Salomon, luy succedant à la couronne, de ne laisser descendre au tombeau quelque certain, qui l'avoit outragé, non que le Roy, et prochain de la mort, et prest à rendre compte devant Dieu, fust

126

RIGHT **The Cranach-Presse** *Hamlet* The opening to Act IV, scene V of the Cranach-Presse's edition, published in Weimar in 1930. Its strikingly bold design and typography used types designed by Edward Johnston, and 80 **woodcuts** and engravings by the artist and dramaturge Edward Gordon Craig.

LEFT **The Doves Press approach** This earlier follower of William Morris believed in simplicity. The owner's quest for "the ideal book" relied on good presswork and beautiful type alone. The Doves *Hamlet* was undoubtedly beautiful—but boring and formulaic, very different from the Cranach-Presse version.

Connections

For other printing of drama, see

Boucher's Molière, pp. 152–153

For books from other private presses, see

Whitman's Leaves of Grass, pp. 216–217

Hunter's Old Papermaking, pp. 238–239

A West-Coast Interpretation of an American Epic

Épinal (France) was noted as a center for popular prints, and in the 20th century, Onitsha (Nigeria) and Recife (Brazil) for street literature. San Francisco became famous as a center for fine printing, and the Grabhorn brothers were admired as West Coast printers. Their edition of Whitman's Leaves of Grass *is a fine example of a limited edition book.*

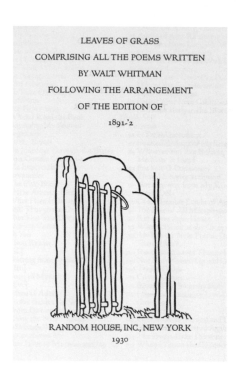

William Morris and the Kelmscott Press were even more influential in the US than they were in Britain. Boston commercial printers such Daniel Berkeley Updike at the Merrymount Press, or the typographer Bruce Rogers, at first followed the Morris style and their books were admired and bought by American book collectors.

In the 1920s, there was a boom in fine printing on both sides of the Atlantic. At the New York firm of Random House the shrewd publisher Bennet Cerf in 1927 obtained the US marketing rights for Golden Cockerel, Nonesuch and other British fine presses. Cerf also commissioned the publication of a fine edition of the great American epic, Walt Whitman's *Leaves of Grass*, from the relatively new Grabhorn Press.

San Francisco had long been a center for the book arts, fostered by the Book Club of California, founded in 1912. The work of Edward and Robert Grabhorn was admired on the West Coast. But the Grabhorn Press was not like the austere **private presses** owned by rich aficionados, for whom sales were not important. The Grabhorn Press was more like commercial firms (such as Chiswick Press in London, or the Riverside Press in Massachusetts), who printed well but also needed to be profitable. The Grabhorn brothers, like Bruce Rogers, practiced allusive typography, marrying the text and typography in a way that up until then was rare in private presses.

In the boom years of the 1920s, expensive **limited editions** sold well. In an audacious gamble,

Cerf's persuasiveness ensured the success of *Leaves of Grass*, with nearly 2,000 would-be subscribers competing to buy the 400 copies, priced at the unheard-of sum of US$100. (Cerf had originally planned a larger edition priced at US$15!)

Production took over a year. The Grabhorns printed the book well, setting the text in Newstyle **type**, by the American type designer Frederic W. Goudy. Having originally planned an unillustrated text with elaborate initials, and disappointed by the effect, the Grabhorns decided to have simple, evocative illustrations instead. Their chosen artist was Valenti Angelo, a self-taught Italian artist who had been working for the Grabhorn Press since 1926. Angelo's simple **woodcuts** were ideal for the Whitman text, and the merits of this edition, which the Grabhorns later recalled as "the most perfect book we ever printed," have been widely recognized.

Connections

For other books from private presses, see

Cranach-Presse's Hamlet, pp. 214–215

Hunter's Old Papermaking, pp. 238–239

LEFT **A Random House edition** The Grabhorn's outstanding edition of Walt Whitman's poems bears the imprint of Random House, who commissioned the work. Like the bold typography, the deceptively simple, fluid woodcuts by Valenti Angelo were perfectly married to Whitman's verse in this most successful of the Grabhorn brothers' fine printing.

RIGHT *Leaves of Grass* Title page of the Grabhorn Press edition of 1930, heavily impressed in black and red using the muscular Goudy Newstyle typeface by the eminent American typographer. Edwin Grabhorn maintained he saw in Frederic Goudy's new typeface, "the strong vigorous lines of Whitman... simple printing— printing like mountains, rocks and trees, but not like pansies, lilacs and valentines."

LEAVES OF GRASS

Come, said my Soul,
Such verses for my Body let us write, (for we are one,)
That should I after death invisibly return,
Or, long, long hence, in other spheres,
There to some group of mates the chants resuming,
(Tallying Earth's soil, trees, winds, tumultuous waves,)
Ever with pleas'd smile I may keep on,
Ever and ever yet the verses owning—as, first, I here and now,
Signing for Soul and Body, set to them my name,

Walt Whitman

Tangoing Toward the Revolution

Some important steps toward modern design came from Italy and Russia,
in the troubled, uneasy period before World War I.

The fine printers of about 1900 (and since) often looked backward to typographical styles of the 15th century—much as, in the fine arts, the Pre-Raphaelite Brotherhood sought to revive art by turning to older styles. Others, wanting to change the book arts of the 19th century, looked forward to reform through radical experimentation. The Italian futurists such as Filippo Marinetti defined it concisely in 1909: "We want no part of it, the past."

Marinetti's *Futurist Manifesto*, published in 1909, attracted wide attention, but was particularly successful in Russia, where the lost war with Japan (1904–05) and the failed 1905 revolution caused disillusion in many parts of the Russian Empire, particularly among the intelligentsia. The Moscow-based literary group Hylaea, founded in 1910 among the disillusioned elite, was attracted and encouraged by Marinetti. They issued a manifesto themselves, entitled *A Slap in the Face of Public Taste*.

In book terms, Hylaea's slap was a very hard and disconcerting one. *Tango with Cows*, written by the poet Vasily Kamensky and designed and produced by

ABOVE ***Tango with Cows*** This small book of "Ferro-Concrete Poems" by the Russian poet Vasily Kamensky was made using commercially produced wallpaper (reflecting bourgeois taste) and three drawings by fellow cubo-futurists David and Vladimir Burlyuk. The spatial arrangements of the typography reflect their subjects: hymns to urban life and modernity.

David Burlyuk, was clearly influenced by Marinetti's *Zang Tumb Tumb* (1912). It is famous for the way it ignores all the normal tenets of printing or how to make books easily readable. Kamensky used *zaum*, the Russian futurist poets' deliberately incoherent and anarchic blend of words used for their sound alone, and stripped of their meaning. Its title tied the vibrant new urban Russia (to which the Argentinian tango was introduced via Paris) to the old traditional agricultural life that would later be destroyed by Soviet collectivism.

Printed roughly on the back of unused wallpaper, deliberately cut to a nonrectangular shape, with the use of large, brutal display **types** used for visual impact, not for meaning, the book mystified many people, but over time its importance was realized. The type-as-pattern was later exploited by El Lissitzky, whose work greatly influenced the Bauhaus and constructivist movements and, in many ways, dominated 20th-century graphic design. *Tango with Cows* is still a stimulating book to see.

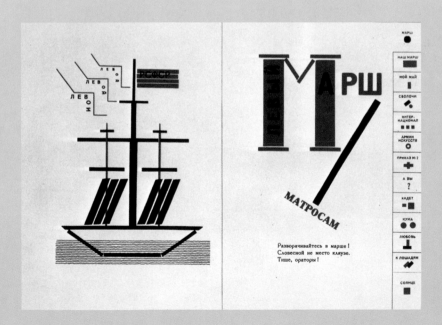

ABOVE **Left march!** Expelled, like David Burlyuk, from Moscow Art School for his political activities, was fellow futurist Vladimir Mayakovsky, whose poems *Dlya golosa* (*For the Voice*) were illustrated by El Lissitzky. This seminal work is typical of the dynamic, angular and asymmetric designs reflecting the group's ideas; though now a century old, its modernist elements are still hugely influential today.

Connections

For other modernistic books, see

Sterne's Tristram Shandy, *pp. 166–167*

Borges' Garden of Forking Paths, *pp. 210–211*

Ernst's Une Semaine de Bonté, *pp. 220–221*

For other artists' books, see

Prieto's Antibook, *pp. 250–251*

Time-Travel Surrealism

The effects of World War I were disastrous for all combatant countries, and this is reflected in their art and typography. In France (as in Germany), book arts were swept away by new approaches such as Dada and surrealism. In the hands of Max Ernst, some beautiful and disturbing books were produced.

BELOW ***Une Semaine de Bonté*** Max Ernst's *Week of Kindness* is a surrealist landmark in publishing. Using the technique of collage (so popular with an earlier generation as découpage, for decorative effect), Ernst reassembles Victorian engravings to construct numerous "exquisite corpses"—to intriguing, and at times unsettling, narrative effect. The newly emerging psychoanalysis was of much influence in this dreamlike world.

Like Russian futurist artists and writers, many in Western Europe responded to pre-war discontents (and later the horror of trench warfare) by seeking new ways to express their beliefs. At first, the Dada movement (which started in Zurich) rejected logic and reason, and prized irrationality—beliefs held by the post-war surrealists based mainly in Paris.

Although it was by no means limited to Dada and surrealism, **collage** was an artistic technique that became much used in modern art. It had existed long before (it was first used at the time of the invention of **paper** in China), but at the beginning of the 20th century Georges Braque and Pablo Picasso adopted and popularized the method, using pasted-on elements in their work. Among the Dadaists, Kurt Schwitters was perhaps the best-known and most influential collagist, but his work was of individual assemblages to create his pictures. Such work could be reproduced in books and articles, but few artists took up the method to facilitate mass production, in the way the Russian futurists produced their books.

In Paris, the German Max Ernst (1891–1976), already an artist, developed collage into a means of illustrating books, first in three books for the poet Paul Éluard. He later used it in three **graphic novels**, using a technique that was superficially quite simple—taking a range of 19th-century wood engravings, cutting and pasting other discordant images onto them to create the picture he wanted, and then using photomechanical means to make new printing plates.

Une Semaine de Bonté (*A Week of Kindness*), 1934, was named after a French

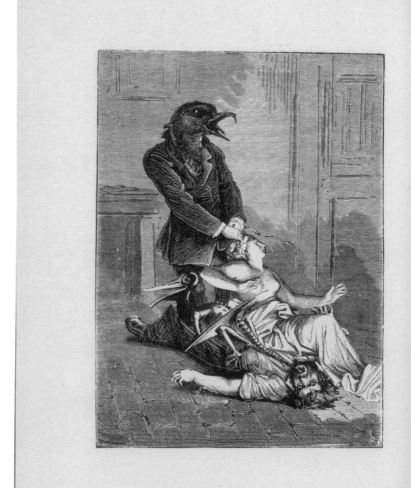

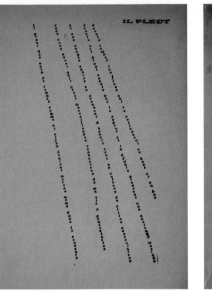

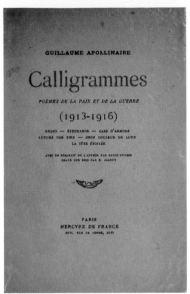

LEFT **Calligrammes** The term *surréalisme* was coined by the poet and foremost member of the French avant-garde Guillaume Apollinaire, whose posthumously published **concrete poems** of 1918 (he died in the influenza pandemic that year) look back to the playful typography of *Tristram Shandy*. They were created using the automatic writing technique beloved by the surrealists.

philanthropic organization. The third of Ernst's graphic novels, it was created in three weeks in Italy. To prepare it, Ernst cannibalized several books, including *Les damnées de Paris*, a cheap French sensational novel by Jules Mary. Originally published in five parts (but actually comprising seven sections, one for each day of the week), Ernst's macabre and sometimes horrifying book built up a story, the meaning of which is still debated by many critics. The 19th-century engravers, often with great technical skills, used anti-clericalism, eroticism and violence in their images. By dislocating and substituting elements in the pictures, Ernst's collages (which drew on theories from the emerging science of psychology) suggested ideas that had been suppressed. The influence of *Une Semaine de Bonté* is marked in the work of such later illustrators as Edmund Gorey, and Ernst's book still haunts many readers.

Connections

For other disconcerting works, see

Sterne's Tristram Shandy, **pp. 166–167**

Kamensky's Tango with Cows, **pp. 218–219**

Prieto's Antibook, **pp. 250–251**

For other brilliant wood engraving, see

Bewick's British Birds, **pp. 172–173**

Cranach-Presse's Hamlet, **pp. 214–215**

Street Literature—The Voice of the People

Many countries once had flourishing trades of books produced by the people for the people. These traditions are only a memory in Europe, but in Nigeria and Brazil the production of street literature still prospers.

Connections

For other Central- and South-American books, see
Caral Khipu, *pp. 20–21*
Codex Mendoza, *pp. 130–131*
Borges' Garden of Forking Paths, *pp. 210–211*
For other African books, see
Moroccan Sefer Abudarham, *pp. 112–113*
For a different self-help book, see
Stopes' Married Love, *pp. 230–231*

ABOVE **Romances on a string** An anonymous engraving published in 1850, depicting a stall adjoining the convent of San Agustín (Barrio de la Ribera, Barcelona) selling *romanços*—the Spanish forerunner of the *cordel*. The two lads are perhaps attracted to one of the more sensational of the titles on offer.

LEFT *Beware of Harlots* This admonitory pamphlet by Joseph O. Nnadozie is typical of Onitsha productions of the 1970s, printed on a vertical platen press, with a card cover featuring a **woodcut**. In fact, the cuts were generally made with a razor blade into thick flooring rubber mounted on wood.

In the first few centuries of printing, before the book trade became systematized and books began to be sold through bookshops, there was an undergrowth of publishing—of the **chapbooks** sold widely by traveling salesmen (colporteurs or chapmen) at fairs and markets. They were designed to appeal to the newly literate or poorly educated people and, like the **dime novels**, they were cheap.

Improving education, higher incomes and the publication of more sophisticated books meant that the production of chapbooks all but disappeared in Europe. But in two third-world countries this tradition continued well into the 20th century—in northeastern Brazil and in the southern part of Nigeria around the great market town of Onitsha. Seventy years ago, it was alleged that it was possible to buy anything and everything at Onitsha. Enterprising printers and aspiring authors started to produce small books for people moving from traditional tribal society to an English-speaking and Western-thinking world, as once had been the case in India. The **type** for the Onitsha books was set by female as well as male **compositors**, rare for Nigeria (and many other countries).

Many of these small books were simple self-help guides, often with a distinctly moral tone (such as

Sunday O. Olisah's *Life Turns Man Up and Down* [1964], with crude rubber-cut illustrations). Others were clearly aimed at young men, such as J. Abiakam's useful-sounding *How to Make Friends with Girls* (1965), using an incongruous half-tone of a knitting pattern for the cover illustration. The production of these Onitsha books was disrupted by the bloody Biafran war of 1967–70, and the trade declined thereafter.

The idea of the Brazilian *literatura de cordel* (so named because copies for sale were displayed in stalls hanging on a cord) was probably derived from the Portuguese *papéis volantes* (paper flyers) and traditionally these pamphlets were produced in the same ways and with the same limited equipment of the Onitsha printers. But there were differences: the *literatura de cordel* was often poetry intended to be sung; but also increasingly the cordel writers recorded current events (rather like the Trinidadians with their calypsos). Frequently markedly left wing in tone, the *literatura de cordel* is increasingly popular to buyers, and its writers and artists are still a vital part of Brazilian culture.

FAR LEFT *How to Make Friends with Girls* An example of street literature from Nigeria, published by the J.C. Brothers Bookshop, 1965, when the Onitsha market for literature was at its peak. Religious tracts, how-to manuals, drama, fiction and social etiquette were popular themes. The cover illustration appears to have been lifted from a knitting pattern for a sweater, hardly suitable for Nigerian weather.

LEFT Brazilian *cordel* Rooted in folklore, religion and song, often the street "string" literature is also political. This pamphlet is suggestive of pulp fiction; in fact it commemorates the shooting Dr Evandro, a Pernambuco lawyer involved in land reform, who was gunned down in front of his family in 1987.

Twentieth-Century Solutions to Publishing Needs

In the 1930s, paperbacks started to replace clothbound editions as the norm. Much of this was due to the effects of World War II, and the good business sense of Allen Lane, who took other people's ideas and improved them at Penguin Books.

The enormous success of Penguin Books sometimes suggests that founder Allen Lane's venture in publishing cheap books created the paperback revolution. The real innovation in marketing good-quality paperbound books came much earlier, from the success of Tauchnitz's continental editions; and they were dependent on publishers to sell them the rights to reprint such cheaper editions. Another later continental series started in 1932; Albatross Books (soon to absorb the Tauchnitz company) also attracted attention. Using modern layouts with new **fonts** developed by Stanley Morison, among others, with color coding on its books by genre (orange for fiction, green for travel), it took innovative approaches to publishing and publicity. Had it not been for the growth of Nazi rule in 1933, which disrupted trade, it is likely that Albatross Editions would have come to dominate the world market.

Several major London publishers attempted to produce up-market books in paperback—for example, Ernest Benn with his innovative series of Yellow Books—but London publishers were reluctant to sell reprint rights to other British firms, and bookshops were hesitant to stock them. The genius of Allen Lane (1902–70) was not the idea of good paperbacks, nor their design (which was closely copied from Albatross volumes), but in his success in persuading publishers to sell their reprinting rights to him and in finding distributors to market his books.

Lane had a long association with publishing, having worked for years with his uncle John Lane, founder of the Bodley Head imprint; by 1930, Allen Lane had become chairman of the board. Well known and liked in the publishing trade, he was regarded as a bit of a maverick, while his notion of distributing his sixpenny paperbacks through using slot-machines at railway stations was regarded as ridiculous. But bulk sales of the first 10 Penguin titles sold by Woolworths ensured Lane's success. In 1937 Lane started a non-fiction

series, Pelican Books, and then Penguin Specials. The huge success of these books in the late 1930s was crucial: when **paper** rationing was introduced in Britain during World War II, their earlier good sales ensured Penguin Books were allocated a substantial paper allocation, allowing them to dominate the growing paperback market. (The **format** of Penguin paperbacks was ideal for soldiers to carry with them.)

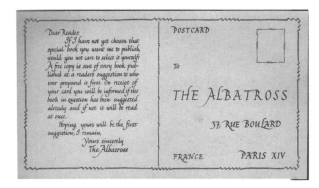

ABOVE **Reader interaction** The Albatross Modern Continental Library attracted many outstanding writers of English literature, its first list in 1932 including Joyce, Woolf and Huxley. This postcard, tucked inside Rosamond Lehmann's *Invitation to the Waltz*, right (published in 1934), is an effective bit of "soft" marketing, encouraging the reader to feel involved in the editorial selection.

INVITATION
TO THE WALTZ

by
ROSAMOND
LEHMANN

THE ALBATROSS

COPYRIGHT EDITION

NOT TO BE INTRODUCED INTO THE BRITISH EMPIRE OR THE U.S.A.

LEFT Birds of a feather The striking design and typography of Albatross editions by the German Max Christian Wegner, formerly of Tauchnitz, were widely copied, particularly by Penguin. Writing in 1953, Hans Schmoller, head of design at Penguin Books, described Albatross Editions as "the pinnacle among paper-covered books."

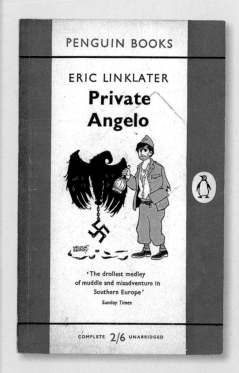

ABOVE *Private Angelo* This deceptively simple cover, what would become ubiquitous Penguin style, bears no hint of the change in printing the book heralded. Its forerunner, Allen Lane's 1957 Christmas edition, was printed on McCorquodale's Intertype Fotosetter— a move away from mechanical setting and letterpress toward filmsetting and, eventually, computer setting.

Connections

For other technical advances, see

Gutenberg's 42-Line Bible, **pp. 98–99**

Perkins' Patent, **pp. 182–183**

For other successful publishers' series, see

Dickens' Pickwick Papers, **pp. 190–191**

Boldrewood's Robbery Under Arms, **pp. 204–205**

LEFT *Kamienie na Szaniec*
Stanisław Kunstetter, a
member of the Home Army's
Bureau of Information and
Propaganda, designed the
cover for this first edition,
in 1943, featuring the Polish
szabla (saber) device adopted
by TWZW, the publishers.
The book was released in
English translation in 1945
by the Polish Boy Scouts'
and Girl Guides' Association.

Never Surrender! Clandestine Presses in War

Resistance presses sprang up in most occupied countries in World War II.
The Polish endeavor in Warsaw was the biggest of all.

Most people think of a clandestine press working in wartime as a small and highly secret operation, hidden in cellars, attics or farm sheds where the authorities would never find it. There were such presses, and their personnel were sometimes caught and then executed. In most countries occupied by the Germans in World War II, there were many attempts, fostered by the British Air Force, to drop small and portable presses by parachute for use by the Resistance. In France, the books secretly printed in Paris by Les Éditions de Minuit, including Vercors' *Le silence de la mer* (*The Silence of the Sea*, 1942), were important for raising the morale of Resistance fighters.

Though significant, these efforts did not compare with the Resistance printing in Poland after the invasion by the Germans in 1939. Ever since their country had been carved up by the Russians, Austrians and Germans in 1795, Poles had sought freedom, and secret publishing was part of it. In World War II, the TWZW (Tajne Wojskowe Zakłady Wydawnicze, or Secret Military Printing Works) emerged as probably the largest underground publisher in the world, with 12 printing centers working by 1944, producing many thousands of copies of newspapers, as well as posters useful for psychological warfare.

Like Vercors' *Le silence de la mer*, Aleksander Kamiński's *Kamienie na szaniec* (*Stones for the Rampart*) was fiction, published under the pseudonym Juliusz Górecki. It was closely based on real events in the Polish Resistance. The plot tells of the way members of the underground scout movement carried out minor acts of sabotage; Kamiński was one of the leaders of the heroic scout group and his book had the ring of truth about it. Published secretly in Warsaw in 1943, it was reprinted again in Poland before the end of the war; and in England in translation in 1945. Under the communist rule of Poland, Kamiński's book was thought dangerous so reprinting was discouraged, but it is now regarded as a minor classic, and on the recommended reading lists for the Polish secondary school curriculum.

ABOVE **Undercover printing** Though perhaps rather posed for the camera, this photograph, which appeared in *Le Point* in 1945, shows the claustrophobic conditions in which the resistance publishers had to work, on equipment that could be readily moved.

Connections

For other subversive publications, see

Bulgakov's Master and Margarita, *pp. 228–229*

The Greatest Samizdat Book

Russian government and state censorship always ran together. The secret publications of the Stalinist era—samizdat or self-published works—produced some remarkable works of literature.

Because of the history of oppression in Russia, there was a long tradition of resistance by the intelligentsia, through secret means of publication. In imperial times, there were severe punishments (including exile to Siberia); after the 1917 revolution many hoped for a new, more tolerant approach to publication. Instead, under Lenin (and particularly his successor Stalin) controls became much stricter: Solzhenitsyn's *Gulag Archipelago* (published in the West in 1973, but in Russia available only in samizdat form until 1989) caused the author to be stripped of his nationality and expelled. This almost happened to the Nobel Prize-winner Boris Pasternak for daring to have his *Doctor Zhivago* (1957) smuggled abroad for publication—and his Italian publisher was expelled from the Communist Party for accepting it. A later dissident, Vladimir Bukovsky, who spent many years imprisoned in a *psikhuska* (Russian psychiatric hospital), ostensibly for owning samizdat, distilled the experience of such authors, saying he wrote, edited and censored his own work; he then produced and distributed the book, knowing imprisonment would follow.

Perhaps fortunately, Mikhail Bulgakov (1891–1940) died before his greatest book was published, even in

samizdat form. Having trained in medicine and served as a doctor after the 1917 revolution, he was a marked man—his brothers served in the White Army. Bulgakov's earliest writings were blameless (medical stories written in 1925–27 and partly autobiographical), but his dramatic work got him into trouble, all his plays were banned at the Moscow Arts Theater.

Very boldly, he wrote personally to Stalin, asking for permission to emigrate: remarkably, Stalin found him work at the Arts Theater, and as a librettist at the Bolshoi, but further publication of his plays or fiction was impossible. *The Master and Margarita*, Bulgakov's sardonic, Menippean novel, was an indictment of the form of the Soviet world. There were many early drafts, some burned, before the book was completed in 1938–39; but it was only with the easing of censorship in 1967 that publication was possible, and still with substantial cuts made by the censors. A full version was published in 1973, and the genius of the author was soon recognized, in the Russian naming of a minor planet for him in 1982.

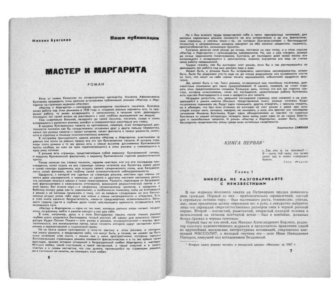

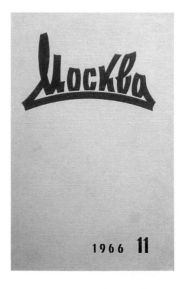

LEFT **The *Master* in Moscow** Written between 1928 and 1940, this first official publication (1966–67) in *Moskva* magazine was heavily censored, omitting about 12 percent (100 pages) of the text. The censored sections were available in the Soviet Union only through samizdat copies and the novel wasn't published in full there until 1973.

Михаил Булгаков

МАСТЕР

И

МАРГАРИТА

LEFT *The Master and Margarita* As in war-torn Europe, many writers in the Soviet bloc were forced underground; Bulgakov's great novel was at first distributed only in samizdat form. In 1969 the Frankfurt publishers Possev published one of the earliest book editions—here, with its striking cover— restoring much of the censored material.

Connections

For other subversive novels, see

Borges' Garden of Forking Paths, *pp. 210–211*

For another revolutionary Russian book, see

Kamensky's Tango with Cows, *pp. 218–219*

Married Love

A NEW CONTRIBUTION TO THE SOLUTION OF SEX DIFFICULTIES

BY

MARIE C. STOPES

*Doctor of Science, London; Doctor of Philosophy,
Munich; Fellow of University College, London;
Fellow of the Royal Society of Literature,
and of the Linnean and Geological
Societies, London*

Federal Judge Lifts Ban

*on the famous book dealing with the
intimate contacts of love in marriage*

In lifting the ban on "Married Love" Federal Judge
John M. Woolsey said that this famous book "was
neither immoral nor obscene, but highly informative . . .
it pleads with seriousness, and not without some elo-
quence, for a better understanding by husbands of the
physical and emotional side of the sex life of their wives.

. . . I cannot imagine a normal mind to which this book
would seem to be obscene or immoral within the proper
definition of those words, or whose sex impulses would
be stirred by reading it. . . . The book before me here
has as its whole thesis the strengthening of the centri-
petal forces in marriage, and instead of being inhospit-
ably received, it should, I think, be welcomed within
our borders."

ABOVE *Married Love* The book that
"crashed into English society like
a bombshell" in 1918 was widely
published. This edition by Eugenics
Publishing in New York, 1931, used
the US controversy to sell copies, a
tactic much used in marketing today.
Stopes was a moderate supporter
of eugenics, like many progressive
thinkers of her day.

ABOVE RIGHT *Maisie's Marriage*
In 1923 came a film adaptation
of *Married Love*, starring silent-
screen actress Lillian Hall-Davis.
Again using of the book's
controversy to promote the film,
and suggestive of a "sex romp"
(rather than the serious marital
guide as intended), the film was
also subject to an aggressive
censorship campaign.

Connections

Guidance in the Marital Home

*A significant sector of publishing includes guides for people trying to improve themselves.
In its day,* Married Love *was hugely important in changing ideas.*

Many writers regard *Self-Help* (1859) by the Victorian writer Samuel Smiles (1812–1904) as the foundation stone for all attempts to provide guide and instruction. In fact, since the invention of printing (and possibly since the start of writing) authors have written manuals on how to succeed in a particular field— such as some of the Onitsha street literature. Smiles' book was enormously successful (a quarter of a million copies were sold in the author's lifetime), partly because his prescriptions matched the ethos of the time; his book has been described as "the Bible of mid-Victorian liberalism." It paved the way for the "self-help" industry that was to come.

Discontent with the treatment of women was nothing new, but by the early 20th century, educated women were often expressing their frustration about their role in life. In many cases, this led to the women's suffrage movement; for others, their interest was concentrated on their own personal lives and the burdens of childbearing. The work of Margaret Sanger (1879–1966) in distributing contraceptive information in the US forced her in 1915 to flee to Europe to avoid prosecution, and her situation attracted Marie Stopes (1880–1958), an eminent paleobotanist working at University College London. Possibly dissatisfied by her marriage to a Canadian botanist (annulled in 1915), Stopes started to devote more time to sexological matters—work in which she was influenced by Havelock Ellis' seminal series of *Studies in the Psychology of Sex* (1897–1928).

Stopes wrote *Married Love*, she said, to increase the joys of marriage and to show how sorrow could

be avoided. It was too frank for many publishers to consider (and until 1931 its distribution in the US was banned as obscene by the US Customs Service). Its publication early in 1918 from Fifield & Co., a small publisher in London, came only because Humphrey Roe (1878–1949) underwrote the production costs. It was followed in November 1918 by *Wise Parenthood*, which dealt explicitly with contraception. Humphrey Roe was a forgotten pioneer: marrying Marie Stopes in 1918, he joined her in setting up the first British birth-control clinic in Islington, north London, in 1921, and he worked tirelessly to administer and fund the work while his wife publicized the spread of birth-control clinics to other cities.

Scandalous by the standards of the time, and found offensive by the Anglican Bishops as well as the Roman Catholic Church, *Married Love* was issued just as the floodgates of feminist emancipation started to open. It was an enormously successful book in Britain, widely read by many middle-class women, while the contraceptive advice in *Wise Parenthood* was important for poorer classes. In 1935, an American survey judged *Married Love* to be among the 25 most influential books of the previous half-century, and over a million copies were sold.

RIGHT *How to be Personally Efficient* Two years before the issue of *Married Love* was this efficiency guide, published in New York by System: The Magazine of Business. With illustrations and underscored by a previous reader, it describes how to run a "tickler" file, foreshadowing today's business bible, *Getting Things Done*.

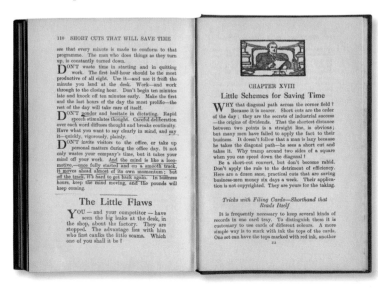

The Limits of Political Propaganda

Enlightenment and 19th-century thinkers looked forward to steady improvements in the civilized world. However, the 20th century plumbed new depths of barbarism, and new totalitarian rulers learned to exploit the media. Others found subtle ways to resist.

BELOW **"Dear Kitty"** The cheerful red-plaid cover of this child's notebook masks its provenance: the first journal given to Anne Frank on her 13th birthday, June 12, 1942. She began writing it two days later, shortly before the family went into hiding in the "Secret Annexe." She maintained her journal, in three volumes, throughout their confinement, until August 1, 1944, when the family were arrested. These pages show Anne with her sister Margot; both were to succumb to typhus in Bergen-Belsen camp.

Stalin reputedly commented that, "Death solves all problems. No man, no problem," and the organization of open and systematic mass killings against the bourgeoisie became USSR policy in the Red Terror of the 1920s. After he obtained power in Germany in 1933, Hitler developed similarly oppressive policies. Between them, Hitler and Stalin were responsible for tens of millions of deaths in Europe, often of the most horrible kind.

Dictators often resorted to printing to justify their objectives, using skilful and persuasive propaganda. There were many Western apologists (such as Walter Duranty or Beatrice Webb) for the Soviet regime and Hitler's *Mein Kampf* (1925) sold in the millions in Germany and elsewhere.

Resistance publishing is an active response to tyranny (see Kamiński's *Stones for the Rampart*, pages 226–227). Books written by Jews sent by the Nazis to the death camps are particularly memorable, including Primo Levi's *If This is a Man* (1947), about his incarceration at Auschwitz, or Aleksandr

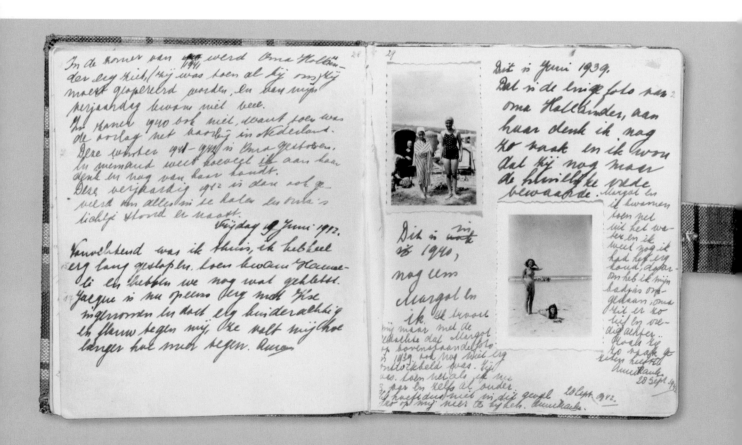

Solzhenitsyn's *One Day in the Life of Ivan Denisovich* (1962), about life in a Soviet labor camp.

Irène Némirovsky's (1903–42) *Suite Française*, a novel portraying the early period of the German occupation of France, was written secretly in 1940–42 before Némirovsky died in Auschwitz in 1942. Rediscovered by her daughter over fifty years later, it was published in 2004, when it won the French literary award, the Prix Renaudot, and has been made into a film. In many ways the history parallels that of the better-known *Diary of a Young Girl*, by Anne Frank, first published in the Netherlands as *Het Achterhuis* (*The Secret Annexe*) in 1947.

Anne Frank (1929–45) was a Jewish child, whose parents emigrated from Frankfurt when Hitler gained power in 1933. Anne's diary was written while the Franks were hiding in Amsterdam, and she continued it until the family were captured in 1944. She was sent to the Bergen-Belsen concentration camp, where she died of typhus early in 1945, a few weeks before the camp was liberated by the British army. Remarkably,

the diary survived, and after the war her father Otto Frank (the only family survivor) prepared it for publication. It was an immediate success, with countless editions and dramatizations drawn from her work. Hated by holocaust-deniers (who still claim it to be fake) the diary has been an inspiration to many. Nelson Mandela, who read it while in prison, said he gained much encouragement from it: "It kept our spirits high, and reinforced our confidence in the invincibility of the cause of freedom and justice."

Connections

For other resistance publishing, see

Kamiński's Stones for the Rampart, pp. 226–227

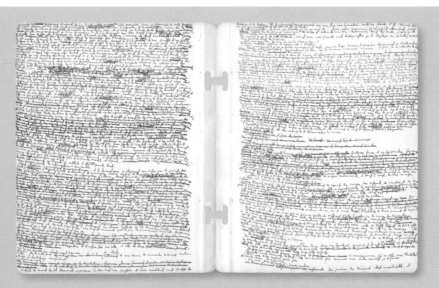

ABOVE ***Het Achterhuis*, 1947** Anne's notebooks were rescued by Miep Gies, who helped shelter the Franks. Since this first edition, abridged and published by her father Otto Frank (it translates as *The Annexe: Diary Notes 14 June 1942–1 August 1944*), the diary has appeared in numerous revised editions and many languages.

ABOVE ***Suite Française*** The miniscule writing covers the pages of Irène Némirovsky's notebook, in which all volumes of her book were recorded. The Kiev-born Jewish emigré was unable to obtain French citizenship and, despite her conversion to Catholicism, in 1942, as "a stateless person of Jewish descent," she was deported to Auschwitz.

CHAPTER

11

Digitization & the Future of the Book

Some people believe that the coming of e-books will replace traditional books and change publication forever. But will it really be much different from the challenges the printed book has faced in the past?

RIGHT **Robotic adventures**
In her book, *One Thousand Years of Manga* (Flammarion, 2007, page 151 shown here), Brigitte Koyama-Richard discusses the phenomenon of *Astro Boy*: First published in graphic novel **format**, then serialized for newspapers, translated (with its illustrations flipped for English reading from left to right), televised, made into a film and finally adapted for video gaming, merchandising and as an e-book, this popular manga character is an example of the fluid and interactive nature of modern publishing. See pp. 248–249.

259
Tezuka Osamu, *Astro Boy*, 1960 © Tezuka Production

The historian of the telegraph, Tom Standage, used the word chronocentricity to reflect the belief that our generation is on the cusp of history. Much writing about the future of communication and the ways in which new technologies will create a rosy future, is of the kind he described. It is hyperbole (see pp. 238–239). Naturally, those pushing for new processes like to believe that their changes will result in improvements. The notion that digitizing the texts of books would remove all the problems of care and maintenance of physical books is common. It has been taken as a decisive argument for those in Project Gutenberg, Open Library or the obsolete Universal Digital Library to put much money and effort into such scanning, although the projects largely ignore the realities of copyright and rights of ownership, and they are oblivious to the need for the best texts (see pp. 240–241 and 242–243).

THE INTERNET

There is no doubt that the coming of the Internet has increased the range of sources of information to users. To have to rely on only the *Encyclopedia Britannica* rather than tools such as Wikipedia would be a great loss for many searchers of information. But it is good to remember what Diderot wrote about the contributors to the great *Encyclopédie* (see pp. 158–159), that some "were weak, mediocre or completely bad." He concluded that the work was full of things "badly observed, half digested, good, bad, detestable, true, false and uncertain, and always incoherent and disparate." Despite the best efforts of those in charge of Wikipedia, or even much more tightly controlled works such as the *Oxford Dictionary of National Biography*, errors, omissions, biases and misinformation are still prevalent.

ACCESS TO INFORMATION

In retrospect, the free-for-all piracy in 19th-century publishing seemed good for book buyers and readers, but one of the most troubling features of the current scene has been the growth of privately owned copyrights and permissions, often reducing access for potential readers. The publishing world is concentrated in a small number of agents, able to fix prices unnecessarily high, as has been shown by the huge increases in the costs of subscriptions to scientific journals—so libraries' purchasing policies are skewed.

Many book lovers bemoan the increasing rarity of independent booksellers. For writers, getting their

books accepted through an agent is increasingly difficult. At the same time it seems much easier to self-publish than ever before. Authors who choose to take this course have to bear the production costs themselves and give large discounts to Amazon and other distributors, or create their own means of selling their publications. **Subscription publishing** is now common again and direct personal publishing outside the regular book trade is on the increase (see pp. 244–245).

The information explosion—too many books being published—means that libraries can afford to buy fewer. Fremont Rider's old prediction of the exponential growth of research libraries is reflected by increasing costs in all libraries. Even national libraries have to trim their sails and resort to sometimes highly undesirable cost-cutting measures. The idea of free public library service throughout Britain is being abandoned, and in the US public libraries', roles are being reassessed. Clearly, public libraries must have computers and provide access to a range of expensive online services—but do they need **paper** books? Some foolhardy administrators think not: the first *deliberately* bookless public library was opened in Texas in 2013.

Many writers favor the switch to electronic publishing, but it is also argued by some that the failures of UNESCO (and governments) to alter the developed world's dominance of the world media system ensures that poorer countries remain inadequately served. Few of the online reports about the coming of the e-book address the needs of would-be readers in countries that are computer poor, or may even still lack a reliable supply of electricity. The gap between information-poorer people and the well-informed is increasing. And in all developed societies, there are always large bodies of people unable to use online information sources. The Internet has brought many benefits for the computer savvy, but it has also greatly increased the possibility of scams, frauds, deceptions and deliberate misinformation, just as the introduction of the telegraph did in the 19th century.

A PROFITABLE TRADE?

For publishers, there are risks of bankruptcy from switching to publishing e-books too soon, or at the wrong price, just as it is risky for publishers who stay with physical books alone. Prudent businessmen hedge their bets and introduce fresh charges when they can. All major publishers now allow libraries to make unlimited loans of e-books, as had always been

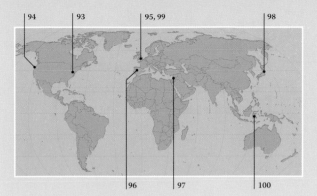

possible with traditional physical books. But will this last? HarperCollins recently announced that it would allow libraries to circulate their e-books only 26 times, after which the text will be deleted. Good for publishers; not so good for libraries or readers.

None of us can foresee the future of the book. In the short term digitization has brought enormous benefits in facilitating improvement in some tools (see pp. 246–247). Being able to scan through many other online services is good for readers. For the scholars in charge of such materials, their ability to do fresh things (as with the Archimedes Palimpsest, or in editing the Marciana *Iliad*) has been exhilarating. But such digitization involves costs, and though at present governments are still providing funding, it is at levels that will probably not be maintained (any more than libraries' book funds are being supported now).

Optimists see the future as bright: in a few years, they say, there might be fewer books being published, but they believe these books will be better edited, better designed and better printed (see pp. 248–249 and 250–251). This may become true, but there is little evidence yet to support it. Some critics take a much more pessimistic view. One states bluntly that the book is dead, and has been dead for some time—that it has succumbed to antibooks, that is, the "marketing-driven, ideas-free" creations from the book trade, which will sell but will also trivialize publication. Many pulp fiction and even manga titles can equally be described as antibooks. There are plenty of these published in hard copy, and for centuries critics have complained about the poor taste of readers, but the proportion of e-books of this kind seems uncomfortably high.

In poorer countries, and for the information-poor segments of populations who want to read, traditional forms of publication have a long future. The tradition in many countries of food stalls, or the Western development of fast-food services, have not wiped out peoples' desire to eat well. So publication of traditional books will still flourish (see pp. 252–253). Undoubtedly e-publication is to last (but not perhaps in its current hamburger-like style); and by the end of the 21st century, electronic publishing will perhaps be creating books as good as have been produced in the past few thousand years.

ABOVE **The craftsman-publisher** Dard Hunter examining an impression of *Old Papermaking* in his letterpress workshop at the Mountain House Press, Chillicothe, Ohio, in 1922.

RIGHT *Old Papermaking* The title page of Dard Hunter's extraordinary "one-man book," printed on his own paper with a typeface designed and cast by himself. His printer's mark, with its branch and leaf design, incorporates a bull's head—an old **watermark** device used as early as 1310.

OLD PAPERMAKING

BY
DARD HUNTER

MCMXXIII

All His Own Work

Industrialization has replaced hand methods in producing books for ever. Or has it? Individualists like Dard Hunter went successfully in the opposite direction.

The early 20th-century dissatisfaction with some aspects of modern life took many forms. Production of books intended to change people through political or social means was common in the early 1900s; others sought to change people's artistic beliefs and practices. Even traditionalists, who wanted only to make handsomer books, were also mild revolutionaries.

Dard Hunter (1883–1966) could have been one of these. Growing up in an Ohio family owning a newspaper and with artistic interests, it was natural that, in 1904, Hunter should join Elbert Hubbard at The Roycrofters, Hubbard's artistic arts-and-crafts community in upstate New York. There he made wood carvings, bound books, did calligraphy and made stained glass, jewelry and furniture. Hunter had a strong sense of design and his art-nouveau creations are now highly valued by collectors. Dissatisfied by the commercialism he saw in The Roycrofters, in 1910 he took himself to Vienna to study at the Wiener Werkstätte (then probably the most important of all craft workshops in the world), and included printing among his courses of study. In 1911 he moved to London, working as an advertising designer—and there, in the Science Museum, he saw a display of papermaking equipment and the punches, molds and matrices needed for casting printing **type**.

Hunter became an expert on the history of papermaking, exploring widely in Europe and Asia to see the various methods traditionally used. (His collection later formed the basis for the American Museum of Papermaking.) For years in the 1920s, he ran a papermill at Marlborough-on-Hudson, producing the only handmade paper in the US. And in Marlborough he printed his own books about papermaking, using types designed, cut and cast by himself to print (on paper he had made) the books that he then bound and published.

Individual hand labor, using age-old methods instead of the best modern processes, seems to many to be mere willfulness. It is not. Many people still set type and print by hand; others make their own paper, and some even build their own printing presses and cut punches for type—and their publications are eagerly sought and bought. Few, however, emulate Hunter's amazing work.

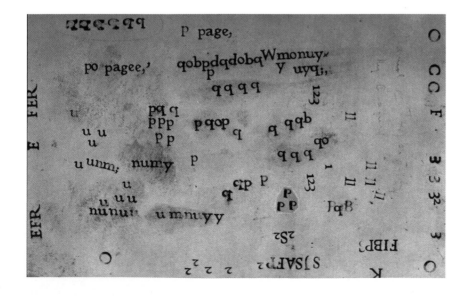

LEFT The smoke proof Hunter spent four years handcutting 63 punches to cast his **font**. His smoke proof (using soot from an open flame to leave an impression on a partially filed punch) shows his success in capturing the lively, free strokes found in early typefaces but often lost in machine-cut modern types.

Connections

For another interpretation of arts and crafts, see

Cranach-Presse's Hamlet, *pp. 214–215*

For another American interpretation of the arts and crafts message, see

Whitman's Leaves of Grass, *pp. 216–217*

Star charts, logarithms and many other tables were difficult to prepare, and equally hard to print accurately in the old days before computers. RAND's 1955 manual marked the move to automation, and is still widely used today.

Charles Babbage's difference engine of 1832 (now in the Science Museum in London) was designed to automate production of error-free mathematical tables. Babbage's machine never worked satisfactorily, and was regarded almost beyond the capabilities of early Victorian engineering; it employed almost all the concepts of the modern electronic computer.

The need for absolute accuracy in the calculations and in the printing of these tables was vital; it was slow, laborious work, making it likely for errors to be overlooked when proofreading. In the intensified mathematical calculations for cryptography in World War II, or in the scientific and engineering work for the Manhattan Project, large numbers of random numbers were vitally useful, but also hard to produce.

Work on *A Million Random Digits* started in 1947 at the Project RAND (then an offshoot of the Douglas Aircraft Company). This was long before reliable electronic computers were available, and RAND staff used an electronic "roulette wheel" and a random-frequency pulse source to generate the numbers. These numbers were transposed into an IBM card punch (IBM

The Last of the Old,

```
230                         TABLE OF RANDOM DIGITS

11450   74643 91686   64861 13547   47668 02710   11434 82867   40442 23126
11451   30774 56770   07259 58864   02002 78870   29737 79078   03891 96198
11452   52766 31005   71786 78399   41418 73730   44254 81034   81391 60870
11453   30583 57645   02821 46759   21611 81875   75570 71403   95020 90567
11454   11411 87781   95412 14734   68216 24237   64399 57190   62003 08072

11455   65154 65573   06505 85246   28223 48663   84092 80996   62804 25062
11456   71484 49166   54358 28045   90602 26369   18826 34129   11186 02587
11457   36886 15978   25701 88856   99666 72497   28170 74573   66399 98915
11458   31911 32493   55851 22810   77446 47338   58709 00366   76974 89213
11459   57668 83978   67201 95886   02009 87160   63753 12256   84441 23567

11460   20180 80993   05486 83908   29691 75989   16955 24709   66116 55376
11461   29450 78893   24478 40084   96185 64091   74278 19220   59232 79651
11462   10645 25607   05493 66388   14886 10433   13541 60814   84317 56135
11463   86989 65289   55234 46428   57719 18708   88916 98692   40281 81694
11464   81822 31790   27929 60106   04794 50792   52855 69708   54471 98480

11465   57260 73820   40482 50328   08141 63218   92180 33241   88052 99353
11466   03162 15444   20152 57789   87027 24196   69223 03376   28451 60351
11467   03883 01325   75192 63458   69469 82978   39120 56925   58287 37961
11468   20476 36163   49805 39896   40557 89825   99027 68148   68330 14547
11469   04097 82269   13198 82429   30119 06488   40897 77511   82718 20536

11470   03150 81213   38131 72824   38659 60749   64581 64225   07982 13359
11471   41868 08277   15733 03512   66062 55144   42684 92562   95855 18976
11472   19019 75509   82239 46407   80331 67153   97832 07365   78527 25388
11473   66762 65374   73880 42723   52871 61036   35039 70330   19690 65487
11474   56984 25574   51915 47671   32288 94925   46278 62789   66452 20813

11475   62919 32771   60512 67786   62409 25006   15544 27585   41141 07056
11476   80152 53210   58708 63052   29172 61110   50802 61103   31451 73705
11477   14609 03458   36701 61286   55876 76651   12026 57579   63041 00518
11478   69685 96134   85288 20667   85030 25703   24172 75414   94525 98963
11479   37653 41665   23805 16495   50566 92923   58570 37989   14454 96483

11480   97333 40313   38311 79632   88471 94287   18842 56481   10727 78168
11481   46918 35923   43219 89408   42015 70960   39767 33981   00896 62632
11482   77647 92375   95821 56223   20137 50993   01956 37476   65479 37315
11483   84557 54389   92845 66027   25750 75426   74213 54278   87040 87720
11484   50184 53941   77795 47527   99423 48280   94101 96132   65778 55536

11485   62994 33610   61432 81063   07104 72979   67234 51208   58087 64686
11486   74536 61392   54720 01452   23781 37295   24279 36401   84360 97841
11487   24945 28226   08113 79223   78135 43679   40184 67041   13070 51304
11488   76597 61745   07848 59773   88922 31500   89386 01970   31954 74586
11489   21739 73880   84999 71712   20223 04734   05297 38494   57925 83158

11490   76373 36578   07987 73464   86703 43769   38113 85094   76527 89307
11491   75771 17498   31380 65347   86809 22856   80806 83634   08719 34906
11492   37509 95478   66738 53649   66346 55218   73532 43708   97621 39974
11493   26800 77759   78505 67784   64526 05422   54794 98671   74839 79856
11494   65925 13968   71642 98512   87510 56434   93220 76328   53413 17961

11495   50573 71610   48683 29869   32535 75387   22438 84636   94631 27382
11496   83160 02118   84936 15513   18912 48738   72173 28797   17683 88883
11497   80436 58377   66896 58495   27405 17933   89367 75965   93790 58615
11498   74836 84165   82436 68509   23923 12254   28278 69602   49651 70140
11499   80971 88014   58161 70037   08593 81048   90612 70159   47830 03778
```

the First of the New

```
                          TABLE OF RANDOM DIGITS                        231

11500   88473 86062   26357 01678   05270 80406   62301 23293   85734 32590
11501   00677 42981   84552 44832   67946 61532   79109 32073   13354 78578
11502   25227 51260   14800 19101   03146 12068   18261 06193   45909 65339
11503   15386 68200   21492 71402   76801 35235   49676 75306   52969 77447
11504   42021 40308   91104 34789   93269 77750   51646 95883   27282 26277

11505   63058 06498   49339 33314   49597 95931   44854 67348   91633 79473
11506   32548 69104   89073 32037   14556 70568   58821 37003   04390 86496
11507   03521 52177   24816 01706   79363 84378   70843 02090   85945 64113
11508   39575 90626   35889 82962   93759 92582   20979 57479   65739 11110
11509   58252 56687   60412 05060   95974 50183   88659 76568   45373 54231

11510   56440 69169   05939 57516   85127 74159   53295 29028   07409 28140
11511   16812 18195   88209 39856   03187 05605   43348 65589   51283 68224
11512   56503 14023   69475 37217   11465 15872   05551 37231   68175 18132
11513   96508 90101   11990 61199   75399 78214   84891 01376   05039 43632
11514   68958 56862   60433 07784   37721 96521   85412 13941   63969 45395

11515   26721 12583   44793 12071   83645 44062   86684 80890   09152 60050
11516   01476 19255   58656 26401   27356 38443   55210 61493   89832 07578
11517   45924 27655   27730 78321   45402 46568   64053 39814   74960 60944
11518   79516 79027   96227 72473   21231 68748   90204 92330   16216 09483
11519   59946 54123   38645 56734   87427 38049   88471 07421   53080 28515

11520   89056 71858   84058 44154   47929 94196   90847 40905   39151 12029
11521   07056 34611   45456 68268   31718 09715   80414 64095   24464 52799
11522   66189 03099   16595 30601   31691 38657   59600 24443   47978 35730
11523   85281 53288   58972 51531   02406 72117   85547 27445   79581 61608
11524   34761 22435   75006 61241   48628 62840   62633 34982   79051 76314

11525   45549 16045   96353 80376   64802 46062   39519 08688   18254 09915
11526   29337 45746   00844 79084   45838 22246   11095 05209   05113 83895
11527   44509 72387   39414 01011   46568 25718   62591 00174   38633 52966
11528   15068 41200   32705 47327   64465 50395   97110 31292   02965 37147
11529   59253 23492   55166 76780   33945 90298   39736 62674   00787 98482

11530   17140 07016   53376 07582   06899 32503   24412 29650   97759 02905
11531   87048 20624   23285 78268   13122 78242   40515 18454   97122 29628
11532   90254 79631   05936 68057   22760 38809   29233 81372   49252 28497
11533   66090 41296   19263 10253   33878 80280   33407 44464   23229 60740
11534   54672 30805   03962 93237   40900 90912   20746 63914   65456 32138

11535   99080 08088   99211 80001   88691 58425   52324 11449   18830 45387
11536   22859 21563   17374 20731   42124 17219   99392 63681   20452 19714
11537   65013 58031   22092 79881   34695 01615   28233 68809   35091 82223
11538   87296 05362   95779 54816   80032 94335   71581 72691   84058 39495
11539   61336 19425   24408 74091   19730 39832   49166 84284   01851 29579

11540   93134 41529   85992 45493   68165 02129   73858 54280   29281 12449
11541   80388 28010   93018 21652   32608 88409   63041 77051   93107 68856
11542   80214 71603   52837 90272   52141 58642   93933 25183   30994 54332
11543   74165 63881   77261 69394   29194 25046   23948 13048   57594 58886
11544   31361 68333   55171 96461   20694 31275   88884 71366   13054 03764

11545   48570 53579   64703 97498   67888 07817   34223 61667   43474 29179
11546   97894 36631   14389 59041   32600 08865   69364 99415   81194 82304
11547   77563 53771   54527 83456   23914 57808   67250 92991   91474 96012
11548   39903 34555   47585 70546   15704 61087   81728 03973   80652 22179
11549   83877 07815   14813 40666   43906 85802   42125 07164   13056 83161
```

LEFT **A "Bible" of randomness** Deceptively difficult to produce, *A Million Random Digits*, with its unusual random "text," was developed from RAND Corporation's pioneering work in computing, to meet a need for random numbers and deviates that could be used for experiments in probability. It is still widely used today in engineering and econometrics, and employed by statisticians, physicists, market analysts and lottery administrators.

punched cards were then a state-of-the-art digital storage medium). The sets of digits produced by the equipment were checked (it was said) for statistical meaninglessness, but "because of the very nature of the tables, it did not seem necessary to proofread every page of the final manuscript;" other IBM equipment was used to print out the numbers, and the resulting pages used to make printing plates.

Published in 1955, *A Million Random Digits* became widely used in the scientific community, and second-hand copies have a high value for collectors, though RAND's work is totally unreadable to the regular reader. It is almost a perfect example of the "books" described by Charles Lamb: "books which are not books, biblia a-biblia," and he would undoubtedly have included *A Million Random Digits*. The second edition, published in 2001, produced some splendid satirical reviews: "with so many terrific random digits," one reviewer wrote, "it's a shame they didn't sort them to make it easier to find the one you're looking for."

Connections

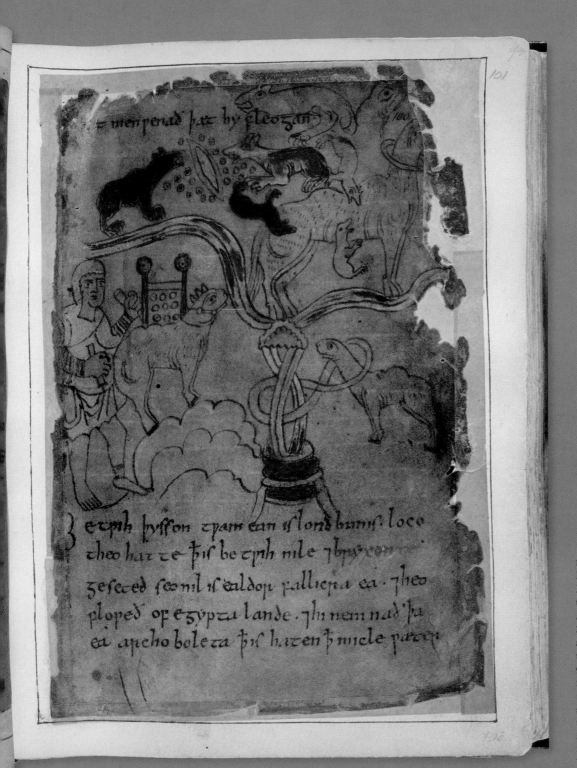

LEFT *Beowulf* The British
Library's Cotton Vitellius A.
XV (shown, fo. 101) contains
the unique manuscript of this
Anglo-Saxon epic—some
3,182 lines about King Scyld
and his struggle against
the monsters Grendel and
Grendel's mother. Dating
from around AD 1000 the
manuscript, copied by two
scribes, was badly damaged
through time and by fire.
Attempted restoration caused
further loss of text.

Modernizing Medieval Manuscripts

A key book in the history of English literature, the surviving early manuscripts damaged
by fire have deteriorated badly. What is the best way to make them usable for scholars?

Beowulf, like Homer's *Iliad* and Virgil's *Aeneid*, is one of the great classic works in European literature and has been widely translated into many languages, as well as modernized for English readers—for the Anglo-Saxon text of this anonymous poem, written in King Canute's reign about 1000 CE, can now be read only by Anglo-Saxon scholars.

The oldest manuscript to have survived, on which all editions are based, is in the British Library, among other important manuscripts collected by Sir Robert Cotton (c. 1570–1631), whose library was by far the most important private collection in England. Disaster struck the Cotton library in 1731: a fire destroyed many of the books, and Cotton Vitellius A.XV (as the *Beowulf* manuscript is known) was badly damaged. Despite the best efforts of conservators over the past 280 years, much of the text of the manuscript's outer leaves was lost. To learn about some of the missing words, scholars have to turn back to an Icelandic scholar, Grímur Jónsson Thorkelin, who transcribed the manuscript in 1786.

Like the Marciana manuscript of the *Iliad* (see pp. 48–49), the manuscript of *Beowulf* was an ideal subject for modern forensic examination

and electronic publishing. Edited by Kevin Kiernan, a scholar at the University of Kentucky, the *Electronic Beowulf* was first released as a freely available download in 1999. It was replaced in 2011 by a DVD edition published by the British Library as *Electronic Beowulf 3.0*. We are now dealing with a computer product, not a book. It reflects the problems of new media: *Electronic Beowulf 3.0* does not support earlier versions, and (because of rapid changes in computer technology in recent years) its presentation is still based on aging software, and reviewers may quibble at the effectiveness of the interface.

Other doubts surface, some similar to those expressed by Johannes Trithemius questioning how long-printed books would last without decaying. (The known longevity of DVDs is still open to debate, but with periods of 2 to 15 years being suggested, long-term survival seems unlikely.) Other Internet alternatives (such as the Project Gutenberg provision of an outdated text) are not useful. *Electronic Beowulf 3.0* was a bold and largely successful attempt to provide a really useful version—though most readers will prefer to read a modern interpretation, such as that of Seamus Heaney.

LEFT *Beowulf* on disk
In 1993 Professor Kevin Kiernan, the leading authority on the manuscript, initiated the digitization of *Beowulf*, which was finally completed in 1998. Transferred to publicly available DVD, the full-color scans of each folio, key supporting documents and a new modernized version of the poem by Seamus Heaney provided readers with unprecedented access to this fragile manuscript.

Connections

The First E-Book?

E-books developed because of the availability of PCs or other cheap, reliable readers. But the ideas were forming many years before advances in technology made them practicable, and a farsighted Spanish school teacher had a brainwave.

Many developments in computing have come from the US, and while it seems unlikely that the first "e-book" should have been invented by a school teacher in Spain, many think that it was. In 1949 Ángela Ruiz Robles (1895–1975) filed a patent application for her new "mechanical encyclopedia." Arranged like a book, with preloaded reels of text that could be easily manipulated by the user, it is very different from the modern e-book readers, but Ruiz's ideas were essentially what an e-book might be. The idea seems to owe something to the design of microfilm readers, and her intention was to provide a single tool that pupils could carry in place of a load of school books. Ruiz was unable to find backers for the production of her *Mechanical Encyclopedia* and, like the American Dynabook of the 1970s, it was never developed beyond its prototype—but the ideas behind it were similar. Inventors often concentrate on the technical requirements and disregard other problems. The prototype of the *Mechanical Encyclopedia* was rather clunky (but so were early pre-electronic calculators) and the problems of copyright, marketing and other matters seem not to have been addressed. But with the Internet and digitization came the potential of a lightweight and mobile new media.

Many writers of fiction, from Laurence Sterne to Georges Perec, have experimented with the book, all using traditional media. At the start of the 21st century, many writers have been attracted to the (apparently new) ways of expression offered by the new media; the rise of desktop publishing and publishing online, with its potential for giving a voice to everyone, has appealed. Publishers scramble to keep up with the demand for the e-book, noting (for the cynically minded) the marketing opportunities and low overheads it offers. In 2000 the successful writer Stephen King's novella, *Riding the Bullet*, was the first to be mass marketed, at first exclusively in e-book **format**. In the first 24 hours, more than 400,000 copies were downloaded by King devotees—a revolution in terms of book sales.

"Crowd-sourcing" was used for the *Oxford English Dictionary* in the 19th century, and it is a method now widely employed. In September 2012, the writer Silvia Hartmann began to write a fantasy novel online (using Google Drive). Her widely publicized "Naked Writer" project attracted input from over 13,000 people who commented on her progress online. She wrote the final part live, before (and in collaboration with) delegates to a conference she organized. *Dragon Lords* (published in 2012 as an e-book and a traditional book on paper) attracted considerable attention, being perhaps the first example of crowd- (and cloud-) sourced fiction. It remains to be seen what effect this experiment has on the future of writing.

It's time to change the world ...

Dragon Lords

Silvia Hartmann

RIGHT *Dragon Lords* The rise of social media, in which everyone has a voice (at least, those with ready access to the Internet) influenced this crowd-sourced venture, written collaboratively online.

Connections

For other educational publications, see

Newbery's Little Pretty Pocket-Book, **pp.** *156–157*

Haüy's Education of the Blind, **pp.** *176–177*

For other reel-to-reel books, see

Sulawesi Lontar, **pp.** *252–253*

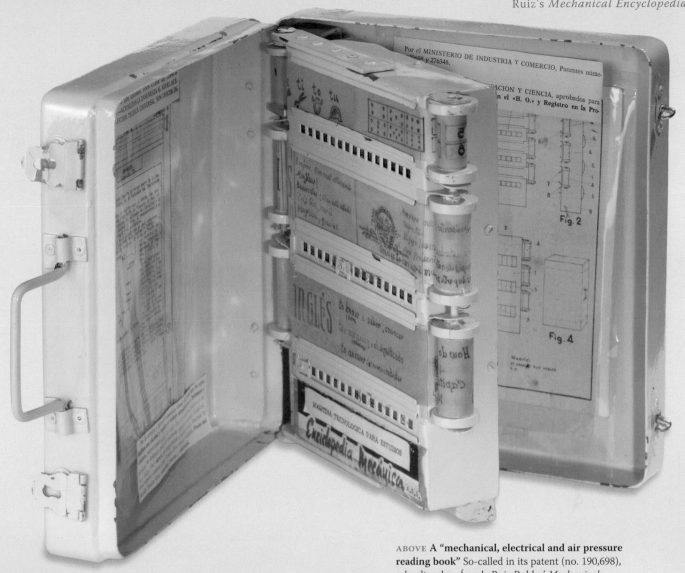

Por el MINISTERIO DE INDUSTRIA Y COMERCIO, Patentes núme-
...0698 y 276346.

...ACION Y CIENCIA, aprobados para
...en el «B. O.» y Registro en la Pro-

Fig. 2

Fig. 4

ABOVE **A "mechanical, electrical and air pressure reading book"** So-called in its patent (no. 190,698), schoolteacher Ángela Ruiz Robles' *Mechanical Encyclopedia*, invented for her pupils, was possibly the world's first e-book. Equipped with coils incorporating what would today be called hypertexts, these moved through the (multilingual) topics. Like the modern e-reader, Robles' contraption had a zoom function, with which the reader could focus on a specific text.

LEFT **The e-reader** The modern e-reader is a marketing success story; its compact form for storing information lends itself to the modern mobile age. Yet it is a reductive process largely focusing on text alone; for many people, reading is about more than just text—and the aesthetic enjoyment of handling traditionally formatted books is lost in transfer.

Multum in Parvo—the Smallest Books

Technical developments have enabled publishers to miniaturize books, creating a new field for collectors. Will nanotechnology create new forms of books quite different from today's e-books?

Miniaturization has long intrigued people. To celebrate the 500th anniversary of Gutenberg's invention, several typefounders produced and gave away single pieces of **type**, with the text of the Lord's Prayer on the head of them—demonstrating their competence in cutting and casting. Many engravers and calligraphers undertook similar feats of creating minute texts, readable only with the use of a magnifying glass. Producing small books for children also appealed, though the technical problems were considerable.

Collecting miniature books is a well-known hobby, and there is even an international society devoted to the collection and study of small books, generally defined as books no more than 3 inches (76 millimeters) in height, width or thickness. The earliest known printed book of such a small size is a religious text printed in 1475.

One firm of publishers seized on producing miniatures as gift books for a niche market. In the late 19th century, such "small thinking" was made

practicable because of improvements in **lithography** and photo-engraving. David Bryce & Son of Glasgow developed a series of such small books, including a dictionary and poetry and a New Testament: all issued with a locket and a magnifying glass. Their edition of the Koran was inspired, for some Muslim soldiers liked to carry one as a talisman. Many Muslim soldiers in the Indian army serving in the trenches of World War I carried these into battle.

The idea of books as talismans is an old one and emerges sometimes in unexpected ways. One of the great advantages of modern technology is the ability to store a huge amount of information in a tiny space. In his seminal 1945 article "As We May Think," the influential American inventor Vannevar Bush foresaw a world with nanotechnology in which the size of the *Encyclopedia Britannica* could be compressed to the size of a matchbox. Recent work in Israel, drawing upon the earlier work of Pawan Sinha of the Massachusetts Institute of Technology, demonstrates the possibilities clearly: at the Technion-Israeli Institute of Technology, in Haifa, staff and students at the Russell Berrie Nanotechnology Institute created a nano-Torah, holding the whole text of the Hebrew Bible, etched using a focused ion beam onto a 0.5 mm^2 gold-plated silicon chip. As a way of interesting students in nanotechnology, the intention could hardly be bettered. The Technion Nano Bible was a unique gift, presented by Israel's President Shimon Peres to Pope Benedict XVI during the Pope's 2009 visit to the Holy Land. At the moment, this is only one example of what can be done, but the possibilities in the future of information science for nanotechnology are enormous. What will be the future for the e-book?

LEFT **Miniature Koran** This fine miniature Koran, gold-stamped red or black morocco with gilt edges, was produced by David Bryce & Sons between about 1900–10. Like their Bibles, it was issued with a metal locket and magnifying glass, and served as a talisman for some Muslim soldiers in the trenches of World War I.

RIGHT **A Bible on a pin head** The entire text of the Hebrew Bible was inscribed by Technion students at the Russell Berrie Nanotechnology Institute on a 0.5 mm^2 gold-etched silicon chip. Using the digitized source text, which was translated into a suitable **font**, more than 1.2 million letters, 0.0002 mm in height, were incised into the chip using a focused beam of gallium ions.

Connections

For other advances in information storage, see

Carlson's Lab Book, **pp.** *212–213*

Electronic Beowulf, **pp.** *242–243*

Modern Technology and Manga

A new form of publishing developed in Japan in the 1950s, manga techniques were widely copied throughout the world—and new methods of color printing are changing all book production methods as well.

Since the middle of the 20th century, advances in printing technology have made the publication of profusely illustrated books of all kinds much simpler and more affordable. In earlier times, very few printers could reliably reproduce color and colored illustration could be prohibitively expensive. The complexity of the logistics often discouraged publishers from working together to produce illustrated editions in more than one language. The lack of a worldwide market prevented economies of scale being used, except for special categories such as travel guides or Tauchnitz's paperbacks, which were not picture-based editions.

Advances in letterpress printing encouraged publishers to use color photographic illustration— for example, in such different magazines as *National Geographic* and *Playboy*, both printed in large editions in several countries. The logistical difficulties of a generation ago have been removed by the emergence of the Internet and the development of high-quality four-color offset-litho presses (as used in this book). Accurate color reproduction can be guaranteed and a huge range of well-illustrated books can be published at modest prices. We could have chosen books on gardening, natural history or travel to represent this category; instead we use a historical survey of a modern Japanese publishing phenomenon: manga.

In France and Belgium, **graphic novels** or **bds** (***bandes dessinées***), such as the Asterix and Tintin series, with text and pictures intermingled, became widely popular, just as comics were in the US. There was a strong 18th-century tradition for picture books, known as *kibyōshi*, in Japan—often seen as the ancestor of manga. Manga production emerged in Japanese publishing during the American occupation after World War II, and was strongly influenced by Disney. One of the most famous series, Astro Boy, started in 1952, was written by Osamu Tezuka, a writer who was strongly influenced by Disney. Its

142
Kawanabe Kyōsai, *La Bataille de Naoba, après 1871* © Kawanabe Kyōsai Memorial Museum
Cette bataille fut menée par Tokugawa Ieyasu contre les partisans de Toyotomi Hideyori, en 1615. Il avait toujours été interdit, à l'époque d'Edo, de représenter le *shōgun*. Quatre ans après le début de l'ère Meiji, ce sujet est donc nouveau. D'une remarquable puissance, les lignes provenant de la droite font ressentir la violence de l'explosion qui a réduit en miettes le *Tōzi*.

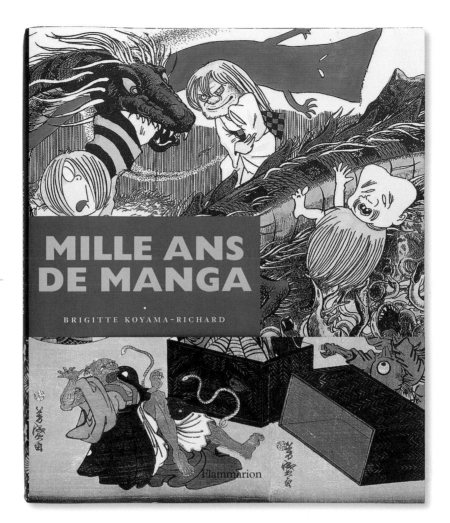

RIGHT *One Thousand Years of Manga* Brigitte Koyama-Richard's scholarly book was researched in Japan, edited in France, and a French and an English edition were simultaneously printed in Singapore. Like many other books produced by the use of computer-based files and four-color printing, it is an example of the effective authorial/editing/printing methods used by publishers today.

LEFT **Kawanabe Kyōsai** (1831–1889) was perhaps the last virtuoso in traditional Japanese painting, and his portrayal of historical events got him into a lot of trouble with the authorities. His memorable **woodcut** depiction (after 1872) of an explosion in a 1615 Osaka battle pointed forward to the style of art used in manga, as discussed in Koyama-Richard's book.

theme, though concerned with atomic energy, was essentially peaceful; similarly another famous and popular manga series, Hiro Arikawa's *Toshokan Sensō* (Library War), was developed as an argument for free libraries and freedom of expression.

This book, *One Thousand Years of Manga*, represents the best of modern printing and publishing methods. The development of anime, animated films, and the creation of subsidiary industries (producing computer games, dolls and manga-based soft toys) have changed the nature of publishing in Japan and beyond, just as four-color printing has revolutionized our concept of what books should look like. Will it be manga, not e-books, that overtake traditional books?

Connections

For earlier Japanese publications, see

Shōtoku's Dharani, pp. 30–31

Murasaki's The Tale of Genji, pp. 82–83

For other books intended for popular reading, see

Powell's Old Grizzly Adams, pp. 192–193

Nnadozie's Beware of Harlots, pp. 222–223

Are "Artists' Books" Books?

"Books" are much more than just vehicles for text; their place in people's minds can vary wildly from love through indifference to hatred. When a book becomes a vehicle for an artist's imagination, it can sometimes take an unexpected form.

Some readers see a book merely as a vehicle for text, the same thinking that was behind the initiatives of Kindle and other e-readers. Many others believe that having the text is only the starting point for further imaginative work, exploiting illustrations and other aspects of a book's production through materials, color and tactile qualities. Fine printing is part of this—texts whose material form is intended to be viewed, touched and enjoyed on an aesthetic level, as well as read.

Other artists' books are prepared primarily as a channel for artists to express their aesthetic beliefs. All are planned to be viewed, but many such creations cannot be read at all. These works are also often signed and deliberately limited in number and availability. These books are usually sold to dealers and collectors, rather than stocked in bookshops or provided to be read in libraries: they seem unlikely ever to be replaced by e-books.

Writing about almanacs and directories, Charles Lamb categorized them as "biblia a-biblia," books that could not be read. Some artists' books question and undermine the physical and conceptual foundations of books. In the work of Pablo Neruda and Nicanor Parra, Chile has a long tradition of thoughtful bookish poetry, sensitive to typographic traditions; and the "antibook" (shown here to represent artists' books in general) is very different from Lamb's categories. Its author, Nicanor Parra Sandoval (b. 1914), wrote his Chilean antibooks to challenge traditional concepts of what a book of poetry should be. Parra's "*Me retracto de todo lo dicho*" ("I take back everything I said") is usually repeated at his recitations.

Parra's poem formed the ideal starting point for a London-based Chilean book artist, Francisca Prieto, to make another interpretation of the "antibook." Prieto's work often takes the form of intricately cut paperwork, using origami traditions to create low-relief paper constructions. Her antibook took a rather different form; in her series of "Between Folds," she has used pages from Victorian maps, books and magazines to provide windows through which the Victorian illustrations can be glimpsed. These bring to mind the nightmarish surrealist work of Max Ernst, whose **collages** were also derived from 19th-century engravings (see pp. 220–221).

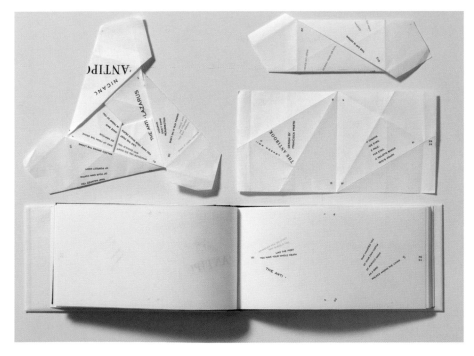

FAR LEFT AND LEFT **The *Antibook*** The interaction between artists and books is traditional, even when the art itself is not. Yet the line between book and artwork varies: Ernst (see pp. 220–221) creates an entirely new but conventionally formatted book, while others such as Francisca Prieto use an existing text (here, Parra's *Antipoems*) as a starting point. Her paper origami icosahedron measures 6 x 6¾ x 7½ inches (15 x 17 x 19 centimeters).

Is it a Book, or is it a Book?

Differing needs dictate different formats to service those needs.
What do readers need from their books?

Of course, it is cheating to include this amazing production from Sulawesi (Indonesia) in a chapter concerned with digitization and e-books. We include it because the **format** is immediately recognizable— not entirely unlike the **scroll** form for Torahs in Jewish worship, or the now obsolete reel-to-reel recording tapes. One would wonder why the Bugis people in Sulawesi adopted this format. Indeed the Bugis and Makassarese were exposed to other forms used in other cultures, and they used the **codex** form as well— so even if you are unable to read the script, you can infer that this book was intended to be read from beginning to end, and that it was probably a book for formal use in ceremonies.

For easy consultation, the scroll format is difficult to use, and any modern researcher working with microfilm hates having to scroll through hundreds of pages to find the ones he or she needs to read. In the ancient times of writing on **papyrus**, the use of the scroll form was understandable, but the Greeks and

Romans rapidly switched to the codex format that we use today because it was much easier to consult and to be able to turn back to the beginning (or to skip to the end). It seems obvious, but people using e-books (whether online or in the e-reader format) still lack the ability to skip around easily. Only the careful design of the layout gives the reader of e-books the contextual information always available in books in codex form.

It needs to be repeated that books are much more than merely vehicles for text. Awareness of the way a book is created, the materials of which it is made, flipping through the volume to see how it is arranged, the intended readership, the clues of the previous ownership and use, and potential problems in its conservation—all these become almost instinctive for experienced readers. (For rare-book custodians, such things as smelling a volume or shaking a leaf to hear the rattle provide further "forensic" information.) This is like an extension to the metadata (such as a book's Dewey class number), which is still largely absent from

e-books. Searching the Amazon "look inside" facility when buying books is useful, but it is a poor substitute for browsing through a printed volume.

The discussions in previous chapters show many instances of the importance of this metadata. It is clear that many custodians of rare books work hard to see that when they digitize books in their collections, potential readers are provided with this metadata. It is not simple: how can a digitized version of the text in this Sulawesi manuscript shown here provide all these clues? It is discouraging that many providers and purveyors of e-books still do not do this, or see the need for it. Until it is done far better than today, the future of e-books will be to survive only as a complement to paper-based books, which will continue to be produced and read.

LEFT Sulawesi reel-to-reel
This *lontar* manuscript, created in South Sulawesi, Indonesia, before 1907, resembles a fishing reel more than a "book" as most of us know them. Using strips of palmyra palm (rather like Ángela Ruiz Robles' *Mechanical Encyclopedia*, see pp. 244–245), its text (an episode of *La Galigo*, a Buginese epic) is rotated between spools.

ABOVE Reels of text The text of another *lontar* manuscript, from Bulukumba in South Sulawesi, is a letter written in Buginese by the queen of Tanette, before 1887.

Connections

A

ABUGIDA (or alphasyllabary): A segmental writing system with characters for consonants plus vowels, so that one would be for "ba," another for "be," a third for "bi" etc., written as a unit. The name comes from the first four characters in the Ethiopian Ge'ez script, just as alphabet is named from the first letters (alpha, beta) in Greek.

ALIM: The agarwood tree (*Aquilaria malaccensis*). Its inner bark is used as a writing surface in Sumatra and other Indonesian islands.

AMHARIC: The Semitic language used in Ethiopia and Eritrea. An ancient language, written with a broad pen in the Ge'ez script, it has its own system of punctuating the text with word divisions and other pointers.

A page of AMHARIC *text on vellum, written in black and red Ge'ez or Ethiopic script, Ethiopia.*

17th century printers' flowers used here to form an abstract ARABESQUE *pattern.*

ARABESQUE: Decorative motif, originally comprising a flowing and stylized representation of acanthus leaves. Widely used in Islamic art (for example, on glazed tiles), the fashion was imported for book decoration, particularly those from Venice. Many of the early printers' flowers or fleurons were derived from abstract arabesque designs.

ATELIER: French for "workshop." In English, the word is used principally to mean the workshops of artists in the fine or decorative arts in which a principal master, with a series of assistants, apprentices and other students, works collaboratively in producing pieces issued in the master's name. In the old guild system, technically every master printer and his workmen and apprentices ran ateliers; but the term usually means those whose work, by master and workmen, was of exceptionally high quality, as in the cases of Michael Wolgemut and Wilhelm Pleydenwurff in Nuremberg, and Thomas Bewick in England. *See:* Schedel's *Nuremberg Chronicle,* pp. 100–101; Bewick's *British Birds,* pp. 172–173.

ASCENDERS: Capital letters in the roman alphabet are all the same height and sit on a uniform baseline (except the Q). Lower-case letters sit on the same baseline. Ascenders are lower-case letters that ascend above the x-height (b, d, f, h, k, l, t). In rare cases (the italic f), letters extend above and below the x-height. *See also:* DESCENDERS.

B

BANDES DESSINÉES (bds): French term used for the popular graphic books published in France and Belgium by, for example, Hergé.

BASTARDA (or *lettre bâtarde*): a Gothic script used in the 14th and 15th centuries in Western Europe. Used for copying of books or documents in the vernacular languages (and very seldom for Latin texts), the scripts use a simplified letterform that could be written at speed. In France and Flanders, the design was good; Caxton's first types in England were a poor interpretation of this style. The use of the French *lettre bâtarde* was superseded by **roman** and **italic** designs in the 16th century, but the German styles developed into the use of **Schwabacher** and **Fraktur** type for printing in German and remained in use until the mid-20th century. *See:* Cristoforo's *Liber Insularum Archipelagi,* pp. 70–71; Caxton's *Chesse Moralysed,* pp. 102–103.

BLACKLETTER: The writing styles and typefaces used in the earliest days of printing. Often used to mean the "Old English" styles used for printing books in English. *See:* Wynkyn's *Demaundes Joyous,* pp. 104–105.

BLOCK BOOKS (also XYLOGRAPHICA): Short books of up to 50 leaves, with both text and illustrations cut on wood, instead of using printing type. Produced in the later 15th century (after Gutenberg's invention of printing), they were usually produced for religious purposes for distribution to a popular audience.

BOUSTROPHEDON: Greek, from *bous* (ox) and *strophē* (turn)— that is, to turn like oxen plowing a field. A bi-directional text, seen in some ancient Greek and Etruscan manuscripts and inscriptions, where alternate lines of writing are reversed. Rather than running from left to right (as in modern European languages), or from right to left as in Semitic languages, alternate lines and characters "turn" to run the other way, being read in the opposite direction.

C

CALENDERING: **Paper** that has been passed through polished rolls to give a smooth surface is called calendered (or hot-pressed) paper. Introduced in the 18th century, its use was well suited for printing **intaglio** prints or **modern-faced** roman types. *See also*: HOLLANDERING.

CAMERA OBSCURA: An optical device used to catch an image through a pinhole into a closed box or chamber, known in ancient times and was used widely as an aid by artists from the 17th century onward. Louis Daguerre's pioneering method of photography employed a camera obscura to make **daguerrotypes**; the use of the word "camera" as a device for photography is derived from this.

CANGJIE: The mythological inventor of the Chinese system of writing. His name is used for a computer inputting system, invented in Taiwan in 1976, with which the ordinary QWERTY keyboard can be used to generate all the characters used in Chinese text.

CAROLINGIAN MINUSCULE: Name given to the style of formal writing developed in the **scriptoria** under Alcuin of York in the reign of Charlemagne in the eighth century. The style became widely used in Western Europe, and the "lower-case" letters we use today (a, b, c, d etc.) are derived from the Carolingian styles. *See*: St. Gall *Cantatorium*, pp. 114–115.

CHANSONS DE GESTE: French epic poems forming the core of legends about the reign of Charlemagne and his successors in the eighth to ninth centuries. Many of them, sometimes thousands of lines long, survived in manuscripts from the 12th to the 15th centuries. There is a very faint echo of them in the Brazilian cordel literature.

CHAPBOOKS: Small booklets, stitched but often unbound cheap lowbrow publications of a popular nature printed in the 18th and early 19th centuries. Sold through pedlars and chapmen in rural areas, or by booksellers in provincial towns as well as in London, chapbooks were similar to the French work issued in Épinal. Sold by the thousands, chapbooks covered similar material as in the *Newgate Calendar* (see pp. 164–165) or penny bloods, and had similarities to the more recent street literature of Nigeria and Brazil (see pp. 222–223).

CHOLIAMBIC: A metrical form in poetry, used in both Greek and Latin poetry in the Classical period.

CODEX/CODICES: Manuscripts in which written sheets were gathered

A **CHAPBOOK** *containing a play,* The Devil's Auction, *printed by letterpress on natural groundwood paper, with an etching by the popular illustrator José Guadalupe Posada, published in Mexico between 1890 and 1932.*

and folded and fastened together in the modern book form. (In classical times, *codex* was used to describe books gathered in this way; *volumen* was used to describe books in which the sheets were fastened to make a **scroll**, as in the Egyptian **papyrus** manuscripts.)

COLLAGE: An artistic technique in which the artist assembles pieces of paper (or other materials) and pastes or mounts them onto a surface to create new works. The late 18th-century flower pictures by Mrs. Delany are an early example, but the method is more closely associated with modern art—particularly surrealists such as Max Ernst and Cubist painters Pablo Picasso and Georges Braque. *See*: Ernst's *Une Semaine de Bonté*, pp. 220–221.

COLOPHON: (1) Text printed at the end of early printing before title pages were introduced, giving the printer's name and the date. In some modern finely printed books, the colophon also includes the statement of limitation and details on typefaces or paper used; (2) Often used (incorrectly) for the printers' devices or publishers' marks, traditionally placed in the colophon or more recently on title pages.

COMPOSITOR: The printer who sets (composes) the texts assigned to him by the master printer. Specialists were employed to set the type for books in Greek or Hebrew, or to compose mathematical texts, but all compositors were necessarily literate, and had to be able to make sense of authors' often illegible manuscripts, and supply correct spellings and punctuation.

CONCRETE POETRY: Verse in which the typographical arrangement of words is as important in conveying the intended effect as the conventional literary content of the poem, as in the work of Marinetti and the Dadaists. *See*: Kamensky's *Tango with Cows*, pp. 218–219; Prieto's *Antibook*, pp. 250–251.

CUNEIFORM: An ancient writing system used in Mesopotamia from about 3300 BCE until about 75 CE, when it was replaced by the Phoenician alphabet and dropped out of use. Using a wedge-shaped reed to press marks into damp clay tablets, the writing system was widely adopted and developed. Of the hundreds of thousands of these tablets that have been excavated, many remain to be deciphered. See: *Epic of Gilgamesh*, pp. 18–19.

CYANOTYPE: A contact photographic process invented by Sir John Herschel in 1842 using

potassium ferricyanide to create prints (the blueprints often used by engineers). For books, the technique was most closely associated with Anna Atkins and some followers. *See*: Atkins' *Photographs of British Algae*, pp. 184–185.

D

DAGUERREOTYPE: An early form of photography developed in France in the 1830s, named for its inventor, Louis Daguerre. It was the first commercial photographic process. The process involved exposing a copper plate with a polished silver surface sensitized by iodine fumes in a camera, and then developing the image over heated mercury vapor. It became a popular process, in particular for portraiture, as refinements in technique allowed for shorter exposure times. *See*: Duperly's *Daguerian Excursions in Jamaica*, pp. 186–187.

Printer's DEVICES: the dolphin and anchor of Aldus Manutius, adapted in 1501 from a motif on the back of an ancient Roman coin given to him by Cardinal Bembo.

DESCENDERS: Lower-case letters that descend below the baseline (g, j, p, q, y). *See also*: ASCENDERS.

DEVICE (or PRINTER'S MARK): A trademark included in a **colophon** or on a title page to allow readers to recognize that it was produced by a particular firm.

DIDOT: (1) The name of a famous dynasty of printers/publishers in France from the 18th to the 19th centuries. (2) The name for a **modern-face roman type** used extensively in France. (3) The European measurement of the sizes of printing type (as **Pica** was used for type sizes in the Anglo-American trade).

DIME NOVEL: A term, used pejoratively, for popular literature produced in the US in the late 19th century. *See*: Powell's *Old Grizzly Adams*, pp. 192–193. *See also*: PENNY DREADFUL.

DISS (distribute/ed): A printing term to mean type that, having been assembled and used, has to be sorted back into the typecases for reuse. The need for dissing was a significant cost until mechanical methods of casting and setting type eliminated the process.

DLUWANG (or DULUANG): Writing surface of the inner bark of the paper mulberry (*Broussonetia papyrifera*) and some other tropical plants, made by stripping it out and beating it to form sheets that, when burnished, are ready for writing.

RIGHT *A plate illustrating letterpress printing, from Didérot and d'Alembert's* L'Encyclopédie, *1751–57, showing: top,* COMPOSITORS *composing and distributing type; center, pieces of type and spaces; below, a composing stick; bottom, type justified to the chosen length.*

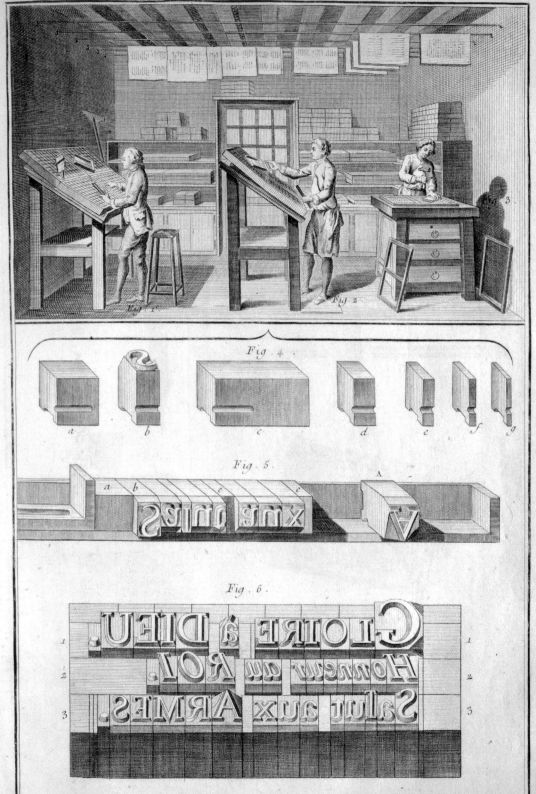

Pl. I.

Fig. 4.

Fig. 5.

Fig. 6.

Goussier Del.

Benard Fecit.

Imprimerie en Lettres, L'Operation de la Casse.

Highly susceptible to insect attack, this bark **paper** was until recently made widely throughout Indonesia and the Philippines, and at earlier times in south China and Southeast Asia. It is still made in the South Pacific, where it is known as **tapa**, and from different plants in Mexico, where it is known as *amate*. *See*: *Boke van Bonang*, pp. 92–93.

DUODECIMO (or 12mo or 12°): A book printed on sheets of pages to make 12 leaves. The **formats** for most early paperbound books were duodecimo *See*: Lehmann's *Invitation to the Waltz*, pp. 224–225.

E

ELECTROTYPE/-ING: The process of making copies on thin sheets of copper by electrolysis for printing purposes, using parallel inventions from St. Petersburg and Liverpool in the late 1830s. (1) Used to make exact copies taken from founders' punches/matrices, facilitating the mass production of Chinese types and enabling Western typefounders to pirate other founders' designs. (2) Used to make copies of engraved **intaglio** plates for printing, as in mid-19th century **nature-printing** processes. (3) Used to make exact copies of relief surfaces (such as pages of printing type or wood engravings) to enable more extensive publication. Widely used from about 1840 until the second half of the 20th century. *See also*: STEREOTYPE/-ING.

EMBLEM BOOKS: A category of illustrated books popular in Western Europe in the 16th and 17th centuries, in which (censors suspected) readers could read meanings in the pictures that were not necessarily stated in the texts. *See*: Erasmus' *De ratione conscribendi epistolas*, pp. 126–127.

F

FASCICLE: A part of a book, often issued to purchasers as a separate item so that readers could use the first parts of the book while editorial work was still in process; frequently in massive reference books and books illustrated with **intaglio** engravings.

FLAP-BOOK *See*: HARLEQUINADE.

FOLIO (or fo or 2°): A sheet of handmade paper, folded in half. Depending on the size of the sheets of paper used, books printed as folios are relatively large, as compared with other **formats** such as **quarto** and **octavo**.

Dragon devouring itself by the tail, with an epigram. From Michael Maier, Atalanta fugiens *[Atlanta fleeing], an alchemical* EMBLEM BOOK *with poems and text and 50 musical fugues (a pun on the title), with engravings by Johann Theodor de Bry, published in Oppenheim, 1618.*

FONT (or fount): The family of types cut and designed to be used together. A fount has characters for each letter in the alphabet: A–Z in the capitals (plus Æ and Œ), a–z in **lowercase** (plus other special characters such as ß), A–Z in small capitals; and capitals and lowercase for **italic**; plus punctuation marks and special characters such as *, & and $. The word **font** often is taken to mean all these "sorts" (different pieces of type), in every different size (as 12-point, 24-point, etc.). Only the largest printing firms had all these; and to be "out of sorts" (often because used type was waiting to be dissed) was a serious problem, unless the printer had ready access to a type foundry.

FORMAT: (1) The size and shape of a book, as determined by the number of times the original sheet of paper has been folded to form the leaves; *See also*: DUODECIMO; FOLIO; OCTAVO; QUARTO. (2) The general physical appearance of a book or other publication, including the paper quality, margins, typefaces and binding.

FRAKTUR: A handsome formal German **blackletter** type used for printing in German (and some other vernacular languages) from the early 16th century to World War II. Its use for printing in Latin and other languages was largely replaced by the use of Antiqua (**roman**) typefaces from the 18th century onward, but many German literary texts continued to be printed in Fraktur. It had no equivalent for **italic** (used for emphasis for books printed in roman types), so printers used either a different blackletter face (**Schwabacher**) or else letterspaced. *See*: Gustav Vasa Bible, pp. 124–125.

*One of the first uses of the **FRAKTUR** type, printed in red on the cover of the Bible of Christian III, known as the Reformation Bible, published in Denmark in 1550. The surrounding wood engraving (detail) is by Erhard Altdorfer.*

G

GRAPHIC NOVEL: A story intended for use by adults (as well as children) in which the plot and action are portrayed by pictures (as in the novels of Lynd Ward); or a combination of pictures and a limited amount of text, as in **bandes dessinées** (bds) or manga.

H

HARLEQUINADES: Known also as metamorphoses, flap-books or turn-up books, harlequinades were first devised by a London publisher, Robert Sayer, and were popular from about 1765 until the early 19th century. A **format** used for books for children, it consisted of two single sheets (usually engraved). The first sheet was folded perpendicularly into four sections. The second sheet was cut in halves, and hinged at the top and bottom edges of the first sheet, so that each flap could be lifted up separately. The sheets were folded into four, and a verse on each section of the flap told a simple story, usually concluding with instructions to turn a flap to continue. When it was turned up or down, the reader saw that half of the new picture fits onto the half of the unraised flap. Lifting one flap after another exposes a surprise unfolding of the story. *See:* Meggedorfer's *Grand Circus*, pp. 198–199.

HIEROGLYPHICS: A formal writing system used by the ancient Egyptians using both **ideographic** and alphabetic elements. For religious literature written on **papyrus** and wood, Egyptians used cursive hieroglyphs. *See: Book of the Dead of Ani*, pp. 22–23.

HOLLANDER: A beating machine developed by the Dutch in 1680 to reduce plant fibers such as linen or hemp to paper pulp for papermaking. It replaced the stamp mills used earlier in European paper mills because it was much faster, but the **paper** made in the hollander was weaker.

HOT-PRESS/ING
See: CALENDERED.

HYPERTEXT: Text displayed on an electronic device in which information (text, tables, images, links to further webpages, etc.) is stored in multiple layers. References to the additional information are displayed in hyperlinks, clickable links often highlighted in a color other than the main text. Clicking the links takes the reader to the new information. The form is increasingly used, for example, in essays, online news bulletins, CVs, and even novels (see *Afternoon, a story*, p. 210). In the latter, hyperlinks act as a virtual crossroads, leading to one plot development over another.

I

IDEOGRAM/IDEOGRAPHIC: Ideograms are symbols that represent ideas directly, rather than words or morphemes, as in alphabets and **abugidas**. The **hieroglyphics** of ancient Egypt and the earliest Chinese systems of writing were of **pictograms** or ideograms, but in the passage of time the symbols attract other more abstract meaning. The earliest Phoenician alphabet from which all modern Western forms descended were pictographic in form—for example, aleph, an ox; beth, a house; gimel, a camel; and daleth, a door.

INCUNABULA: "Cradle books," a word used to describe printed books produced in Europe after Gutenberg's invention. Usually limited to mean those printed in the 15th century, but sometimes taken to include all books printed by 1520.

INSULAR: The art forms of the British Isles and Ireland between about the years 600 and 900 CE. In manuscripts, the *Book of Kells* and the *Lindisfarne Gospels* are the best known examples of this style. *See*: *Book of Kells*, pp. 60–61.

INTAGLIO: Printing processes in which the lines of a picture are engraved or etched into the surface of a metal plate; ink is forced into the recesses of the cut, and paper pressed with great force onto the plate so that the image is transferred to the paper. Much finer detail is possible from intaglio prints than from blocks printed by letterpress, and so the process became fashionable for good work. *See*: Linschoten's *Itinerario*, pp. 132–133; Tomlinson's *Art of Dancing*, pp. 146–147.

ISOLARIOS: "Books of islands," cartographical books produced for sailors and travelers, particularly in Venice and elsewhere in Italy in the 15th and 16th centuries. *See*: Cristoforo's *Liber Insularum Archipelagi*, pp. 70–71.

ITALIC: Humanistic cursive style of writing developed in northern Italy in the 14th century, first cut as a typeface by Aldus Manutius in Venice, using sloped **lowercase** with (upright) roman capitals. A very successful style, **italic** was often used instead of **roman**, but in time became a subsidiary face used with roman. The slope varies from one **font** to another, and upright italics were also cut. *See*: Aldine Virgil, pp. 108–109.

A detail from the Lindisfarne Gospels, *the opening of St. Luke. This parchment gospel book was written and decorated at the end of the seventh century by the monk Eadfrith at the priory of Lindisfarne, an island off the northeast-coast of England. It is one of the finest examples of the* INSULAR *Anglo-hibernian style, using animal, vegetable and mineral pigments from both local and imported sources. The Latin text, in iron gall ink, has a gloss in Old English.*

K

KAMAWA-SA: The most sacred of Burmese manuscripts, consisting of excerpts from the Buddhist Pali Vinaya, written in special scripts on lacquered and gilded lontar leaves.

KHIPU/QUIPU: A memory device made from knotted and twisted fibers as a substitute for writing. Used extensively in Andean civilizations until Spanish colonial times, the system was also reported as used in China as a "rope knot-tying" system when the Yellow Emperor Huangdi ordered the invention of writing about 2625 BCE. *See*: Caral khipu, pp. 20–21.

L

LIMITED EDITION: A statement printed in the book that the size of the edition has been limited. In **private press** books, it is often written or printed in the **colophon**—for example, "This is copy 19" or "19/250" (meaning "this is copy no. 19 of an edition limited to 250 copies").

LINOTYPE: A machine designed in 1886 in the US by Ottmar Mergenthaler to set and cast text on metal slugs (hence "Line o' type"), with the advantage that the type cast could be discarded after printing, without a need to distribute the type for fresh use. With its competitors, the Linotype became standard equipment used in newspaper and magazine printing and also for book work, until superseded in the 1960s by filmsetting machines.

LITHOGRAPHY: A

planographic printing process invented by Alois Senefelder in Bavaria in the late 18th century, using Bavarian limestone slabs as the vehicle in his process, based on the fact that oil and water do not mix. A drawing sketched on the stone with a greasy pencil, then wetting the stone with water ensures that ink will adhere only where the greasy marks have been made. Lithography had the great advantage that prints from relief or **intaglio** processes can be transferred to the stones, allowing prints that can be made cheaply. Rapid developments in the early 19th century made lithographic printing of almost equal importance to letterpress printing, and in the mid-20th century it replaced letterpress. *See*: Duperly's *Daguerian Excursions in Jamaica*, pp. 186–187 and Meggendorfer's *Grand Circus*, pp. 198–199.

LIVRES D'ARTISTES:

Sometimes translated as "artists' books," these are books in small editions illustrated by major artists, and produced in the better printers **ateliers** (usually) in Paris. Published at very high prices and usually bound by the best avant-garde binders, these books are designed as works of art to be admired but seldom to be read. All outside the main book trade, the differences between **private press** books, artists' books and livres d'artistes are often hard to distinguish and depend on the philosophy of the artists and printers concerned.

LONTAR: Manuscripts made out of dried leaves in India and Southeast Asia taken from either palmyra or lontar palms (*Borassus flabellifer*) or talipot palms (*Corypha umbraculifera*). These palm-leaf

manuscripts served as the normal writing surface in parts of Asia as far back as the fifth century BCE, and possibly earlier; their conservation is a continuing problem. *See*: Nalanda *Perfection of Wisdom Sutra*, pp. 34–35.

LOWERCASE (or L.C.): The smaller **minuscule** letters (a, b, c etc.). The name is derived from the fact that in printing houses these were kept in the lower case (drawer), with capital letters (or caps) kept in the upper case above them.

M

METAMORPHOSES *See*: HARLEQUINADES.

MINUSCULE/MINISCULE:

A small cursive script used in ancient Greek manuscripts (especially Biblical texts), which in the seventh century developed into minuscule cursive of the **roman** alphabet as Carolingian (Caroline) minuscule. Used in later forms. Used also to refer to printers' **lowercase** letters, as distinct from capitals.

Decorated initial with Greek MINUSCULE *script, in a Psalter written by Matthaios, hieromonk of the monastery of St. Catherine, Mount Sinai (Egypt) in 1661. The initial is picked out in red and yellow penwork decoration.*

MISSAL: A liturgical book providing instruction, according to the rites of the Church, on the celebration of Mass throughout the year, often containing Psalms (sung as Graduals with musical notation), Gospels, Epistles and prayers. These were often ornamented or illustrated.

MODERN FACE: Design of **roman** typefaces produced from the mid-18th century onward, with the shapes of serifs and other aspects of the designs closer to engineers' drawing than the scribal forms written with a broad pen, which were the models for **old-face** type. Modern face became normal throughout the world into the late 19th century, when old-face designs started to be used again in the English-speaking world.

MONOTYPE: A machine designed in 1890 in the US by Talbot Lanston to set and cast types already justified. With some technological advantage over **Linotype**, Monotype came to be the main machine used for book composition and scientific printing in Britain, until it was superseded by filmsetting machines in the 1960s.

N

NATURE PRINTING: (1) Printing processes using natural objects such as leaves, flowers or feathers to produce an image. The ink is applied directly to the object, which is then impressed onto the paper. The hand print is the very oldest form of nature print. (2) Processes used in the mid-19th century to impress natural objects, lace, leaves and so on into a lead plate, which was then **electrotyped** to make a copper plate that could be printed **intaglio** or by letterpress.

Cai Lun, the patron saint of papermaking. An 18th-century woodcut copying a Qing dynasty design.

NEUMES: From the Greek, *pneuma*, meaning "breath." Developed from Greek textual accents modified into shapes showing pitch direction and vocal ornament, neumes became the notation form for plainchant (notes sung on a single syllable, and in successive musical pitches) in Gregorian and Byzantine liturgical and secular chant as well as for early medieval polyphony (music in several voices). Neumes were the predecessor to the modern musical note.

O

OCTAVO (or 8vo or 8°): The **format** of a book resulting from folding a single sheet of paper three times to make eight leaves, and printing both sides to make 16 pages of text. Thus each octavo page is one eighth of the original paper size. Often the smaller common book size is referred to as an octavo, (roughly 8 to 10 inches, 20 to 25.5 centimeters, tall), the larger formats being **quartos** and **folios**—although whether a book is technically one or the other depends on the size of the original sheet of paper.

OLD FACE: The **roman** typefaces produced by early printers in Europe, in which the designs were closely based on the humanistic scripts used in Renaissance manuscripts. The designs began to be changed by French punchcutters in the early 18th century, but a late version, Caslon Old Face, remained in regular use in Britain and in the US until the end of the century, and became popular again in the late Victorian period.

P

PALIMPSEST: From the Greek *palimpsēstos* (scraped again), a manuscript, typically of **papyrus**, **vellum** or **parchment**, that has had its surface scraped to erase existing text and has been reused. The Archimedes Palimpsest is one of the most famous examples, where unwanted texts by classical writers were erased and reused in the Byzantine era to make a prayer book.

PAPER: From the Latin, *papyrus*, a material traditionally made by reducing vegetable fiber (such as flax and hemp) by beating in mills. Suspended in water, the fibers are put into papermaking molds, and sheets are then dried and sized. In the earliest paper (developed in China around 105 CE by Han courtier Cai Lun), papermaking molds were sewn of fine bamboo; in Europe paper molds were made of rows of fine brass wire supported by stronger wires at right angles, so that the distinct wireline pattern could be seen when a sheet was held to the light. From the 18th century onward, woven wire was used to make the molds, and after papermaking was mechanized in the early 19th century the use of wire molds became universal, except for the expensive handmade papers preferred by **private presses** and artists. Most modern paper is based on using wood as the source for pulp, but increasingly recycled papers form part of the mix; this provides inferior surfaces whose conservation is a continuing problem.

PAPYRUS: A writing surface formed of two layers of strips of the inner pith of the papyrus sedge (*Cyperus papyrus*, also known as Nile Grass, for the area where it was once widely cultivated). These were beaten together, dried and polished, and usually cut to a standard size. It was in use as early as the fourth millennium BCE.

PARABAIK: A Burmese manuscript book made of a thick, glued and folded **paper**, either made black, to support writing (particularly of nonreligious texts), or white or cream, for paintings and drawings.

PARCHMENT: A writing surface deriving its name from Pergamon (now Bergama in Turkey), where it is thought to have originated under the Attalid King Eumenes II, when exports of **papyrus** ceased. Properly referring to a medium made from sheepskin (**vellum** being calfskin or goatskin), the term is now often loosely applied to refer to any animal skin or even vegetable parchment. Like vellum, the skins were cleaned with lime, stretched and scraped, and finely pumiced, to produce a fine and long-lasting writing surface.

PECIA: A section of a manuscript, generally of four folios, that scribes would be hired to copy, often in conjunction with another scribe working on a different section or pecia from the same book. This was a medieval form of a production line, by which means copies could be produced more quickly than by a single person working alone. The system, using institutionally approved texts called exemplars, originated in Italian university cities and by the late 13th century had become a regulated procedure at the University of Paris.

PENNY DREADFUL [also known as penny bloods, penny awful, etc.]: A 19th-century, typically British, cheaply produced publication usually featuring sensational stories in serialized form and costing one penny. Sweeney Todd, the demon barber, first appeared in this form. The term was later used more widely for the booklet type of pulp fiction in general.

PERIPLUS: Name used in classical Greek times for sailing directions.

PICA: (1) The Anglo-American point system, named for the commonest size of type called Pica. *See also*: DIDOT; TYPE/TYPEFACE. (2) The equivalent unit of measurement used by book designers and type **compositors** to determine the dimensions of lines, illustrations or printed pages.

PICTOGRAPH/ PICTOGRAM(ME): A graphic symbol conveying its meaning through visual resemblance to the idea it represents (rather than through letter forms). Unlike the Roman and Arabic alphabets, **cuneiform** and **hieroglyphics** are pictographic, as, for example, are many Chinese characters (in Chinese the character niú—a cow or ox—for example, is based on a very simplified drawing of the horns).

PLANOGRAPHIC: The name for printing processes in which the area to be printed and the background are

The Mandarin Chinese character niú (shown right) is a PICTOGRAM, *based on an earlier more recognizable drawing of cattle horns.*

on the same surface, in distinction from relief (or letterpress) printing and **intaglio** (recessed) surfaces. The commonest form of planographic printing is **lithography**.

POLYGLOT: A multilingual text or person. A polyglot lexicon or Bible (such as the Complutensian) has text printed concurrently in several languages, often on the same page. An early instance is the Old Testament Scriptures of Origen of Alexandria, in Hebrew and differing Greek variations (although just two languages). One of the most famous polyglots was Giuseppe Mezzofanti, a 19th-century Italian cardinal reputed to speak 72 languages.

PORTOLAN: Nautical charts, often drawn on sheepskin, which were based on compass directions and estimated distances observed by navigators. They originated in Italy in the 13th century (the oldest extant example being the *Carta Pisana*, dating from approximately 1296) and were later commonly employed by Spanish and Portuguese seafarers. *See also*: RUTTER.

LEFT *A* REBUS *from America to Britannia, headed "[America toe] her [miss]taken [moth]er", published by M. Darly, Strand, May 11, 1778.*

PROVENANCE: The record (explicit or inferred from signatures, library stamps, bookplates, inscriptions and other sources) of previous ownership of a particular volume. For "important" books such as, for example, the First Folio of Shakespeare, the provenance is always important, and as with fine arts, the previous ownership by a famous person increases the book's value.

PRIVATE PRESS: The production of fine printing at a privately owned press sometimes operated in person by the owner. Private presses had been operated from the 15th century onward, but the movement gained ground at the end of the 19th century under the influence of William Morris and the Arts and Crafts Movement, where an appreciation of traditional skills and fine craftsmanship in book production were paramount. *See*: Cranach-Presse's *Hamlet*, pp. 214–215; Whitman's *Leaves of Grass*, pp. 216–217; Hunter's *Old Papermaking*, pp. 238–239.

PSALTER/PSALTERIUM: A Book of Psalms, particularly in the Middle Ages, often also containing other devotional material such as a liturgical calendar or litany of saints. Many, like the Luttrell Psalter, were privately owned and commissioned and often contained very fine illumination or decorations. Latin psalters date from the early eighth century, Coptic psalters, undecorated, are older; the earliest complete example, from al-Mudil in Egypt, dates from the fourth century.

Q

QUARTO (or 4to, or 4°): A sheet of paper folded twice to make a gathering of 4 leaves or 8 pages. Books of this size are often referred to as Quartos. *See also*: FOLIO; OCTAVO.

QUIRE: Four sheets of **paper** or **parchment** folded to form 8 leaves and 16 pages (called a signature), as in medieval manuscripts. Now also used to refer to one-twentieth of a ream of paper; and 24 (or now more commonly 25) sheets of paper of the same size and quality, unfolded or having a single fold.

R

REBUS: Like the **pictograph** this uses images, but to represent a syllabic sound, which stands in for a part of a word—for example, images of an eye, a can, the sea and a ewe, for the sentence "I can see you." Widely used in heraldry and popular as puzzles or coded letters in the 18th and 19th centuries.

RECTO *See*: VERSO.

ROLL *See*: SCROLL.

ROMAN/ROMANCE: A literary genre of prose or verse that developed out of the medieval epic and was often connected with wondrous tales of chivalry, particularly of courtly love, popular in aristocratic circles of high medieval and early modern Europe. During the early 13th century, these were increasingly written as prose, in Old French, Anglo-Norman and Occitan (*lengue d'òc*), and later in German and English (*Sir Gawain and the Green Gome*—or Knight—is a notable example). The genre fell out of favor around 1600, but was revived for a while in the Victorian Gothic Revival in the work of writers such as Alfred Lord Tennyson, and the imagery of the medieval romance was a source of much material for the Pre-Raphaelites. *See also*: CHANSON DE GESTE.

ROMAN (type): One of the three primary historical typefaces in the Latin script, together with **blackletter** and **italic**. Based on a European manuscript style of c. 1400, this upright roman face combines square capitals found in ancient Roman texts with **Carolingian minuscule**. Up until the Renaissance, one or other typeface was used, either roman or italic. Nowadays, roman and italic types are often combined within the same text, for different grammatical or functional purposes.

RUBRIC: A word or section of text that is traditionally written or printed using red ink to highlight it.

RUTTER (also *periplus*, *portolan*): A navigational pilot book used by medieval mariners before the advent of nautical charts. Usually containing information on ports and coastal landmarks, with approximate distances. From the French, *routier*.

S

SCHWABACHER: Named after the town of Schwabach in Germany, a **blackletter** typeface much used from 1480–1530 in Germany, notably for the printing of the works of Martin Luther; in use (less widely) up until the 20th century. It is derived from Gothic bookhand (also known as textualis or textura), which was common throughout France, England, Germany and the Low Countries. *See also*: FRAKTUR.

SCRIPTORIUM/SCRIPTORIA: A room for writing; particularly, a place set aside in medieval European monasteries for the mass copying by scribes of manuscripts (particularly religious works) in pre-printing days, although much writing was probably conducted in the monks' cells or in cubicles within the cloisters. By the 13th century, secular copy shops also existed. Copying, in dimly lit rooms, was overseen by the *armarian* (*armarius* meaning "cupboard"), who provided the scribes with materials such as the **parchment**, **vellum** and inks.

SCROLL (also, roll): The earliest form of editable record-keeping (dating from the ancient Egyptian period), a scroll is a writing surface for text or art made of **papyrus**, **parchment** or **paper**. Usually divided into pages, scrolls sometimes comprise separate sheets of papyrus or parchment glued together, or one continuous roll with marked-up page divisions. Pliny, in his *Natural History* in 1 CE, describes commercial papyrus rolls as being of about 20 sheets (15 feet or 4.5 meters) in length, whereas book rolls (*volumen*) were often 30–35 feet (9–10.5 meters). Scrolls were simply rolled and often tied (or sealed) or, like many Torah scrolls, had supporting wooden or ivory rollers.

SIDEROGRAPHY: A process of reproducing steel-engraved designs for **intaglio** printing, invented by Jacob Perkins. It was used to create dies for making duplicate images on printing plates for banknote printing.

SIZING: Used in relation to papermaking to denote a method of preparing the surface of the paper, to make it less absorbent and more suitable for writing and printing, by applying a glue-like substance such as modified starches, gelatine (and, after 1850, resin). The process was developed early on by the Chinese (using starch). Although early sizing

undoubtedly improved the printing surface and the strength of the sheet, modern sizing often weakens it, and many sizes produce a chemical reaction that hastens deterioration.

STEATITE (or soapstone): A mineral that can be used to leave white marks on dark surfaces, as in Burmese black **parabaik**.

STEREOTYPE/ STEREOTYPING: A process invented by William Ged in Scotland in the early 18th century, comprising taking a mold from a page of set type using plaster or papier mâché and taking a cast of this in typemetal. The action frees the type for resetting and preserves the text for later impressions—the process used for almost all cheap reprint series such as Tauchnitz and Everyman's Library. *See also*: ELECTROTYPING.

SUBSCRIPTION LIBRARY: (1) A library financed from membership fees or endowments. (2) Commercially run circulating lending libraries. Both developed in the English-speaking world in the 18th century. (The oldest surviving is the Library Company of Philadelphia, founded in 1731; the London Library is the best known in Britain). Commercially run libraries tended to be replaced by public library services, but survive as film and DVD libraries.

SUBSCRIPTION PUBLISHING: A method of publishing in which authors or publishers can place (subscribe for) prepublication orders, before the text has been printed, and possibly even written. Developed in England in the 17th century, and very popular in the 18th century, such books frequently included the names of the people who subscribed. In more modern times, many owners of **private presses** or

producers of artists' books publish their books by subscription; and the method is being modified by firms like Unbound for future publishing.

SYLLABARY: A phonetic writing system consisting of symbols representing syllables. A syllable is often made up of a consonant plus a vowel or a single vowel—but other phonographic mappings occur. Cherokee (Tsalagi) and Hiragana (Japanese) syllabaries are still in use, while Mycenaean Greek (Linear B) and Mayan are no longer used.

T

TALLY STICK: A memory device used to note quantities and numbers, even messages. Usually cut on bone or wood, such systems were used in prehistoric and classical times in Europe and China, and they continued to be used as late as the 19th century. *See also*: KHIPU. *See:* Ishango bone, pp. 16–17.

TAPA: Polynesian name of barkcloth. *See also*: DLUWANG.

TYPE/TYPEFACE: (1) The metal castings bearing the letters forming printing type. (2) The appearance of the letters when printed. Punchcutters and typefounders created **fonts** of different sizes of type, using traditional names for the sizes (such as Bourgeois, Nonpareil, English in Britain) until the early 19th century, but it was difficult to match types from different typefounders. When their size became standardized, in the English-speaking world, the commonest size (**Pica**) was taken as

RIGHT *A specimen sheet of* TYPEFACES *and languages by William Caslon, from* Ephraim Chambers' Cyclopaedia *or* An Universal Dictionary of Arts and Sciences *(London: James & John Knapton, 1728).*

A SPECIMEN

By WILLIAM CASLON, Letter-Founder, in Chiswell-Street, LONDON.

ABCD
ABCDE
ABCDEFG
ABCDEFGHI
ABCDEFGHIJK
ABCDEFGHIJKL
ABCDEFGHIKLMN

French Cannon.

Quousque tan-
dem abutere,
Catilina, pati-
Quousque tandem
abutere, Catilina,
patientia nostra?

Two Lines Great Primer.

Quousque tandem
abutere, Catilina,
patientia nostra?
quamdiu nos etiam
Quousque tandem a-
butere, Catilina, pa-
tientia nostra? quam-
diu nos etiam furor

Two Lines English.

Quousque tandem abu-
tere, Catilina, patientia
nostra? quamdiu nos e-
tiam furor iste tuus elu-
Quousque tandem abutere,
Catilina, patientia nostra?
quamdiu nos etiam furor

DOUBLE PICA ROMAN.

Quousque tandem abutere, Catilina, patientia nostra? quamdiu
nos etiam furor iste tuus eludet?
quem ad finem sese effrenata jac-
ABCDEFGH JIKLMNOP

GREAT PRIMER ROMAN.

Quousque tandem abutere, Catilina, patientia nostra? quamdiu nos etiam furor iste tuus eludet? quem ad finem sese effrenata jactabit audacia? nihilne te
nocturnum præsidium palatii, nihil con-
ABCDEFGHIJKLMNOPQRS

ENGLISH ROMAN.

Quousque tandem abutere, Catilina, patientia
nostra? quamdiu nos etiam furor iste tuus eludet?
quem ad finem sese effrenata jactabit audacia? ni-
nihilne te nocturnum præsidium palatii, nihil
urbis vigiliæ, nihil timor populi, nihil consensus bonorum omnium, nihil hic munitissimus se-
ABCDEFGHIJKLMNOPQRSTVUW

PICA ROMAN.

Melium, novis rebus studentem, manu sua occidit.
Fuit, fuit ista quondam in hac repub. virtus, ut viri
fortes acrioribus suppliciis civem perniciosum, quam
acerbissimum hostem coërcerent. Habemus enim senatusconsultum in te, Catilina, vehemens, & grave:
non deest reip. consilium, neque autoritas hujus ordinis: nos, nos, dico aperte, consules desumus. De-
ABCDEFGHIJKLMNOPQRSTVUWX

SMALL PICA ROMAN. No 1.

At nos vigesimum jam diem patimur hebescere aciem horum
autoritatis. habemus enim hujusmodi senatusconsultum, verumtamen inclusum in tabulis, tanquam gladium in vagina
reconditum: quo ex senatusconsulto confestim interfectum te
esse, Catilina, convenit. Vivis: & vivis non ad deponendam, sed ad confirmandam audaciam. Cupio, P. C., me
esse clementem : cupio in tantis reipub. periculis non dif-
ABCDEFGHIJKLMNOPQRSTVUWXYZ

SMALL PICA ROMAN. No 2.

At nos vigesimum jam diem patimur hebescere aciem horum
autoritatis. habemus enim hujusmodi senatusconsultum, verumtamen inclusum in tabulis, tanquam gladium in vagina
reconditum : quo ex senatusconsulto confestim interfectum te
esse, Catilina, convenit. Vivis : & vivis non ad deponendam,
sed ad confirmandam audaciam. Cupio, P. C., me esse
clementem : cupio in tantis reipub. periculis non dissolutum
ABCDEFGHIJKLMNOPQRSTVUWXYZ

LONG PRIMER ROMAN No 1.

Verum ego hoc, quod jampridem factum esse oportuit, certa de
caussa nondum adducor ut faciam. tum denique interficiam te, cum
jam nemo tam improbus, tam perditus, tam tui similis inveniri po-
terit, qui id non jure factum esse fateatur. Quamdiu quisquam erit
qui te defendere audeat, vives: & vives, ita ut nunc vivis, multis
meis & firmis præsidiis obsessus, ne commovere te contra rempub.
possis. multorum te etiam oculi & aures non sentientem, sicut adhuc
fecerunt, speculabuntur, atque custodient. Etenim quid est, Cati-
ABCDEFGHIJKLMNOPQRSTVUWXYZÆ

LONG PRIMER ROMAN. No 2.

Verum ego hoc, quod jampridem factum esse oportuit, certa de caussa
nondum adducor ut faciam. tum denique interficiam te, cum
jam nemo tam improbus, tam perditus, tam tui similis inveniri pote-
rit, qui id non jure factum esse fateatur. Quamdiu quisquam erit
qui te defendere audeat, vives: & vives, ita ut nunc vivis, multis
meis & firmis præsidiis obsessus, ne commovere te contra rempub.
possis. multorum te etiam oculi & aures non sentientem, sicut adhuc
fecerunt, speculabuntur, atque custodient. Etenim quid est, Catil-
ABCDEFGHIJKLMNOPQRSTVUWXYZÆ

BREVIER ROMAN.

Novem. C. Manlium audaciæ satellitem atque administrum tuæ? num me fefellit,
Catilina, non modo res tanta, tam atrox, tam incredibilis, verum, id quod multo
magis est admirandum, dies? Dixi ego item in senatu, cædem te optimatum contulisse in ante diem v Kalend. Novemb. tum cum multi principes civitatis Rom.
non tam sui conservandi, quam tuorum consiliorum reprimendorum caussa profugerunt. num infciari potes, te illo ipso die meis præsidiis, mea diligentia circumclusum, commovere te contra rempub. non potuisse, cum tu discessu ceterorum,
nostra tamen, qui remansissemus, cæde contentum te esse dicebas? Quid? cum te
ABCDEFGHIJKLMNOPQRSTVUWXYZÆ

Nonpareil Roman.

O dii immortales! ubi-nam gentium sumus? quam rempub. habemus? in qua urbe vivimus?
hic, hic sunt in nostro numero, P. C. in hoc orbis terræ sanctissimo gravissimoque consilio, qui
de nostro omnium interitu, qui de huius urbis, atque adeo de orbis terræ exitio cogitent. hos
ego video consul, & de republ. sententiam rogo, & quos ferro trucidari oportebat,
eos nondum voce vulnero. Fuisti igitur apud Lecam ea nocte, Catilina : distribuisti partes Ita-
liæ : statuisti quo quemque proficisci placeret : delegisti quos Romæ relinqueres, quos tecum
educeres : descripsisti urbis partes ad incendia : confirmasti te ipsum jam esse exiturum : dixisti
paulum tibi esse etiam tum moræ, quod ego viverem. Reperti sunt duo equites Romani, qui te
ista cura liberarent, & tibi illa ipsa nocte paulo ante lucem me in meo lecto interfecturos polli-
cerentur. Hæc ego omnia, vix dum etiam cœtu vestro dimisso, comperi : domum meam majoribus
ABCDEFGHIKLMNOPQRSTVUWXYZÆ

Pearl Roman.

Pearl Italick.

O dii immortales! ubi-nam gentium sumus?

Double Pica Italick.

Quousque tandem abutere, Catili-
na, patientia nostra? quamdiu
nos etiam furor iste tuus eludet?
quem ad finem sese effrenata jac-
ABCDEFGH JIKLMNO

Great Primer Italick.

Quousque tandem abutere, Catilina, pa-
tientia nostra? quamdiu nos etiam fu-
ror iste tuus eludet? quem ad finem sese
effrenata jactabit audacia? nihilne te
nocturnum præsidium palatii, nihil ur-
bis vigiliæ, nihil timor populi, nihil con-
ABCDEFGHI JKLMNOP QR

English Italick.

Quousque tandem abutere, Catilina, patientia no-
stra? quamdiu nos etiam furor iste tuus eludet?
quem ad finem sese effrenata jactabit audacia?
nihilne te nocturnum præsidium palatii, nihil ur-
bis vigiliæ, nihil timor populi, nihil consensus bo-
norum omnium, nihil hic munitissimus habendi se-
ABCDEFGHI JKLMNOPQRSTVU

Pica Italick.

Melium, novis rebus studentem, manu sua occidit.
Fuit, fuit ista quondam in hac repub. virtus, ut viri
fortes acrioribus suppliciis civem perniciosum, quam
acerbissimum hostem coërcerent. Habemus enim senatus-
consultum in te, Catilina, vehemens, & grave: non deest
reip. consilium, neque autoritas hujus ordinis: nos, nos,
dico aperte, consules desumus. Decrevit quondam senatus
ABCDEFGHIJKLMNOP QRSTVWXYZ

Small Pica Italick. No 1.

At nos vigesimum jam diem patimur hebescere aciem horum
authoritatis. habemus enim hujusmodi senatusconsultum, verum-
tamen inclusum in tabulis, tanquam gladium in vagina recon-
ditum: quo ex senatusconsulto confestim interfectum te esse, Ca-
tilina, convenit. Vivis: & vivis non ad deponendam, sed ad
confirmandam audaciam. Cupio, P. C., me esse clementem:
cupio in tantis reipub. periculis non dissolutum videri: sed jam
ABCDEFGHIJKLMNOP QRSTVWXYZ

Small Pica Italick. No 2.

At nos vigesimum jam diem patimur hebescere aciem horum au-
toritatis. habemus enim hujusmodi senatusconsultum, verumtamen
inclusum in tabulis, tanquam gladium in vagina recondito, con-
quo ex senatusconsulto confestim interfectum te esse, Catilina, con-
venit. Vivis: & vivis non ad deponendam, sed ad confirman-
dam audaciam. Cupio, P. C., me esse clementem: cupio in tantis
reipub. periculis non dissolutum videri: sed jam meipsum inertiæ
ABCDEFGHIJKLMNOP QRSTVWXYZ

Long Primer Italick. No 1.

Verum ego hoc, quod jampridem factum esse oportuit, certa de caussa
nondum adducor ut faciam. tum denique interficiam te, cum jam
tam improbus, tam perditus, tam tui similis inveniri poteris, qui id
non jure factum esse fateatur. Quamdiu quisquam erit qui te defen-
dere audeat, vives: & vives, ita ut nunc vivis, multis meis &
firmis præsidiis obsessus, ne commovere te contra rempub. possis. mul-
torum te etiam oculi & aures non sentientem, sicut adhuc fecerunt, spe-
culabuntur, atque custodient. Etenim quid est, Catilina, quam amp-
ABCDEFGHIJKLMNOP QRSTVWXYZÆ

Long Primer Italick. No 2.

Verum ego hoc, quod jampridem factum esse oportuit, certa de caussa
nondum adducor ut faciam. tum denique interficiam te, cum jam nemo
tam improbus, tam perditus, tam tui similis inveniri poteris, qui id non
jure factum esse fateatur. Quamdiu quisquam erit qui te defendere
audeat, vives: & vives, ita ut nunc vivis, multis meis & firmis
præsidiis obsessus, ne commovere te contra rempub. possis. multorum te
etiam oculi & aures non sentientem, sicut adhuc fecerunt, speculabuntur,
atque custodient. Etenim quid est, Catilina, quid jam amplius expectas,
ABCDEFGHIJKLMNOP QRSTVWXYZÆ

Brevier Italick.

Novem. C. Manlium audacia satellitem atque administrum tuæ? num me fefellit,
Catilina, non modo res tanta, tam atrox, tam incredibilis, verum, id quod multo magis
est admirandum, dies? Dixi ego item in senatu, cædem te optimatum contulisse in ante
diem v Kalend. Novemb. tum cum multi principes civitatis Rom. non tam sui conser-
vandi, quam tuorum consiliorum reprimendorum caussa profugerunt. num inficiari potes,
te illo ipso die meis præsidiis, mea diligentia circumclusum, commovere te contra rempub.
non potuisse, cum tu discessu ceterorum, nostra tamen, qui remansissemus, cæde contentum
te esse dicebas? Quid? cum te Præmeste Kalend. ipsis Novembris occupaturum nocturno
ABCDEFGHIJKLMNOP QRSTVWXYZÆ

Nonpareil Italick.

O dii immortales! ubi-nam gentium sumus? quam rempub. habemus? in qua urbe vivimus? hic, hic

Pica Black.

And be it further enacted by the Authority
aforesaid, That all and every of the said Exchequer Bills to be made forth by virtue of
this Act, or so many of them as shall from
ABCDEFGHIJKLMNOPQRST

Brevier Black.

And be it further enacted by the Authority aforesaid, That all and every
of the said Exchequer Bills to be made forth by virtue of this Act, or so
many of them as shall from time to time remain undischarged and uncan-
celled, until the discharging and cancelling the same pursuant to this Act

Pica Gothick.

ATTA NNSAR ÞN ÍN HIMINAM VEIHNAI
NAMÔ ÞEIN ÛIMAI ÞIUDINASSUS ÞEINS
VAIRÞAI VIÂA ÞEINS SVE ÍN HIMINA

Pica Coptick.

ⲂⲈⲛ ⲟⲩⲁⲣⲭⲏ ⲁϥⲧ ⲑⲁⲙⲓⲟ ⲁⲧⲫⲉ ⲛⲉⲙ ⲡⲕⲁ-
ϩⲓ· ⲡⲕⲁϩⲓ ⲇⲉ ⲛⲉ ⲟⲩⲁⲑⲛⲁⲩ ⲉⲣⲟϥ ⲛⲉ ⲟⲩⲟϩ
ⲛⲁⲧⲥⲟⲃⲧ ⲟⲩⲭⲁⲕⲓ ⲛⲁϥⲭⲏ ϩⲓϫⲉⲛ ⲫⲛⲟⲩⲛ ⲟⲩⲟϩ
ⲟⲩⲡⲛⲁ ⲛⲧⲉϥⲧ ⲛⲁϥⲛⲓⲟⲩ ϩⲓϫⲉⲛ ⲛⲓⲙⲱⲟⲩ

Pica Armenian.

Սկզբն արար Աստուած զերկին և զերկիր. որ և երկիրն
և ամենայն բուսանէ զի անդ են թագաւորն երկնաւոր
եկ ամենայն զ զ զ ամենին.զ ի հեր բան արի
Բարագանդ. և միայն արմատ, որդ երկրն

English Syriack.

ܡܢ ܪܝܫܝܬܐ ܐܬܒܪܝ ܫܡܝܐ ܘܐܪܥܐ
ܘܚܫܘܟܐ ܣܚܝܦ ܥܠ ܐܦܝ ܬܗܘܡܐ

Pica Samaritan.

ﬡﬡﬢﬤﬥ ﬦﬧﬨ ﬩ ﭏ ﭑ ﭒﬢﬤﬥﬧﬨ

English Arabick.

ﺑﺴﻢ ﺍﻟﻠﻪ ﺍﻟﺮﺣﻤﻦ ﺍﻟﺮﺣﻴﻢ
ﻭﻻ ﺗﻘﺘﻠﻮﺍ ﺍﻟﻨﻔﺲ ﺍﻟﺘﻰ ﺣﺮﻡ ﺍﻟﻠﻪ

Hebrew with Points.

בְּרֵאשִׁ֖ית בָּרָ֣א אֱלֹהִ֑ים אֵ֥ת הַשָּׁמַ֖יִם וְאֵ֥ת הָאָֽרֶץ׃ וְהָאָ֗רֶץ
הָיְתָ֥ה תֹ֙הוּ֙ וָבֹ֔הוּ וְחֹ֖שֶׁךְ עַל־פְּנֵ֣י תְה֑וֹם וְר֣וּחַ אֱלֹהִ֔ים
מְרַחֶ֖פֶת עַל־פְּנֵ֥י הַמָּֽיִם׃ וַיֹּ֥אמֶר אֱלֹהִ֖ים יְהִ֣י א֑וֹר
וַֽיְהִי־אֽוֹר׃ וַיַּ֧רְא אֱלֹהִ֛ים אֶת־הָא֖וֹר כִּי־ט֑וֹב
וַיַּבְדֵּ֣ל אֱלֹהִ֔ים בֵּ֥ין הָא֖וֹר וּבֵ֥ין הַחֹֽשֶׁךְ׃ וַיִּקְרָ֨א אֱלֹהִ֤ים ׀ לָאוֹר֙ י֔וֹם וְלַחֹ֖שֶׁךְ קָ֣רָא לָ֑יְלָה

Hebrew without Points.

בראשית ברא אלהים את השמים ואת הארץ׃ והארץ
היתה תהו ובהו וחשך על פני תהום ורוח אלהים
מרחפת על פני המים׃ ויאמר אלהים יהי אור ויהי אור׃
וירא אלהים את האור כי טוב ויבדל אלהים בין האור
ובין החשך׃ ויקרא אלהים לאור יום ולחשך קרא לילה

Brevier Hebrew.

בראשית ברא אלהים את השמים ואת הארץ׃ והארץ היתה תהו
ובהו וחשך על פני תהום ורוח אלהים מרחפת על פני המים
ויאמר אלהים יהי אור ויהי אור׃ וירא אלהים את האור כי טוב
ויבדל אלהים בין האור ובין החשך׃ ויקרא אלהים לאור יום ולחשך

English Greek.

Πρόεδρος ὁ σοφὸς ὃ τῷ συγγράμματι τῷ περὶ τῦ Ἡρακλέος (ὅπερ δὴ ὡς πλείςου τιμώμενος ἐπιδείκνυσι) ἔτυχε περὶ τῆς
ἀρέτης ἀποφαινόμενος, ὧδέ πως λέγων, ὅσα ἐγὼ μεμνημαι.
φησὶ μὲν Ἡρακλέα, ἐπεὶ ἐκ παίδων εἰς ἥβην ὡρμᾶτο,
(ἐν ᾗ οἱ νέοι ἤδη αὐτοκράτορες γιγνόμενοι δηλοῦσιν, εἴτε τὴν

Pica Greek.

Πρόεδρος ὁ σοφὸς ὃ τῷ συγγράμματι τῷ περὶ τῦ Ἡρακλέος
(ὅπερ δὴ ὡς πλείσου τιμώμενος ἐπιδείκνυσι) ἔτυχε περὶ τῆς ἀρετῆς
ἀποφαινόμενος, ὧδέ πως λέγων, ὅσα ἐγὼ μεμνημαι. φησὶ μὲν
Ἡρακλέα, ἐπεὶ ἐκ παίδων εἰς ἥβην ὡρμᾶτο, (ἐν ᾗ οἱ νέοι ἤδη
αὐτοκράτορες γιγνόμενοι δηλοῦσιν, εἴτε τὴν δι' ἀρετῆς ὁδὸν τρέψονται

Long Primer Greek.

Πρόεδρος ὁ σοφὸς ὃ τῷ συγγράμματι τῷ περὶ τῦ Ἡρακλέος (ὅπερ δὴ ὡς
πλείσου τιμώμενος) ἔτυχε περὶ τῆς ἀρετῆς ἀποφαινόμενος, ὧδέ πως λέγων,
ὅσα ἐγὼ μεμνημαι. φησὶ μὲν Ἡρακλέα, ἐπεὶ ἐκ παίδων εἰς ἥβην ὡρμᾶτο,
(ἐν ᾗ οἱ νέοι ἤδη αὐτοκράτορες γιγνόμενοι δηλοῦσιν, εἴτε τὴν δι' ἀρετῆς

Brevier Greek.

Πρόεδρος ὁ σοφὸς ὃ τῷ συγγράμματι τῷ περὶ τῦ Ἡρακλέος (ὅπερ δὴ ὡς πλείσου
τιμώμενος ἐπιδείκνυσι) ἔτυχε περὶ τῆς ἀρετῆς ἀποφαινόμενος, ὧδέ πως λέγων, ὅσα
ἐγὼ μεμνημαι. φησὶ μὲν Ἡρακλέα, ἐπεὶ ἐκ παίδων εἰς ἥβην ὡρμᾶτο, 1734.

Long Primer Saxon.

Ða he þa mid grummum 7 mid
nexum þæcede þæt þ he ealle þa
þreo he hæт morgenlice ahreas 7
7 geþeode þone nexum almet ap

Pica Saxon.

Ða he þa mid grummum 7 mid
þingum 7 nexum þæt nexum þæ
ceð ꝥ he ealle þa þu

the norm and measured at 12 points, and all other sizes of type were cast on the same point system such as 10-point, 14-point, 24-point etc. In Europe, where under Napoleonic rule the standardization came earlier, the point system was **didot**; until the end of the production of metal types, a 12-point didot piece of type would be appreciably different from a 12-point Pica piece.

U

UNCIAL: Developed from late Old Roman cursive, uncial was originally a rounded, single-stroke formal pen script, found, for example, in the *Book of Kells*. In a more complex style, with **ascenders** and **descenders** being introduced around AD 600, it found favor with Pope Gregory the Great, who commissioned many works by the Church fathers. Uncial letters were sometimes ornamented with Christian symbols, such as a fish or the Cross.

V

VELLUM: From Latin, *vitulinum*, "from calf," and Old French, *vélin*, a writing surface much used historically for **scrolls** and **codices** due to its smooth and durable surface. Made from calfskin and goatskin that has been cleaned, stretched on a "herse" and scraped with a moon-shaped blade (*lunarium*), the quality varies depending on the skin used and the skill in preparation. True vellum differs from modern "paper (vegetable) vellum," which is a synthetic material.

VERSO: **Recto** and verso are the names for the "front" and "back" of a leaf of paper in a bound item such as a manuscript **codex**, a printed book or a broadsheet. In languages written

A Merovingian UNCIAL, *with rustic capitals, from a book of Homilies, a parchment codex produced probably in Corbie, northern France, last quarter of the seventh century. (British Library, MS Burney 340, fo. 11.) Some of the capitals in this are zoomorphic, with fish decorations.*

from left to right (such as English) the recto is the right-hand page, and the verso the left-hand page; in languages written right-to-left, the order is reversed.

VOLVELLE (Also, wheel chart): A computational device made of paper disks resembling an astronomer's astrolabe. The volvelle probably originated in ancient Babylon, but as a paper device, from 11th-century Persia, where it was used to depict the movement of the planets and stars. Often taking the form of perpetual calendars or planetary devices, they were probably introduced to the West by Ramon Llull in his *Ars Magna* in the late 13th century.

W

WATERMARK: In book terms, a pattern or image created during the **paper**-manufacturing process, using a wire sewn onto the paper mold, causing a variation in the thickness of the paper to make the pattern, which is visible when the paper is held against the light. Watermarks first appeared in Italy

A WATERMARK *in* Quodlibets, Lately Come Over from New Britaniola, Old Newfoundland *by Robert Hayman (perhaps the first Newfoundland poet) published in London in 1628. Identifying watermarks were often found in the gutter (the paper fold) of books, particularly quartos, owing to their position on the sheet of paper.*

Danse Macabre, or Death at the Printer's Workshop—*a* **WOODCUT** *by Mathias Huss, published in Lyons, February 18, 1499/1500. Huss's woodcut depicts a French 15th-century workshop, with the compositor at his table, with copy-holder (visorum) and composing stick, the inking balls and the press itself. The books are sold in the small bookshop at right.*

during the 13th century, and were simple shapes, sometimes Christian in origin, such as an anchor, or lamb and cross. First used by the paper mill, guild or patron as an identifying mark, watermarks quickly found favor across Europe, and are still widely used in paper manufacture (and money) today. Owing to their longstanding widespread use, they can be useful in dating historical documents.

WOODCUT (or XYLOGRAPHY):
A printing technique, used in the East since antiquity and from about 1400 in the West, on cloth and, later, paper. The image is carved into the surface of a block of wood and then inked and impressed onto the surface. As a relief print, it prints "in negative"—that is, the area to remain white is gouged away and the lines or areas to be inked remain uncut as the surface. Often they were designed by an artist and cut by a block cutter or *formschneider*, but these days printmakers often design, cut and print the blocks themselves. In the West, Albrecht Dürer is perhaps the most famous artist working with woodcuts.

WOOD ENGRAVING:
A fine form of wood relief-printing that developed in the late 18th century with the work of Thomas Bewick. Using the ends of a hard wood, such as boxwood or lemonwood, and a fine engraving tool (a burin) in place of the traditional woodcutters' blade, a finer line can be achieved than with traditional woodcut techniques. It is still a popular form of book illustration today.

X

XYLOGRAPH *See:* WOODCUT.

Y

YELLOWBACKS (also "mustard-plaster" novels): A style of cheap popular fiction that developed in the 1840s with the rise of the railway bookstalls. Dominated by George Routledge's Railway Library (from 1849), they reached their peak in the 1870s and 1880s. Often cheap reprints of bestsellers of the day, they earned their name from their yellow paper or board covers, block-printed with lively illustrations in an attempt to compete with the **penny dreadful** market.

Z

ZAUM (Russian, *заумь*). Derived from the Russian за (beyond) and ум (the mind) to denote "beyond sense"or "trans-rationality". Applied to linguistic experiments, particularly of the Russian futurist poets, characterized by indeterminacy in meaning. Coined in 1913 by the poet Alekei Kruchenykh, who in his 1921 *Declaration of Transrational Language*, described language as "binding." The use of zaum, with its rhythmic sounds and imagery, was to capture larger concepts.

Bibliography

In preparing this very selective bibliography, we have become very conscious of the information explosion in writings traversing from ancient manuscripts to contemporary electronic books. We include some sources available only on the Internet. Seeking printed books, one would naturally use library catalogs; it is assumed that readers will also search on-line through Google or other search engines and will find some treasures. We all know that printed sources often have errors or omissions, and can easily identify their weaknesses. It is more difficult with electronic sources, and these range from excellent to very bad indeed.

One of the better sources to turn to is Jeremy Norman's *From Cave Paintings to the Internet: Chronological and Thematic Studies on the History of Information and Media* (www.historyofinformation.com).

For many "important" books, the websites of national and other research libraries often provide digital images of many of their treasures—for example, the British Library (http://www.bl.uk/onlinegallery/index.html). Similarly, the Bavarian State Library and the Bibliothèque Nationale de France—to name just two European libraries—offer very rich collections of digitized images of books in their collections, and these can often be downloaded as PDFs.

As well as noting general books, the entries here for both printed books and on-line sources are arranged thematically by each chapter.

GENERAL

Nicholas A. Basbanes, *On Paper: the Everything of its Two-Thousand-Year History* (New York: Knopf, 2013)

Michael Bhaskar, *The Content Machine: Towards a Theory of Publishing from the Printing Press to the Digital Network* (London: Anthem Press, 2013)

Wilfrid Blunt and William T. Stearn, *The Art of Botanical Illustration*, rev. ed. (Woodbridge, Suffolk: Antique Collectors' Club, 1994)

Christine L. Borgman, *From Gutenberg to the Global Information Infrastructure: Access to Information in the Networked World* (Cambridge, MA: MIT Press, 2000)

Joseph A. Dane, *What Is a Book? The Study of Early Printed Books* (Notre Dame, Indiana: University of Notre Dame Press, 2013)

Simon Eliot and Jonathan Rose (Eds), *A Companion to the History of the Book* (Chichester: Wiley-Blackwell, 2009)

Stuart Kelly, *The Book of Lost Books* (London: Viking, 2005)

David Pearson, *Books as History; the Importance of Books Beyond Their Texts*, rev. ed. (London: British Library/New Castle DE: Oak Knoll Press, 2012)

CHAPTER 1: IN THE BEGINNING...

El Castillo Cave, pp. 14–15
Kevin Sharpe and Lesley Van Gelder, *Evidence for Cave Marking by Palaeolithic Children* (www.ksharpe.com/word/AR86.htm)

Ishango Bone, pp.16–17
Laurence Kirby, *Plimpton 322: The Ancient Roots of Modern Mathematics* (http://media.baruch.cuny.edu/mediacenter/Plimpton_322.mov)

Epic of Gilgamesh, pp.18–19
Vybarr Cregan-Reid, *Discovering Gilgamesh: Geology, Narrative and the Historical Sublime in Victorian Culture* (Manchester: Manchester University Press, 2013)

Caral Khipu, pp. 20–21
Guaman Poma website (www.kb.dk/permalink/2006/poma/info/en/frontpage.htm)

Gary Urton, *Signs of the Inka Khipu: Binary Coding in the Andean Knotted-String Records* (Austin: University of Texas Press, 2003)

Book of the Dead of Ani, pp. 22–23
Richard Parkinson and Stephen Quirke, *Papyrus* (London: The British Museum Press, 1995)

James Wasserman, *The Egyptian Book of the Dead: The Book of Going Forth by Day*, rev. ed. (Chicago: University of Chicago Press, 2008)

CHAPTER 2: EASTERN APPROACHES

Guodian Chu Slips, pp. 28–29
Jiang Guang-hui, "Guodian and Early Confucianism" (http://www.lunwentianxia.com/product.free.3455418.1/>)

Joseph Needham, *Science and Civilisation in China: Chemistry and Chemical technology. Part 1 Paper and Printing*, by Tsien Tsuen-Hsuin (Cambridge: Cambridge University Press, 1985)

Tripitaka Koreana, pp. 32–32
Research Institute of Tripitaka Koreana (RITK), *The Tripitaka Koreana Knowledgebase Project* (http://kb.sutra.re.kr/ritk_eng/intro/introProject03.do)

Batak *Pustaha*, pp. 38–39
Ann Kumar and John F. McGlynn, *Illuminations: the Writing Traditions of Indonesia* (Jakarta: Lontar Foundation/New York: Weatherhill, 1996)

Teygeler, René, "Pustaha; A study into the production process of the Batak book" *Bijdragen tot de Taal-, Land- en Volkenkunde* (Manuscripts of Indonesia 1949, no: 3, pp. 593–611)

Parabaik, pp. 40–41
Stephanie Watkins, *Hand Papermaking in Central Burma and Northern Thailand* (http://cool.conservation-us.org/coolaic/sg/bpg/annual/v11/bp11-41.htm)

CHAPTER 3: THE GREAT CLASSICS

Aesop's Fables, pp. 46–47
Anne Stevenson-Hobbs (Ed.), *Fables* (London: Victoria and Albert Museum, 1986)

Homer's *Iliad*, pp. 48–49
Casey Dué, ed, *Recapturing a Homeric Legacy: Images and Insights from the Venetus A Manuscript of the Iliad* (Washington: Center for Hellenic Studies, Harvard University, 2009). Also available as http://www.homermultitext.org/Pubs/Due_Recapturing_a_Homeric_Legacy.pdf

Garima Gospels, pp. 50–51
Martin Bailey, *Discovery of Earliest Illuminated Manuscript*, (http://www.ethiopianheritagefund.org/artsNewspaper.html)

Lester Capon, *Extreme Bookbinding: a Fascinating Preservation Project in Ethiopia* (http://www.hewit.com/skin_deep/?volume=26&article=1#article)

Richard Pankhurst, *How to Lose Your History: the Microfilming of Ethiopian Manuscripts* (http://www.linkethiopia.org/guide-to-ethiopia/the-pankhurst-history-library/the-microfilming-of-ethiopian-manuscripts-a-nostalgic-view/)

Apicius, pp. 52–53
Apicius (http://penelope.uchicago.edu/~grout/encyclopaedia_romana/wine/apicius.html)

Eric Quayle, *Old Cook Books, an Illustrated History* (New York: E.P. Dutton, 1978)

Archimedes Palimpsest, pp. 54–55
Archimedes Palimpsest Project, *The Archimedes Palimpsest* (http://archimedespalimpsest.org/about/history/archimedes.php)

Reviel Netz and William Noel, *The Archimedes Codex* (London: Weidenfeld & Nicolson, 2007)

CHAPTER 4: MEDIEVAL WORLDS & THE BOOK

Book of Kells, pp. 60–61
Faksimile Verlag, *Book of Kells* (http://www.faksimile.de/werk/Book_of_Kells.php?we_objectID=17)

Trinity College Dublin, Digital Collections (http://digitalcollections.tcd.ie/home/#searchresults)

St. Gallen, *Codices Electronici Sangallenses Virtual Library* (http://www.cesg.unifr.ch/en/index.htm)

Chludov Psalter, pp. 62–63
Robin Cormack, *Writing in Gold, Byzantine Society and its Icons* (London: George Philip, 1985)

Dioscorides' *De Materia Medica*, pp. 64–65
Wilfrid Blunt and Sandra Raphael, *The Illustrated Herbal*, rev. ed. (London: Frances Lincoln, 1994)

Encyclopaedia Romana, *Dioscorides De Materia Medica* (http://penelope.uchicago.edu/~grout/encyclopaedia_romana/aconite/materiamedica.html)

T'oros Roslin Gospels, pp. 66–67
Christopher De Hamel, *Scribes and Illuminators*
(London: British Museum Press, 1992)

Ptolemy's *Geographia*, pp. 68–69
Ralph E. Ehrenberg, *Mapping the World: an Illustrated
History of Cartography* (Washington: National Geographic
Society, 2006)

Cristoforo's *Liber Insularum*, pp. 70–71
Sullacrestadellonda.it ("Riding the wave"), *The Aegean Sea:
The Books of Islands* (http://www.sullacrestadellonda.it/
cartografia/mar_egeo1_en.htm)

Bruges *Roman de la Rose*, pp. 72–73
Roman de la Rose Digital Library
(http://romandelarose.org/)

University of Glasgow Special Collections, *Roman de la Rose*
(http://special.lib.gla.ac.uk/exhibns/month/feb2000.html)

Farnese *Hours*, pp. 74–75
J.J.G. Alexander (Ed.), *The Painted Page: Italian
Renaissance Book Illumination, 1450–1550* (Munich:
Prestel, 1994)

CHAPTER 5: LIGHT FROM THE EAST

Dunhuang *Diamond Sutra*, pp. 80–81
British Library, *Diamond Sutra* (http://www.bl.uk/
onlinegallery/sacredtexts/podsusanwhitfield.html)

British Library, On-line Gallery, *The Diamond Sutra*
(http://www.bl.uk/onlinegallery/ttp/sutra/accessible/
introduction.htm)

International Dunhuang Project: The Silk Road Online
(http://idp.bl.uk/)

Dorothy C. Wong, *Personal Devotional Objects of Buddhist
Asia* (http://people.virginia.edu/~dcw7a/articles/Personal-
Devotional-Objects-of-Buddhist-Asia.pdf)

Murasaki's *The Tale of Genji*, pp. 82–83
Peter Kornicki, *The Book in Japan: A Cultural History*
(Honolulu: University of Hawai'i Press, 2001)

Panchatantra, pp. 84–85
Bodleian Library, *Kalilah wa-Dimnah* ("The Fables of
Bidpai") (http://treasures.bodleian.ox.ac.uk/The-Fables-
of-Bidpal)

Al-Jazari's *Mechanical Arts*, pp. 88–89
Ahmad Y. al-Hassan (Ed.), "Al-Jazari and the History of the
Water Clock" (http://www.history-science-technology.com/
articles/articles%206.htm)

Mansur's *Anatomy*, pp. 90–91
National Library of Medicine, *Historical Anatomies on
the Web: Mansur* (http://www.nlm.nih.gov/exhibition/
historicalanatomies/mansur_bio.html)

David J. Roxburgh (Ed.), *Turks; a Journey of a Thousand
Years, 600–1600* (London: Royal Academy of Arts, 2005)

Boke van Bonang, pp. 92–93
Teygeler, René, *Dluwang, a near-paper from Indonesia*
(http://www.scribd.com/doc/39391411/Dluwang)

CHAPTER 6: WHEELS OF CHANGE

General
K. Lesley Knieriem, *Book-Fools of the Renaissance*
(Champaign, IL: University of Illinois, Graduate School
of Library and Information Science, 1993)

Alberto Manguel, *A History of Reading* (London:
Flamingo, 1997)

Andrew Pettegree, *The Book in the Renaissance*
(New Haven: Yale University Press, 2010)

Southern Methodist University, Bridwell Library, *Invention
and Discovery: Books from Fifteenth-Century Europe* (http://
www.smu.edu/Bridwell/Collections/SpecialCollections
andArchives/Exhibitions/InventionDiscovery)

Gutenburg's 42-Line Bible, pp. 98–99
Lucien Febvre and Henri Jean Martin, *The Coming
of the Book: The Impact of Printing 1450–1800*, 3rd. ed.
(London: Verso, 2010)

Morgan Library & Museum, The Morgan Gutenberg Bible
Online (http://www.themorgan.org/collections/works/
gutenberg/provenance)

Eric Marshall White, *Peter Schoeffer: Printer of Mainz*
(Dallas, TX: Bridwell Library, 2003)

Schedel's *Nuremberg Chronicle*, pp. 100–101
Cambridge Digital Library, *Nuremberg Chronicle*
(http://cudl.lib.cam.ac.uk/view/PR-INC-
00000-A-00007-00002-00888/1)

Caxton's *Chesse Moralysed*, pp. 102–103
John Rylands University Library, *Jacobus de Cessolis* (http://www.library.manchester.ac.uk/firstimpressions/assets/downloads/07-Jacobus-de-Cessolis-The-game-of-chess-translated-by-William-Caxton.pdf)

Euclid's *Elementa Geometriae*, pp. 106–107
University of British Columbia, *Images from the first (1482) edition of Euclid* (http://www.math.ubc.ca/~cass/euclid/ratdolt/ratdolt.html)

Aldine Virgil, pp. 108–109
Bartolomeo Sanvito: The Life and Work of a Renaissance Scribe (http://www.paulshawletterdesign.com/2011/04/bartolomeo-sanvito-the-life-and-work-of-a-renaissance-scribe/)

Martin Davies, *Aldus Manutius: Printer and Publisher of Renaissance Venice* (London: British Library, 1995)

Garamond, *Aldus Manutius and his Innovations* (http://www.garamond.culture.fr/en/page/aldus_manutius_and_his_innovations)

Gregorio's *Book of Hours*, pp. 110–111
Miroslav Krek, "The Enigma of the First Arabic Book Printed from Movable Type" (http://www.ghazali.org/articles/jnes-38-3-mk.pdf.)

Paul Lundes, "Arabic and the Art of Printing" (http://www.saudiaramcoworld.com/issue/198102/arabic.and.the.art.of.printing-a.special.section.htm)

***Sefer Abudarham*, pp. 112–113**
Jewish Virtual Library, *Judaic Treasures of the Library of Congress: First Book in Africa* (http://www.jewishvirtual library.org/jsource/loc/Africa.html)

St. Gall *Cantatorium*, pp. 114–115
Jenneka Janzen, *Pondering the Physical Scriptorium* (http://medievalfragments.wordpress.com/2013/01/25/pondering-the-physical-scriptorium/)

D. W. Krummel and Stanley Salie, *Music Printing and Publishing* (New York: Norton, 1990)

Virtual Manuscript Library of Switzerland, Cod Sang. 359, (http://www.e-codices.unifr.ch/en/description/csg/0359)

Constance Gradual, pp. 116–117
Newberry Library Chicago, *Apocolypse Block Book* (http://www.newberry.org/apocalypse-block-book)

Bernstein: The Memory of Paper (http://www.memoryofpaper.eu:8080/BernsteinPortal/appl_start.disp)

Complutensian Polyglot Bible, pp. 118–119
Pecia Complutense, *The Pinciano and his Contribution to the Edition of the Alcalá Polyglot Bible* (1514–1517) (http://biblioteca.ucm.es/pecia/56309.php)

CHAPTER 7: A DANGEROUS INVENTION

Erasmus' *De ratione conscribendi epistolas*, pp. 126–127
Glasgow University Emblems Website, "Andrea Alciato's *Emblematum liber*" (http://www.emblems.arts.gla.ac.uk/alciato/books.php?id=A31a&o=)

Jewish Virtual Library, *Christian–Jewish Relations: The Inquisition* (http://www.jewishvirtuallibrary.org/jsource/History/Inquisition.html)

Bay Psalm Book, pp. 128–129
Dick Hoefnagel, *The Dartmouth Copy of John Eliot's Indian Bible (1639): Its Provenance* (http://www.dartmouth.edu/~library/Library_Bulletin/Apr1993/LB-A93-Hoefnagel.html?mswitch-redir=classic)

Sotheby's, *The Bay Psalm Book: America's First Printed Book* (http://www.sothebys.com/en/news-video/videos/2013/11/The-Bay-Psalm-Book-America-First-Printed-Book.html)

***Codex Mendoza*, pp. 130–131**
Frances Berdan and Patricia Anawalt, *The Essential Codex Mendoza.* (Berkeley: University of California Press, 1997)

Vesalius' *De humani corporis fabrica*, pp. 134–135
National Library of Medicine, *Historical Anatomies on the Web, Andreas Vesalius* (http://www.nlm.nih.gov/exhibition/historicalanatomies/vesalius_home.html)

Andreas Vesalius, *On the Fabric of the Human Body* (http://vesalius.northwestern.edu/flash.html)

Brahe's *Astronomiae*, pp. 136–137
Museum of the History of Science, Oxford, *The Noble Dane: Images of Tycho Brahe*, (http://www.mhs.ox.ac.uk/tycho/index.htm)

Newton's *Principia*, pp. 138–139
Levenson, Thomas, *Newton and the Counterfeiter: The Unknown Detective Career of the World's Greatest Scientist* (London: Mariner Books, 2010)

Markham's *Cavelarice*, pp. 140–141
Gervase Markham, *Cavalarice* (http://www.
classicrarebooks.co.uk/sports/cavalarice_book.html)

Helm's *Art and Industry*, pp. 142–143
Moira Thunder, "Deserving Attention: Margaretha Helm's
Designs for Embroidery in the Eighteenth Century",
Journal of Design History, December 2010, p. 409
(http://connection.ebscohost.com/c/articles/55370545/
deserving-attention-margaretha-helms-designs-
embroidery-eighteenth-century)

Blackwell's *Curious Herball*, pp. 144–145
British Library Online Gallery, *Blackwell's Herbal*
(http://www.bl.uk/onlinegallery/ttp/blackwells/accessible/
introduction.html)

Bruce Madge, "Elizabeth Blackwell—the Forgotten
Herbalist?," *Health Information & Libraries Journal*, vol. 18,
no. 3, pp. 144–152, September 2001 (http://onlinelibrary.
wiley.com/doi/10.1046/j.1471-1842.2001.00330.x/full)

Tomlinson's *Art of Dancing*, pp. 146–147
Baroque Dance Notation Systems, (http://www.baroque
dance.com/research/dancenotation.htm)

Library of Congress, *Dance Instruction Manuals* (http://
memory.loc.gov/cgi-bin/ampage?collId=musdi&fileNa
me=158/musdi158.db&recNum=183&itemLink=r?ammem/
musdibib:@field(NUMBER+@band(musdi+158)))

CHAPTER 8: PRINTING & THE ENLIGHTENMENT

Boucher's *Molière*, pp. 152–153
Bland, David, *A History of Book Illustration: the Illuminated
Manuscript and the Printed Book* (Cleveland: World
Publishing Company, 1985)

Metropolitan Museum of Art, *Gravures de Boucher pour
les Oeuvres de Molière* (http://www.metmuseum.org/
collections/search-the-collections/346508)

Metropolitan Museum of Art, *Dangerous Liaisons: Fashion
and Furniture in the Eighteenth Century* (http://resources.
metmuseum.org/resources/metpublications/pdf/
Dangerous_Liaisons_Fashion_and_Furniture_in_the_
Eighteenth_Century.pdf)

Johnson's *Dictionary*, pp. 154–155
Beryl Bainbridge, "Words count" (http://www.theguardian.
com/books/2005/apr/02/classics.wordsandlanguage)

Dictionary of the English Language: *A Digital Edition
of the 1755 Classic by Samuel Johnson* (http://johnsons
dictionaryonline.com/)

Technische Universität Berlin, *A Brief History of
English Lexicography* (http://classic-web.archive.org/
web/20080309181613/http://angli02.kgw.tu-berlin.de/
lexicography/b_history.html)

Newbery's *Little Pretty Pocket-Book*, pp. 156–157
Virginia Haviland and Margaret Coughlan, *Yankee Doodle's
Literary Sampler... Selected from the Rare Book Collections
of the Library of Congress* (New York: Thomas Y. Crowell
Company, 1974)

Library of Congress Digital Collections, *A Little Pretty
Pocket-Book* (http://lcweb2.loc.gov/cgi-bin/ampage?collId=rb
c3&fileName=rbc0001_2003juv05880page.db&recNum=10)

Morgan Library & Museum, *A Little Pretty Pocket-Book*
(http://www.themorgan.org/collections/collections.
asp?id=130)

South Australia State Library, Treasures, *Orbis sensualium
pictus* (http://www.samemory.sa.gov.au/site/page.
cfm?u=965&c=3702)

Diderot's *Encyclopedie*, pp. 158–159
BBC Radio 4, "In our time," *The Encyclopédie*,
(http://www.bbc.co.uk/programmes/p0038x93)

Philipp Blom: *Encyclopédie: the Triumph of Reason
in an Unreasonable Age* (London: Fourth Estate, 2004)

Massachusetts Institute of Technology, Library Exhibits,
*Technology and Enlightenment: The Mechanical Arts in
Diderot's Encyclopédie* (http://libraries.mit.edu/exhibits/
maihaugen/diderots-encyclopedie/)

Linnaeus' *Species Plantarum*, pp. 160–161
Staffan Müller-Wille and Sara Scharf, "Indexing Nature:
Carl Linnaeus (1707–1778) and his Fact-Gathering
Strategies," *Working Papers on The Nature of Evidence*
no. 36/08 (http://www.lse.ac.uk/economicHistory/pdf/
FACTSPDF/3909MuellerWilleScharf.pdf)

Natural History Museum, *A Film about Carl Linnaeus*
(http://www.youtube.com/watch?v=Gb_IO-SzLgk)

Uppsala Universitet, Linné on line (http://www.linnaeus.uu.se/online/life/8_3.html)

Playfair's *Commercial and Political Atlas,* pp. 162–163
enlightenment-revolution.org., *William Playfair* (http://webcache.googleusercontent.com/search?q=cache:http://enlightenment-revolution.org/index.php/Playfair,_William)

Rosalind Reid, "A Visionary and a Scoundrel" (http://www.americanscientist.org/bookshelf/pub/a-visionary-and-a-scoundrel)

Ian Spence, "William Playfair and the Psychology of Graphs" (http://www.psych.utoronto.ca/users/spence/Spence%20(2006).pdf)

Edward R. Tufte, *The Visual Display of Quantitative Information* (Cheshire, CT: Graphics Press, 1993)

Newgate Calendar, pp. 164–165
British Library, *Learning, Dreamers and Dissenters* (http://www.bl.uk/learning/histcitizen/21cc/crime/media1/calendar1/calendar.html)

oldbaileyonline.org, *The Proceedings of the Old Bailey, 1674–1913* (http://www.oldbaileyonline.org/)

Sterne's *Tristram Shandy,* pp. 166–167
Jesus College, Cambridge, *Laurence Sterne* (http://www.jesus.cam.ac.uk/about-jesus-college/history/pen-portraits/laurence-sterne/)

Laurence Sterne Trust, "The First Publication of *Tristram Shandy*" (http://www.laurencesternetrust.org.uk/wp/sterneana/first-publication-of-tristram-shandy/the-first-publication-of-tristram-shandy/)

Cleland's *Fanny Hill,* pp. 168–169
Julie Peakman, *Mighty Lewd Books: the Development of Pornography in Eighteenth-Century England* (Basingstoke: Palgrave Macmillan, 2012)

Banneker's *Almanack,* pp. 170–171
Inventors.about.com, *Benjamin Banneker,* (http://inventors.about.com/od/bstartinventors/a/Banneker.htm)

Bewick's *British Birds,* pp. 172–173
Thomas Bewick, *My life,* ed. by Iain Bain (London: Folio Society, 1981)

Bewick Society, *Thomas Bewick* (http://www.bewicksociety.org/index.html)

Diana Donald, *The Art of Thomas Bewick* (London: Reaktion Books, 2013)

Repton's Red Books, pp. 174–175
gardenhistorygirl, *Humphrey Repton and Accessible Gardening History* (http://gardenhistorygirl.blogspot.co.uk/2013/02/humphrey-repton-and-accessible.html)

Morgan Library & Museum, *Humphry Repton's Red Books* (http://www.themorgan.org/collections/works/repton/#self)

Haüy's *Education of the Blind,* pp. 176–177
Emmy Csocsán and Solveig Sjöstedt, *Learning and Visual Impairment* (http://www.isar-international.com/_files/didaktikpool_9_20090710102624.pdf)

Royal London Society for Blind People, *RLSB Archive Exhibition, Celebrating 175 years of RLSB* (http://www.rlsb.org.uk/175years)

John Rutherford, *William Moon and his Work for the Blind* (London: Hodder & Stoughton, 1898; https://docs.google.com/document/d/1Rg0lW6DCpcm8Fwk5qYdkDxX-POZ5XCA9ZGKl0wr__RM/edit#)

Sobre a Deficiência Visual, *Essai sur l'Éducation des Aveugles par Valentin Haüy* (Paris, 1786; http://deficienciavisual9.com.sapo.pt/r-Hauy.htm)

CHAPTER 9: PRINT & STEAM

General
Ann M. Blair, *Too Much to Know: Managing Scholarly Information before the Modern Age* (New Haven : Yale University Press, 2010)

Tom Standage, *The Victorian Internet: the Remarkable Story of the Telegraph and the Nineteenth Century On-line Pioneers.* (New York: Berkley Books, 1999)

Perkins' Patent, pp. 182–183
Baker Perkins Historical Society, "Jacob Perkins in the Printing Industry" (http://www.bphs.net/GroupFacilities/J/JacobPerkinsPrinting.htm)

hevac-heritage.org, "The Perkins Family" (http://www.hevac-heritage.org/victorian_engineers/perkins/perkins.htm)

Stephen Van Dulken, *Inventing the 19th Century: the Great Age of Victorian Inventions* (London: British Library, 2001)

Atkin's *Photographs of British Algae,* pp. 184–185
Roderick Cave, *Impressions from Nature: A History of Nature Printing* (London: British Library/New York: Mark Batty, 2010)
Liz Hager, "Anna Atkins" (http://venetianred.net/2010/05/08/anna-atkins-mistress-of-blueprint-manor/)

Naomi Rosenblum, *A History of Women Photographers*, 3rd edition (New York: Abbeville, 2010)

Duperly's *Daguerian Excursions in Jamaica,* pp. 186–187
National Library of Jamaica, "The Beginning of Photography in Jamaica" (http://nljblog.wordpress.com/2011/11/25/the-beginning-of-photography-in-jamaica/)

Evans' *Syllabic Hymnbook,* pp. 188–189
Bruce Peel, *Rossville Mission Press: The Invention of the Cree Syllabic Characters, and the First Printing in Rupert's Land* (Montreal: Osiris Publications, 1974)

Dickens' *Pickwick Papers,* pp. 190–191
John Siers, ed., *The Culture of the Publisher's Series*. 2 vols (Basingstoke: Palgrave Macmillan, 2011)

Powell's *Old Grizzly Adams,* pp. 192–193
Albert Johannsen, *The House of Beadle & Adams and its Dime and Nickel Novels*, (http://www.ulib.niu.edu/badndp/bibindex.html)

Thomas L. Bonn, *UnderCover: an Illustrated History of American Mass Market Paperbacks* (Harmondsworth: Penguin, 1982)

Robert J. Kirkpatrick, *From the Penny Dreadful to the Ha'penny Dreadfuller: A Bibliographical History of the British Boys' Periodical* (London: British Library, 2013)

Library of Congress, "Dime Novels" (http://www.loc.gov/exhibits/treasures/tri015.html)

Monash University, Library, "Yellowbacks" (http://monash.edu/library/collections/exhibitions/yellowbacks/xyellowbackscat.html)

worldwidewords.org, "Penny Dreadful" (http://www.worldwidewords.org/qa/qa-pen2.htm)

Aikin's *Robinson Crusoe,* pp. 194–195
publidomainreview.org, *Nursery Lessons in words of one syllable*, (http://publicdomainreview.org/2013/08/01/nursery-lessons-in-words-of-one-syllable-1838/)

Hoffman's *Struwwelpeter,* pp. 196–197
curiouspages.blogspot.co.uk, *Strewwelpeter* (http://curiouspages.blogspot.co.uk/2009/10/struwwelpeter-or-shock-headed-peter.html)

Meggendorfer's *Grand Circus,* pp. 198–199
Ana Maria Ortega, *Pop-Up, Mobile and Deployable Books* (http://emopalencia.com/desplegables/historia.htm)

University of Florida, Baldwin Library, "Always Jolly; Movable Book by Lothar Meggendorfer" (http://www.youtube.com/watch?v=yWzrGpp7DGo)

University of North Texas, Libraries, *A Brief History of Movable Books* (http://www.library.unt.edu/rarebooks/exhibits/popup2/introduction.htm)

Baedeker's *Switzerland,* pp. 200–201
Richard Mullen and James Munson, "*The Smell of the Continent*": The British Discover Europe (London: Macmillan, 2009)

oldguidebooks.com, "History of Guide Books" (http://oldguidebooks.com/guidebooks/)

Frank Werner, "Collecting Baedeker Travel Guides" (http://www.ilab.org/eng/documentation/197-collecting_baedeker_travel_guides.html)

Soyer's *Modern Housewife,* pp. 202–203
Michael Garval, "Alexis Soyer and the Rise of the Celebrity Chef," (http://www.rc.umd.edu/praxis/gastronomy/garval/garval_essay.html)

Nancy Mattoon, "Britain's Original Celebrity Chef: Alexis Soyer" (http://www.booktryst.com/2010/12/britains-original-celebrity-chef-alexis.html)

Boldrewood's *Robbery Under Arms,* pp. 204–205
Paul Eggert, "*Robbery Under Arms*; the Colonial Market, Imperial Publishers, and the Demise of the Three-Decker Novel," *Book History* vol. 3, 2003, pp. 127-46, (http://www.jstor.org/discover/10.2307/30227345?uid=3738032&uid=2&uid=4&sid=21102980036937)

CHAPTER 10: THE BOOK IN THE TURBULENT TWENTIETH CENTURY

General
Federation of British Industry, *Oxford University Press and the Making of a Book* (http://www.slate.com/blogs/lexicon_

valley/2013/11/07/oxford_english_dictionary_a_1925_
silent_film_about_the_making_of_a_book.html)

Borges' *Garden of Forking Paths*, pp. 210–211
Adam Lee, "How Big is the Library of Babel?" (http://www.
patheos.com/blogs/daylightatheism/2006/03/how-big-is-
the-library-of-babel/)

Carlson's Lab Book, pp. 212–213
David Owen, *Copies in Seconds: Chester Carlson and the Birth
of the Xerox Machine* (New York: Simon & Schuster, 2004)

Cranach-Presse's *Hamlet*, pp. 214–215
John Dieter Brinks, *The Book as a Work of Art: the Cranach
Press of Count Harry Kessler* (Laubach: Triton Verlag/
Williamstown: Williams College, 2005)

Roderick Cave, *The Private Press*, 2nd. ed. (New York:
R.R. Bowker Co., 1983)

Kamensky's *Tango with Cows*, pp. 218–219
Tim Harte, "Vasily Kamensky's 'Tango with Cows': a
Modernist Map of Moscow" *Slavic and East European
Journal*, vol. 48 no. 4 (Winter, 2004), pp. 545–566
(http://www.jstor.org/discover/10.2307/3648812?uid=3738
032&uid=2&uid=4&sid=21102983729067)

Museum of Modern Art, *Tango s korovami.
Zhelezobetonnye poemy* (http://www.moma.org/collection/
object.php?object_id=11018)

tangowithcows.com, *Tango with Cows* (http://www.
tangowithcows.com/)

Ernst's *Une Semaine de Bonté*, pp. 220–221
Elza Adamowicz, *Surrealist Collage in Text and Image:
Dissecting the Exquisite Corpse* (Cambridge: Cambridge
University Press, 1998)

Dorothy Kosinski, *The Artist and the Book in Twentieth-
Century France* (Dallas: Bridwell Library, 2005)

Musée d'Orsay, "Max Ernst, 'Une semaine de bonté'—the
Original Collages" (http://www.musee-orsay.fr/en/events/
exhibitions/in-the-musee-dorsay/exhibitions-in-the-musee-
dorsay-more/article/les-collages-de-max-ernst-20484.
html?cHash=83c594fbdb)

M. E. Warlick, "Max Ernst's Alchemical Novel: 'Une
Semaine de bonté'" *Art Journal* vol. 46, no. 1, Spring, 1987,
pp. 61–73 (http://www.jstor.org/discover/10.2307/776844?
uid=3738032&uid=2&uid=4&sid=21102984022587)

Nnadozie's *Beware of Harlots*, pp. 222–223
Mark J. Curran, *Brazil's Folk-Popular Poetry—"A
Literatura de cordel"* (Bloomington, Ind.: Trafford
Publishing, 2010)

Mark Dinneen, ed., *Brazilian Popular Prints* (London:
Redstone Press, 1995)

McCarthy, Cavan "Printing in Onitsha" (http://www.lsu.
edu/faculty/mccarthy/OnitshaText.htm)

University of Florida "Onitsha Market Literature"
(http://ufdc.ufl.edu/onitsha)

University of Kansas, "Onitsha Market Literature"
(http://onitsha.diglib.ku.edu/index.htm)

Lehmann's *Invitation to the Waltz*, pp. 224–225
University of Bristol, Library, *Penguin Book Collection*
(http://www.bristol.ac.uk/library/resources/
specialcollections/archives/penguin/penguinbooks.html)

Kamiński's *Stones for the Rampart*, pp. 226–227
Grzegorz Mazur, "The ZWZ-AK Bureau of Information &
Propaganda" (http://www.polishresistance-ak.org/13%20
Article.htm)

Bulgakov's *Master and Margarita*, pp. 228–229
Middlebury College, *Master and Margarita* (http://
cr.middlebury.edu/bulgakov/public_html/intro.html)

Frank's *Diary of a Young Girl*, pp. 232–233
Anne Frank Museum, Amsterdam
(http://www.annefrank.org/)

Robert Gellately, *Lenin, Stalin and Hitler: the Age of Social
Catastrophe* (London: Vintage, 2008)

Website devoted to Irene Nemirovsky (http://www.
irenenemirovsky.guillaumedelaby.com/en_biography.html)

CHAPTER 11: DIGITIZATION & THE FUTURE OF THE BOOK

General
Nicholson Baker, *Double Fold: Libraries and the Assault
on Paper* (London: Vintage, 2002)

Nick Bilton, *I live in the Future & Here's How it Works:
How Your World, Work, and Brain are Being Creatively
Disrupted* (New York: Crown Business, 2010)

Ian F. McNeely, *Reinventing Knowledge; from Alexandria to the Internet* (New York: W.W. Norton, 2009)

Janet H. Murray, *Hamlet on the Holodeck: The Future of Narrative in Cyberspace* (New York, Free Press, 1997)

polarstarfilms.com, *Google and the World Brain* (http://shop.polarstarfilms.com/?product=dvd-google-and-the-world-brain)

Abigail Sellen and Richard Harper, *The Myth of the Paperless Office* (Cambridge, MA: MIT Press, 2003)

Sherman Young, *The Book is Dead* (Sydney: NewSouth Publishing, 2007)

Hunter's *Old Papermaking*, pp. 238–239
Cathleen A. Baker, *By His Own Labor: The Biography of Dard Hunter* (New Castle, DE: Oak Knoll, 2000)

www.dardhunter.com, "Mountain House Press" (http://www.dardhunter.com/mhpress.htm)

www.pbs.org,"Elbert Hubbard: an American Original" (http://www.pbs.org/wned/elbert-hubbard/index.php)

RAND's *Million Random Digits*, pp. 240–241
www.wps.com, "Book review: *A Million Random Digits*" (http://www.wps.com/projects/million/index.html)

Electronic *Beowulf*, pp. 242–243
Grant Leyton Simpson, Review of *The Electronic Beowulf* (http://www.digitalmedievalist.org/journal/8/simpson/)

Benjamin Slade, ed., *Beowulf on Steorarume* (<http://www.heorot.dk/)

www.audioholics.com, "Data Longevity on CD, DVD Media: How Long Will They Last?" (http://www.audioholics.com/audio-technologies/cd-and-dvd-longevity-how-long-will-they-last)

Ruiz's *Mechanical Encyclopedia*, pp. 244–245
Robert McCrum, "The Dragon Lords, world's first 'cloud-sourced' novel, prepares to land" (http://www.theguardian.com/books/booksblog/2012/dec/17/the-dragon-lords-novel-silvia-hartmann)

unbound, "How to Crowdfund a Book" (http://unbound.co.uk/about)

Technion Nano Bible, pp. 246–247
Simon Beattie, "Used in the Trenches" (http://www.simonbeattie.kattare.com/blog/archives/843)

Louis W. Bondy, *Miniature Books, their History from the Beginnings to the Present Day* (Farnham: Richard Joseph, 1994)

Martin Chilton, "Is this the World's Smallest Book?" (http://www.telegraph.co.uk/culture/books/booknews/9927200/Is-this-the-worlds-smallest-book.html)

Brant Rosen, "Nano-Torah Technology?" (http://rabbibrant.com/2007/12/26/nano-torah-technology/)

University of Indiana, Lilly Library, *4,000 Years of Miniature Books* (http://www.indiana.edu/~liblilly/miniatures/earlyprinted.shtml)

Prieto's *Antibook*, pp. 250–251
Harry Polkinhorn, "From Book to Anti-book" (http://www.thing.net/~grist/lnd/hp-book.htm)

Francisca Prieto, "My Life with Paper" (http://uppercasemagazine.com/blog/2012/11/29/my-life-with-paper-francisca-prieto#.UpOCCcR7KSp)

Victoria and Albert Museum, "Artists' Books and Books as Art" (http://www.vam.ac.uk/vastatic/wid/exhibits/bookandbeyond/case1.html)

Acknowledgments

The authors would like to thank all those who have so generously given their time, expertise, material and enthusiastic support; in a book of this scope they are, of course, too many to mention individually. In particular we would like to thank David Chambers, Ray Desmond, Ross Harvey, Pia Ostlund, John Randle and Boyd Rayward; also Julie Farquhar and Gary Haines for their feedback and encouragement. We would also like to thank the staff of Quarto, in particular Victoria Lyle and Sarah Bell. Especial thanks are due, of course, to Dawn Cave, for her advice and feedback on our many drafts and revisions, and unstinting support throughout the writing of this book.

Picture credits

The publishers wish to thank the institutions, scholars and private collectors who have so generously made available their texts and information. All attempts have been made to clear copyright and we apologize for any unwitting copyright infringement. Images from The British Library, London are © The British Library Board; all others are as stated below.

pp. 2–3 Esther scroll, 18th century
Pen and ink on parchment
with engraved *repoussé* silver
case. From Italy, silvermark
denoting import control to the
Netherlands. Israel Museum,
Jerusalem, Israel, Stieglitz
Collection, donated with
contribution from Erica and
Ludwig Jesselson.
© The Bridgeman Art Library

pp. 4, 11, 15 Hand prints
and buffalo, El Castillo cave,
Puente Viesgo, Spain, probably
Neanderthal.
Colored mineral pigments
applied with a blowpipe.
Courtesy Marcos Garcia Diez.

pp. 4, 25 Batak divination book,
c. 1855.
Bones, shells and bark paper.
Sumatra, Toba region.
Tropenmuseum, Amsterdam,
coll. no. A.1389.

pp. 4, 43 After Homer, *Iliad*,
10th century.
Shown: 24r, detail of Greek
Minuscule.
Biblioteca Marciana, Venice,
MS Homer Venetus A/B., Gr Z.
454 (= 822), f. 1v.
By permission Ministero per i
Beni e le Attività Culturali.

pp. 5, 57 T'oros Roslin, Gospels,
1262. Shown: fo.104r, St.
Matthew. Ink, colored pigments
and gold leaf on parchment.
Turkey: Hromklay, in Gaziantep.
Courtesy The Walters Art
Museum, Baltimore, W.539.

pp. 5, 77 Traveling monk, Northern
Song Dynasty, 851–900 CE.
Silk painting, ink and colors
on paper. Gansu province,
China, Mogao, near Dunhuang:
Cave 17, The caves of the
Thousand Buddhas.
© The Trustees of the British
Museum, OA 1919,1-1,0.168.

pp. 6, 95 Hartmann Schedel,
Liber Chronicarum, 1493.
Shown: fo.xii, Secundas etas

mundi. Gothic Rotunda
type; numerous woodcuts by
Michael Wohlgemut, Wilhelm
Pleydenwurff and workshop.
Nuremberg: A. Koberger.
Bayerische Staatsbibliothek
München, BSB-Ink A-195,94

pp. 6 ,121 Andreas Vesalius,
*De humani corporis fabrica libri
septem*, 1543.
Shown: page 190: figure hanging
from a gibbet. Latin medical
text with woodcuts probably by
Jan Stephan van Calcar. Basle:
Johannes Oporinus.
Wellcome Library London,
L0031739.

p. 6, 149 Samuel Johnson,
*A Dictionary of the English
Language*, 1755–56.
Shown: title page of the
second edition. London:
J. & P. Knapton, etc.
The British Library, London,
680.k.12,13.

pp. 7, 179, 194 Mary Godolphin
(pseud. Lucy Aikin), *Robinson
Crusoe in Words of One Syllable*,
1882.
New York: McLoughlin Brothers.
Collection the author.

p. 7, 207 *Architecture at
VkhUTEMAS*, 1927.
Jacket design by El Lissitzky
Moscow: VkhUTEMAS
Russian National Library,
St. Petersburg
© Heritage Image Partnership
Ltd/Alamy

pp. 7, 235, 248–249 Brigitte
Koyama-Richard, *Mille Ans de
Manga*, 2008
Shown: pp. 150–151; 94–95;
cover of French edition.
Paris/London: Flammarion.
© Flammarion and (pp. 150–151)
© Tezuka Production; (pp.
94–95) © Kawanabe Kyôsai
Memorial Museum; (cover
of French edition) © Mizuki
Shigeru Production/© Kumon
Institude of Education/© Chiba
City Museum of Art/© Mizuki
Shigeru Production.

p. 14 Hand prints, Cuevas de las
Manos, Santa Cruz Province,
Argentina, c. 9500 BCE.
Colored mineral pigments.
Mariano Cecowski. Creative
Commons Attribution Share
Alike 2.5 Generic license.

p. 16 Tally sticks, exchequer
receipts,13th century.

Split hazel, notched and
inscribed.
© National Archives, Kew, E402.

p. 17 Ishango Bone, 25,000–
20,000 BCE.
Inscribed baboon fibula;
Belgian Congo.
The Royal Belgian Institute of
Natural Sciences, Brussels.

p. 18 Epic of Gilgamesh,
7th century BCE.
Clay tablet fragment with Neo-
Assyrian cuneiform inscription.
Iraq: Library of Ashurbanipal,
Kouyunjik, Ninevah.
© The Trustees of the British
Museum, K.3375.

p. 19 Assyrian scribes, relief from
the Palace at Nimrud, 730 BCE.
Gypsum stone relief.
British Museum, London,
ME 124955.
© Zev Radovan/BibleLandPictures/
© www.BibleLandPictures.com/
Alamy.

p. 20 Caral khipu, 4600 BCE.
Knotted cotton wrapped round
sticks. Peru: sacred city of Caral
Supe archaeological site.
© Archaeological Zone Caral,
Peru, courtesy Dr Ruth Shady.

p. 21 Felipe Guamán Poma de
Ayala, *Nueva corónica y buen
gobierno*, 1615.
Shown: p. 335 [337], man with
khipu in a storehouse. Spanish
and Quechua manuscript; ink on
paper. Lucanas Ayacucho, Peru:
for King Philip III of Spain.
© The Royal Library,
Copenhagen, GKS 2232.

pp. 22–23 Book of the Dead
of Ani, c. 1250 BCE.
Painted papyrus. Thebes, Egypt:
from the Tomb of Ani.
© The Trustees of the British
Museum, EA 10470/3.

p. 23 Ptahshepses the scribe,
5th Dynasty, c. 2450 BCE.
Painted limestone statue.
Saqqara, Egypt, found in
Mastaba C10.
Egyptian National Museum,
Cairo.
© The Art Archive/Collection
Dagli Orti.

p. 28 Oracle bone, probably late
Shang Dynasty, China, c. 1400 BCE.
Petrified tortoise shell, inscribed.
Museum of East Asian Art, Bath.
© Heritage Image Partnership Ltd/
Alamy.

p. 29 Chu slips of Laozi (Version A),
c. 300 BCE.
Painted bamboo. Guodian,
Jingmen, Hubei Province: from
Chu tomb no. 1.

Private collection.
© Archives Charmet/The
Bridgeman Art Library.

p. 30 Hyakumanto pagoda with
printed dharani, c. 770 CE.
Pagoda (originally painted) with
central cavity containing a block-
printed dharani scroll; pine wood
and hemp paper. Japan: Nara.
Courtesy Bloomsbury Auctions,
London, UK.

pp. 32–33 *Tripitaka Koreana*,
13th century.
Shown: view of the Hall, Haein
Buddhist temple; some of the
81,258 wooden printing blocks
with Hanja script. Haein Buddhist
temple, South Gyeongsang
province, South Korea.
© Image Republic Inc./Alamy.

pp. 34–35 *Ashtasahasrika
Prajnaparamita sutra*, c. 1112.
Painted palm leaf manuscript,
from Bengal.
© Victoria & Albert Museum,
London, IS.8-1958.

p. 36 Chieh Ming, et. al., *Yongle
Dadian*, 1562–67.
Third copy, Jianqing period.
Shown: fos 44–45r, discussing
flood management.
The British Library, London,
Or.14446.

p. 37 Papermaking, c. 1800.
Watercolor from a Chinese
export album depicting trades.
The British Library London,
Or. 2262, no.69.

p. 38 Batak divination book,
c. 1855.
Painted bark paper, inscribed.
Sumatra, Toba region.
Tropenmuseum, Amsterdam,
coll. no. A.1389.

p. 39 Divination bone, late
20th century.
Buffalo bone, inscribed. Jakarta.
Collection the author.

p. 41 Parabaik tattooing manual,
19th century.
Manuscript on paper, illustrated
with black and red inks. Burma.
© Trustees of the British
Museum, inv. 2005,0623,0.5.

p. 46 "The bear and the bee
hives", 17th century.
Etching by James Kirk after
Francis Barlow for *Aesop's Fables*.
Wellcome Library, London, 39904i.

p. 47 Valerius Babrius, after Aesop,
Mythiambi Aesopici, 11th century
Shown: fo.3r, text with Greek
choliambic verse. Manuscript on
parchment. Probably Syria
The British Library, London,
Add MS 22087.

pp. 64–65 Bihnam bin Mus
bin Yusuf al-Mawsili (after
Dioscorides), *De Materia
Medica*, 1228.

p. 48 After Homer, *Iliad*,
10th century.
Shown: fo.1v, Helen, Paris
and Aphrodite sailing to Troy.
Probably Greece.
Biblioteca Marciana, Venice,
MS Homer Venetus A/B.,
Gr Z. 454 (= 822).
By permission of the Ministero
per i Beni e le Attività Culturali.

p. 50–51 Garima Gospels, 330
and 650 CE.
Illuminated manuscript on
parchment (probably goatskin);
2 vols. Adwa, northern Ethiopia:
Abba Garima Monastery.
Courtesy Ethiopian Heritage
Fund © Lester Capon and
Jacques Mercier.

p. 52 After Apicius, *De Re
Culinaria*, c. 830 CE.
Shown: fos 24-25r. Manuscript
on parchment. Monstery of
St. Fulda, Germany.
Courtesy of the New York
Academy of Medicine Library.

p. 53 Roman school, kitchen
hands gutting a hare, 50–75 CE.
Fresco, from a villa near Boscoreale.
Getty Villa, Malibu, 79.AG.112.
© Alex Ramsay/Alamy.

p. 54 Johannes Myronas et. al.,
Archimedes Palimpsest, 1229 CE.
Illustrated Greek prayer book
(Euchologion), overwriting
ancient texts (287–212 BCE) by
Archimedes, Hyperides and
others; ink on parchment.
From Jerusalem.
Private collection. Courtesy
the Rochester Institute of
Technology, Archimedes
Palimpsest Imaging project.

p. 61 Anglo-Saxon author, Book
of Kells (*Leabhar Cheanannais*),
c. 800.
Shown: fo.34r, Chi-Ro. Iron gall
ink and colored pigments on
vellum; Insular majuscule script.
County Meath, Ireland: Abbey
of Kells.
Trinity College Library, Dublin,
MS A. I. (58).
© The Board of Trinity College,
Dublin/Bridgeman Art Library.

p. 63 Chludov Psalter, 850.
Shown: fo.67r, Psalm 69 and
the iconoclast John VII. Ink,
cinnabar, gold and tempera on
parchment; uncial and later
minuscule script. Constantinople:
probably monastery of St. John
Studios.
© State Historical Museum,
Moscow, GIM 86795 Khlud. 129.

p. 124 Bible, 1541.
Bible in Swedish translated by Andreae Laurentius and Olaus and Laurentius Petri. Uppsala: for King Gustav Vasa of Sweden. The British Library, London, 1109.kk.5.

p. 125 *The Byble in Englyshe*, 1539. Printed in red and black ink; woodcuts depicting Henry III, Thomas Crowell and Archbishop Cranmer and the laity. London: John Cawood.
The British Library, London, C.18.d.1.

p. 125 *Die Heilige Bibel* (Luther's Bible), 1681–82.
Shown: titlepage (vol. 1), with J.S. Bach's monogram. Wittenberg: Christian Schroeder.
Courtesy Special Collections, Concordia Seminary Library, St. Louis

p. 126 Desiderius Erasmus, *Ratione Conscribendis Epistolis*, 1522.
Shown: pp. 80 and 83, with censorship and registration by the censor of the Inquisition, 1747. Basle: Johannes Froben. Episcopal Library, Barcelona
© PRISMA ARCHIVO/Alamy.

p. 127 Hans Holbein, marginal sketch of Erasmus in a copy of his *In Praise of Folly*, 1511.
Ink sketch on paper.
Kupferstichkabinett, Basle.

p. 128 *The Whole Booke of Psalmes...* , 1640.
Cambridge, Mass.: S. Daye.
Private collection.
Courtesy Sotheby's.

p. 129 *The Whole Booke of Psalmes...* , 1640.
Shown: pp. 59–60, Psalm XXVII. Cambridge, Mass.: S. Daye. American Imprint Collection, Library of Congress, Washington, D.C., BS1440 .B4.

p. 129 *The Holy Bible: Containing the Old Testament and the New. Translated into the Indian Language*, 1663.
Cambridge, Mass.: Samuel Green and Marmaduke Johnson.
Rare Book and Special Collections, Library of Congress, Washington, D.C., BS345 A2E4.

p. 130 Codex Mendoza, early 1540s.
Shown: fo.65r, six stages in the career of successful priest-warriors (calmecac); below, two sets of imperial officers. Aztec manuscript, summarized soon after Spanish conquest of Mexico. Bodleian Library, Oxford, Arch. Seld. 1.
© The Art Archive/Bodleian Library, Oxford.

p. 131 Samuel Purchas, *Haklvytvs posthumus, or, Pvrchas his Pilgrimes*, 1625.
Shown: reproduction of the Codex Mendoza. London: William Stansby for Henrie Featherstone. Library of Congress, Washington, D.C., G159 .P98.

p. 132 Jan Huygen van Linschoten, *Itinerario*, 1595–96. Shown: plates 80–88, natives collecting coconuts. Three parts, with hand-colored plates. Amsterdam: Cornelius Claesz. The British Library, London, 569.g.23.
© The British Library Board/ Art Archive.

p. 133 Jan Huygen van Linschoten, *Itinerario*, 1595–96. Shown: fo.544b, title page. Three parts, with hand-colored plates. Amsterdam: Cornelius Claesz. Bodleian Library, Oxford, THETA.
© The Art Archive/Bodleian Library, Oxford.

p. 134 Andreas Vesalius, *De humani corporis fabrica libri septem*, 1543.
Shown: title page, illustrating a dissection at Vesalius' anatomy lesson.
Latin medical text, with woodcuts probably by Jan Stephan van Calcar. Basle: Johannes Oporinus. Bibliothèque de l'Academie de Médecine, Paris.
© The Art Archive/CCI.

p. 136 William Cheselden, *Osteographia, or The Anatomy of the Bones*, 1733.
Shown: title page spread; frontis depicting Galen, and vignette of the camera obscura used to make the drawings for the plates. London: William Bowyer.
The British Library, London, 458.g.1.

p. 137 Tycho Brahe, *Astronomiae instauratae mechanica*, 1598. Shown: Tycho Brahe in his observatory. Wandesburgi: Tycho Brahe.
The British Library, London.
© The British Library Board/The Art Archive, London.

p. 138 Isaac Newton, *Philosophiæ Naturalis Principia Mathematica*, 1687.
London: S. Pepys, for the Royal Society.
The British Library, London, C.58.h.4.
© The British Library Board/ The Art Archive, London.

p. 139 Isaac Newton, *Philosophiæ Naturalis Principia Mathematica*, 1687.

Shown: p. 402, Hypotheses, with Newton's annotations. London: Jussu Societatis Regiæ ac Typis Joseph Streater. Cambridge University Library, Adv.b.39.1.

p. 139 Francesco Algarotti, *Il Newtonianismo per le dame*,1737. Shown: frontispiece engraving by Marco Pitteri after Giambattista Piazzetta. Naples.
Biblioteca Marciana, Venice
© The Art Archive, London/DeA Picture Library.

p. 141 Gervase Markham, *Cavelarice, or the English Horseman*, 1607.
London: for Edward White.
The British Library, London

p. 142–143 Margaretha Helm, *Kunst- und Fleiss-übende Nadel-Ergötzungen oder neu-erfundenes Neh-und Stick-Buch*, c. 1725. Shown: a design for gloves; title page. Nuremberg: Johann Christoph Weigel. Bayerische Staatsbibliothek München, 4 Techn. 41 gf.

p. 144 Mary Delany, Album of flower collages, 1778.
Shown: vol. 1, 1, *Acanthus Spinosus* (*Dydinamia Angospermia*, Bear's Breech). Colored papers, with bodycolor and watercolor, on black ink background.
© The Trustees of the British Museum, AN330030001.

p. 145 Elizabeth Blackwell, *A Curious Herball*, 1737.
Shown: plates 1, Dandelion. London: Samuel Harding
The British Library, London, 34.i.12.

p. 146 Kellom Tomlinson, *The Art of Dancing Explained*, 1775. Shown: plate VI, "The Regular Order of the Minuet."
The British Library, London, K.7.k.8.

p. 147 Kellom Tomlinson, *A small treatise of time and cadence in dancing*, 1708–c. 1721. Shown: manuscript notebook cover; "Measures of Common and Triple Time"; "*Saraband a deux*."
© Alexander Turnbull Library, Wellington, New Zealand.

pp. 152–153 Jean-Baptiste Poquelin (Molière), *Oeuvres de Molière*, 1734.
Shown: *Le Malade Imaginaire*; title page. With engravings by Laurent Cars and others after drawings by François Boucher. Courtesy Le Feu Follet, Paris.

pp. 154–155 Samuel Johnson, *A Dictionary of the English Language*, 1755–56.
Shown: pp. 114–115, annotated pages; entry for "Bandog." London: W. Strahan, for J. & P. Knapton.
Beinecke Rare Book and Manuscript Library, Yale University, IIm J637 755D.

p. 156 Isaiah Thomas, *A curious hieroglyphick Bible...*, 1788. After T. Hodgson, London, 1783. Worcester, Mass.: Isaiah Thomas Rare Book and Special Collections, Library of Congress, Washington, D.C., BS560 1788.

p. 157 Isaiah Thomas, *A little Pretty Pocket-book*, 1787. Shown: title page; p. 43 "Base-ball." Worcester, Mass.: Isaiah Thomas Rare Book and Special Collections, Library of Congress, Washington, D.C., PZ6.L7375.

p. 158–159 Denis Diderot, Jean Baptiste Le Rond d'Alembert, *L'Encyclopédie*, 1751–57.
Shown: "Paper Marbling", engraved by Prévost; title page. Paris: André le Breton, Michel-Antoine David, Laurent Durand, and Antoine-Claude Briasson.
© The Art Archive/ Gianni Dagli Orti.

p. 160 Carolus Linnaeus, *Praeludia sponsaliorum plantarum in quibus physiologia...*, 1729.
Uppsala University Library, Sweden
© The Art Archive/Gianni Dagli Orti

p. 161 Carl Linnaeus, *Species Plantarum*, 1753.
Shown: title page; detail of p. 491, "Polygynia", with annotations. Stockholm: Impensis Laurentii Salvii.
Linnean Society of London, BL.83.

pp. 162–163 William Playfair, *The Commercial and Political Atlas*, 1786.
Shown: plates 5 & 20, "Exports... from all North America" and "National Debt of England." London: for J. Debrett.
The British Library, London, 8247.de.2.

p. 164 *The Malefactor's Register; or, the Newgate and Tyburn calendar*, 1779.
Shown: "The convicts making their way near Blackfriars Bridge..." London: Alexander Hogg.
The British Library, London.
© The British Library/Robana/ Getty Images.

p. 165 *The Newgate Calendar...*, 1824–26.
London: J. Robins and Co.
The British Library, London.
© British Library/Robana/Getty Images.

p. 166 Thomas Sterne, *The Life and Opinions of Tristram Shandy, Gentleman*, 1760.
Shown: pp. 152–153, Chapter XL. York: Ann Ward.
The British Library, London, C.70.aa.28.

p. 167 State National Lottery advertisement in the form of a rebus, c. 1805.
Printed sheet with engravings. Amoret Tanner Collection.
© The Art Archive.

p. 168 [Michel Millot], *L'Escholle des Filles*, 1668.
Fribourg: Roger Bon Temps. (False imprint, probably Amsterdam).
The British Library, London, P. C.29.a.16.

p. 169 John Cleland, *Memoirs of a Woman of Pleasure*, c. 1765. London: for G. Fenton; (false imprint).
Private collection.
Courtesy David Chambers.

p. 169 *Whitehall Evening Post* or *London Intelligencer*, 6–8 March, 1750.
Shown: advertisement for *Fanny Hill*. London: C. Corbett.
The British Library, London, Burney collection, issue 635.
© The British Library Board.

p. 170 Benjamin Banneker, Pennsylvania, *Delaware, Maryland and Virginia Almanack and Ephemeris, for the Year of Our Lord 1792*, 1791. Shown: pp. 6–7 zodiac anatomy; title page. Baltimore: William Goddard and James Angell. Rare Book and Special Collections, Library of Congress, Washington, D.C.

p. 171 Phillis, Wheatley, *Poems on various subjects, religious and moral*, 1773.
Shown: portrait of Wheatley, engraved by Scipio Moorhead. London: Archd. Bell.
Rare Book and Special Collections, Library of Congress, Washington, D.C., LC-USZC4-5316

pp. 172–173 Thomas Bewick, *A History of British Birds*, 1804. Shown: "The Nightingale"; uncaptioned tailpiece ("The fiend"); title page for vol. II, "History and Description of Water Birds." Newcastle: Edward Walker for T. Bewick.

© Courtesy of the Natural History Society of Northumbria, Great North Museum: Hancock.

p. 174 Humphrey Repton, *Wimpole Red Book*, 1801. Shown: estate view, with overlay, showing Wimpole Hall entrance, front elevation, Church and new planting. The National Trust, Wimpole Estate, Cambridgeshire. © The National Trust Photolibrary/Alamy.

p. 176 Valentin Haüy, *Essai sur L'Éducation des aveugles*, 1786. Shown: pp. 445–445, type embossed on heavy paper. Paris: les Enfants-Aveugles, sous la direction de M. Clousier. Courtesy of the Museum of the American Printing House for the Blind, Louisville, Kentucky, 2004134502.

p. 177 William Moon, *Dr. Moon's Alphabet for the Blind*, 1877. Embossed alphabet page. Brighton: Moon Printing Works. Courtesy of the Museum of the American Printing House for the Blind, Louisville, Kentucky, 1992313.

p. 177 John Bunyon, *The Pilgrim's Progress*, 1860 Shown: page of text printed in raised Lucas type. Courtesy of the Museum of the American Printing House for the Blind, Louisville, Kentucky, 1998.66.

p. 182 Specimen banknote, c. 1821. A specimen of the siderographic plan for preventing the forgery of banknotes. Patent. London: Perkins, Fairman & Heath. Courtesy Heath-Caldwell Family Archive.

p. 183 Jacob Perkins, Patent for Apparatus and means for producing ice and in cooling fluids, 14 August 1835. The British Library, London, GB 6662/1835.

p. 183 Thomas Campbell, *The Pleasures of Hope with Other Poems*, 1821. "New Edition": reprint with steel plates by Richard Westall and Charles Heath. London: Longman, Hurst, Rees, Orme and Brown; Edinburgh: Stirling and Slade. Courtesy Heath-Caldwell Family Archive.

pp. 184–185 Anna Atkins, *Photographs of British Algae: Cyanotype Impressions*, 1843–50. Shown: title page; fo.55, "Dictyota

dichotoma, in the young state; and in fruit." The British Library, London, C.192.c.1.

pp. 186–187 Adolphe Duperly, *Daguerian Excursions in Jamaica*, 1840. Shown: title page; lithograph, "A View Of The Court House." Kingston, Jamaica: Adolphe Duperly. The British Library, London, Maps.19.b.12.

p. 188 James Evans, *Cree Syllabic Hymnbook*, 1841. Elk-skin wrapper with syllabary printed front and back. Norway House, Manitoba: James Evans. Victoria University Library, Toronto, AS42 .B49 no.4.

p. 189 Jacob Hunziker, *Nature's Self-Printing...*, 1862. Shown: title page in Canarese with *Lycopodium cerium* (staghorn clubmoss) nature print. Mangalore: J. Hunziker, Basel Mission Press. © Basel Mission Archives/Basel Mission Holdings, C.325.I.004.

p. 189 *Chinese Recorder and Missionary Journal*, 1875. Shown: advertisement for the American Presbyterian Mission Press. Shanghai: American Presbyterian Mission Press. Collection the author.

p. 190 *The Tauchnitz Magazine*, August 1892. Leipzig: Bernhard Tauchnitz. Courtesy Alistair Jollans.

p. 191 Charles Dickens, *The Posthumous Papers of the Pickwick Club*, 1836–37. Serialized in 20 monthly parts (19 & 20 in one), April 1836 to November 1837; plates by R.W. Buss, H.K. Browne ("Phiz") and Robert Seymour (including cover). London: Chapman and Hall. Copyright © 2013 Bonhams Auctioneers Corp. All Rights Reserved.

p. 192 Dr. Frank Powell, *Old Grizzly Adams, The Bear Tamer, or, The Monarch of the Mountains*, 1899. Beadle's Boy's Library of Sport, Story and Adventure, vol. II, no. 23, 11 June, 1899. New York: M.J. Ivers & Co. Johannsen Collection, Rare Books and Special Collections, Northern Illinois University Libraries, 23.

p. 193 *The Indian Queen's Revenge*, 1864. Munro's Ten Cent Novels,

no. 55. New York: George Munro & Co.; Philadelphia: J. Trenwith. Johannsen Collection, Rare Books and Special Collections, Northern Illinois University Libraries, 241.

p. 195 Anne and Jane Taylor, *Rural scenes, or, A peep into the country: For children*, 1825. Shown: pp. 48–49, "Angling" etc. London: Harvey & Darton. Collection the author.

pp. 196–197 Heinrich Hoffmann, *Struwwelpeter*, 1848. Shown: cover; p. 16, "The Story of Little Suck-a-Thumb." Glasgow: Blackie & Sons. Collection the author.

p. 197 Mark Twain, *Slovenly Peter* (*Der Struwwelpeter*), 1935. Shown: cover (second edition). New York: Harper & Brothers. Collection the author.

pp. 198–199 Lothar Meggendorfer, *Le Grand Cirque International*, 1887. Pop-up book. Paris: Nouvelle Librairie de la Jeunesse, 1887. Collection Ana Maria Ortega. Photo © Álvaro Gutiérrez.

p. 199 Ramón Llull, *Ars Magna*, 1305. Shown: volvelle. Facsimile (1990) after the original in the Biblioteca El Escorial, Madrid. Madrid: Kaydeda Ediciones in Madrid. Collection Ana Maria Ortega. Photo © Álvaro Gutiérrez.

p. 199 Robert Sayer, *Harlequinade with Adam & Eve*, 1788. Flap book; hand-colored engravings, drawn and engineered by James Poupard; text after Benjamin Sands, "The Beginning, Progress and End of Man" (London, 1650). Philadelphia: James Poupard. Collection Ana Maria Ortega. Photo © Álvaro Gutiérrez.

p. 200 Baedeker's *Äygyten*, 1928. Travel guide, with maps and illustrations; a revision of the earlier German edition. Koblenz: Karl Baedeker. Courtesy Karl Baedeker Verlag.

p. 201 *Rheinreise von Strassburg bis Düsseldorf*, 1839. Yellow pictorial Biedermeier boards. Koblenz: Karl Baedeker. Courtesy Karl Baedeker Verlag.

p. 201 *Der Schweiz*, 1844. First edition in yellow pictorial Biedermeier boards. Koblenz: Karl Baedeker. Courtesy Shapero Rare Books, London.

p. 202 Alexis Soyer, *The Modern Housewife or Menagere*, 1849. Shown: title page; advertisement for "Soyer's Sauce." London: Simpkin, Marshall. Collection the author

p. 203 Soyer's camp and bivouac kitchen in the Crimea, 1855. Engraving in *Illustrated London News*, 22 September 1855. London: Herbert Ingram. © 19th era 2/Alamy.

p. 204 Rolf Boldrewood, *Robbery Under Arms*, 1927. London: MacMillan and Co. Courtesy Ian Riley.

p. 205 Sir Arthur Conan Doyle, *The Hound of the Baskervilles*, 1902. First Colonial Edition; plates by Sydney Paget. London: Longman, Green and Co. Courtesy Adrian Harrington Rare Books, London.

p. 205 Playbill advertising *Robbery Under Arms*, 1896. For a production at the Theatre Royal, Hobart. Hobart: John Hennings. Tasmaniana Library, LINC Tasmania. © Tasmanian Archive and Heritage Office.

p. 210 Michael Joyce, *Afternoon, a story*, 1987. Interactive e-book, using hypertext authoring system Storyspace. Watertown, Mass.: Eastgate Systems. © Eastgate Systems.

p. 211 Jorge Luis Borges, *El Jardin de Senderos Que Se Bifurcan*, 1942. Buenos Aires: Sur. Courtesy Ken Lopez Bookseller, Massachusetts.

p. 212 Chester Floyd Carlson with his first 1938 Xerox model copier, c. 1960. © Pictorial Press/Alamy

p. 213 Chester Carlson, Lab notebook, 1938. Shown: pp. 4–5 manuscript notebook A4, with notes on electrostatic printing. The New York Public Library, Chester F. Carlson papers, MssCol 472.

p. 214 William Shakespeare, *The Tragedie of Hamlet Prince of Denmarke*, 1930. Shown: p. 126 Act IV, scene iv. With 80 woodcuts and engravings by Edward Gordon Craig. Weimar: The Cranach Press. The British Library, London, C.100.l.16.

p. 214 William Shakespeare, *The tragicall historie of Hamlet, Prince of Denmarke*, 1909. Shown: p. 138, Act V, scene i. Hammersmith : Doves Press. The British Library, London, C.99.g.30.

p. 215 Edward Gordon Craig, "The First Gravedigger", 1927. Representing Harry Gage-Cole, pressman for the Cranach Hamlet. From *Matrix* 12, 1992 (f.p. 97). Courtesy of John Randle.

pp. 216–217 Walt Whitman, *Leaves of Grass*, 1930. Shown: leaves printed in black and red, illustrated with woodcuts by Valenti Angelo. New York: [Grabhorn Press for] Random House Inc. The British Library, London, RF.2003.c.9.

p. 217 Vladimir Burliuk and Vasilii Kamenskii, *Tango with Cows: Ferro-concrete Poems*, 1914 . Book with three letterpress illustrations and wallpaper cover. Moscow: D. D. Burliuk, Fo.12. Museum of Modern Art, New York, Gift of The Judith Rothschild Foundation, inv. 74.2001. © Digital image, The Museum of Modern Art, New York/Scala, Florence.

p. 218 Vladimir Mayakovsky, *For the Voice*, 1923. Design by El Lissitzky for "To the Left." Berlin: R.S.F.S.R. gos. izd. © Image Asset Management Ltd./ Alamy

pp. 220–221 Max Ernst, *Une Semaine de Bonté*, 1934. "Collage novel", with collages by Ernst executed 1933–34. Paris: Éditions Jeanne Bucher, printed by Georges Duval. The Louis E. Stern Collection, Museum of Modern Art (MoMA). © Digital image, Museum of Modern Art, New York/Scala, Florence © ADAGP, Paris and DACS, London 2014.

p. 221 Guillaume Apollinaire, *Calligrammes; poèmes de la paix et da la guerre, 1913–1916*, 1918. Concrete poems with typographical arrangements, published posthumously. Paris: Mercure de France.

p. 222 Joseph O. Nnadozie, *Beware of harlots and many friends, the world is hard*, c. 1970. Revised and enlarged by J.C. Anorue; includes several simple linocut illustrations.

Onitsha (Nigeria): J.C. Brothers Bookshop.
Courtesy Cavan McCarthy.

p. 223 Unknown artist, Stall selling 'Romanços' by the convent of St. Augustine, Barcelona, c. 1850. Engraving in a sainete or one-act drama, published 1850.

p. 223 J. Abiakam, *How to make friends with girls*, c. 1965. Cover illustration originally from a knitting pattern. Onitsha (Nigeria): J.C. Brothers Bookshop. Courtesy Cavan McCarthy.

p. 223 Olegário Fernandes da Silva, *A morte do Dr. Evando, Veriador de Surubim*, 1987. With a woodcut or linocut cover Caruaru (PE): publisher unknown. Courtesy Cavan McCarthy.

p. 224 Rosamond Lehman, *Invitation to the Waltz*, 1934. Albatross Modern Continental Library, vol. 223. Hamburg: The Albatross. Collection the author.

p. 225 Eric Linklater, *Private Angelo*, 1958. Paperback, following the 1957 limited photo-set Christmas edition. Middlesex: Penguin Books Limited. Courtesy Penguin Books Ltd.

p. 225 Postcard for the Modern Continental Library readers, c. 1934. Paris: The Albatross. Collection the author.

p. 226 Aleksander *Kamiński, Kamienie na szaniec*, 1944. Published under the pseudonym Julius Gorecki; cover design by Stanisław Kunstetter. Warsaw: TWZW. Warsaw Uprising Museum, Warsaw

p. 227 Resistance press photograph in *Le Point*, 1945. Photographer unknown. Collection the author.

p. 228 Mikhail Bulgakov, *The Master and Margarita*, 1966-67. Serialization in Moscow magazine. Shown: cover; text (1966) Courtesy Helix Art Center, San Diego www.russianartandbooks. com; Courtesy Shapero Rare Books, London.

p. 229 Mikhail Bulgakov, *The Master and Margarita*, 1969 Shown: jacket from the 1974 reprint, reproducing the original. Frankfurt: Possev Verlag. Courtesy Possev Verlag, Frankfurt.

p. 230 Marie Stopes, *Married Love, A New Contribution To The Solution Of Sex Difficulties*, 1931.

Jacket advertising "Federal Judge Lifts Ban." New York, Eugenics Publishing Company. Collection the author.

p. 230 Playbill for *Maisie's Marriage*, 1923. Page Hall Cinema, Pitsmoor, Yorkshire; film loosely based on *Married Love*. Leeds and London: John Waddington Ltd. © National Archives, Kew, HO45/11382.

p. 231 *How to be Personally Efficient*, 1916. System "How-Books", for *System: The Magazine of Business* . Shown: chapter 18, "Little Schemes for Saving Time." London and Chicago: A.W. Shaw & Company. Collection the author.

p. 232 Anne Frank, *Diary*, 1942–44. Shown: pages of the first notebook, dated 19 June 1942. © Anne Frank Fonds—Basel via Getty Images.

p.233 Anne Frank, *Het Achterhuis*, 1947. First published edition of Anne Frank's diary, edited after her death by Otto Frank. Amsterdam: Contact Publishing. © Allard Bovenberg/Anne Frank Fonds—Basel via Getty Images.

p.233 Irène Némirovsky, *Suite Française*, 1940–41. Manuscript notebook. © Fonds Irène Némirovsky/ IMEC, by permission of the Estate.

p. 238 Dard Hunter printing *Old Papermaking* at the Mountain House Press, Chillicothe, Ohio, 1922. Courtesy Dard Hunter III.

p. 238 Dard Hunter, *Old Papermaking*, 1923. Chillicothe (Ohio): Mountain House Press. Courtesy Dard Hunter III.

p. 239 Dard Hunter, Smoke proof of Hunter's typeface, c. 1922. Courtesy Dard Hunter III.

pp. 240–241 Rand Corporation, *A Million Random Digits with 100,000 Normal Deviates*, 1955. Glencoe (Illinois): Free Press Publishers. Photo courtesy Tom Jennings, by permission of Rand Corporation.

p. 242 Anglo-Saxon author, *Beowulf*, c. 1000 CE. Shown: fo.101, a miniature of gold-digging ants in the land of

Gorgoneus, from the "Marvels of the East", Beowulf manuscript. The British Library, London, MS Cotton Vitelius A. XV.

p. 243 Electronic Beowulf CD, version 2, 2011. CD after the Anglo-Saxon manuscript of Beowulf and other works, MS Cotton Vitellius A. XV. Third edition, 2011. London: British Library Publishing.

p. 244 Silvia Hartmann, *The Dragon Lords*, 2013. Cover of the paperback edition, from the online crowd-sourced novel. Eastbourne: DragonRising Publishing. Courtesy of Silvia Hartmann (www.SilviaHartmann.com) and DragonRising Publishing (www.DragonRising.com).

p. 245 Angela Ruiz Robles, *Enciclopedia Mecánica*, 1949. Shown: prototype as preserved today, property of the heirs of Ángela Ruiz Robles. Spanish National Museum of Science and Technology. Photo © Luis Carré.

p. 245 Turning page of e-book reader on an iPad mini tablet computer. © Iain Masterton/Alamy.

p. 246 Miniature Qur'an with metal locket and magnifying glass, c. 1900–10. Glasgow: David Bryce & Sons. Courtesy Simon Beattie, www.simonbeattie.co.uk.

p. 247 Jewish Bible on a pin-head, 2009. Nano-Bible developed at the Technion Russell Berrie Nanotechnology Institute. Tel Aviv: Technion, Israel Institute of Technology. © Technion, Israel Institute of Technology, Tel Aviv.

pp. 250–251 Francisca Prieto, *The Antibook*, 2003. Paper origami icosahedron: 15 x 17 x 19 cm, using Nicanor Parra's "AntiPoems"; origami process. Artist's collection. All rights reserved. Copyright © Francisca Prieto, 2001–13.

p. 252 Reel manuscript from South Sulawesi, Indonesia, before 1907. Lontar paper. Tropenmuseum, Amsterdam, coll. no. 673-4.

p. 253 Reel manuscript, from Bulukumba, South Sulawesi, Indonesia, before 1887. Written in Buginese, lontar paper.

Tropenmuseum, Amsterdam, coll. no. A-4515b.

p. 254 Ethiopic script, Ethiopia, date unknown. Black and red Ge'ez or Ethiopic script on vellum. © The Art Archive.

p. 254 Arabesque, printing ornament, 17th century. Collection the author.

p. 256 Device Printers device of Aldus Manutius, c. 1501. Collection the author.

p. 257 Denis Diderot, Jean Baptiste Le Rond d'Alembert, *L'Encyclopédie*, 1751–57. Shown: "Letterpress printing", engraved by Bernard after Goussier; title page. Paris: André le Breton, Michel-Antoine David, Laurent Durand, and Antoine-Claude Briasson. © The Art Archive/DeA Picture Library.

p. 258 Michael Maier, *Atalanta fugiens*, 1618. Shown: Ouroboros devouring itself by the tail. Alchemical emblem book; poems, text, musical fugues; engravings Johann Theodor de Bry. Oppenheim: Hieronymi Galleri, 1618. Prints and Photographs Division, Library of Congress, Washington, D.C., LC-USZ62-95263.

p. 259 Christian III's Bible, 1550. Shown: title page (detail) with Fraktur titling and a woodcut by Erhard Altdorfer. First full translation of the Bible into Danish. Copenhagen: Ludowich Dietz.

p. 260 *Lindisfarne Gospels*, c. 700. Shown: fo.139r (detail), initial page of the Gospel of St. Luke. Colored pigments and ink on vellum. The British Library, London, Cotton MS Nero D.IV.

p. 261 Psalter, 1661. Shown: fo.1 (detail), decorated initial with Greek minuscule script. Written by Matthaios, monastery of St. Catherine, Mount Sinai, for the monk Pachomios. Mount Sinai, Egypt, St. Catherine's monastery. The British Library, London, MS Burney 16.

p. 262 Cai Lun, patron saint of paper making, 18th century. 18th-century woodcut after a Qing dynasty design. Collection the author

p. 263 Mandarin Chinese characters for cattle.

p. 264 "[America toe] her [miss] taken [moth]er", rebus, 11 May 1778. Hand colored etching. London: M. Darly, Strand, May 11. Prints and Photographs Division, Library of Congress, Washington, D.C., PC 1 - 5475.

p. 267 Ephraim Chambers, *Cyclopædia; or, an Universal dictionary of arts and sciences*, 1728. Shown: "A specimen sheet by William Caslon..." London: James & John Knapton.

p. 268 Origen, *Homiliae in numeri 15-19*, 675–700. Shown: fo.11, (detail) Uncial (Merovingian) script, with rustic capitals. France, N. (Corbie?). The British Library, London, MS Burney 340.

p. 268 Robert Hayman, *Quodlibets, lately come over from New Britaniola, Old Newfound-land*, 1628. Shown: watermark in the gutter. London: Elizabeth All-de for Roger Michell. Private collection. Creative Commons, Ambassador Neelix.

p. 269 Matthais Huss, Otto Schäfer, *La Grant Danse macabre*, 1499–1500. Lyons: Matthais Huss. Collection the author.

Index